CELEBRITY SURGEON

This book is dedicated to my mother, Joan
who died 2 September 1997

and to my father, Ray
who died 18 August 2003.

They were the most honest,
most remarkable of people.

CELEBRITY SURGEON

Christiaan Barnard
A Life

CHRIS LOGAN

Jonathan Ball Publishers
JOHANNESBURG & CAPE TOWN

Published in 2003 in trade paperback by
JONATHAN BALL PUBLISHERS (PTY) LTD
P O Box 33977
Jeppestown
2043

ISBN 1 86842 163 5 (soft cover)
ISBN 1 86842 180 5 (hard cover)

Design by Michael Barnett
Cover photograph by Eric Miller
Reproduction and typesetting of cover and picture section
by Triple M Design & Advertising, Johannesburg
Typesetting and reproduction of text by Alinea Studio, Cape Town
Index by Owen Hendry
Printed and bound by CTP Book Printers,
Duminy Street, Parow, 7500, Cape Town, South Africa

Contents

	Foreword	9
1	Beyond the Frontier	11
2	A Karoo Boyhood	15
3	Medical School	39
4	Young Doctor	61
5	Surgeon ... and America	80
6	Ambition	101
7	Transplant	124
8	Aftermath	147
9	Divorce	176
10	Barbara	197
11	Info	232
12	Divorce Again and Karin	263
13	Marriage and Divorce (Again!)	290
14	Homecoming	312
	Bibliography	327
	Index	331

The conditions necessary of the surgeon are four:
First, he should be learned.
Second, he should be expert.
Third, he must be ingenious.
Fourth, he should be able to adapt himself.

Guy de Chauliac (1300-1368)

Taken from a scroll outside Christiaan Barnard's office at the University of Cape Town Medical School.

*

It was a frontier no less important and much more immediate than the stars.

Washington Daily News editorial.
3 January 1968

Acknowledgements

During the two years in which this biography was conceived, researched, written and produced, my wife, Jill, bore each agonising twist and turn with a patience and stoicism which only occasionally teetered on the edge of breaking. She believed in the book from the start and encouraged me to take it on when my own doubts about embracing such a challenge rose up. Quite simply, without her support this book would never have materialised.

In the course of the research I interviewed more than 100 people, many several times. A number of them had never spoken before about their professional or personal relationship with Christiaan Barnard. I am deeply grateful to all who agreed to talk to me – whether or not their names appear in the book, they all had something of value to say – and to those in various parts of the world who corresponded by e-mail. I have listed in the bibliography those books which I used as sources, but three I would like to mention here: *The Transplanted Heart,* by Peter Hawthorne, a mini-masterpiece published within weeks of the first heart transplant; *Chris Barnard – By Those Who Know Him* compiled by David Cooper to mark the 25th anniversary of the operation in 1992; and *King of Hearts – The True Story of the Maverick who Pioneered Open Heart Surgery* by G Wayne Miller. Hawthorne's book is a superb contemporaneous account by a journalist who covered the story; Cooper's book comprises a series of testimonies, some of which, such as the interview with Walt Lillehei, the man who trained Barnard in open-heart surgery, and the contributions of Terry O'Donovan and John Perry, provide priceless insights. (Many of those featured in the Cooper book have since died, making their contributions all the more valuable.) Miller's book tells the life story of Lillehei and vividly portrays the furnace of innovation and surgical ambition Barnard stepped into when he went to Minneapolis in the 1950s.

I have also drawn on material in *One Life*, Christiaan Barnard's autobiography, written with Curtis Bill Pepper; its sequel, *The Second Life*, edited by Chris Brewer; and *Heartbreak*, by Louwtjie Barnard.

In addition I would like to thank the following for their special contributions to the work that went into producing this biography: Johan Brink, Professor of Cardiothoracic Surgery at the University of Cape Town and head of the heart transplant programme at Groote Schuur Hospital, whose expert guidance along the way was of great value and who helped with the more technical aspects of the text. Karin Berman, who supported the project from the beginning. Chris Brewer. Jo Heydenreich, widow of Siegfried Stander, who allowed me free access to his papers. Elizabeth Blane, who allowed me access to papers left by her late former husband, MC Botha. Barbara Cole, for her invaluable help with research. Christine Heydenrych and Pat Heydenrych at the Transplant Museum, Groote Schuur. Sandra Smit and Caroline Bedeker at the Beaufort West Museum. Library staff at the manuscripts and archives department of the University of Cape Town. Karen Klinkenberg in the archives department at the University of Minnesota. Rose Willis, tourism co-ordinator of the Central Karoo. Gillian Carter at Knysna public library. Library staff at the following – Independent Newspapers, Durban; *Die Burger*; *Fair Lady*; *You* and *Huisgenoot*, Cape Town; Associated Newspapers, London; Minneapolis Star Tribune. Alessandra Maggiorani for her research work in Italy. Martin Myers. Andrew Brown. Robert Johnson. Bob Molloy. Roger Williams. Francine Blum, production manager at Jonathan Ball Publishers whose patience was tested to the limit. Barry Streek, editor-in-chief at Jonathan Ball Publishers, whose gentle, painstaking advice as the book developed, especially on the political context, was much appreciated. And, finally, Jonathan Ball, who commissioned this biography and backed it with more than mere words of encouragement.

Foreword

A blustery winter's afternoon in Muizenberg cemetery: not the place, you might think, for extraordinary coincidences. I had gone there to see for myself where the graves of Christiaan Barnard's baby brother Abraham and his mother Maria lay, side by side. As I wandered around the vast collection of stones, many crumbling and worn and unreadable, I came across a smartly dressed man with a bunch of flowers in his hand, tending a well-kept grave. He was the only other person in the cemetery. Did he happen to know where I might find the Barnards? He looked puzzled, then pointed me towards the superintendent's hut in another corner of the cemetery, before returning to his mission. The superintendent duly took me to Abraham's grave, the inscription on its white marble stone decayed and barely visible. Maria's grave was not quite alongside, but close enough. As I tried to make out the words dedicated to Abraham, the man I had approached earlier came running up. 'I don't know why I didn't say before, but my wife was Barnard's first open-heart patient in South Africa! I was at her grave. She died of cancer last year.'

Joan Pick was 15 when Barnard, using for the first time the primitive heart-lung machine he had brought back from America, repaired a defect in her heart. She went on to live a full life, bearing a son and marrying twice. Neville Barlow was her second husband. Until cancer caught her, she was healthy. When she was admitted to hospital with stomach pain, the doctor pronounced the heart Barnard had worked on all those years ago 'as strong as an ox'.

Barnard would go on to tackle far more complex cases than Joan Pick. Babies with hearts no bigger than a walnut. Listless, blue-edged children who grew pink and vibrant after he had operated. Men and women who were so grateful they could breathe freely again that they lavished him with gifts. He would often take on the more difficult cases, the ones other surgeons preferred to avoid. In the main, he succeeded. Then came the first human heart transplant.

Cardiac surgeons, it has been said, are the rock stars of the operating room. In the course of researching this biography I have certainly met some remarkable people. There is something compelling about the heart that seems to attract surgeons of uncommon individuality and drive. Its astonishing work rate – the average heart beats 100 000 times a day, or two-and-a-half-billion times in a life – is one thing. Its symbolic hold over ordinary people is another. By repairing or transplanting a heart, the cardiac surgeon masters its physical and mystical forces. Patients and their loved ones remain in awe.

In July 1958 Christiaan Barnard was setting out on a path that would make him the most famous and infamous surgeon the world has seen. The operation he performed on an ailing teenage girl was technically simple, and deliberately so. Yet in Neville Barlow's voice some forty-four years later, as he spoke of his wife's ox-strong heart, there was more than pride. There was awe.

Chris Logan
June 2003

NOTE: So many of those quoted in this book are or were professors and doctors that I had to choose: include all titles and clutter the text, or, with one or two exceptions, to leave them out. I decided to leave them out.

1

Beyond the Frontier

For the first time in his life, Christiaan Barnard stared into the chest of a patient without a heart. The man lay on the operating table still alive, his blood still coursing through his veins. But the cavity where for 55 years his heart had been beating was empty. In the tall, green-tiled room, under a stark white light, the bloated heart of Louis Washkansky had been cut out.

A few feet away, in a stainless-steel dish, bathed in a cold solution, lay another heart – the small, pink, healthy heart of a 25-year-old woman. Hours earlier, on a bright summer's afternoon, Denise Darvall had stopped to buy a cake. Slammed into the air by a speeding car, she now lay dead in the next theatre, her chest open. Her heart would be Washkansky's heart now.

Barnard took the girl's heart in his hands. It felt cold, firm. It looked too small for the cavern it was supposed to fill. Too weak for the bullish man whose life it would have to sustain. Slowly, he began to sew the heart into its new home.

Few people outside those high walls knew what was going on inside Barnard's operating room in the early morning of Sunday 3 December 1967. There were other surgeons, in other countries, poised to do what he was doing at this moment. All had hoped to be the first to transplant a human heart.

Once secured, the heart was ready to receive the warming blood of Washkansky. It flushed a deep pink. It began to quiver, to fibrillate. It wanted to live, but it could not summon the strength to assume its natural rhythm and begin to beat. Barnard placed two wired paddles on either side of the struggling muscle. A bolt of electricity shot through it, sending Washkansky's back jerking upwards. The quivering stopped. Seconds passed, like minutes. Then the contractions began, a gentle pumping. But the heart-lung machine was still doing the work, pushing the blood around the body. The critical moment would come when it was switched off.

As soon as the pump stopped, the heart began to labour. It lasted just 25 seconds before Barnard ordered: Pump on!

A second failure. The heart would not take over the load. Had they expected too much? Again the heart-lung machine started up. It stayed on longer. The third attempt: bypass off. Wait … Hope … Pray. This time, the warmed heart surged on. It took on its new workload, pumping Washkansky's blood where before it had pumped the blood of a young woman. The tension in the room collapsed. 'Jesus, dit gaan werk!' Barnard announced through his mask, in his native Afrikaans. 'Jesus, it's going to work!'

Barnard reached out over Washkansky. He wanted to shake the gloved hand of Rodney Hewitson, his assistant, whose steady nerves perfectly counterbalanced his own highly-strung temperament. Outside a new dawn had broken in Cape Town, South Africa. It would be several hours before the rest of the world learned of what Barnard had done.

Back in the tearoom it was suggested that the medical superintendent of the hospital, Groote Schuur, should be told. When he answered the phone, Jacobus Burger at first sounded confused. No, it wasn't dogs this time, said Barnard. He had performed a human heart transplant.

Barnard made another call. He told Lapa Munnik, who ran health affairs for the provincial administration, what he had done. Munnik phoned Nico Malan, administrator of the Cape Province. Malan called John Vorster, the prime minister. Within an hour of Washkansky getting his new heart, the government had been informed.

Velva Schrire, head of the cardiac clinic, was also called. He would have to examine Washkansky. As he left his home he gave no indication to his wife and two sons that anything extraordinary had happened. He was often called in on Sunday mornings.

Everything was fine, said Schrire. Washkansky had opened his eyes, and had been moved back to his room, still attached to a ventilator. Now would begin the intensive round of drugs and monitoring to watch for the slightest sign of infection or rejection of the new heart.

In the corridor Barnard ran into Washkansky's wife, Ann. She had been at home and had stayed up all night waiting for news from the hospital, ever since being told that a donor had been found. She had never really understood what Barnard planned to do until it was about to happen. She had even tried to persuade her husband not to go ahead with the operation. If it had to be done, she thought Louis's old heart, the one she had fallen in love with and married, would stay put. She couldn't imagine it being taken out. Now she was told that it would be several days before she could see her husband. She thanked God, then Barnard, that her husband was alive and said she would leave, and wait.

For now Barnard went along with others at the hospital who said it was 'probably' a world first, or that they 'believed' it might be. But he knew it was; he had achieved what he had worked towards his whole career. To be first had been the goal of his life since he was a small boy. His mother had drilled it into him. As he drove home he heard the radio newsreader announce details of the transplant. His name was not mentioned.

Louwtjie, his wife, greeted him warmly. Once inside the house, he called a close friend, Fritz Brink, and put on his best English accent. 'This is the BBC in London. I understand you are a friend of Dr Christiaan Barnard who has performed the world's first human heart transplant ... What kind of man is he?' Brink immediately guessed it was Barnard, and gave a typically blunt appraisal.

But no-one, including Barnard, could have foreseen the impact the news would have. He had long wanted to be famous, but he had in mind the kind of fame that usually went with great medical achievements. Distinction in his field, honour among his peers, maybe even the Nobel Prize. But the international media avalanche that now began to slide towards Cape Town was like nothing seen before on the southern tip of Africa.

Barnard was 45. He lived in a country whose apartheid policies had earned the condemnation of the world. He worked in a place geographically remote from the better-known centres for cardiac surgery in America and Europe. He was unconventional. He did as he pleased. He dressed poorly, most days wearing the same sports jacket patched at the elbows. Sometimes he was mistaken for a hospital porter. But the press reporters and photographers and the television crews who descended on Cape Town now discovered a natural. Barnard was tall and good-looking, with a boyish face and large ears. His features were lean and sharp. He spoke in a high-pitched voice with a strong Afrikaans accent, but with a firm grasp of English. His energy seemed endless. His confidence shone through intense eyes that absorbed the television cameras. His wide, toothy smile would soon beam every day from the front pages of the world's newspapers.

For Vorster and the reviled regime that ran South Africa it was manna from heaven. The country had pulled off a medical first, the biggest. No operation had gripped the world's imagination like this. The trail-blazing work of South Africa's finest doctors would fill the foreign newspapers and television screens for weeks to come. The donor was white – they had made sure of that – and the recipient was white. It had been one of the first questions asked. For once, however briefly, South Africa did not mean riot police and brutal racial oppression. It meant hope.

It was an era when boundaries were being rolled back, on Earth and in space. America would soon put a man on the moon. The human body was being explored and gradually conquered by courageous surgeons determined to overcome disease and even death. In an age of discovery they were all pioneers: astronauts and surgeons. Failing kidneys had for some years been replaceable. Liver transplants were becoming more successful. But the heart held a unique place in Man's affections. It was the seat of emotions, the source of love. Courage and fear were contained there. It was soul and identity. Surgeons in other countries had hesitated to transplant it.

Barnard had not hesitated. To him, the heart was just a pump.

2

A Karoo Boyhood

The surgeon who astounded the world that day was an Afrikaner, the son of a Dutch Reformed Church missionary. As a boy he had gone barefoot and hunted springbok in the semi-desert of the Karoo. His parents had saved and scraped to put him through medical school. His life story would now become as much a draw as the transplant itself. But it was not as simple as it appeared. Christiaan Neethling Barnard was no ordinary Afrikaner.

He was born on 8 November 1922, in Beaufort West, 500 kilometres north-east of Cape Town. In this sheep-farming community the living was harsh. Years of drought, and even a biblical plague of locusts, had fuelled a natural sense of injustice among the Boers. Across the country a deep recession and violent industrial unrest had fanned racial and political tensions. South Africa was seething with the resentment of Afrikaners: they felt oppressed by English-speaking whites, they saw their way of life threatened by coloureds and blacks. Afrikaner nationalism, bent on power, was on the rise.

Beaufort West lies at the foot of the Nuweveld Mountains, named after the new grazing the early trekboers found there. The first human inhabitants of the Karoo plains, which cover most of central South Africa, were the Bushmen and Hottentots, or the San and the Khoi. It is a fossil-rich region renowned for its dry beauty. The first white farmers settled in the area around 1760, and in 1818 the governor of the Cape Colony, Lord Charles Somerset, named the town after his father, the fifth Duke of Beaufort. In 1837 it became the first municipality in South Africa. In good times the sheep farmers grew wealthy selling their meat and wool to traders in Cape Town, usually for the British market.

In the 1920s Beaufort West was a politically volatile town. The white, mainly Afrikaans-speaking community of 3 000 mostly backed the right-wing National Party which fomented Afrikaner nationalism; they bitterly opposed the ruling South African Party of Jan Smuts favoured by Barnard's father. There were also 7 000 coloureds and blacks, whose concerns were largely passed over. To the Afrikaner sons and daughters he mixed with, Barnard – the son of the Smuts-supporting missionary devoted to coloured and black people – came from the wrong side of the tracks.

Racial segregation was an ingrained part of life. At nine each evening a curfew bell tolled to warn any coloured and black person who was still in town to leave. Adam Barnard's simple mission church – its red iron roof did not even boast a steeple – survived in a white area of the town. He preached to his congregation across the road from the Boerekerk, the main Dutch Reformed Church, an impressive white neo-Gothic building with a soaring spire. Coloured and black people were not allowed to worship there. A few of the better-off coloured families, like the Morkels, who ran the butcher's shop, had homes in this area. But generally the whites lived on one side of the Gamka River – usually no more than a dry rocky bed – and the coloureds and blacks on the other.

As a boy Barnard would often join his father to hunt springbok and hare in the bare countryside around the town. He would come to have a deep, lifelong love of the wide, lonely landscape. At first the land seems empty of colour and life; and then, as you grow used to the subtleties of rock and vegetation, appears to teem with both. As Olive Schreiner wrote, some thirty years before Barnard was born, 'In the still, clear air you can see the rocks on a hill ten miles off as if they were beside you; the stillness is so intense that you can hear the heaving of your own breast.' Schreiner's 'motionless, immeasurable silences' are to be found there still today if you take a gravel road through the hills, away from the N1 Cape Town-to-Johannesburg highway that runs through the desert and slices Beaufort West in two.

The best hope of a better future for Afrikaners, many so poor that they were known as Poor Whites, lay in education. None were more certain of this than Barnard's parents, Adam and Maria. Adam, who had scarcely gone to school as a boy, was largely self-taught, while Maria was a teacher by profession. They were determined to push their sons through school and university, no matter what sacrifices they would have to make to pay for it.

*

Anyone walking into the Barnards' rectory sitting room was immediately drawn to three pictures. One showed a chubby-faced boy with large, deep eyes. Dressed smartly for the camera, his pitiful, doomed expression is explained by the next image: a grieving woman standing beside a small stone on a child's grave. Third was a painting of an angel ascending to heaven, wings outstretched, a baby in its arms. Barnard's deeply religious mother Maria would stand in front of these pictures weeping for this child, her lost son: Abraham had died at 18 months from a heart defect.

The pictorial shrine to Abraham gave Barnard his earliest thoughts about death. As a youth he told his brothers he wanted to go into medicine to help 'others with poor hearts'. Later he insisted his career was set by a dream of making money to pay off his father's debts. But the driving ambition that would shape the course of his life was honed by his strong-willed, God-fearing mother, and she doted on the memory of Abraham.

His death was not the only darkness that hung over the household before Christiaan arrived. Before Abraham, Maria had given birth to twins – a son, Johannes, and a daughter. But the girl died during the birth. Never again, the Barnards decided, would they do without a midwife.

*

Maria suffered fearsome, sometimes violent moods that dominated the household. To understand why, it is worth going back to long before Barnard's birth. The outbreak of World War I in 1914 had direct repercussions on life for the Barnards. Adam, despite his poor education, spoke good English (unlike Maria) and was unafraid to give voice to his support for the South African Party (SAP), whose leader, the prime minister, Louis Botha, had persuaded parliament to agree to Britain's request to invade German South West Africa. Adam's views did not go down well in an Afrikaner community heavily in favour of Germany. The bitterness of defeat by the British in 1902 in the South African War still ran deep. On top of this had come the thwarted rebellion of 1914-15, led by Boer War veterans angry at their government's 'imperial' line. In their turn SAP supporters rioted in major cities, attacking businesses owned by German-speakers.

Barnard's older brother Johannes, at first nicknamed 'Boetie' and later Barney, was only four when the war broke out, but he soon became aware of the open hostility towards his father. Years later, in his own account of the family history, written by hand in an exercise book, he recalled: 'The events of the war had a terrifying effect on me, as I dreaded what would happen to me, Daddy and Mammie, if the Germans should win. I remember a night when lots of people walked up and down the streets singing and shouting and Daddy told me they were happy because the Germans were winning the war. Shortly afterwards on going out into the streets on an errand some boys came to me and called me "Boetie Barnard die Hotnot Predikant se seun", "the hotnot preacher's son". They also told me the Germans would come and cut off something between my legs because my father was a "bloody SAP".'

Abraham was born several months before the war started, and was clearly ailing from birth. There was nothing the doctors could do. In a desperate effort to cure him, Adam and Maria used their savings to rent a room by the sea near Cape Town, a 16-hour train journey away. But far from improving, he grew weaker and eventually died. Both parents were consumed with grief over their loss, but Maria took it especially badly. On the tiny grave was placed a white marble stone – still there today – bearing the inscription, in Afrikaans: 'Abraham, beloved son of Reverend and Mrs Barnard of Beaufort West. There is no death in Heaven.'

Adam had given Abraham a small biscuit just before he died. He would treasure this biscuit, showing the boy's tiny teeth marks, along with a matchstick he had used to clean his fingernails before burial.

The family returned to Beaufort West, to a house of 'grief and gloom', said Johannes. For days Maria dressed in black. She never got over the death of Abraham. More than sixty years later, in accordance with her wishes, Maria would be buried alongside Abraham in Muizenberg rather than beside her husband in his home town of Knysna.

*

Soon the three large, framed pictures appeared on the sitting-room wall. This room, proudly preserved for guests, had always been a place where Johannes was forbidden to enter unless invited. But now, if he needed his mother, he knew where to look. 'I would find her standing in front of these three pictures, with tears rolling down from her eyes. Sometimes Daddy would join her and try to comfort her, but he was a man who very quickly became moved to tears, and he would then weep just as much as Mammie.'

Maria would erupt into violent rages, and Johannes bore the brunt. 'She grew more and more severe towards me and started to punish me with beatings even for the smallest misdoings, whether accidental or intentional.' Adam, plagued by ill-health but a man of firm will, would not stand for his son being beaten, and intervened. As a small boy and youth, Johannes recalled, 'I lived in an atmosphere of dread and feared my mother.'

Maria often complained of feeling tired and run-down in the year following Abraham's death, which was hardly surprising. But she also became convinced, wrongly, that she was suffering from a variety of diseases. Some eighteen months after Abraham died, another son, Dodsley, was born. His middle name, Retief, was the surname of the midwife who delivered him.

Dodsley was named after the elderly spinster who lodged with the family, and who became a much-loved figure to the young Barnards, Miss Dodsley-Flamstead. After the deaths of the girl twin and Abraham, Maria became convinced that tragedy would strike again with Dodsley. Before his birth, she and Adam begged God to give them a child 'without deformity or defect'. Maria even grew worried that she might die during her pregnancy. In fact Dodsley's birth went without a hitch and he appeared to be perfect, except to Maria, who could not rid herself of an overwhelming sense of doom. Dodsley had light blue eyes, very different from the dark eyes of Abraham and Johannes. Maria was certain Dodsley was blind. She called in the doctor, who told her she should wait a while – he had no way of establishing whether the baby was blind or not. 'It took many a week, many prayers and much poking of fingers at his face and eyes before everybody was satisfied that the baby's eyesight was normal,' said Johannes.

During her pregnancy with Christiaan, Maria was again haunted by ominous, irrational fears. She told Adam she had had a premonition that the new baby would suffer from some form of congenital disease. Even when Christiaan was born – like his brothers, in his parents' black iron bed – and pronounced 'perfect' by the family doctor, Maria would not be reassured. She insisted that he must be suffering from some illness that could not be detected. (Maria passed on this faith in premonition and intuition to Barnard. Uncommonly in later years it would often influence him as a surgeon: he would postpone an operation if the patient expressed fear.)

In the evenings leading to the births of Abraham, Dodsley and now Christiaan, Johannes would turn the Singer's crank handle as his mother stitched the seams of new bedsheets, made from Irish linen. Like most Afrikaner wives then, Maria was able to make many of the family's clothes herself.

Barnard was delivered by a midwife named Neethling and a GP. The doctor would play an important part in Barnard's life much later, when, in an extraordinary coincidence, he was on a hospital panel interviewing job candidates. For now the doctor's role was confined to making sure the new Barnard boy emerged into the world safely: which he did, in the back bedroom of the rectory in Donkin Street, a surprisingly spacious house adjoining the mission church where Adam preached. Christiaan was named after the eldest son of Dominee Rabie, the minister of the 'white' church.

Adam's pay was low – just £20 a month, a third of the salary of the 'white people's minister'. He would even rise early each Sunday to walk two miles to the town jail to preach to prisoners, thereby boosting his monthly earnings by £1 10s. Maria, although partly deaf, also earned money by playing the organ in the 'European' church if the regular organist was away, or by giving piano lessons. Yet they were able to buy a car the year after Barnard was born, and some years later they bought a seaside holiday cottage. Both were beyond many other white families living in Beaufort West at the time. Adam was a diligent saver, but others felt there must have been another source of income, perhaps from Maria's family. According to Johannes the boys often felt 'very hungry', but this was because their mother – 'brought up as a near Puritan' – would lock the pantry between meals and carefully measure out each day's rations of food, coffee and sugar.

They may not have been well off, but it can hardly be said they lived in poverty.

After his first heart transplant brought him fame, Barnard would always attribute his drive to his mother's relentless pressure 'to be first'. 'My father was the brake, my mother the accelerator,' he would say. Like his three brothers he adored his father, who was the son of a humble woodsman. But he feared his mother, who came from a prosperous farming family near George. Although she had mellowed by the time Barnard was born, she remained a stern, distant and domineering woman who rarely, if ever, kissed or cuddled her sons, and was never seen to passionately embrace her husband. The only time Barnard saw her cry was when she stood before Abraham's picture. Barnard later wrote of his parents in his autobiography, published in 1969: 'Even when older I never imagined either of them kissing with their eyes open or actually making love, other than in the dark. In fact, I had never seen them kiss with the heat of lovers. They were for us two ends of a house, fixed and untouching as different doors – one with an arch, the other with pillars, one who came to you at night, the other who drove you on by day with a hairbrush. One whom you loved, the other whom you loved and feared.'

Maria sometimes hit the boys viciously with the hairbrush. When one of the children cried out at night because they were ill, it was Adam who went to their aid. Maria herself often believed she was sick, and always complained of being tired. Perhaps the tragedies of losing first her twin daughter, and then Abraham, had so wounded her emotionally that she preferred to put herself beyond reach. She could never bring herself to talk about Abraham. It was Adam, often moved to tears, who spoke about the boy they had lost. Maria's unnatural detachment from her sons may well have been partly to blame for Barnard's compulsive need for female company in later life. It may also explain his almost obsessive interest in some of his own children when some of them were very young, a close attention he would then abandon as they grew older, often just as they sought it all the more. He clearly inherited his mother's emotional ruthlessness.

*

If Maria was behind Barnard's drive, Adam taught him to appreciate the simpler things in life, and the importance of believing, if not in God, then in himself. There was drive there too, but of a quieter kind. Born in 1875, Adam was a remarkable self-made man. He had risen from the poorest of backgrounds to marry an educated woman and devote his life to God. He came from hardy stock, but ironically owed what education he received to the fact that he was a sickly child.

The first Barnard to set foot in South Africa was Johannes, a soldier from Cologne, Germany, who arrived in Table Bay in 1708 as an employee of the Dutch East India Company. Two years later he became a 'free burgher', allowing him citizen's rights, and in the same year he married a Dutch girl, Sara Pieterz Strand. They had three children, two sons and a daughter. The second son, Adam, married a girl called Lea le Roux in 1734, and their first son was named Hendrik. Towards the end of the 18th century Hendrik Barnard was granted farming land near what is now Knysna, on the edge of a great natural lagoon where the Indian Ocean sweeps in between two heads of rock. He and another Barnard, Adam, later signed a contract with the Dutch East India Company to supply timber for ships. The forests in the area were nurtured by some of the heaviest rainfall in South Africa, and inhabited by wild elephants and leopards.

The Barnards eventually became simple woodcutters. Adam Barnard's father Jan spent his days chopping down stinkwood and yellowwood trees. He married an Elizabeth Barnard, a lean, wiry woman who was apparently no relation, and who developed a reputation in the area for being an expert in herbal cures. The family lived in a primitive cottage, no more than the size of the average double garage today, built from mud and brick. It had once had a thatched roof, but this was destroyed during the Great Fire of Knysna in 1869.

Adam was one of several boys in the family; but unlike his well-built father and brothers he was small, weak and ailing. Like the other woodcutters who lived in the forest, the Barnards were almost certainly illiterate. Adam's brothers went to work with their father in the forest as soon as they were able. They did not attend school. So big and strong were they that they were known as the 'Giant Barnards'. But Adam was different. As he grew older he suffered increasingly from bronchial asthma, made worse by the area's damp climate, and often had to stay in bed. With many hours alone to kill, and a curious mind, he developed an interest in learning. At a very late age he began attending the village school, his determination to succeed overcoming his embarrassment. Johannes writes: 'In the later years of his life he told his children how humiliated and ashamed he felt when, as a grown-up man, around the age of twenty, he for the first time sat on a school bench and had to rub shoulders with children less than half his age while learning to use the A, B, C and picking up the rudiments of High Dutch and the English language.'

Adam had a good singing voice and had always fervently attended church and Sunday school. In 1895 he joined the Salvation Army as a cadet. When the Boer War broke out in 1899 he was posted to Cape Town; from there he went to East London where he became seriously ill with typhoid fever for two months. A posting to Kimberley followed, where, in 1900, one of his colleagues noted his rapport with children, a trait Barnard would later display. Adam had clearly been taken by religious zeal even as a small boy. According to Salvation Army records, he testified in Kimberley that he had been 'saved at an early age, and grace had kept him'. He went to Bulawayo, the only time he left South Africa, and later he would often display with great pride the dog-eared return rail ticket from that journey.

But once more serious illness struck, and in 1902, now Captain Barnard and back in Cape Town, he was forced to give up his life with the Salvation Army. For the next four years he earned a living in various ways – jailer, salesman and smallholder – before deciding to train as a Dutch Reformed minister at the seminary in Wellington, set up by the missionary Andrew Murray. Adam Barnard did not have the educational qualifications needed to become a DRC minister, or dominee, to white people. He would be a reverend, and preach to the coloureds.

After being ordained in 1909 he took up his first post at Joubertina, a small town near Knysna, where he met Maria, nearly ten years his junior. They married in 1910. Adam was posted to Graaff-Reinet, where Johannes was born in 1911. Later that year, the family moved to Beaufort West. The rectory at the back of the mission church was then much smaller than it was to be at the time of Barnard's birth, too cramped for a family. But Adam and Maria persuaded the church authorities to extend it and switch the front door so that instead of being at the side, it now faced the main street through the town.

*

The extension left them with a fairly large home; Miss Dodsley-Flamstead, the lodger who arrived in 1916, took two of the rooms. She was the principal of the town's high school for girls, and the daughter of a clergyman. She had come to South Africa in the hope that the warmer, drier climate might cure her persistent cough. On cold winter nights she would sit in the dining room in front of the open wood fire – the only one in the house – and entertain the boys with stories of her childhood in England and how she had worked during the war in a hospital tending to wounded soldiers just back from the Front. She left to return to England when Barnard was seven.

The long hall that ran to the front door was covered by linoleum. It was the young Barnard's job to clean it every week. Later, to show how his mother refused to accept second best, he would tell of how he spent hours polishing it only to be told off for missing a spot. There were many other chores, no doubt shared with his brothers, but the hall was the worst: 'It collected dust from the street all week long and, no matter how hard I tried, I could never please my mother,' he later wrote. 'She was a strongly determined woman – insisting everything be perfect, that we boys be first in school, and that we never admit defeat. I was afraid of my mother, of displeasing her and making her angry.'

The Barnard brothers were mercilessly teased and called names by other children; many whites were unashamed to show the contempt they felt for Adam Barnard because he worked among coloured people. The word 'hotnot', an insulting term for coloured people, always featured in the abuse hurled at the boys. They were made to feel inferior, and it hurt deeply. In his autobiography Barnard points out that Dominee Rabie was his father's 'brother in Christ' yet had little to do with him socially. He also describes how his father would be given the cold shoulder as he went about the town: 'He wore a black suit and waistcoat, with a white strikkie, or bowstring tie. He carried his Bible and hymn book, and people in town seeing him would say, "Good morning, sir." There were some, however, who said little more than that, and avoided further contact with him because of his close association with Coloureds.' Some years later, he adds, a lawyer in the town told him: 'I am ashamed to say this, but I avoided shaking your father's hand whenever possible. I knew he shook the hand of thirty or more coloureds every day, and I didn't want it to rub off on me.'

In later life Barnard would be able to use his childhood association with coloureds to give credence to his political views about South Africa and its apartheid policy. In 1977 he wrote: 'The barefoot country boy who grew up in Beaufort West accepted the coloureds as part of his life and, although I always knew that they were different from me – the social strictures in our community made sure of that – they never seemed to me to be unequal or inferior. I felt superior only when I could beat them in a race across the rock-strewn countryside of the Karoo – or shoot more starlings with my catapult! ... I could not understand the laws of the country in which I lived. They defined that not all people were equal in the eyes of those who ruled them, because of skin colour.'

But there was another invidious side to the family's social position. Some of the coloured children abused the Barnard boys too – because they were white. Hercules Morkel, son of the butcher, says, 'We knew the Barnards usually went barefoot, and if we wanted some fun we would put thorns down on the street outside their home. We would wait across the road for them to come out, and when they crossed the street to avoid the thorns we would jump on them and rough them up a bit.' The Morkels were members of Adam's congregation and, like all the coloured families, loved and admired him. They sometimes gave him a large joint of meat for the family's Sunday lunch, and, despite his involvement in the occasional 'roughing up', Hercules played at the Barnards' home.

Johannes, being older, was inevitably more conscious of the attitude of other whites to the family. He recalled: 'We were often called "die Hotnot Predikant se seuns" or "sons of the Hotnot Minister". The bad name was barked at us by some of the young and even older people because we were poor and ill-clad. We had no money to spend freely as could the children of the wealthy wool farmers and rich folks of the town. As the first to bear the nickname I can remember only too well how hurt I felt as a youngster when addressed in this manner.'

The youngest of the four Barnard brothers, Marius, born in 1927, would never forgive the white community of Beaufort West for its treatment of the family. Christiaan's softer stance towards the town in later years would be a source of great friction between them. For decades Marius would refuse to return to the place where he grew up. He was appalled to see his father, a man he revered, not given the respect he deserved. Later he would say of Adam: 'I sincerely believe he went straight to heaven when he died. He was a man whose consideration was only for others. He was the kind of person who would give someone in need the last crumb out of his own mouth.' This view is shared by Barnard's first wife Louwtjie, who, long after Adam's death in 1958, wrote: 'If anybody asks me one day if I ever met a saint on earth, I would be able to say "Yes – a little old man called Reverend Adam Hendrik Barnard."' Her verdict on Maria, on the other hand, was scathing: 'I found her always remote, cold and untouchable.'

*

Home life was permeated by the daily prayers and rituals of the Church. Every evening after dinner, Adam would read aloud from the Bible in High Dutch. The family would then kneel by their chairs and pray. Afterwards they would all sing – usually *Rock of Ages*. After Marius was born, he and Christiaan shared the bedroom next to their parents'. At night their father would kneel at his bed and pray silently. Maria, because of her deafness, preferred to pray loudly. The next day the boys would wake to the sound of their mother's strong voice intoning morning prayers. Then she and Adam would sing together. The solemn, guilt-laden Calvinist doctrine on which the DRC was founded was reflected in the 'severe' interiors of both his father's church and the Boerekerk which, remembered Barnard, 'lacked any art suggesting the children of God could sweat and love and – alas – sin'.

Weekends were taken up with weddings, funerals and services. When Maria played the organ high in the gallery of the mission church, Barnard had to signal to her to start playing. He pumped the handle to keep the bellows full. Maybe this, he would suggest later, was what got him interested in the mechanics of the heart.

Having to sit in on three services a day also put him off attending church in later life.

But it was not all darkly serious. The Barnard boys were musical – Johannes played the ukulele, Christiaan the piano accordion. And in the flickering light from the wood fire Adam, a vivid storyteller, would entertain his sons with tales of ghosts from his boyhood. Barnard was fascinated, but he was easily spooked – he was nervous about using the outside toilet in the dark, and, as an adult, never felt relaxed on his own in a house at night.

All the Barnard brothers were baptised in their father's mission church, but because of the rules of the day they had to be confirmed in the Boerekerk by Dominee Rabie. Adam's services were always well attended. Draped over the front of the pulpit was a cloth embroidered with the words: 'Your Word is a lamp unto my feet.' Hercules Morkel, whose father was a deacon in the mission church, recalls, 'Adam Barnard was a wonderful minister. He was very down to earth in the way he preached. He never used big words. But he was a very spiritual man and a very powerful speaker. He believed in everything he said. The Barnard boys sometimes came and attended our services. They didn't sit with us. There were three benches at the front set aside for them.' Apart from sinners, Adam reserved most of his wrath for Roman Catholicism, the 'Roman danger'.

Tom Appies, son of a railwayman who lived in the coloured quarter of the town, was a boy in the last few years of Adam Barnard's time in Beaufort West. He says, 'We saw Adam Barnard as a great fighter against apartheid. He would come to visit us in our homes and he would visit the coloured people when they were sick in hospital. He would always speak out against what was going on in the country. But he was getting old in those years and his voice was weak. When he preached he wheezed. He looked pale and lean. He used to tell us that Christiaan and Marius were going to become doctors to help the family.'

Adam Barnard travelled regularly outside the town to visit the coloured workers on outlying farms, who could not get in for his services. With often vast distances involved, these trips could take several days by ox cart or on horseback, and he eventually needed an assistant to take some of this work off his hands.

Adam Barnard's moral zeal was unceasing. According to an

account by a local historian, WGH Vivier, Rev. Adam Barnard 'fought against the evils of drunkenness, immorality and the smoking of dagga'. But he clearly did not share his wife's puritanical attitudes to people who suffered weaknesses. In 1976 a friend of Barnard's visited Beaufort West and reported meeting a woman who recalled: 'My father was a drunkard. He would ask Rev. Barnard for a sixpence, and although Rev. Barnard knew he would use the money to get drunk, he would still give him the sixpence.'

It is hard to imagine Maria handing over that sixpence. She loathed anything she thought frivolous: it was sinful. She hated dancing, where Adam enjoyed it. She would tell her sons that if they did not come first in class she would 'whip them'. Yet if they came home with a good report and appeared to be proud of themselves, she would bring them down to earth by taking them out to the garden and standing them before a plum tree. 'There I would show them that the more plums the tree carried, the lower the branches hung,' she said. A branch might snap if it carried too many plums, she told her boys. 'It was a symbolic lesson – to teach them always to be modest in the flush of success.'

In later years, Louwtjie would confront her over this overweening pressure, blaming her for Barnard's ambition which she felt trampled over other people's feelings. Maria had said to her grandson André, after looking at his school report, 'You are only fifth in your class. That is bad. You must be like your father. He was always first.' Louwtjie was furious and told her: 'I don't want my children to destroy the souls of other people with their ambitions. You made your sons ambitious, but you forgot to tell them about a word called love.'

*

Barnard's academic ability helped secure his place as Maria's favourite. Jan Louwrens was at primary school with him and remembers how bright he was: 'He was one of two boys who competed to be top of the class. Once he did two standards in one year. He was clever. One day we were all given detention and told to write 500 lines because one of the boys could not recite the poem he was supposed to have learned. Afterwards Chris went to the principal and asked for five sheets of carbon paper. That afternoon he sat at the back of the class writing out his lines while we did our lessons. As soon as the teacher left the room to go home, Christiaan stood up and said, "Right, boys, I'm off." He'd done his lines with the carbon paper, and, of course, the next day the teacher didn't even look at them.'

Although Barnard was later fond of saying he 'almost always went barefoot' as a child because his parents could not afford to buy him shoes, Louwrens remembers him wearing shoes to school. 'As soon as school was finished we would all take our shoes off. But the rule was you had to wear shoes to school.' They played soccer in the street outside the town hall with a tennis ball, and rugby and cricket. In the public baths they learned to swim and dive with the 'Otters', a local swimming club, and played water-polo.

Each year, on Union Day, there was a town sports festival. Barnard later told of competing against Dominee Rabie's son Daantjie, who was four years older, in the mile race. Daantjie was a champion miler, but in 1940 Barnard was determined to beat him. According to Barnard's account, he had always run barefoot until this point. But Dominee Rabie took pity on him and presented him with a new pair of spiked running shoes for the big race. He was given 150 yards start – only to be pipped at the post by the Rabie boy. This race achieved symbolic proportions later in Barnard's own romanticised accounts of his youth. He would often refer to the pain he felt at coming second in this contest as a constant reminder of his goal in life – to come first. In reality, while he must have undoubtedly been disappointed at not winning, he reacted afterwards in the same way he would often behave later when suffering any form of rebuff. Louwrens – who believes Barnard had by this time owned spiked track shoes for several years – remembers the big race clearly: 'Afterwards Chris laughed about it, and said he had only run the race for a joke.'

At the whites-only Central High School, which Barnard attended from the age of 13, new boys were put through a brutal initiation ceremony. Willie Burger, who was a contemporary of Dodsley's and therefore several years older than Barnard, says, 'The blood really flew. It took place at playtime on the Friday of the first week you started at the school. We had to run between a line of older boys thrashing us with their belts, up some stairs. They were trying to make us fall over before we got to the top of the steps. When you got through this line there was a bucket of water and ash which they forced your head into. It was terrible punishment, and a lot of the young boys couldn't take it. Dodsley was given a fierce beating. There were so many badly injured boys on the day it happened to us that the doctor had to be called to the school and he was furious with the teachers, who had been standing around watching. There was such a row about it that it was the last time it happened.'

Frank Krynauw, who started at Central High on the same day as Barnard, could not recall being beaten with belts, something which is likely to stay in the memory. 'I do remember having my head put in a bucket of water and having to run, and my brother having his face blacked with boot polish, but nothing as brutal as being hit with belts.' Yet it must be assumed that somehow the tradition survived, because in his autobiography Barnard graphically described his initiation ordeal, in which he was thrashed with belts and had his head forced into a bucket of cow manure. He started at Central High three years after Willie Burger believes the beatings had stopped.

The high school building was close to the town's railway station – one teacher who worked there later wrote of having to blow soot off the desks when it was windy. A glimpse of what could be enjoyed if you had money came when the luxurious Blue Train began running between Cape Town and Pretoria, with a stop at Beaufort West, usually in the evenings. Like other children Barnard gawped at the finely dressed men and women on board.

The school's playing fields were barely more than a large expanse of rocky ground. Barnard continued his excellent academic progress, although he was never listed among the school's 'top achievers', and thrived at sports. At 16 he played tennis for the school, using a borrowed racquet, and was vice-captain of the rugby first team. The captain of that team was Willem Krynauw, Frank's brother, who recalls, 'Chris was a very good scrum half. But he had one problem – he wouldn't put his hands in at a scrum, in case they were damaged. He would stick his foot in, but not his hands. He was already planning to go to medical school and he was worried about his hands. It was clear to all of us that he was going to be a doctor.'

Music and dancing were to play a large part in Barnard's life. As a boy he had been taught to play the piano by a blind teacher at school and by his mother. Later he formed a musical trio outside school. He played the piano accordion his father had bought him (and which he played well enough later to impress his first serious girlfriend as a medical student).

The school was mixed, and females had by now started to attract Barnard's attention. But he preferred to keep his interest low-key for fear of arousing the wrath of his mother. It is not clear when he first started going out with girls, but he recalled sending a love poem to one girl in his mid-teens, and kissing another. He often had to slip out of his home through a back window if he wanted to meet someone, or go to a dance which his mother would have forbidden had she known. He made sure he was back by 10 pm to avoid detection. Years later he recalled: 'Dancing, my mother believed, was the quickest way to Hell. For me, it was the only way to teenage popularity. No girl would look twice at anybody who couldn't dance or, worse still, wasn't allowed to go to dances.' One girl who fascinated him, although there is no evidence that he managed to go out with her, was Annatjie. She had the best figure of any girl in the school, and boys fought over her. 'She had breasts like a grown woman. We all stared at them,' said Barnard.

In his final year at Central High he became close to a girl in the same class, Stella Oosthuizen, who had dark hair and green eyes. He would spend a lot of time at her home. In the months following his first heart transplant he received many congratulatory letters from people he had known as a boy in Beaufort West. One came from Stella's mother. In his reply, Barnard wrote: 'I always remember the wonderful time I spent at your home and how in love I was with Stella.'

'In our matric year Chris studied extremely hard in the evenings and my mother would give him a flask of coffee and sandwiches to keep him going,' says Stella. 'She also gave him my brother's old clothes because we knew how poor his family were.' Even then Barnard was a romantic. He carried Stella's books to school and sent her love notes in class. 'He'd tell me how much he loved me and how he hoped we'd get married one day. But we never even talked about sex, never mind did it. We were from a strong religious background and it just wasn't done in those days to discuss these things.'

Barnard felt his lack of money, and being the son of the mission preacher, hampered his chances of impressing girls. In an early outline of his autobiography, which then had the title *The Beat of My Heart*, he wrote: 'One day I fell in love with a girl. I had nothing to give her. I sent her a flower and a long poem. I went barefoot and in short trousers until I was 17. My father bought me a pair of shoes, but I wore them only to go to church and to go walking with a girl. You can't go barefoot when you are accompanying a girl.'

'It was me he sent the poem to,' says Stella. 'He had a chip on his shoulder, an inferiority complex because his family were poor and his father worked with coloured people. He liked to show bravado and make jokes of things. He was obsessed with money – he always said he was going to make something of himself that would bring him money, he was sick of being poor. He usually came third in class behind me and another girl, but our principal said where I had the ability to go far, Chris had the ambition and determination to get wherever he wanted to go.'

His strong feelings for Stella were not fully reciprocated. She was amused by his ardour. 'We became very close and often held hands at school, but I never had romantic thoughts about him. There were other boys more debonair.'

Barnard would one day become famous for his sexual exploits, but the close-knit Afrikaner society in which he grew up gave him little opportunity for carnal adventures. Johannes admitted that his early sexual experiences had been with mischievous friends of the family's black maid, a not uncommon story in Afrikaner households. There is no proof, but it is quite possible that Barnard, good-looking and curious and full of adolescent sexual energy needing an outlet, also enjoyed furtive fumblings, at least, in a similar fashion.

He was attractive to girls – even as a boy, he had a charm that singled him out. He usually wore hand-me-down khaki shorts, cut from his father's trousers and often worn first by his older brothers. Pieta Fourie, whose father was the tailor in Beaufort West, says, 'Whenever there were birthday parties Christiaan would arrive in his khaki shirt and shorts, always with a patch on the seat. I used to feel sorry for him, so I asked my father to make him some shorts for free. Often Christiaan would come into my father's shop and talk for a long time about the antiques he had on display there. Sometimes Christiaan would be allowed to choose some clothes for nothing.'

In boyhood photographs Barnard's early good looks are clear. There are pictures of him at 13 with a school tennis trophy, one – with Marius – when he was a member of a swimming team at about the same age, and one taken of the school rugby side when he was 17. Another shows him in the school cricket team. In all his ears stick out, but his face is fine-boned and his eyes are focused intensely on the camera.

In one picture, taken when Christiaan was just a year old, his moustachioed father is already grey-haired. Despite the ill-health which dogged him throughout his life, he looks bright and sits upright in his jacket, waistcoat and pastor's white tie. His slender fingers bear a wedding ring. Maria, holding Christiaan on her lap, has her dark hair tightly tied behind, and manages the faintest smile. Johannes and Dodsley, also in the picture, are well-dressed in jackets and ties.

*

Barnard would make much in later years of the 'poverty' he endured as a child. On Christmas morning he and his brothers would wake to find their stockings empty, save perhaps for a piece of fruit. His father, he would say, never had money to buy them toys. It was an essential part of the story of how the barefoot boy from Beaufort West had made good. But there are those who lived in the town at the same time who query this account. One photograph shows Johannes, well-dressed, driving a pedal car in the front garden of their home.

Poor or not, the Barnard family often enjoyed the generosity of others. Gifts of food came from farmers to keep the pantry stocked. In *The Beat of My Heart* Barnard painted this scarcely imaginable picture of hardship which did not surface in his published autobiography: 'My father explained the financial problems of the family. I remember very well how he would say grace at the head of the table every evening. We ate bread and salami and drank black tea. Occasionally there was something more on the table, a hard-boiled egg for instance, and we children would compete to have a small bit of it. I know that my father was hungry too, but he always left that extra something for us. He knew how much we desired it.' While this sounds overdone, Pieta Fourie remembers walking into the rectory one day to find Maria standing at the wood-burning stove praying. 'She was praying for food because they had nothing. Farmers often sent them vegetables and meat. A short while after she had prayed a cart arrived from one of the farmers with food. Mrs Barnard said to me, "See, if you pray you will get what you ask for."'

Sometimes the Barnard boys would feel so hungry that they resorted to plundering their father's vegetable garden. They ate raw onions, tomatoes and green beans – and even the bitter fruit of a lemon tree in the back garden. They also stole the fruit from the pear trees that lined Donkin Street.

Yet Frank Krynauw is one who disputes the notion that the Barnards were 'poor'. 'They were never talked about as being poor in Beaufort West. We all ran around in bare feet when we were at primary school, but when you went to high school you had to wear shoes, and we all did, including Chris Barnard. His father would never have stood for him walking round without shoes. The Barnards had a car when only wealthy people had cars, years before my father could afford one. They had a holiday home, and only people with money had those. My father was stationmaster and he earned more than Adam Barnard but he could not afford to put two sons through university. Yet Adam Barnard sent four sons to university.'

Nevertheless a lack of money seemed to weigh heavily on Barnard. It would lead to a craving for wealth throughout his life. He often spent Saturday afternoons walking with his father in the countryside, or sitting on a kopjie (a small hill) above the dam where he and his friends swam just outside the town. His father would teach him about the wildlife in the Karoo, explaining how to tell birds apart by their song and showing him scorpions under rocks. He taught Barnard to appreciate detail, a lesson that helped make the surgeon the perfectionist he became: 'My boy, the man who hasn't time to give to the little things won't be able to find it even for the big ones,' he would tell him. When they hunted, Adam, a good shot, carried a 12-bore while Barnard had a smaller rifle. But they would also discuss the family's financial problems, including the burden of a £500 bond on the holiday cottage at the Wilderness, about 270 kilometres away on the coast near Knysna, which his father had bought with a view to renting it out. Despite his church's disapproval of gambling, Adam even bought a lottery ticket on one occasion, hoping it would rid him of debt. It left a great impression on Barnard.

With his brothers, Barnard earned extra money for the family by catching mice – at the town hall they would pay a penny for each one – and selling sheep bones and bottles scavenged from the surrounding fields. The bones would be crushed in a factory and sold back to farmers to help them fertilise the soil. Caddying at the golf club was another way to bring in some cash. Adam even tried his hand at one stage writing short stories that he sent off to *Die Burger*, the Afrikaans daily newspaper in Cape Town. They were rejected.

*

With so little money to spare, the arrival of the family's first car in 1923, a dark-brown Willys Overland touring model, came as a shock to Maria. Adam had apparently told no-one in the family that he had decided to spend £300 on a car, equal to 15 months' salary. Johannes recalled: 'We two boys jumped with glee but Mammie clasped her hand over her mouth … Her eyes filled with tears.' But Adam said he needed the car to help his work on the farms, and to enable them to take trips to the seaside and broaden his sons' horizons.

In this car they would drive each summer to the Wilderness, a 12-hour expedition along narrow roads, across rivers and through spectacular mountain passes. At first they rented an old double-storey house set among milkwood trees close to the beach. Later they bought the holiday cottage. Maria, showing a combination of favouritism and callousness towards her children that would later manifest itself in Barnard as a father, insisted on calling this cottage 'ChrisMar' after her two youngest sons. What Johannes and Dodsley thought of this can only be imagined. At the Wilderness the Barnard boys could swim in the warm waters of the Indian Ocean and go on long treks through the rich forest that surrounds the resort.

*

There were few signs that the young Barnard was destined to go into medicine. As a youth, though, he often showed a gruesome fascination for the workings of the animal body. Frank Krynauw says he would sometimes arrive at school with a bag of chicken heads collected from the Beaufort West Hotel kitchen, and proceed to dissect them with a penknife on his desk at break time while the other pupils were outside. 'He never really explained what he was trying to do, but it seemed a bit strange. Now and then they would start to stink – we'd tell him to get rid of them, and he'd laugh.' Occasionally he would cut up beetles and other insects to see what went on inside.

But otherwise his experience of medicine seemed to be confined to his grandmother's homespun wisdom, as passed on to his father. According to Johannes, Adam had learned from his mother 'various natural remedies' like the use of weeds and garden herbs to cure ills and heal wounds. She was 'well-known for her skills in treating and attending to the ill, wounded or dying'. Barnard later told of how his father would apply a mixture of paraffin and candle wax to cracks in his sons' feet in winter.

According to Dodsley's second wife Kay, as a boy Barnard sometimes spoke to his brothers about wanting to heal people with heart problems, like Abraham. But when pressed later on why or how he chose to become a doctor, he said it was because Johannes, by now studying engineering at university, told him to go into medicine to 'make a stack of money'. 'He repeated it so often that in the end I decided to become a doctor. I thought that if I made a great deal of money one day I would be able to repay my parents and the friends who had helped me,' was how he put it in *The Beat of My Heart*.

*

The outbreak of World War II in September 1939 again polarised political opinion in South Africa. The sympathies of the Barnards once more came under scrutiny in Beaufort West. The country was now run by the United Party, a union of the SAP and NP. General Hertzog, who argued for neutrality, was prime minister, and the pro-British Jan Smuts was his deputy. By a narrow margin the South African parliament voted to enter the war on the side of the Allies. Hertzog resigned, and Smuts became prime minister. At Central High Barnard and his fellow pupils were still a year away from matriculation. Whether or not Barnard had decided by now on a career as a doctor, the issue most on his mind was the war.

Barnard chose to follow his father's pro-British line rather than take sides with some of those Afrikaners who had made him feel like a second-rate outcast. He would later insist on the Anglicised version of his name to make the point. Frank Krynauw, who later became an advocate, recalls his passionate defence of Smuts in many classroom debates at the time: 'Adam was very political and was always very critical of the NP. We didn't expect that from a mission preacher. Chris was exactly the same. Whenever we had a political debate about what was going on he was the main speaker. He should really have gone into politics. He was totally in favour of Jan Smuts's position and wanted South Africa to go into the war on the side of the British. He felt so strongly about it that when he went on to medical school he insisted on being called Chris. We had always called him Chrisjan, an Afrikaans version of his name. But he decided he didn't like that, so he dropped the "jan" to make it sound English. Yet he didn't go off to fight in the war. Some of the others in our class joined up later, but not Chris.'

More than 300 000 South Africans of all races volunteered to fight for the country on the side of the Allies in World War II – including Dodsley, who dropped out of university to do so, much to the dismay of his parents. He would be taken prisoner at Tobruk, but eventually escape and find his way back to South Africa.

By the time Barnard matriculated in December 1940, he was clearly showing the will to be first his mother had been determined to instil in him. The *Beaufort West Courier* of 22 January 1941 notes in its list of matriculation results that CN Barnard had 'passed first class, with admission to university'. Adam and Maria must have been justly proud, and relieved. Their eldest son, Johannes, had already failed his university engineering exams twice, and the family resources were being stretched to the limit. Dodsley had abandoned his studies to go to war. They prayed that their third son had the ability to become a success, and their hopes now looked to be grounded in something more than parental faith.

There was evidence too that Barnard was a character of many talents, and no dull academic. School records show that he had attained the rank of sergeant-major in the cadets; that his musical trio was 'very popular'; and that his ability as a public speaker, even then, was such that he was chosen by his class to give the farewell address on behalf of the outgoing pupils.

The Helpmekaar Fund, set up by Afrikaans businessmen to support the education of Afrikaners, had agreed to lend money to Adam and Maria to pay medical school fees. Barnard, now 18, was set to spend the rest of the war years in a very different way to his brother Dodsley: training to be a doctor in Cape Town.

3

Medical School

The single-storey beach house at the Wilderness, a beautiful and unspoilt resort 15 kilometres from George on the Cape's Garden Route, had been bought as an investment by Adam Barnard. But his plan to rent it out at £5 a month to provide extra income had failed. At one stage it was let for a whole year, but otherwise the few sporadic rentals that came along barely covered the cost of maintenance. Nevertheless it made an idyllic holiday home, standing as it did almost on top of the dunes and with a stoep, or verandah, looking out towards the Indian Ocean.

As usual, in January 1941 the Barnards arrived at the house ready to enjoy several weeks of sea air, a welcome relief from the merciless midsummer heat of the Karoo. Nature walks in the rich forests that surrounded the Wilderness, led by Adam using his walking stick to point out this flower or that butterfly, were a daily source of enjoyment for the Barnard boys and their holiday friends who tagged along. Maria, stern and serious as ever, preferred to remain in the house preparing meals or mending clothes. This particular holiday was rather different from previous ones, for Dodsley was away fighting in the war and Christiaan was about to fly the nest to begin life as a medical student. The air of fun was overshadowed by fears for Dodsley and, in a different way, apprehension for his younger brother, especially in view of the costs involved in sending him to the University of Cape Town; he would carry the whole weight of his parents' expectations on his shoulders.

For Barnard this holiday was to prove special for another reason. He and a friend had taken to caddying at the local golf club to earn some extra cash. The friend had several sisters, including one known by her nickname 'Ningi', who caught Barnard's eye when she appeared one day on the golf course. He was immediately struck by her good looks and vivacious smile. In his autobiography he recalled this first encounter: 'We came to a green and Ninky (sic) and her sisters started singing, *Boo-Hoo, you've got me crying for you*. Then she did a little dance by herself on the green while they all sang *Begin the Beguine* and I thought, hell, man this is really a fantastic girl.' That night they all went to Ningi's house to dance and 'outside I held her and she came close and kissed me. That was the first time anybody had ever kissed me like that, and I fell madly in love with her.'

Ningi, real name Katharine Stevens, was an art student, a brunette with unusual grey-blue eyes, and just a few months younger than Barnard. But coming from a non-religious 'English' background – her father was a sugar farmer who spoke fluent Zulu (hence her nickname, which means 'handful', given to her as a baby) and her mother British – she was considerably more worldly wise than the young Afrikaner preacher's son. She liked his intense green-brown eyes, energy and sense of fun, but found him 'innocent'. 'We were both innocent really,' she says. 'In those days no-one dared to do the things they do now. I would never have kissed him on that first night.' But she, too, felt an immediate attraction. 'He was full of fun and clearly very ambitious. He seemed star-struck with the world. Everything was great to him, everything was shining. He was lively, very enthusiastic. He could not say my nickname properly with the hard "g" sound because he was Afrikaans, so he called me Ninky instead.'

When Barnard's autobiography *One Life* was about to be published in 1969 Ningi learned of some of the scenes depicting her when a magazine planning to serialise the book approached her for an interview. She and her sisters were appalled by one particular episode in which they were supposed to have bathed naked in a river in front of Barnard and exposed themselves to him, singing *Anchors Aweigh* as they stood on a rock 'like two river nymphs, their bodies white and pink and also dark at mysterious places I hardly dared look upon'. As they slipped into the water, 'their little breasts bobbing like separate suns' and their 'two little bottoms going in double arcs before splashing with all the rest of their delights into the blue water', the soon-to-be medical student kept his trousers on before jumping in after them. 'I had never slept with a girl or even seen one nude,' he wrote. 'Ninky had seen all sorts of nudes because she was an art student and already going to the university. I would see more of them now, as a medical student, but nothing would ever equal the splendour of Ninky's body.' By the time the book was due to come out Ningi was married and the mother of two children. She went to her attorney who had a word with the publisher in South Africa, Howard Timmins, who agreed not to identify her in the book. Her name in the South African edition of the book was changed to Jackie, although it remained 'Ninky' in foreign editions.

She insists now that Barnard had wildly exaggerated the scene. 'Show him my naked body? Not in his wildest dreams! We were swimming naked but the water was so dark you couldn't see anything below the surface. And *Anchors Aweigh*? We didn't even know the song.' But Barnard's memories were clearly coloured by the sexual excitement he felt about her at the time. His only previous romantic experience of any note had been in his final year at school with Stella. 'He told me they had kissed a few times but that was all,' says Ningi. 'He was very innocent with me, and back then you had to be a good girl or you got a bad reputation. He had come from this very strict, strait-laced background. He was still dominated by his mother's moralistic code. But he was very romantic, good-looking and lots of fun to be with.'

Ningi's visits to the Barnard holiday home gave her a glimpse into the suffocating religious routine Barnard had always known. 'I would go over for dinner and it was such a new experience for me because they always said grace before the meal. Then after dinner we'd kneel on the floor while Adam read from the Bible. Yet even then Chris would be making little jokes and smiling at me.' Later the pair would sit on the verandah until dark – when Maria would step out to switch on the light, bringing the evening to an end.

On other evenings they would dance to records with friends at Ningi's house, or to Barnard playing *Begin the Beguine* on his piano accordion. Released from the stultifying atmosphere of the Beaufort West rectory, the young Barnard was overwhelmed by this beautiful, wild creature who knew nothing of the rigid home environment he had grown up in. Soon he was declaring his love. 'It was certainly far more serious for him than for me,' says Ningi. 'It meant a lot to him. He told me he loved me. But for me it was little more than a holiday romance. We never got beyond kisses and cuddles. It was a very child-like love affair.'

Evidence of just how smitten Barnard was with Ningi comes from Johannes, with whom he lodged when he moved to Cape Town to start medical school. So infatuated was he that he would erupt into joyous singing. Writing many years later, Johannes recalled: 'I noticed within a few days after Chris joined us that there was what one might say a twinkle in his eyes. Soon the cat was out of the bag. Chris was in love ... I know that she inspired him and made him burst into song.' Johannes recorded the words of the song belted out by the love-struck Barnard:

I would like to ride a ferry
Where music is so merry
There's a boy who plays the concertina
On the moonlit upper deck arena
Where boys and girls are dancing
And sweethearts are romancing
Life is like a Mardi Gras
Funiculi, funicula
Happy as we swing together
Happy as we sing together
On the ferry boat Serenade.

Such heady love for Ningi may have been understandable amid the heat of summer and at a time of great transition for an inexperienced, emotional teenager; but impulsive desire for an alluring woman was to be a recurring theme in Barnard's life, often with disastrous consequences.

While Barnard's heart was absorbed in romance and having fun during this, his last Wilderness holiday before he began his arduous medical studies in March 1941, his determination to make a name for himself had not been forgotten. 'He was in awe of people who were famous, like film stars,' says Ningi. 'He was particularly excited by people who reached the top, the zenith of their professions. I knew he would do well – there was so much riding on him because his parents had made so many sacrifices. He often talked about how much he wanted to be a good doctor. His mother had encouraged him to be first and he made it clear he wanted to fulfil that ambition, to be Number One. He was extremely single-minded.'

After the holiday Barnard and Ningi continued to see each other in Cape Town. In several poignant scenes in *One Life* Ningi is remembered fondly. Once a month the couple would go to the cinema to watch the latest Hollywood star in action – Gary Cooper was a favourite. According to Barnard's own account, he would spend all his monthly allowance of 10 shillings, which he received from Johannes, on this outing with Ningi. Her recollection differs: 'I always paid my way because my mother knew Chris had no money. I simply wouldn't have let him pay for me. Chris wore hand-me-downs, although he didn't make a thing of it.'

Again, according to Barnard, Ningi is supposed to have told him that he should live more by instinct. Instead he had disciplined himself like a machine that must not fail. Yet he could learn more from defeat than from winning, she told him. There was something inside him unreachable, as if he was 'carrying someone else around inside you who was giving you orders …' More than sixty years later Ningi cannot recall these highly charged conversations. But she does remember clearly the moment when, after a few months of seeing Barnard occasionally, among other boyfriends, she decided to bring it to an end. 'When he came to my house one evening I told him I thought he was getting too serious, and that it wasn't a serious thing for me. He was rather upset and he gave me a long, cynical look, but that was that.'

*

In early 1941, less than two years into the war, UCT Medical School was passing through 'troublesome, momentous, exciting and promising times' in the words of Professor Jannie Louw in his history of the establishment, *In the Shadow of Table Mountain*. It was overflowing with students. The government had let it be known that those studying medicine and engineering would not face conscription because they were seen as 'key' people. Undoubtedly one reason for the bulge in the ranks of both disciplines in the early war years was the fact that they were a bolt hole from the danger of being sent to fight in a war many were dead set against joining. The prime minister, Jan Smuts, who had favoured South Africa siding with the Allies against Germany, was also chancellor of UCT at this time. The proportion of Afrikaners attending this 'English' university – most of whom took the Hertzog line and disagreed with entering the war at all – was higher than it had ever been. Chris Barnard, as he would always prefer to be known from here on, was an Afrikaner who took the Smuts position. Cultural and language ties would inevitably draw him close to some among the Afrikaner set at medical school, like 'Pikkie' Joubert, with whom he would later work in an ill-fated venture as a GP; and Piet Willers, with whom he would form a problematic business partnership in later life. But partly because of his more 'left-wing' or liberal views he also developed close friendships with several from the English-speaking group, such as Harry Webber – who would become a psychiatrist, and was then using his original surname Aufrichtig – and Basil Jaffe, both then members of the Communist Party and of the Students' Socialist Party.

Donald Ross, who had started a year before Barnard but would also qualify in 1946 – and who would go on to perform Britain's first heart transplant in 1968 – recalls a lot of tension between the English and Afrikaans medical students over the war. The Afrikaners, many of whom, like Barnard, were from poorer, rural backgrounds, were clearly driven and had little time for play. They looked upon their better-off English colleagues as arrogant time-wasters. 'We saw the Afrikaners as being a rather dull, hard-working and dedicated bunch, and they thought we were rather frivolous because we liked to party and drink,' says Ross.

'There was quite a lot of ill-feeling about the war. There was a dividing line after which you had to finish your studies or you were free to go off and fight. I was in the year when we were told we had to finish our studies rather than go to war as they thought we would be more use that way. We felt strongly about it. About a dozen of us, English-speakers, went down to Simonstown to see if we could join the navy. They said they were very impressed but that we should finish our studies. That didn't occur with the Afrikaner-speakers because on the whole they didn't want to join the war.'

Barnard's main concern when he arrived at Cape Town railway station, to be met off the Beaufort West train by Johannes and his wife Joyce, was how he was going to survive financially. He wore clothes that had once belonged to Dodsley, suitably adjusted by his mother; he could conveniently lodge for free with his brother in their two-bedroom flat in Rondebosch (a suburb close to UCT), avoiding the fees for staying in residence. But he had books to buy, and the 10 shillings a month allowance from Johannes would not cover this. The Helpmekaar Fund had already assisted Johannes through university, although now, out of his £36 a month salary from South African Railways as a 'pupil engineer', he was having to pay back the loan as well as supporting his younger brother. The Fund would now help the Barnards put Chris through medical school. As the trio drove away from the station in Johannes's 10-year-old second-hand Riley, they were keenly aware of how vital it was that Chris succeeded. The economic screw would be turned tighter at home while he studied to become a doctor. 'It was Daddy, Mammie and Marius who had to bear the brunt,' said Johannes later.

Two days after arriving in Cape Town Chris Barnard was one of around one hundred and eighty 'freshers' who walked onto the UCT campus to enrol for their medical studies. (Another was Rodney Hewitson, who would outshine Barnard at the medical school and would later become his right-hand man for many years at Groote Schuur.) By his own account Barnard walked along the streets up the slopes of Devil's Peak, the back of Table Mountain, towards the magnificent white pillars of UCT's Jameson Hall, feeling rather lonely amid streams of babbling students, all seemingly better dressed than him: 'I walked alone, knowing no-one, conscious of pants that had been worn by my brother, my jacket that had been given to me by my dear friend Michel, and, most important, the bright yellow tie on which I had spent nearly all my money – symbol that I was a freshman and properly dressed. This, at least, was new ...'

His pride in the tie was short-lived. A senior student, with the build of a rugby player, rudely pulled him up before he could enter Jameson Hall. He pointed out, in the true style of the kind of bully Barnard had come up against occasionally at school, that the tie he was wearing was not yellow, but orange. It would make him stand out among the freshers, said the bully threateningly, and must be changed. Barnard recalled being horrified to realise he was right. After registering for classes in the hall – feeling 'confused and humiliated' by now he signed his name twice in the wrong place – he returned to his lodgings to face the problem of retrieving the money he had spent on the tie to buy a new one. Fortunately the shop that had sold him the orange tie relented, and he found a perfect yellow tie elsewhere.

At 18 Barnard's command of English was less than impressive, a weakness he would have to overcome rapidly. In the first year, in which classes were held on the UCT campus, four subjects – Chemistry, Physics, Botany and Zoology – were intended to provide a solid academic grounding. Barnard found himself 'less prepared' than other students, partly because of the language barrier and partly because he had not studied physics at school. It was a 'sad omission for a prospective student of medicine', noted Johannes years later: 'Because I had qualified in Engineering I started tutoring my brother in this subject, which gave him difficulty … It was a pleasure to teach Chrisjan. He was so keen and worked hard.'

Soon after starting medical school, Barnard could see that even with assistance from the Helpmekaar Fund he would struggle to make ends meet. He approached the university registrar. After studying Barnard's record to date the registrar decided he could have a three-year Bolus scholarship to cover the £80 a year tuition fees – but warned that should he fail at any stage, it would be withdrawn.

The pressure on Barnard to succeed had now doubled. Yet the mid-term exam results in his first year delivered a huge shock. With a mark of just 43 per cent he was seven points below the pass rate in physics. 'It was not the final, year-end exam, and two more tests were scheduled for those who had not passed. However, it was the first exam I had ever failed in my life, and I was alarmed,' he wrote later. After a week of intense work, no doubt with the help of Johannes, he achieved 65 in the repeat test. He had passed, but it wasn't good enough for Barnard. He insisted he be allowed to take it a third time, got 73 and 'never again felt like a parrot in physics'. A six-month course in botany, conducted by a lecturer known for her fascination with mushrooms, led to top marks for Barnard, whose knowledge of the subject had been nourished by those long walks in the Karoo and the Wilderness forest with his father. He found chemistry, which he had studied at school, straightforward; but zoology posed another problem. He had scraped through the mid-term exam and the final was expected to be even more difficult.

Showing characteristic initiative and determination, he set about conquering the subject by putting in a vast amount of extra work. With money handed to him by Johannes and his mother, he bought a scalpel, scissors and dissecting forceps. Frogs, dogfish and rabbits were obtained from the university research laboratory attendant, and these were taken back to his brother's flat to be dissected. Often he worked until dawn. In what must have been a gruesome scene for Joyce and Johannes he would sometimes boil a rabbit in caustic soda on the stove to dissolve its flesh from the skeleton.

The hard work paid off. In his finals Barnard achieved three firsts, including – to the delight of Johannes – physics. He got a respectable second in zoology. The real medical training would now begin and continue for five more long, gruelling years.

In this first year Barnard had found little time outside his studies to enjoy himself. He went in for the fresher trials at rugby but was outclassed. He had been something of a star on the school rugby field. Now he could not make the first team. He would, in fact, continue to play rugby occasionally – he was a 'slightly built, unorthodox player with more enthusiasm than skill', says one former student – but only for the third- or fourth-string side.

As a boy Barnard had learned to swim and dive confidently, and in his first year at UCT he pursued these interests, representing the university in three-metre diving competitions. (Years later his diving skills would astonish a party of Spanish dignitaries when he spontaneously stripped off his suit and dived to the bottom of a dam to retrieve a photographer's expensive camera.) He also liked to visit the baths close to his brother's home. But in general the pressure on him to do well and his natural enthusiasm for study ruled out much else.

Barnard may have worn jackets with elbow patches and trousers that didn't always fit well, but he was a handsome, confident student who even then possessed a special charm with women. Charlotte Webber was one of only nine women who started medical studies at UCT in 1941. She recalls dancing with him at the Freshers' Ball in Jameson Hall during their first week: 'All the men wore proper suits so Chris must have found one from somewhere.

It was a real ball where the girls had invitation cards. Chris danced beautifully. He was a very attractive person, outgoing, with a wonderful smile. He seemed to be interested in girls but none of us went out with him. He always seemed to be busy doing other things. From about the third or fourth year he was often doing experiments in the labs.'

He was mischievous. 'As part of our course in medical jurisprudence we attended a murder trial at the Cape High Court,' recalls Charlotte Webber. 'A woman was accused of murdering her husband. While this poor woman was giving evidence Chris was standing behind me trying to make me laugh by tickling the back of my neck.' Basil Jaffe, who much later would become Barnard's GP for a while, says, 'He had a great sense of fun. He used to take the mickey out of some of the more timid lecturers. He had a lot of confidence and cheek. He was never shy or fearful of anyone.'

Micky Baskin was also impressed by Barnard's boldness: 'He had a mind of his own. He was a very forthright, clever chap. He wasn't afraid of anybody – he spoke his mind. He had no fear of the professors whatsoever. He was always asking questions. Everything he did in his work was done with absolute zest.'

By the summer of 1941 Adam Barnard had sold the holiday cottage in the Wilderness – he had always dreamed it would be his retirement home – to pay off his bond. He used much of the rest of the cash to buy a house in the suburb of Pinelands, about four miles from the medical school. The plan now was for Johannes and Joyce to live there, paying Adam the rent. From now on Barnard would have to walk, or catch a bus or train, every morning; to save money, of course, he would mostly walk. In fact, he often ran to make the journey quicker.

While his fellow students rarely saw Barnard with a girlfriend or at a dance, he seemed to be enjoying himself away from medical school. The Barnards entertained themselves musically at home – Johannes with his ukulele, and Chris on his concertina and a piano Johannes had bought for £82 on the 'never-never' at £2 a month. There was no wireless in the house, and the lack of money forced them to be careful about what they spent on food. The three used to joke: 'If you have to die, it is better to die slim.' To save money on petrol, scarce as it was in the war, the car was used just once a week to go to buy vegetables.

For the first time in many years there was to be no refreshing holiday visit to the Wilderness. Instead, lamented Johannes, it was the 'dust storms, blistering summer sun and heat of the Karoo which must be endured'.

The anatomy course which began in the second year – when studies moved to the medical school next to Groote Schuur Hospital – placed Barnard face to face with the chill reality of death. Like many young medical students seeing cadavers for the first time, he felt queasy both from the sight of the corpses and from the smell of formalin, used to preserve them: 'To learn anatomy it was necessary to take the body apart and physically note its separate nerves and muscles and organs. Yet the vision of twenty bodies, each on a marble-top table, was so overwhelming that I almost had to turn back into the corridor of the anatomy building ... I could not breathe, let alone look upon them,' he later wrote.

The man who taught Barnard anatomy, a gentlemanly Scottish professor by the name of Maxie Drennan, would leave a lifelong impression. He was famous for his skilful, colour-coded anatomical drawings on the blackboard: muscles were brown, arteries red, veins blue, nerves yellow, and bones white. 'They were so good some students would take photographs of them,' recalls Piet Willers. 'Drennan was a classic professor, he absolutely lived for his subject.' Unusually perhaps for an anatomy professor, Drennan had an MA degree in natural philosophy; he was also an internationally renowned anthropologist. He was 'the doyen of the medical faculty, greatly respected and loved by students and staff alike', noted Jannie Louw. His lectures were packed with lively anecdotes, and his tendency to repeat words as he searched for a memorised sentence became a tradition at the medical school: 'The joint has a rich ... rich ... rich ... a rich blood supply,' he would declare.

The young Barnard was bowled over by Drennan's powers of communication, attention to detail and, away from the lecture hall, bravery as a hunter. In *One Life*, he wrote: 'Professor Drennan was my ideal – a man of grace and knowledge and physical courage. The corridor of the anatomy building was lined with heads of wild beasts he had shot at close range. He had a knowledge of anatomy that was astonishing. In classes he would illustrate sections of the body by drawing the nerves, vessels, muscles and bones on a blackboard, using coloured chalk and drawing with both hands at the same time. The finished work would resemble an etching from a textbook. With this he had a Victorian elegance we all admired.' It was perhaps from Drennan that Barnard learned the art of turning a science-based lecture into a tour-de-force of anecdote, humour and unexpected visual shocks from slides and illustrations. Barnard's later ability to communicate complex concepts in a vivid and entertaining way would be a major factor in his success as a public speaker, and make him a natural media man.

Drennan's students were split into groups of eight which were each assigned a cadaver. Over the coming weeks the cadaver would be systematically stripped and plundered until each student was intimately acquainted with its nerves, muscles and organs. Harry Webber and Barnard were in the same group, and shared a macabre sense of humour. In later life Barnard would joyfully recall how Webber announced one day that their cadaver, a 40-year-old white man, should be known as 'Chaim', pronounced 'Hy-am', Hebrew for a common salute meaning 'Life!' and a play on the English translation of the reply given by God to Moses when asked His name in Exodus, Chapter 3: 'I am that I am.' A few days later, with the cadavers decimated, Webber declared the body should now be called 'Chaim-Not'.

Barnard had bumped into Webber on his way into Jameson Hall to register on that first day at UCT. Webber, the youngest of a family of ten whose Jewish parents had emigrated to South Africa from what was then Poland in 1926, would be Barnard's closest friend for much of his early period at medical school. 'We seemed to hit it off immediately,' says Webber. 'I came from the Eastern Cape and I could speak very good Afrikaans. On that first day we chatted about our backgrounds and we seemed to have quite a bit in common.' Webber, the son of a shopkeeper, was two years younger than Barnard but found the missionary's son to be 'unsophisticated and naive in a charming way ... he was forthright and straightforward; he had no side to him.'

Webber had a three-year bursary on condition that he achieved at least average seconds. He also had an allowance of £8 a month, thanks to an older brother, and he generously took pity on Barnard as he tried to live on a much smaller sum, albeit with no boarding expenses. During the war there was a marked shortage of textbooks, and students came up with an ingenious way of solving the problem. Virtually verbatim notes of a lecture would be put together by several students, who would then sell copies to others. Webber often paid for sets of notes for Barnard. Occasionally he treated him to lunch in the dining hall – usually Barnard would make do with sandwiches made up by Joyce every morning. Webber also introduced Barnard to culture by taking him to the Sunday evening classical music concerts at the Cape Town city hall in his old Austin 7. 'I don't think Chris had been exposed to any kind of culture at all before then.'

It was Webber who introduced Barnard to communism, discussing Karl Marx and the suppression of the working class. Barnard said later they 'agreed on almost everything', including the need for a better deal for the working man, especially coloureds and blacks. Webber told him the middle-classes had sold out to the rich, which struck a chord with Barnard, for at that time the white 'middle-class' of Beaufort West were trying to close down his father's church and move the coloured congregation out. Webber suggested Barnard meet some of his friends, fellow members of the Students' Socialist Party. After this, he 'seriously considered' joining the group. In the end he didn't, mainly, he claimed, because he could not square Webber's atheistic views with his father's devotion to God: 'I thought only of my father's love of God and how interlaced this was with his work for the Coloured people, and suddenly it was clear that Harry and I could never agree on this subject.' His father's faith in God, however, did not appear to stop him embracing Darwin's evolutionary theories, which formed part of his studies.

Webber confirms that Barnard had been deeply affected by his experience as the son of a missionary to coloured people in apartheid South Africa. 'His family had been looked down upon. He had a chip on his shoulder, but he wasn't bitter about it. He always had a smile.' Nationalist Afrikaner students put pressure on Barnard to side with them in campaigns to elect members of the Student Representative Council, but he always refused and voted instead for the SSP candidates. 'We agitated over various things, such as the absurd treatment of coloured medical students who were not allowed to attend a post-mortem on a white patient, but

Chris didn't really get involved because he was too busy studying. He had fun too, played rugby, liked girls, went out a bit, but on the whole he worked hard,' says Webber.

Physiology, the study of living organisms, was the other main subject in that second year. It was clearly more to his liking than the dissection of dead bodies. He learned to 'pith' a frog – to stick a needle through the animal's brain and spinal column so that while there was no brain function, the heart and nerves continued to work. Barnard was fascinated by what he would come to describe as a 'situation later explored with other animals in studies for the heart transplant'.

Histology, in the examination through a microscope of organic tissues from skin, for example, taught him how 'to be familiar with a functioning organism, to know what to expect from it and thus prepare ourselves to do what every doctor must eventually be prepared to do – leap from the known to the unknown'. Bacteriology, the study of organisms causing disease, and pharmacology, the science of drugs used to fight these diseases, were other key areas of this course. They would pave the way for an 18-month study of pathology which would show how the body copes with disease.

Determined to score firsts, Barnard put in hours upon hours of evening work. He even attended an extra course in chemistry. At home he would slog away at *Gray's Anatomy*, learning by heart page after page. Johannes had bought this essential book for him, as well as other textbooks. He wondered whether it was wise to adopt such a mechanical approach. 'He sat in his little room night after night, week after week until he could recite pages of *Gray's Anatomy* verbatim. I thought this wrong, as in my studies of scientific subjects I believed in memorising the principles, then reproducing it in my own words. So I questioned Chris as to why he was learning things like a parrot. To this Chris replied: "Could you put anatomy in better words than Mr Gray?" This, of course, was quite correct, so I left him to work out his own salvation.'

The walls of Barnard's bedroom were covered in detailed sketches of cross-sections of the human body – limbs, torso and the heart – which he would study while changing his clothes.

Yet, despite the intensive slog, Barnard got only a second in anatomy in the end-of-year exam, which left him 'deeply upset', said Johannes. He had missed a first by just one per cent, and

Johannes told him this must be down to discrimination against his Afrikaner background. He did, however, score a first in physiology at the end of an 18-month course, one of only three awarded to the whole class, whose number had now fallen to around 130 thanks to first-year dropouts and others who had left to join the war effort. His success in physiology showed Barnard was making his mark, although he would never rank among the very brightest of the students such as Hewitson, Willers and Ross.

Halfway through this academic year, in June 1942, the Libyan port of Tobruk fell to the Germans in a catastrophic and unexpected loss for the Allies. Many South African soldiers were killed, injured or taken prisoner. It was to be months, however, before word came through from the Red Cross confirming that Dodsley was still alive and being held as a PoW in Italy. Before his capture, Adam and Maria had sent him regular food parcels and letters. Miss Dodsley-Flamstead, now living back in England, also sent him food packages. At medical school Barnard often spoke warmly to friends about his brother. 'He was very fond of Dodsley,' recalls Harry Webber. Yet when in the following year the Afrikaans rugby players chose to break away from the main UCT team in protest at a plan by the Western Province Rugby Football Union to donate ticket money to the war effort, Barnard would strangely opt to support their protest by turning out for the third- or fourth-string team in the new league, according to Piet Willers. It was typical of the kind of enigmatic stand Barnard would sometimes take in later life, and in truth probably had more to do with wanting to get a game of rugby than making a political statement about the war. Yet while his friends Webber and Jaffe readily enlisted in the 1st Medical Officers Training Ambulance, a unit of medical students who volunteered to man ambulances in place of staff who had been sent to war as members of the SA Medical Corps, Barnard did not. Later he and Dodsley – who would eventually escape from PoW camp and make his way back to South Africa via England – would fall out bitterly for long periods. When Dodsley died in a car crash in 1975, the brothers had not spoken for several years.

Barnard was staunchly and openly opposed to the racist views of the more right-wing Afrikaners. There were a handful of coloured students in the class – only three would eventually qualify – and he often sat with them during lectures. Later he would publish a novel, *The Unwanted*, which would draw on his observations of the discrimination faced by coloured medical students at this time. 'There was no racism in him at all,' recalls Webber. One well-known right-wing Afrikaans professor gave extra tuition to students of a like mind, and Barnard was certainly not among the chosen.

Towards the end of 1942 a new family moved in across the road from Johannes's and Joyce's home. They were a Greek-Afrikaner couple who had a particularly attractive young daughter, Hendrika, although at this stage she was still carrying a little 'puppy-fat'. Johannes recalled: 'One hot day Chris took Hendrika with him to the varsity swimming baths. He later told us he had been somewhat embarrassed when at the baths he bumped into some of his friends he did not expect to find there at that hour of the day. So he tried to talk to them, by leaving this girl where she was sitting and walked over to his friends, as he was afraid that they would pull his leg, because his swimming companion was a bit plump. Within a few minutes there was a loud thump and a splash of water to all sides! Hendrika had dived off the highest spring board and landed like a bomb. She was winded and dazed so Chris had to jump in and save her.'

Other female visitors to the Barnard house would be disappointed if they didn't find Chris there, and they would leave small notes on his desk in his room to let him know they had been. Another new family, by the name of Kelly, moved into the road. They had one unmarried daughter, Rowena. She and Barnard decided to take ballroom dancing classes together, and both became experts. There was one small snag – Rowena's boyfriend. He grew increasingly jealous, and after a while the dancing classes came to an end.

Barnard was often teased by his older brother about 'not being the bravest of men'. The fear of the dark he had had as a boy had not left him, and his powerful imagination made him nervous. After his first contact with the 'cold, bloodless limbs' of the cadaver in anatomy it had taken him a week to steel himself to touch the body again. Such experiences inevitably sowed self-doubt in the minds of young would-be doctors. One woman student in Barnard's class gave up her ambitions to be a doctor completely after feeling repulsed by her first post-mortem. Now Barnard was to face another experience that would lead him to think he might not have what it took to become a surgeon.

During his return to Beaufort West in the summer months Barnard would help out a local GP, Jacobus van der Merwe, who would take him on his rounds at the hospital and out to remote farms. 'It was valuable training,' wrote Barnard later, 'for I learned from him that acute attention to the smallest details, to the tiniest clues, can lead to success – and also that no doctor knows it all.' Van der Merwe also offered him the chance to witness his first operation, an appendicectomy on a young girl. Barnard was excited at the prospect, and dreamed that an emergency would occur and he would be called on to help. But as Van der Merwe began to make the incision in the girl's abdomen, it was Barnard who caused the emergency: 'At the sight of blood pulsating from the open wound I became nauseated. The odour of ether was suddenly oppressive, my knees went weak, and bells began to ring in my ears. There was a chair in the corner, and I staggered over to it just in time, sitting there with my head spinning, and dimly aware that I was about to faint.'

Shaken, Barnard tried to work out why he had reacted in this way. How could he ever become a surgeon if he could not face the sight of blood? By now he had dissected three bodies at medical school, and handled living tissues and organs from animals. The difference, he decided, was not just that the girl had been alive and her blood had come out pumped by a beating heart. There was something more. One of the nurses attending the operation told him it always happened to students with too much imagination. Van der Merwe assured him it was normal – surgeons identified with their patients and his experience until then had involved only dead bodies. This was 'the real thing'. Was it also, Barnard wondered, to do with a fear of death on his part, the death of the patient?

Back at medical school, he was in for a further shock – his first post-mortem, part of the pathology course that began in his fourth year. The pathology professor had a pale, yellow complexion, as though 'constant search through the entrails of the dead was investing him as well with their own special colour', wrote Barnard. In front of him lay the body of a young woman who had died of cancer. He watched the professor slice into the skin around the skull, peel it back over the face, and then use a hand-saw to cut into the skull itself. He then used a hammer and cleaver to sever the brain from the skull. The brain had to be removed first in all post-mortems, explained the professor. His next move was to slit the woman's body from the vagina to the throat. With this, Barnard got up to leave.

His inability to sit through the post-mortem plunged him into despair. According to his account in *One Life* he walked out into the fresh air, up past Groote Schuur and into a small chapel. There he agonised over his horror. He described coming to the conclusion that his 'anguish and rage – and, yes, my fright' was the result of a fierce reaction to the 'loss of life before it had run its span'. Death, he decided, was to be feared as an enemy when it prematurely cut life short, but welcomed when the time was right. How this explains Barnard's perfectly natural queasiness, which he would have gone on to overcome in any case, is not clear. His friends at the time doubt that he would have spent too long analysing his feelings in this way. 'Chris wasn't a philosopher,' says Webber. 'We were all rather disturbed by the post-mortem. It was the first time I had seen a dead body. But you got over it.'

Barnard duly recovered to go on and witness many more post-mortems. He also assisted in a minor way in some operations at Groote Schuur. While other students were enjoying themselves on the rugby field or in the bar, he spent many hours hanging around the operating theatres; occasionally he would be called upon to help in some small way. His confidence grew. Students normally wore used gloves, but when there were none available they were given new ones and this gave them the 'exciting sense of being more like real surgeons'.

Now the students were given their first taste of looking after real patients. Barnard's first was an old lady crippled by rheumatoid arthritis, an image that would haunt him later when he would be diagnosed with the same disease. Under the guidance of men like John Brock and Frank Forman – both renowned for their scrupulous attention to detail and almost inspired clinical abilities – Barnard learned the importance of spending time with patients and putting their needs first. It was training of the highest calibre, and it stayed with him throughout his career. Forman in particular had legendary status in the South African medical world.

But at home problems were starting to surface. Friction between Barnard and Joyce was creeping into what had been a friendly set-up in Pinelands. There were frequent arguments between the pair, and Johannes found himself having to act as arbiter. 'There were also, as I saw it, distinct signs of jealousy because Chris and I were close brothers,' said Johannes. Barnard finally decided it was time to move out, and he took a room in a house with other students in a road close to the medical school. Later, when Marius arrived to start medical studies, they would share lodgings.

In 1945, his fifth year, another striking character entered Barnard's world. Professor Cuthbert Crichton, a fiery Irishman, taught obstetrics and gynaecology, which would involve students assisting at deliveries at the Peninsula Maternity Home in District Six, a 'coloured' area where the rapid rate of births made it an excellent training ground. Crichton terrified most of the students but was an excellent teacher, one of the medical school's 'Big Three' as they were known, and he would exert a great influence over Barnard. He was renowned for 'loving his patients' and would drop in on them at unexpected times to check on their progress, something Barnard would also become known – and feared by his staff – for. One medical graduate described Crichton in the following terms: 'He is lovable, Irish and explosive, charming ... He who would brook no interference or dispute – anything that savoured of argument would cost the "impudent young buck" six months' further study!' Unlike his colleagues, however, Barnard refused to be cowed. 'Chris was fearless of people,' says Webber. 'We would all be hoping Crichton wouldn't ask us to perform because he liked to humiliate you. He wanted you to give the wrong answer so that he could use it as a way of demonstrating the right answer. He was a bully. But Chris would walk in and go up to him, shake him by the hand, and say, "How are you?" Crichton loved him. Chris had complete confidence and an ability to disarm people with his naive friendliness. This fearlessness was a characteristic that was responsible for a lot of his personality, a lot of his achievements in later life.' Willers recalls: 'Everybody was frightened of Crichton – he could tear you apart – but Chris was one of his favourites.' Barnard later described Crichton as 'a man I respected and enjoyed and who often reminded me of my father …'

Apart from the experience of growing up with his little brother Abraham's death in the background, Barnard had so far had no direct encounter with the loss of a loved one or friend. But now one of his closest boyhood friends, Michel Rossouw, died from tuberculosis. As boys in Beaufort West the pair had played together, and Rossouw, whose father ran a shop, was a kind soul. 'Everything he had he divided with me whether it was a sweet, a toy, a flower,' said Barnard. His early death bitterly upset Barnard, and on the day of the funeral he was one of the pallbearers who carried the coffin to its rain-soaked grave. According to Barnard Rossouw had wanted to see him one last time but he did not respond to the message until it was too late.

Barnard would soon meet his first real love, the woman he would marry. But before this he enjoyed a bizarre romantic escapade with twins. Adam and Maria had rented a holiday house at the Strand, a resort 30 kilometres from Cape Town. Johannes, Joyce and Chris joined them, and it was there he met the attractive twin sisters, who were lively blondes. It's not clear from Johannes's account of this episode whether Barnard dated both girls at the same time or individually. But when the holiday was over he was keen enough to travel back to the Strand regularly at weekends – sometimes in his brother's Riley but usually by bicycle – to see them. 'Chris was so sure of himself that he was willing to bet one pound against ten that one of these damsels – he did not say which one – would become his wife. So high was his fever,' wrote Johannes.

But it was during this fifth year at medical school that he met 'Louwtjie', or Aletta Louw, then a raven-haired young nurse who worked at Groote Schuur. She had injured her back while tending to an overweight patient and was recovering in Ward C2 – the same ward where the first heart transplant patients would be cared for years later. Barnard recalled going to the ward to visit another nurse he was seeing, a 'cute blonde'. Instead his attention was caught by Louwtjie, lying in a bed, who asked him to post a letter for her. He liked her eyes – 'big and brown and full of wonder' – and her 'cute little nose'. For her part, she liked his 'big ears and beautiful hands', she said later. Barnard visited Louwtjie several times a day over the following week, and before she was ready to leave hospital they had arranged their first date, a trip to the Savoy cinema to see Charles Laughton in *The Private Life of Henry VIII*.

As a student Barnard's love life seems to have been surprisingly tame, especially in view of his later notoriety; as a young man his parents' vehement disapproval of loose sexual behaviour, set against the heavy Calvinist backdrop of his boyhood and youth, perhaps held him back. He had had the fun of dating twin sisters, and there had been one married woman student who had pursued him openly. It may well have been this woman he was caught kissing in his lodgings one day when her husband climbed through a window brandishing a pistol. But Harry Webber believes Barnard may have remained a virgin until he met Louwtjie. There is a strong suggestion in *One Life* that he and Louwtjie may have slept together on the night of his graduation in December 1946. But Louwtjie was apparently furious with him when the book was published containing this insinuation. According to Louwtjie's account they did not sleep together until their wedding night in 1948, more than two years after they met. Harry Webber recalls a weekend spent with his girlfriend, Barnard and Louwtjie at a house in Llandudno, a hamlet with a secluded beach close to Cape Town: 'We all slept separately in sleeping bags. It was terribly innocent. For my last three years at medical school I was living with my girlfriend, but Chris was the type of chap then who might sleep in the same bed as a girl but not make love to her.' In later life friends of Barnard would say he boasted of having 'lots of girlfriends' at medical school; they simply refuse to believe he did not sleep with them.

In her book *Heartbreak,* written in the bitter aftermath of their divorce, Louwtjie described the way their relationship developed: 'Chris was an ordinary, personable young man. He was ambitious, had a zest for living and a determination to succeed. We were simply two small-town people who met accidentally, were attracted to each other and gradually fell in love. This was no whirlwind romance, it just happened slowly and surely. There is no doubt that Chris possesses an irresistible charm for women and I was no exception.'

Even the strong differences in their political views were no hindrance. Louwtjie, the daughter of a wealthy farmer, came from solid middle-class Afrikaner stock. Her uncle was Eric Louw, who would become an influential foreign minister in the government. 'We had lots in common except for our political views, but when you are in love, politics do not make any difference,' said Louwtjie. The couple would pool the money they had so that they could afford to go out to dinner or to see a film. By doing odd jobs at weekends and by helping as a 'demonstrator' in some classes, Barnard had managed to scrape enough money together by now to buy an old car, a blue Austin. Later, after he had qualified, this would be sacrificed to provide the cash to buy a diamond engagement ring.

Graduation Day, 13 December 1946, saw Louwtjie sitting proudly with Barnard's parents in Jameson Hall as he collected his Bachelor of Medicine and Bachelor of Surgery degrees. He had hired a car to fetch Adam and Maria from Beaufort West for the big day. His finals results must have come as a disappointment – seconds in obstetrics and surgery, a third in medicine, above average but hardly sparkling – especially after the months of cramming he had put in with Harry Webber, night after night. But he had qualified and could now look forward to beginning his career. He did not appear to have a firm goal in mind, and had certainly not expressed any particular ambition to become a surgeon that anyone can remember.

Whatever lay ahead, he was in a rush to get started. Charlotte Webber recalls that the usual practice then was for qualified students to apply to the SA Medical and Dental Council for registration after graduation. Barnard wired his registration fee as soon as his finals results were known, and was registered immediately. He had already arranged to start a six-month internship in gynaecology with Crichton, but that was not due to begin for another month. In the meantime he had decided to gain valuable experience, and a little money, by filling in for a GP in a country town, Usakos, in what was then South West Africa (now Namibia). Adam Barnard suggested he might enjoy a rest, but Maria typically agreed he should get going. They planned a celebration that night – 'Louwtjie squeezed my hand to say that half the night it was not going to be with everybody. Then she dug her nails into my palm and whispered it into my ear,' he wrote in *One Life*. But the next day he was on a train, heading for Usakos.

4

Young Doctor

Three days later Barnard stepped off the train at Usakos, a desert town between Windhoek and the coastal resort of Swakopmund. Usakos was a lively centre of mining and sheep farming; it was also the hub of the country's railway industry. Barnard would stand in for a local GP while he took a month's holiday. As a newly qualified doctor plunged into the maelstrom of general practice in a remote part of Africa, he would be forced to cope with a series of crises with no-one to turn to for advice. 'Good luck, old chap,' the gentlemanly GP told him after showing him the list of patients and handing over the keys. He then drove away to begin his holiday. Within 24 hours Barnard had removed two teeth from a screaming boy, dealt with a complicated birth using forceps, and treated another boy bitten by a snake. He discovered his anaesthetist was a Roman Catholic nun who had to be called away from prayer whenever there was an emergency.

Usakos was a hard lesson for the confident young doctor, grounding for his future spell as a country GP. By the time the older doctor returned to reclaim the practice Barnard was relieved to be heading back to Cape Town, 'more than ever glad to have before me the collective security of Groote Schuur, beginning under so wise a man as Professor Crichton'.

Barnard moved into a lodging house attached to Groote Schuur to begin his 12-month period as a houseman, or intern, on a salary of £150 a year. If he really thought the 'collective security' of the hospital would make life easier he was in for a shock. He found himself in the front line as the casualties of violence, drunkenness and disease, fostered by often dire living conditions, poured in through the doors of the state hospital. Donald Ross, who started as a houseman on the same night as Barnard, recalls: 'There was a shortage of beds for the doctors and we were told we'd both have to sleep in the same bed. But we were so busy dealing with head injuries and the like that we didn't get the chance to sleep.'

One case in particular remained with Barnard for many years: a cancer patient who pleaded with doctors to end her agony. When older he would become a strong advocate of euthanasia, arguing that it was a doctor's job to improve the quality of life, not simply to prolong it for its own sake. The desperation of this woman, who appeared to be dying in great pain from cervical cancer, was too much to bear for the young houseman. Deciding to answer her prayers for relief one night, after her screams had filled the hospital corridors once more, he loaded a syringe with a lethal level of morphine and walked towards her as she lay dozing from the effects of an earlier painkiller. But as he held her arm ready for the injection that would end her hell, and cast him as a murderer, he was seized by the conviction that it was wrong. He turned away and released the morphine into a nearby sink. As he did so, the woman awoke looking brighter. She thanked him for making her feel better, unaware of how close she had come to death at his hand. Several weeks later she walked out of the hospital, her pain gone and her cancer seemingly beaten back for years to come.

Barnard's confidence in his judgement and ability showed itself even at this age. He was just 24, and working with many nurses of much greater experience. But his insistence on getting things right, which marked him out throughout his career, was already making him a hard taskmaster. 'He would slap down the nurses for any form of delinquency,' says Richenda Fry, one of the women who had gone through medical school with Barnard. 'He hadn't been among the very brightest of medical students but he was very firm about what he believed in. He was a go-getter even as a houseman. If the nurses did anything that was not right he told them off.'

After six months in gynaecology Barnard got the chance to do six months in general surgery. As an intern he was allowed to perform only minor operations such as appendicectomies or hernia repairs. He and two other interns, including Pikkie Joubert, would compete to do as many of these as possible in the hope of being allowed to tackle more complicated operations. Barnard would later recall how he typically 'jumped the gun' during an operation to remove a gall bladder. As the intern it was his job simply to prepare the patient for surgery by making sure he was properly anaesthetised and opening the abdomen. But when the moment came when the surgeon should have taken over there was no sign of him. Barnard continued dissecting until the bladder was ready to be removed. When the surgeon finally arrived he found the operation almost complete, and he told Barnard to finish it while he watched. (The surgeon was Jannie Louw who would later become head of the surgery division at Groote Schuur and play a crucial role in Barnard's development.) Barnard was immensely excited by his success and was determined not to let things go wrong. He sat up all night with the patient. Few interns had ever been allowed to perform such an operation.

His relationship with Louwtjie, who was training to be a theatre nurse, was going well. After more than two years together they had become engaged. With the proceeds of the sale of his Austin Barnard bought a solitaire ring with what Louwtjie described as 'a diamond as big as a pea cut into four sections'. Each night Louwtjie was supposed to be back in her room at the nurses' home behind the hospital by 10 pm or midnight, depending on the day. Invariably, like the other young nurses, she failed to reach the entrance in time before the doors were locked. She would stay overnight in the doctors' lodgings, rising at 5 am to scramble back to her room to change and report for duty. Barnard always insisted they were not sleeping together at this time. But they were certainly set on marriage, despite their differences. Like his mother, Louwtjie did not like dancing, according to his account, whereas he enjoyed it; she was also jealous and volatile.

Only once did Louwtjie assist Barnard in an operation. She remembered it as an appendicectomy, he as a leg amputation. Louwtjie was the instrument sister. At one stage the forceps clamping an artery slipped off, allowing blood to pump out, and a tense exchange followed between surgeon and nurse. They didn't speak for several days afterwards.

An operation to remove a leg from a small boy with cancer prompted misgivings in Barnard about the destructive nature of much surgery. He felt there should be something he could do to replace the leg rather than just cut it off. Again for him it came down to the quality of life. A similar case is described in *The Unwanted,* Barnard's first novel, in 1974, written with Siegfried Stander, in which a three-year-old girl with cancer has much of her lower abdomen removed to rid her of the disease, leaving her unable to have children, and dependent on a colostomy bag. Barnard always questioned the worth of destroying or removing large chunks of the body to preserve life. Medicine, and surgery especially, had to have a more positive purpose.

Perhaps with the more creative nature of birth in mind he was 'greatly relieved' to be offered a doctor's residency, once his year's housemanship was up, at the Peninsula Maternity Home, an elegant former private home in District Six. He had already worked there as a student. Now he would move into the doctors' quarters and experience the daily tumult of what was probably Cape Town's most vibrant, violent and volatile area, a mix of whites, coloureds, Malays and Indians bustling together on the narrow streets, their often large families crammed into bursting slums. District Six would later be flattened by the bulldozers of the apartheid regime, and its extraordinarily varied inhabitants evicted, most to populate the bleak Cape Flats.

The doctors of the Peninsula Maternity Home were loved and respected by the community, but they made sure they wore their stethoscopes around their necks at all times to be safe. District Six was dangerous but Barnard was often out working late at night. He went into tiny, overcrowded homes where the woman giving birth was often penned into one corner of a room, while the rest of the family watched from another. Rats, cockroaches and fleas infested these hovels, and the baby often had to be delivered by candlelight.

Yet Barnard found the work here deeply rewarding. His upbringing among the coloureds of Beaufort West had left him with an instinctive ability to communicate with people of other races in a way most Afrikaners, especially in the South Africa of 1948 with the Nationalists about to take control and racial attitudes hardening, would have found impossible. There was no superiority in his tone when he spoke to a young coloured mother struggling to have her baby in conditions the majority of whites could not have imagined. He could talk their language, the street Afrikaans he had picked up as a boy. He felt immensely satisfied at having brought a child into the world: 'There was a clean and wonderful feeling, walking back at dawn through the narrow, empty streets, knowing that you had left behind another human being …' he recalled later.

He began to consider specialising in obstetrics and gynaecology. But with marriage to Louwtjie on the horizon, and a family perhaps, he had to earn more money. A call from Pikkie Joubert, then a GP in Ceres, a small country town 130 kilometres from Cape Town, offered an unexpected opportunity. Joubert had been left in sole charge of the practice while his senior partner, Tim O'Molony, went abroad for a year. The work, explained Joubert, was too much for one man. There was great potential too. A small hospital allowed them to carry out minor operations. Ceres was prosperous, old-fashioned, the centre of a fruit-farming area and popular with Capetonians searching for clean mountain air. It looked the perfect place for a young doctor to make a good living and bring up a family.

Barnard mulled it over for a few days, trying to clarify in his own mind whether it was the right move. Joubert had been persuasive about the income possibilities, and that now had to be the key factor. As a youth he had dreamed of earning a lot of money as a doctor, enough even to help his father. Louwtjie was enthusiastic. Barnard decided to take up the offer. It was to prove one of the most bitter experiences of his life.

*

Determined to make the right impression on the people of Ceres, Barnard obtained a bank loan to buy a car, a dark blue Chevrolet sedan. It was, he said later, the first 'major investment' of his life. Loaded with books and bags, he drove into the town – accessible only via a winding mountain pass – buoyed up by the challenge ahead.

According to his own account, the very first day in Ceres brought a woman about to give birth, a child with measles, and a leopard attack. In *One Life* Barnard described in great detail how Marie van Rensburg, still in shock and barely conscious, arrived in a truck driven by her husband. Her dress was ripped down the front and 'matted with blood'. Her body, said Barnard, was 'cut and clawed in a way which could only have been caused by a beast such as a leopard'. He described how he and a nurse 'began to slowly sterilise and suture 57 wounds'. Once the woman's wounds had been closed and she had been placed in a private room to recover, the husband told Barnard the story. He said he and his son had been tracking the leopard because it had been killing their sheep. They found it and shot at it but only managed to wound the animal. In a frenzy the leopard had run off towards their farmhouse and sought refuge in their kitchen. The wife had been at the doorway when it appeared – it leaped at her, knocking her off her feet. A powerful woman, she managed to grab the weakening animal by its throat. The farmer's dogs had by now reached the kitchen and were snapping at the leopard – until it 'went limp and expired' just as the woman lost consciousness.

It was a remarkable and dramatic start to the new job, except that the evidence suggests Barnard had played, at best, only a minor role in a much smaller drama. He had not taken care of Mrs van Rensburg but had stitched a thumb wound sustained by her son Andries. O'Molony recalls tending the bite wound in Mrs van Rensburg's arm, with the help of Pikkie Joubert, and believes Barnard 'was not involved at all'. Barnard's account was also inaccurate on other fronts. The leopard was not shot, but killed with repeated blows by Mrs van Rensburg's two sons using a piece of bluegum tree and rocks. Pikkie Joubert's widow Truida says the stuffed skin of the leopard was already in O'Molony's house when Barnard arrived in Ceres. But Andries van Rensburg, now 86, is adamant that Barnard was the doctor who stitched his thumb.

Barnard no doubt discussed the story with the family on occasion, and his gripping 'account' of the incident found its way verbatim into a history of Ceres published in 1988.

Barnard relished the intimate contact with patients he found in this small town. It was completely different from working in a hospital, where a doctor saw a relentless stream of patients and rarely got to know them. In Ceres he 'became part of the total experience of human beings I would treat – part of the web, the corner, the roof of their existence'. Coming from another small country town, he was able to ease into the social side of life effortlessly. He played rugby, cricket and tennis. But Barnard's obvious ambition soon began to stir uneasy feelings in Joubert as he set about establishing himself in what he quickly saw was a lively business.

They lived in O'Molony's house – even sharing the one double bed because the only telephone was next to it – and agreed to split cases, income and expenses from the practice 50-50. The surgery was in a cottage at the back, and had two consulting rooms – one, spacious and well-equipped for whites, with chairs, desk and a couch; and one for coloureds, with just one chair and a couch, where the doctor usually stood while carrying out the examination. There were also, of course, two waiting rooms: one for whites inside and comfortably furnished, the other outside beneath a canopy. The whites were mostly private patients who paid their fees on account; the coloureds, if they could afford it at all, paid 7s 6d cash a visit, or up to £1 if they needed special medicines. Only a letter from the local magistrate confirming they were too poor to pay would absolve them of the charge, in which case the government picked up the bill. According to Barnard's own account, under a government medical scheme coloureds were also entitled to have minor operations paid for by the state – '£5 for abdominals and two guineas for the anaesthetic' – and with a backlog of such cases the two young doctors could make a lot of money. O'Molony had also handed over to Joubert his two roles as district surgeon and railways medical officer, the latter bringing in a salary of £8 a month. For every mile the doctors travelled on government business as district surgeon they were paid one shilling in expenses. In such a rural area the miles could be clocked up swiftly.

As a district surgeon Barnard had to take on his share of the more unpalatable work. At the jail the district surgeon had to be present once a month when convicts were lashed as punishment for crimes dealt with at the magistrates' court. Younger criminals, those under 16, were brutally caned at the police station rather than sent to jail. None of those beaten were white.

Barnard could see that here, in Ceres, was an opportunity to make his mark – and to make money. The hardships of his upbringing had not left him. The afternoons he had spent with his father discussing the family's financial problems would never fade from memory. As far as Truida Joubert was concerned, he made it clear that he intended to harvest the wealthier patients for himself. 'At the start he would whine when the work got too much and talk about going off to specialise,' she says. 'Then Pikkie talked to him and said if they carried on building up the work they could both become partners in the practice when O'Molony returned. Pikkie later told me it was the worst thing he could have said. Chris stopped whining. Instead he started trying to build up a practice within a practice, concentrating on the wealthier, white patients wherever possible.' Barnard made disparaging remarks about O'Molony to his former patients. 'He didn't seem to appreciate how well-loved O'Molony was in the town. O'Molony was a gentleman with a wonderful sense of humour. His patients were extremely loyal to him.'

Barnard's casual approach to dress in a town where the rather strait-laced residents were used to seeing their doctors in suits did not always go down well. 'Sometimes he would turn up at our house in dirty sand shoes after playing tennis,' said one. Yet Barnard and Joubert worked well together as a team, especially when performing the many small operations they tackled in their six-bed hospital. 'They could do some things in record time,' says Truida. Barnard typically showed more daring than Joubert, who was sometimes keener to refer cases to Cape Town than take them on himself. Tonsils were whipped out in five to ten minutes; appendices seven to ten; hernias were repaired in 20. Barnard's willingness to act too quickly provoked rows. After Barnard died, Joubert told a newspaper: 'His big thing was that he was daring. He was the most daring doctor I ever knew. He would do things that no other person would do. One day he wanted to take out a man's kidney, just because he believed that the man had kidney stones. He did not even look to see whether the man perhaps only had one kidney. When I told him that he could not do something like that, he was furious with me.'

There was the usual range of emergencies on outlying farms that required a fast drive over poor mountain roads, often in bad weather. Barnard gained invaluable experience tackling difficult births, pneumonia cases, farm accidents and, on one tragic occasion, delivering a baby boy to his surgery nurse, which died within an hour from a heart defect.

The death of this baby had a profound effect on him, he was to write 20 years later; it marked the moment he saw his future lay in working with the heart. It appeared to have been caused by a common condition known as transposition of the great vessels, in which the two major arteries to the heart are swapped, leaving the child with two distinct circulatory systems. Ironically only if there is a further fault, a hole in the heart wall, the septum, allowing the blood to be mixed together, will the child live for a short while, perhaps several years. Otherwise the baby is usually aborted or born dead. It was this same condition, believed Barnard, which probably killed his younger brother Abraham.

Louwtjie had returned to her parents' farm in South West Africa (Namibia) to prepare for their wedding day. Barnard was working seven days a week, but he was not prepared to wait for female company. He began seeing a girl in Ceres. This girl knew nothing of Louwtjie until one evening when Pikkie Joubert walked in on the couple as they cuddled on the sofa. Joubert made a remark about Barnard's forthcoming wedding, and the girl was never seen again.

The wedding day duly arrived: 6 November 1948. It was, according to Louwtjie's recollection, a 'gloriously sunny' Saturday afternoon. Both sets of parents were there, and two of Louwtjie's four sisters were bridesmaids. 'Chris got his moral support from his brother Marius,' recalled Louwtjie. 'Marius was rather amusing because his trousers were a little long and he kept pulling them up.' It took place at the Groote Kerk in Cape Town, appropriately for two staunchly Afrikaner families. Afterwards they held a small reception at a nearby coffee house, with Barnard's friend and mentor Cuthbert Crichton proposing the toast. Louwtjie left with her father, as was the custom, to change for going away. Barnard fetched his car, only to find that a boyhood friend, Fanie Bekker, who had attended the wedding, had mischievously punctured a tyre, causing an hour's delay while the morning-suited bridegroom got out and changed the wheel in the centre of one of Cape Town's busiest streets.

They were to honeymoon at the Wilderness. But they had decided to stop along the way to spend their wedding night in a small hotel in Elgin. Barnard's account of this night was a source of bitterness in Louwtjie in later years. In *One Life* he described how his new bride had fallen asleep in their room after dinner and he had slipped downstairs to listen to a boxing match between the South African and British champions. When the South African was knocked out he returned to the room, said Barnard, to find Louwtjie awake and sitting up in bed, clearly angry. She spurned his advances, until he was able to smooth things over.

But Louwtjie recalled things rather differently. In *Heartbreak* she asks whether it was 'probable' that she would have been asleep at 9.30 pm on her wedding night, the time the fight started. Instead she remembered that after a 'delicious dinner' her new husband had asked if she would mind if he listened to the fight because there was no radio in the room. 'I was delighted and said "Yes, of course." This would give me ample time to relax in a bath, change into the extravagant new negligee I had indulged in and make myself attractive for my husband on my first night of marriage. There would be no scuttling and hurrying. I would be able to take my time. I had barely stepped out of the bath before Chris returned to our room. The fight was over and Johnny Ralph had been knocked out. But boxing gloves, rings and seconds were soon forgotten. Everything was exactly the way I had imagined. That is the one memory I shall always treasure.'

Written in the acrid months after their divorce, Louwtjie's version of events is tinged with nostalgia for that simple first night of married love. She adds: 'It was perfect and beautiful – the love between a man and a woman in love. It was the most beautiful night of my marriage.'

After two 'enchanted weeks' in the Wilderness, during which Barnard shared with Louwtjie 'long-forgotten secrets and incidents' he remembered from his many childhood holidays there, they drove back to Ceres. Louwtjie felt apprehensive about what was to come, but the welcome she received from Pikkie Joubert soon put her mind at rest. She was, in fact, a second cousin of Truida and knew her family. Louwtjie would later say that the years she spent in Ceres 'were amongst the happiest days of my married life'.

O'Molony returned, and was pleased to see the practice had continued to grow in his absence. He agreed there was enough work for all three doctors. The Barnards had been living in his home and now had to find a place of their own. After a spell renting another house, they decided to buy their first home, an attractive, single-storey, tin-roofed house on a corner plot with an ideal garden. It was also just across the road from the surgery. Louwtjie was now expecting their first child, and for her life seemed about as perfect as it could get.

Barnard, however, sensed trouble ahead. O'Molony says he found Barnard extremely ambitious from the beginning, and did not like his volatile temperament. 'We could hear him from the house screaming at some of the patients, things like "You bloody fool, why didn't you come here before? Do you want to die?" My mother-in-law had to ask him to stop screaming at the patients. It became clear to me that he wanted to run the practice. I was told he would ask my patients what I had prescribed for them, and tell them he would give them something better.' On his return O'Molony also found Barnard 'working with patients he had acquired for himself, mostly white, the wealthier ones'. The situation would grow increasingly tense.

In April 1950 Louwtjie gave birth to Deirdre at the Booth Maternity Home in Cape Town, where she had gone to be under the care of Crichton's successor at UCT, James Louw. Knowing that things were coming to a head in Ceres, Barnard spent the hours before the birth consulting his former colleague Jannie Louw about whether there might be a surgical post available at Groote Schuur. Jannie Louw agreed to keep his eyes open.

When Barnard saw his daughter later that day, less than an hour after she was born, he was overcome with a father's love and pride: 'I had never felt anything like this before, and was surprised at the suddenness of its arrival,' he recalled. The baby girl was to be named Dedrika Johanna after Louwtjie's mother, but Barnard preferred the French version of the name, Deirdre Jeanne, which they settled on. (She was almost named Scarlett after Vivien Leigh's character in *Gone with the Wind*, which was and remained one of Barnard's favourite films.)

As Barnard feared, his problems at the practice grew worse. It went on for a few more months, but before an escape route had opened up O'Molony decided to confront him. By now Louwtjie was pregnant again, and the need for financial security was that much greater. 'Chris realised there was something building up, not only from us but from the patients too,' says O'Molony. 'I think he expected he and Pikkie to tell me to push off. In fact I had started looking round for something else in Cape Town because my wife didn't like Ceres. But I could find nothing. I decided Pikkie and I would stay.'

Barnard was devastated at being told he must leave. Now he had a wife, a daughter and another child on the way. There was still no opening for him at Groote Schuur, and he told O'Molony and Joubert he would stay in Ceres and run a rival practice. However, after canvassing the views of a number of patients he had come to know well he discovered their loyalty to O'Molony was stronger. There was no future for him in Ceres. It was a humiliation – perhaps the only defeat of his professional career, and one he would never forget.

Later Barnard always spoke bitterly about the affair, claiming Pikkie Joubert had betrayed him, and portraying O'Molony as a dour, crotchety, grey-haired figure with a limp when in truth he was only eight years older than Barnard, often joked, and only limped because of a childhood illness. Oddly, in view of his feelings, he remained in occasional contact with Joubert, sometimes returning to Ceres to shoot with him or watch Deirdre waterskiing. He also often spoke fondly of the medical experience he gained in the town, writing to one former patient many years later: 'It certainly prepared me well for my future career, as it taught me to work with patients as human beings.' Yet towards the end of his life, when he was invited to address the town's women's agricultural society, and with Joubert – who had formally introduced him – seething in the audience, he devoted much of his speech to how badly he had been treated there some fifty years before, and how he had been 'chased out'.

Thanks to Louwtjie's parents and their small holiday home in the Strand, the Barnard family at least had somewhere to go when they left Ceres. Driving away Barnard felt a 'sense of guilt, of failure'. A few friends had made a point of inviting them round to say goodbye and wish them luck, but most of the patients he had come to know so well had, he felt, turned their backs. The rejection sat heavily on him. They were leaving behind their first home, and the first proper job he had held. Louwtjie was five months pregnant and Barnard had no job to go to. No wonder they felt a 'sense of bewilderment and bitterness'.

*

After settling into their new temporary home, Barnard decided he would not immediately search for a job. Instead he would study to pass the examinations needed to become a Fellow of the Royal College of Surgeons in London. Such a prestigious degree would help him obtain whatever surgical posts he set his sights on. He told Louwtjie if he worked flat out he could achieve the degree in four months. It would mean a spell in London after initial studies back at his old medical school. But what about money? Louwtjie was understandably worried. They had left the keys to their house in Ceres with friends who were trying to sell it for them. But nothing was moving on that front. If necessary, Barnard told his wife, they would get a loan.

Each day he travelled the 50 kilometres into Cape Town by train so he could study on the way. At the medical school it was vacation time, and he worked alone on cadavers left out for students, like him, doing special studies. In the anatomy museum he found himself working on a table next to a display case filled with human hearts, all diseased or with valve defects. He looked at them: each had once been the beating, blood-filled pump that had maintained the life system of a person, a personality. Now they were sitting there, cold, grey pieces of muscle preserved in formaldehyde. Symbols of death, not life. 'I never forgot that assembly of hearts,' he wrote in *One Life*, 'and recalled it vividly years later when critics attacked the rectitude of putting a heart in another human being yet did not question the arbitrary placement of one in formaldehyde on a museum shelf.'

Barnard's plan might have worked. But with the house at Ceres still unsold, money began to run out. Louwtjie was only weeks away from giving birth, and bills were piling up. Whether or not he would ever have the letters FRCS after his name, he must find a job.

His salvation came in the form of an advertisement in the *South African Medical Journal*. The City Hospital for Infectious Diseases in Cape Town needed another doctor to help cope with the relentless tide of victims of serious diseases particularly rife in the townships, where poverty and lack of health care created fertile ground for tuberculosis, diphtheria, hepatitis, scarlet fever and measles. Barnard had not planned to work in this field, but the need to earn money was paramount. When he attended the interview he had a stroke of good luck – one of the five-strong panel was Dr Fehrson, who had delivered him 30 years earlier. He got the job: senior resident medical officer. With the long hours of work and research to come, and a growing fondness for extramarital affairs, the ambition to become a FRCS fell by the wayside.

Working at the City Hospital (today a medical museum) opened Barnard's eyes to the raw horror of diseases which at that time had no cure. Many patients were children whose illnesses left them with appalling deformities. 'Never in my life had I seen such a field of human suffering,' he recalled. He was assigned, among other duties, to the care of children with tuberculous meningitis, a vicious condition, who filled an entire ward. The TB germ had travelled through these children's lungs and up into the brain where it infected the membranes, causing inflammation which in turn produced a protein deposit blocking the free movement of cerebral fluid. Their heads were swollen like balloons, their limbs rendered stiff or paralysed. They lay in rows of cots with iron sides, waiting to die or become vegetables.

Barnard had always been sensitive to the pain of children. In Beaufort West as a teenager he had once crossed a road to scold a frustrated young mother who had slapped her screaming baby in anger. Now the sight of so many of them doomed and deformed by a disease he felt should have been controllable left him determined to find a way to ease their agony. He would set out to find a new drug to stop the swelling in the brain. As almost always with Barnard, his efforts to help others would also combine with an opportunity to further his career: his work on TB meningitis would become the subject of his thesis to obtain a Doctor of Medicine degree. Moved as he undoubtedly was by the sorrowful plight of these children, he had no intention of being deflected from his longer-term goal, a surgical post at Groote Schuur.

The job at City Hospital came with accommodation, an apartment above the administration offices. Meals for the family were also free in what was renowned as the best canteen of any hospital in the city. The frictions of Ceres had been left behind, and when a son, André, was born in March 1951, the Barnards felt complete.

But if Chris Barnard had a major weakness, it was women. He had grown up under the suffocating umbrella of Calvinism. His mother and father had made it clear that in their eyes there were few worse sins than sex outside marriage. The moral climate of South Africa in the early 1950s was vehemently against adultery, and Louwtjie came from a highly moralistic Afrikaner family. An Afrikaner husband who strayed had sinned not only against his wife, but against God. None of this seemed to matter to Barnard. Energetic, with a charismatic smile and a brutally direct approach, he revelled in the impact he made on the young nurses he worked with. Louwtjie may have been living in the grounds of the hospital, caring for their children and known to all the staff, but her husband flirted and carried on affairs as if his marriage meant little to him.

Often he worked late into the night on research for his thesis, carrying out post-mortems to establish why the latest new drug he had tried had not worked on another tiny victim of TB meningitis. But Louwtjie began to grow suspicious, and her fears were confirmed when she found a letter written to Barnard by a nurse who was leaving the hospital and felt emotional about losing her lover. The nurse, wrote Louwtjie years later, 'described vividly her meetings with him while on night duty ... She told him how sad and lonely her life would be now that she could no longer wait for him "in the dark passage"...'

Trapped by motherhood – André was just six months old, Deirdre 18 months – Louwtjie was distraught, and desperate to believe it was not true. 'My little world was shattered ... I was heartbroken, angry and disgusted. Did Chris set such little store by our marriage vows?' Barnard, when he chose, could be a gifted liar. He persuaded Louwtjie the nurse was deranged and had made up the story. 'I fell for his supernatural charm,' admitted Louwtjie. 'It was the first of many times that I was to believe his explanations. My love blanketed all my doubts. Time and again I would be called upon to overlook my nagging suspicions that he was being unfaithful to me. He was the father of my children and I felt very strongly that if humanly possible they must have a father to ensure their happiness and normality ... I do not believe there is another man in the world who has the ability to charm a woman like Chris. In fact, he charmed me so well that in the end I was the one who apologised, ashamed at having thought him capable of such a thing as infidelity. But in the years that followed, I realised that Chris was a man with urgent physical needs.'

If Louwtjie was forced to convince herself her husband was faithful, his hospital colleagues were under no such illusion. Barbara Fortuin was one of the coloured nurses there who, under apartheid, were allowed to care for only coloured patients. 'Chris was such a hungry, tactile man,' she says. 'He always said to me, "Live life with passion, no matter what you do." I would often be asked to stand guard in the corridor while he and one of the sisters popped round the corner for a kiss and a cuddle. All the young nurses adored Chris. We found Louwtjie very withdrawn. She lived in her own private world, one you couldn't enter.'

According to Fortuin, Barnard's partner for these impromptu 'cuddling' sessions was usually Gene Gillespie, the sister on the TB meningitis ward. She was beautiful – tall, blonde and blue-eyed with an athletic body and the grace of a model. In *One Life* Barnard leaves little room for doubt that his interest in her was far more than professional. In one extraordinary passage he describes Gillespie holding a small girl, Flavia, while he prepared to draw fluid from her spine: 'Gene did it beautifully, holding Flavia against her magnificent thighs as I drew out the liquid.' There are other incongruous references to her 'blonde hair touching her shoulders' as they stand over the same girl's brain, removed from its skull, during the post-mortem. Over late-night coffee afterwards he felt 'close and intimate' with her and a 'sudden sense of identity'.

Doctors at other hospitals were aware of his work on TB meningitis, and called him if they had a case. Hannah-Reeve Sanders, who would later become medical superintendent at Groote Schuur, was an intern when she first met Barnard in this way: 'I remember how impressed I was that he did not mind coming out, travelling across the city at that unearthly hour.' He was 'thin, drawn – but bristling with energy'.

The work at the City Hospital was demanding and emotionally draining, and he was earning perhaps no more than £75 a month. Yet Barnard found the time to satisfy his spontaneous sexual appetite, and the money to indulge a new interest – dabbling in shares. John Sonnenberg, a junior doctor who trained under Barnard for six months in 1953, says, 'Barnard was very active. He had quite a few affairs with the nurses. I remember one nurse saying, "His shoes were under my bed last night."'

A clerk at the hospital was well known for his share-dealing activities, and may have introduced Barnard to them. In Ceres Truida Joubert had often heard her husband and Barnard discussing the stock market but she believed it was purely a common interest, and neither man owned shares. At the City Hospital Barnard often failed to attend the lunch-time meetings in the medical superintendent's office to discuss patients' progress because he had popped into town to see his broker, according to Sonnenberg.

'He never got into trouble for this,' he says. 'He was a law unto himself. The medical superintendent was rather in awe of him.'

Barnard continued to try to find solutions to the terrible suffering of TB meningitis victims. He discussed the problem with a friend, Mark Horwitz, a wealthy bachelor physician known for giving financial help to struggling doctors and students (including, it's believed, Barnard), and he suggested using the steroid cortisone. It could be injected into the child's spine along with the antibiotic already being used, streptomycin. This was only partially successful, and Barnard decided to try another drug, first in the spine, and then – highly controversially, because there was no knowing the effects on the nervous system – injected directly into the brain. He argued that without this these children had no hope, and any hope was better than none. He was right – it worked better this way, allowing the drug to start acting earlier, preventing the build-up of congealed fluid. The children lived longer, and in some cases returned to normal, but Barnard failed to achieve the real breakthrough he had wanted. Other new drugs came along soon afterwards that overtook much of what he had done.

What he did achieve was to produce a thesis containing the most detailed study ever made at that time on TB meningitis, some 259 cases over two years, which duly earned him the MD degree he craved. He also showed a remarkable ability to enlist help from others. He persuaded a porter to sew up the bodies after all the post-mortems, saving him time; several adult patients readily agreed to compile graphs from post-mortem results; Louwtjie wrote up many of the case histories and an intern, Eugene Dowdle, helped him put the thesis into perfect English. 'I was impressed by the originality of the man,' says Sonnenberg. 'He had a very incisive, very calculating mind. He used people unashamedly, but he had such an engaging personality that although you were aware he might be using you for his own selfish ends, he left you feeling he had done you a favour by asking for your help. He came across as someone with an exceptional brain, but he was ruthless and single-minded in pursuit of his goal. You could see that the City Hospital was just a stepping stone. Once he got the MD he was off.'

Barnard's superior at the hospital, Rachel Rabkin, was a forceful character with an encyclopaedic knowledge of infectious diseases. She lived in the apartment next to the Barnards' and they often ate together in the evenings. She was André's godmother. 'Rabkin was disappointed when Barnard said he was leaving,' says Sonnenberg. 'She was well aware of his shortcomings. He would rush his ward rounds, wouldn't turn up at meetings, wasn't doing the humdrum parts of his job properly, but she recognised he was something of an original.'

His temperament was rather more fragile than that of most doctors. He had already acquired a reputation for screaming at nurses and throwing instruments. Fortuin recalls: 'If he was handed a faulty syringe he wouldn't just ask for another, he would walk across the room, open a window and throw it out. But he trained you to do things the correct way and if you did he was wonderful.' He made plain his opposition to the rigidly enforced apartheid rules. 'He couldn't abide the fact that coloured nurses weren't allowed to run wards then. He said we should have the best nurses holding these positions, never mind what colour they were.'

His rapport with the children, so many crippled by incurable diseases with little time left, was genuine and striking. 'He was not a sophisticated man, he was rather child-like himself,' says Fortuin. 'When he went to a child he didn't just look, he would pick them up and play, spend time with them.'

After the fame that followed the first heart transplant, Barnard became a dandy, wearing nothing but the finest handmade Italian suits, supplied free by a designer in Rome. But as a young man with little money he wore the same brown sports jacket every day. To Cathy Cavvadas, another junior doctor at the City Hospital, he was 'totally uncultured.' 'He didn't worry about his appearance. But he had an enormous rapport with his patients. He was a tremendously talented doctor and he had vision.'

By now, his early thirties, Barnard had discovered his true talents – the drive to see a way forward where others saw only obstacles, a fascination with research and new ideas, the nerve to take a step others might ponder. It would all come together early one December morning, some years later. But now his mind was set on moving on and up, and he found his persistence had paid off. He was offered a post as resident doctor in medicine at Groote Schuur. This would allow him to work for his Master of Medicine degree, and it took him closer to what he wanted most of all – a surgical post.

5

Surgeon ... and America

For Louwtjie and the children, the job at Groote Schuur meant a new home. After several unsuccessful moves they found a house in Pinelands, not far from the hospital, where they would settle for the next three years. Barnard wasted no time in obtaining his Master of Medicine degree. He could have stayed a physician – he was now riding high – but he saw surgery as his future. A surgical post opened up for him as registrar to Jannie Louw, a man he admired immensely, and he took it although it meant he was back near the foot of the ladder again.

Louw later told the story of how Barnard's patience had snapped during the lengthy oral examinations for the MMed degree: 'He became so frustrated that he rose and said, "Gentlemen, you know enough about me by this time to either plug me or pass me. I leave it to you." And he walked out!'

It was a dynamic and revolutionary period in surgery. The first successful kidney transplant, between identical twins, would soon be done in Boston. And the bravest of new worlds was opening up: surgery inside the heart. Until now the heart had been thought of as virtually untouchable, a belief going back to the ancient Greeks. Hippocrates, 'the father of medicine', declared in the 5th century BC that any wound to the heart must prove fatal. The heart's power as a religious and poetic symbol of faith and love resounded through the centuries. Even for the modern surgeon, the physical obstacles were daunting.

In the first decade of the century the Nobel Prize-winning Frenchman Alexis Carrel had embarked on a series of pioneering surgical experiments. He had transplanted dog and cat kidneys – initially grafting them onto the neck – and grafted ovaries, the thyroid gland and a dog's heart. He discovered that animals which were given their own organs back survived much longer than those given other animals' organs, proof, though he did not know it, of rejection. His work, condemned as evil by anti-vivisectionists, established organ transplantation as a potential reality.

Forty years later the heart remained the organ most beyond reach for anything but the simplest repairs. Operating inside the heart meant interfering with blood circulation, and risked the danger of depriving the brain of oxygen. If the brain went without oxygen for more than three or four minutes it caused serious damage. Much longer could cause brain-death.

But in America, around the same time Barnard began work under Louw, momentous advances were being made. Cardiac surgeons were determined to find a way to operate inside the heart for long enough to fix more complex faults. Cross-circulation would soon be used in which a live 'donor' was attached to the patient so that blood flowed between the two during the operation, and the patient's breathing and circulation were maintained. (The surgeon behind this, Walt Lillehei, was warned he had devised the first operation with a potential fatality rate of 200 per cent. In fact the patient, a baby boy, survived the operation in 1954 but died 11 days later from pneumonia. The donor had been his father.) The year before another surgeon, John Gibbon, had for the first time successfully used a heart-lung machine to keep oxygenated blood circulating round the patient's body during a cardiac operation. Another method being tried was hypothermia. Lowering the patient's temperature by placing him in a bath of ice-cold water, or wrapping him in a blanket with water-cooled pipes, meant the brain could safely go without oxygen for up to twice the normal period.

Cape Town was a medical backwater, but Barnard could not have missed the worldwide publicity given to Lillehei's first cross-circulation operation. Events were moving fast at Groote Schuur, too. Velva Schrire, a quiet visionary who would one day play a central role in the drama of the first heart transplant, and his colleague Maurice Nellen had persuaded the hospital authorities to allow them to set up a cardiac unit. Schrire had gained valuable experience in cardiology abroad, both in London and America, and had returned to South Africa convinced that the treatment of cardiac defects through open-heart surgery was within reach. He defied initial resistance to his ideas and was eventually given a room in which to work – a 10-by-8-feet office with no windows. Schrire became known as 'the broom cupboard pioneer'. Using primitive electrocardiographic machines and facing a daily battle to raise funds for their work, Schrire and Nellen began building what would become, in 15 years, the most famous cardiac unit in the world.

Barnard was not then part of Schrire's team, but his hunger for research drove him to spend long hours in the animal house experimenting with another method of hypothermia. He reasoned that a balloon filled with cold water could be inserted into the stomach, with its rich blood supply, to rapidly bring down the patient's body temperature. Linen and surgical instruments had to be 'borrowed' from the wards every night for the operations on a succession of dogs, then cleaned and returned by 4 am. Barnard was then not skilled enough to open the dogs' hearts and sew them up again in the eight minutes they had to work; this was done by a thoracic surgeon. One after the other the dogs died after a few hours. But for the first time Barnard found himself working on a 'live heart' and it excited him. When one of the dogs finally survived the operation, he was vindicated.

Jannie Louw now approached him about a problem that would lead Barnard to the greatest breakthrough of his early career, and it had nothing to do with the heart. Nine out of ten babies born with a condition known as intestinal atresia – a blockage in the bowel – were dying, and no-one knew the cause of it. Louw believed it might be the result of a lack of blood to that part of the bowel, which then withered and died. But how to confirm this? Barnard told him he would set about proving it with dogs, by artificially producing the condition in a puppy foetus inside the womb of its mother. Louw was impressed. But after committing himself, Barnard began to wonder what he had done. In *One Life* he recalled how he had promised 'a medical discovery of world importance ... this was going to be far more difficult than anything I had ever attempted'.

His fears were justified. Night after night in the animal house Barnard carried out the most intricate of operations on the wombs of pregnant mongrels obtained from the city dog pound. At first he would remove the puppy foetus from the womb before opening its stomach, only to find that when he tried to return it the uterus had contracted and there was no room. In other cases the puppies began to breathe and again could not be returned. Sometimes the mother aborted her entire litter. He decided against removing the puppy, but to move the uterus out of its cavity so as to make operating easier. Once the puppy was opened, a section of the bowel was deprived of oxygen by tying off a pair of blood vessels. The puppy was then sewn up with black silk stitches that would not be absorbed and would identify it after birth.

Barnard had not reckoned on the natural instincts of the mother. Sensing there was something wrong with the puppy, she killed and ate it. This happened repeatedly, and months passed, with Barnard desperately trying small variations on the operation. With more than forty failures it was beginning to look as if the challenge he had set himself was beyond him. But then, guessing that any disturbance could be a trigger for problems, he decided to leave the uterus in its place. It worked – on the 43rd attempt. A year had passed since he began the work, but now he had a living puppy which, he hoped, would provide the evidence he had been looking for.

'We put it to sleep and opened it up – and there it was,' he wrote. 'I began to tremble. We had made it. It lay in a little spotted puppy on a wooden kitchen table – the end of a bitter parade of the death of dogs and dreams. It was the promise of life for thousands of babies. It was a devascularised puppy bowel with proximal and distal blind ends – classic intestinal atresia.'

Barnard went on to succeed in eight out of ten cases to prove the point beyond doubt. His findings showed Louw and other surgeons that they had to cut away a far larger section of the intestine before joining up the healthy parts of the bowel than they had realised. It was a major breakthrough in the treatment of what had until then been an almost certain killer. It had been a relentless slog, but the repercussions of Barnard's work were immense. 'It converted a 90 per cent mortality rate into a 90 per cent survival rate,' said Louw. Babies are still being saved today as a result of Barnard's work.

Countless nights spent on research work in the animal house had not helped his marriage, especially as Louwtjie was aware of his inability to resist the lure of other women. Barnard's colleagues at Groote Schuur remember how he often badgered them for the keys to their rooms so he had somewhere to take a willing nurse. However long he worked in the animal house overnight, there was often a young nurse waiting for him outside when he finished. His marriage was already a sham. Louwtjie put up with his behaviour, she said later, because she loved him and because she wanted her children to have a father. Rightly or wrongly, she chose not to confront her wayward husband. 'I never interfered with Chris and his women. I never telephoned, wrote or went to see any of them.' But the humiliation, for a married Afrikaner woman in a society ruled by the tenets of Calvin, ran deep.

Barnard's success with intestinal atresia confirmed his growing reputation as a man who was set for big things. A South African surgeon, Alan Thal, had spent the past two years training under Owen Wangensteen in Minneapolis. Wangensteen was already a legendary figure. He had built up one of the world's leading surgical training and research centres in a highly unfashionable place. Minneapolis was in the front line of the development of open-heart surgery. Thal was now coming to the end of his time there, and Wangensteen wanted to know if there were any more like him.

Barnard had originally hoped to go to London to further his career in general surgery, but he failed to win a Nuffield Scholarship, a blow made all the worse because a younger, less experienced colleague was granted it. When he was asked by John Brock, head of the department of medicine at Groote Schuur, if he would like to go to Minneapolis and 'see medical history being made every day', he did not dither.

Louwtjie was worried about the prospect of being left alone with the children while he went to America. The plan was for Barnard to go immediately and for Louwtjie and the children to join him later. He had applied for a Charles Adams Memorial Scholarship but it would take a while for it to come through. He would also receive a Dazian Foundation Bursary to cover two years of study in the US. By now, to boost their income, Louwtjie had taken a job as a nurse in a department store and they had a lodger, Syd Cywes, who would later work closely with Barnard at the Red Cross Children's Hospital. In *Heartbreak*, Louwtjie described how they both saw America as a 'magnificent opportunity' that could be the turning point of Barnard's career. But, with hindsight, she laments, 'Minneapolis was to be the start of the climb to world fame and the descent to a broken home.'

*

Trafalgar Square on Christmas Day, 1955, was a lonely place for a man who had left behind his wife and children. Barnard was 33 and had never before been overseas. He had decided to spend a few days in London on the way to America. He looked around at Nelson's Column and the famous lions, watched the couples walking together and the children chasing pigeons, and wondered if he had done the right thing.

*

A few days later Barnard touched down in Minneapolis on a typically snow-driven night. It was colder than he had ever imagined, the icy wind tearing through his clothes. He had seen snow on the mountains around Ceres but never anything like this. This was a city steeped in snow.

He linked up with Alan Thal, who got him settled into the doctors' bungalow at the University of Minnesota Hospital. The next day he met Wangensteen. White-haired, bespectacled, exuding wisdom, Wangensteen was a deeply impressive figure. His drive and imagination had succeeded in building up a surgical and research centre with a $1 million a year budget. The American government had declared war on heart disease, the country's biggest killer, and Wangensteen's team of pioneering cardiac specialists, men like Walt Lillehei and Richard Varco, led the advance party. They had tried various ways of maintaining a patient's breathing and circulation while repairing complex defects inside the heart, a staggering achievement in the face of the long-held belief that opening the heart to surgery would always prove fatal. By the time Barnard arrived, the heart-lung machine in the form of the DeWall-Lillehei bubble oxygenator was the preferred method. Lillehei, undaunted by early failures, had just completed his 100th open-heart operation.

But for Barnard the excitement of open-heart surgery would have to wait. He had gone to Minneapolis to make progress in general surgery. Wangensteen was fascinated by his work on intestinal atresia and wanted him to carry out a project to improve ways of joining the oesophagus after surgery. It sounded less than thrilling, but Barnard had little choice but to accept. He left the meeting 'feeling somewhat lost and depressed'.

The next day was New Year's Eve, and Barnard went with a group of doctors to a party at the home of Lillehei and his wife Kaye. Lillehei, also celebrating his wedding anniversary, was a renowned party animal. He wore alligator shoes and gold jewellery, drove a flashy Buick convertible and liked spending time in all-night jazz clubs. He was, though, a brilliant surgeon, a maverick who went his own way. In theatre he wore an improvised head-lamp to focus light where he needed it most. He lived, too, under a death sentence, having been given a 25 per cent long-term survival chance after an operation by Wangensteen to remove a cancerous tumour in his neck several years earlier. Barnard's first impressions of Lillehei, who was just four years his senior, were ironic in view of the way his own life developed: 'I thought he was a bit of a playboy – and he drank quite a bit too,' he told G Wayne Miller, who wrote Lillehei's life story. 'He didn't appear to be very serious.'

But Lillehei was deadly serious. He would come to be known as the 'father of open-heart surgery' for his talent, vision and determination to repair the most difficult of heart defects. Barnard was to spend more than a year working under him, learning vital skills he would take back to Cape Town. Later he would look back on Lillehei as another Daantjie Rabie, someone who had been ahead of him on the track. 'He wore a head-lamp, and he was out there ahead of all of us. But the race was only beginning ...' he wrote in *One Life*. Barnard would also claim in conversations with his closest friends that Lillehei had one day told him: 'I will do the first heart transplant.' It was a challenge Barnard would not let go.

Barnard settled into life in Minneapolis. He slogged on with the work on dog gullets but found it unrewarding. He was growing homesick, devouring any letters he received from Louwtjie, although they were more factual than passionate. 'We had never learned to write love letters,' he admitted. But, as was always the case with Barnard, he was not short of company.

Minneapolis teemed with blonde, blue-eyed Nordic types – in the 19th century the city had seen the mass immigration of Scandinavians hoping to work in Minnesota's booming timber and mining industries. (At one stage more Swedes lived in Minneapolis than in Stockholm. Wangensteen and Lillehei were both descendants of Scandivanian immigrants.) Shortly after arriving in Minneapolis Barnard began seeing an attractive young nurse, Trudy Nordstrom. Trudy, in her early twenties, had left her home in Sweden to work as a scrub, or theatre nurse in Minneapolis, and fell for the wit and charm of the South African surgeon. He failed to mention his wife and children.

Trudy, who later returned to Sweden, recalls how far-reaching Barnard's ambitions became when he moved into cardiac surgery. 'Chris was very charming, and he was very ambitious. He wanted to be first in things. He talked about wanting to achieve something in heart surgery. He even talked about wanting to do a heart transplant. But he didn't talk about his children and I don't remember him mentioning his wife.' Her friend Dolores Erikson, an operating room supervisor then, says, 'When Chris came he didn't tell anyone he was married. He had a real roving eye – he propositioned everybody. He started going out with Trudy not long after he arrived. He was crazy about her. She had dark blonde hair, blue eyes and a very shapely figure. All the men were after her. She and Chris went out together for quite a time. Trudy knew nothing about him being married until his wife and children arrived in Minneapolis. She was furious and didn't want to have anything to do with him after that.'

Jim Story was one of Barnard's closest friends in his early months in Minneapolis. They went on double dates with Trudy and Story's girlfriend, later his wife, usually to piano bars like Diamond Jim's where they could dance to live Dixieland jazz, music which would become a lifelong passion for Barnard. 'I don't recall him making a secret of the fact that he was married, but I got the feeling his marriage was shaky,' says Story. 'He was lonesome and had the normal drives. It was clear that Trudy had strong feelings for him.'

Story was impressed by Barnard: 'He was very assertive and definitely interested in advancing surgery in whatever field he was in. It was clear he was going to prevail, and he couldn't have picked a better place to be. It was a hotbed of innovation.' It was a standing joke among the young surgeons under Wangensteen that 'you practically have to invent an operation to get on the schedule'. Story and Barnard later drifted apart when Story went into neurosurgery. 'He was good fun to be around, friendly and gregarious. There was an ego there, but he had an enormous amount of drive, energy and ambition. In the end I sensed an obsession. He could be a very pressing fellow.'

Between dates with Trudy Nordstrom, Barnard went out with another nurse, Marilyn Lande. 'We had very little money so it was a movie at best or a place on campus, The Bridge, for an ice cream and hours of conversation,' she says. 'We went dancing a few times too.' He did, however, talk to her about Louwtjie and the children.' He wanted them to come to America desperately.'

The research laboratory next to Barnard's belonged to Lillehei. Vincent Gott was a young resident surgeon working under Lillehei, and he was using the latest heart-lung machine in his research with dogs. Barnard had seen Gott working with the heart-lung machine when he was given his first tour of the laboratories by Marilyn Lande. He had been 'full of questions and wide-eyed with interest,' she says. Now he helped out as Gott's assistant from time to time. 'He came in more and more frequently,' says Gott. 'He was very bright, and in those days he didn't seem to me to have an ego, he was an ordinary guy. It was an exciting period – we had surgeons from Asia, Europe and South America visiting all the time to watch Walt operate with the heart-lung machine and then they would come into the lab to see the research we were doing. There was a constant flow of people.'

Barnard gladly accepted Gott's invitation to see the heart-lung machine working in the operating theatre. He was taken aback by the impact his first open-heart operation made on him. He witnessed what he later described as 'the life of a human being held in a coil of plastic tubes and a whirling pump'. Barnard saw, once again, where his destiny lay: with the heart.

But first he had to tell Wangensteen. Barnard explained that rather than continuing the work with dogs he wanted to achieve his PhD in surgery so that he could work as a specialist surgeon back in South Africa. Wangensteen told him it would take him at least five years to complete the work needed, including learning two foreign languages. Barnard said he would do it in two. Dutch, close to Afrikaans, could be one language and German the other. His thesis would be based on his work already done on intestinal atresia. He would work in the hospital during the day to achieve the required clinical experience for his major, and do post-mortems at night towards his pathology minor. The languages could also be mastered at night, he assured an incredulous Wangensteen. Barnard got his way, and the future looked clear and bright.

The Adams scholarship had come through, and Louwtjie wrote to say she and the children would be travelling out on a cargo ship, the cheapest way, to join him. Barnard was earning little more than $125 a month so the Adams money was essential. He rented one half of a duplex near the airport and, with the help of colleagues from the university, set about filling it with second-hand furniture. To raise more cash he did odd jobs like washing cars and shovelling snow. Then he hit on the idea of working as a night nurse at the hospital where wealthy cancer patients were prepared to pay $5 a night for extra care. He could study there between duties.

Louwtjie, Deirdre and André duly arrived in Boston. They missed their flight to Minneapolis and went to New York instead. Then they were forced to change planes in Chicago. When they finally arrived in Minneapolis, Louwtjie, who was on her first overseas trip, and struggling to cope with two tired children, was shattered and in tears. It was an ominous start to their new life. She was, though, relieved to set foot inside the home her husband had prepared, and moved by the presents he had bought for the children: a doll's pram for Deirdre, and toy cowboys and Indians for André. 'Everything had been done with love, tenderness and hard work,' said Louwtjie. 'Chris had gone to tremendous lengths to make our arrival something memorable.' She especially liked the television set, unknown in South Africa, and the automatic washing machine, something she had never owned. She was less happy with the planes coming in to land directly over their heads.

Barnard's account in *One Life* of Louwtjie's experience in Minneapolis was one of her most bitter complaints about the book. 'I was nearly driven to insanity by it,' she said. The picture painted is one of a small-minded woman refusing to adapt to a new country, and constantly carping about her husband's absence from home while he pursues his life's work. To illustrate her negative approach, Barnard made great play of an incident that took place only days after Louwtjie and the children had settled into their new home. On 9 June 1956 a US Navy jet crashed into three homes close to their duplex, killing six people, including three children, seriously injuring 14, and destroying a row of houses in a fireball. It happened on a Saturday morning, around 9.30, when families were going about their normal weekend activities. One boy escaped the fate of his family, who were all killed, because he had decided to go fishing. It was a terrifying event, and one which would unnerve anyone living on the edge of an airport with a navy airbase attached. People in Minneapolis today still remember it vividly. Louwtjie does not even mention the incident in her account of her time in the city, but Barnard has her calling him hysterically as he sits in the cancer ward, saying, 'Only in America could this happen. The whole house shook. The iron nearly fell off the board. It's awful ... How can people live like this? That's America for you – aeroplanes crash on houses.'

Louwtjie failed to settle in Minneapolis. She said later that she felt 'like a lost child'. She was upset, according to Barnard, when Deirdre and André returned home from their first day at school 'bruised and beaten' after being bullied because of their accents. (Again, Louwtjie makes no mention of this.) Inevitably she found herself alone most of the time, not always because her husband was working. But the demands of the goal Barnard had set himself were huge. He would be called at all hours to attend post-mortems, even at night. Louwtjie joined some women's clubs and gave talks about South Africa, but grew tired of the ignorance she encountered. People asked her about the Mau Mau and whether she was speaking Zulu when she spoke Afrikaans. She also found it hard to stomach critical comments about apartheid when racial segregation was a fact of life in America. Minneapolis, in the Midwest, did not have the rigidly enforced race laws they had in the South, but whites and blacks lived in different areas and their children went to separate schools.

Leontine Day (then Hans) ran Wangensteen's office. She says she found Louwtjie unfriendly and unwilling to mix from the start. 'About a week after she arrived we held the department picnic in one of the many lakeside parks in the city,' she recalls. 'I took it upon myself to introduce her to all there. Food was brought in. We played games and everyone made an effort to include

Louwtjie and the children, but she refused to associate.' Leontine and her then husband, a wealthy company executive, often invited the lowly-paid resident surgeons round to dinner. They lived in a large house in an up-market neighbourhood. Louwtjie had been used to the comforts of South Africa and was unimpressed with the half-duplex Barnard had rented in Minneapolis. When they arrived at Leontine's home for dinner one evening she made her envy plain. 'We were all seated in the living room when they arrived. Louwtjie came in, looked around, and walked to the adjoining sun porch. She then said, "If I lived in a house like this, I'd be happy to stay here." I had to say something, so I told her that "when you and Chris have worked as long as the rest of us, you'll have a much more impressive home".'

The two women clashed again when Louwtjie told her she wanted to return to South Africa. People in Wangensteen's department had been talking about the Barnards' 'constant home turmoil'. 'I told Louwtjie the children loved their school. They loved playing in the snow. I said she should consider the fun the children were having, doing well in school and making friends. It would be a shame to disrupt their education.'

Minnesota is known as the 'land of 10 000 lakes'. In the bitterly cold winters when the lakes freeze over the favourite sport is ice-skating. Barnard would take Deirdre and André skating, but came home one day complaining of unusual pain in his feet. It persisted, then spread to his hands, which began to swell. He went to see a rheumatologist, and heard the devastating diagnosis: rheumatoid arthritis, a potentially crippling disease which, at worst, threatened to curtail his career as a surgeon. He and Louwtjie tried several medicines, including the less conventional such as guava leaves and brake fluid. The disease appeared to stabilise, and he returned to the specialist for a follow-up examination. Time and again in later life Barnard harked back to this day, when the specialist gave him hope: he seemed to have a high resistance to the disease, he said, and perhaps he would not be crippled after all.

Marilyn Lande, however, suggests Barnard may have been aware of his arthritis well before Louwtjie and the children arrived. She recalls one 'miserably cold night' after they had finished rounds and had walked together to The Bridge. 'It was way below zero that night and we warmed our hands on cups of hot chocolate. He had never been so cold before. When he picked up the hot chocolate I noticed the arthritis in his hands. When I asked if he had injured the fingers on his left hand, he was quick to say, "No, it's nothing, I must have bumped into something." It was only years later that I learned how crippling his arthritis had become.'

Gil Campbell would meet up with Barnard at 6 am to breakfast on pancakes with maple syrup and to down some strong coffee, before they both went to the pathology department to study their slides. It was during this period that Barnard says he was diagnosed with rheumatoid arthritis, an incurable disease, but Campbell recalls not one mention of it over breakfast, despite their friendship. 'He was a very likeable person, but he wasn't a party guy tossing down beers with the boys – he preferred to chase the ladies,' he says.

In his autobiography Barnard described graphically the pain and anguish he suffered from arthritis in Minneapolis. Louwtjie, he said, had to help him dress at one point. But few of his close friends from that time recall him talking much about it. Barnard may have confided in Wangensteen, who also suffered from arthritis. When operating, Wangensteen had to stand for comfort on a thick rubber pad which his staff called 'God's Little Acre'.

John Perry was also working under Wangensteen and became another close friend of Barnard's. Perry's girlfriend Genevieve, later his wife, shared an apartment with three nurses. She sometimes cooked a spicy Asian curry and Barnard would join them at the flat for a meal. Perry later recalled his impressions of Barnard on their first meeting in his laboratory: 'He was a tall young man with prominent ears and was not particularly impressive in appearance. He was dressed in a nondescript sports coat, tie, slacks and a nylon wash-and-wear shirt.' Later they travelled together to a medical congress and shared a hotel room to save money. 'Those nylon shirts aged after repeated washings and they soon became a uniform grey colour. After a long day Chris was able to take a shower in his hotel – still wearing his shirt, undershorts, and socks. He washed them as he bathed, and then removed them and hung them up to dry to be ready for the next morning.'

Genevieve became Louwtjie's closest friend in Minneapolis. The two couples, with Deirdre and André, spent Christmas together that year. 'Louwtjie was a wonderful seamstress,' says Genevieve. 'I took her once to a beautiful fabric store and she went wild. But she had trouble adapting to the American way of life. She was unhappy and very homesick. She was isolated. Chris was too busy to be at home with her and I don't think she ever got to know her neighbours. She didn't have a car. I would take her out grocery shopping.'

Tensions between Louwtjie and her husband came to a head, and she told him she was returning to Cape Town with the children. 'He was crushed,' says Marilyn Lande. 'He didn't know what to do. He wanted to go with them but he couldn't leave his residency. I found him in the hospital cafeteria leaning on his elbow and staring into space.' It had been a sudden decision by Louwtjie. 'I just heard one day that she'd gone. She hadn't told me anything,' says Genevieve Perry.

Barnard decided to drive his family to New York to see them onto the cargo ship that would take them back to South Africa. They took a detour to Washington DC where they spent four days sightseeing. A visit to the Lincoln Memorial – the American Civil War remained a lifelong fascination – gives Barnard a platform in *One Life* for stating his views then about equality. The words of Lincoln's Gettysburg Address in 1863 in which he said that 'all men are created equal' are inscribed on a wall at the memorial. Barnard appears to condone apartheid as the only immediate solution to South Africa's problems: 'Apartheid, as a holding action – as a no-search – was wrong. As a system of continuing separate development towards equal rights for all, it was something else. Perhaps it was not the best answer, but for the moment it was the only one we could handle.'

Louwtjie later claimed that she had decided to go after becoming worried that Wangensteen wanted Barnard to stay in Minneapolis permanently. Her fears were confirmed when Leontine Day 'tried to persuade me to stay, but the way she went about it only made me more determined to return to South Africa'. She had said South Africa 'had no good schools and universities', recalled Louwtjie. Her patriotic pride wounded, Louwtjie decided she had had enough and booked her passage. 'Chris was not quite ready to return yet and he said he would follow us within four to six months.'

But Barnard had no intention of following so soon. In fact, he told the latest woman to enter his life, another beautiful blue-eyed blonde, that his marriage was finished. They had been seeing each other for three months already when Louwtjie decided to return home. Had she found out? After seeing him looking so 'crushed' in the cafeteria that evening, Marilyn Lande did not set eyes on him again for three weeks. When she did, he was having a 'very entertaining chat' in The Bridge with a beautiful girl.

Sharon Jorgensen was a 20-year-old sociology student who worked part-time in the surgery division photo-lab at University Hospital. Barnard met her when he needed slides developed for his research work. She fell instantly for the 34-year-old surgeon. 'He was looking for someone to type his PhD thesis and I said I would do it,' she says. 'He was very attractive, very charming, a great guy.' Conveniently, Sharon lived with her widowed mother, Hertha, on Barnard's way home. Most evenings, despite Louwtjie's loneliness and her struggle to get used to a new life, he would drop in for dinner with the Jorgensens before driving home. 'He never seemed to want to go home. He said his wife hated living in America and took it out on him.'

Once Louwtjie had gone – she had been in Minneapolis just ten months – Barnard took a room in a large house owned by an elderly widow, Henrietta Shearer, in a wealthy suburb. He could come and go as he pleased and he seemed happy there. His relationship with Sharon intensified. 'I was very much in love with him. We went dancing on Saturday nights in places where they played Dixieland jazz, his favourite. He told me his marriage was over and I believed him. I think he believed it was.' Many years later, Barnard, without identifying Sharon, would recall 'the many dreams' they had shared as they danced romantically to Dean Martin's *Memories are Made of This*' on those Saturday nights when I could afford to take her out'. Barnard was also on good terms with Hertha Jorgensen, and liked to go pheasant shooting in the country with a cousin of hers. Hertha vividly recalls how Barnard struggled with a 'noticeable limp' at times, and complained of pain in his hands which were often swollen.

Barnard knew he would have to return to Groote Schuur once his allotted time under Wangensteen came to an end, unless he decided to stay permanently. He had always been determined to return to South Africa, partly out of love for his country. But he also knew he could make his mark there. America, after all, seemed to be packed with pioneering heart surgeons. He told Sharon he would divorce Louwtjie and they could marry in Cape Town.

He rarely wrote to Louwtjie, but his love for his children, especially Deirdre, was a strong pull. 'He always talked about his "wonderful" daughter rather than about his son, that was very noticeable,' says Sharon. 'When he came back from seeing his family off in New York, he kept talking about how Deirdre had stood on the deck crying and clutching her doll.'

Barnard had now moved from Wangensteen's service to work for three months as a senior resident under Richard Varco, one of the great early innovators and teachers of open-heart surgery. It meant he would be able to assist at operations. From Varco he learned 'respect for the human body and its tissues', he said later. Varco told him: 'Nothing must be crushed or tied or burned unless there is a reason for it. Eventually the body must repair every trauma you create. If it has to use energy to recover the damage you have done it cannot use it to fight the essential disease we want to cure.'

But it was under Lillehei, who had trained under Varco, that he learned how to operate the heart-lung machine. He had to help assemble it every morning before an operation. When Lillehei let him assist at the operating table, and made him chief resident in the ward, he was finally 'in the thick of it', as he put it. 'Dr Lillehei was a great teacher, an inspiration – and, above all, a sensitive human being,' Barnard wrote in *One Life.*

Lillehei, who had battled through a bloody trail of disasters as he developed techniques to make open-heart surgery possible, stopped Barnard giving up almost before he had begun. With Lillehei not yet in theatre, Barnard had opened the heart of a seven-year-old boy whose father watched intently from above in the dome gallery. Blood suddenly gushed from a hole in the heart's left atrium, drowning the cardiac field in a sea of red so that Barnard could not see what he was doing. As the boy's blood pressure dropped rapidly and Barnard floundered, Lillehei appeared, 'scrubbed in' and stopped the bleeding by sticking his finger in the hole. Once the defect was fixed the pump was turned off, but the boy's heart failed to take over. They tried to shock it into motion, then turned the pump on again several times, but the boy was dead. He had lost too much blood. Marilyn Lande, who was there, recalls, 'Dr Lillehei told Chris to close the chest, and left. There was a terrible silence throughout the room – the only noise was from the dismantling of the pump and the taking down of the surgical set-up. I looked up into the dome to see a man peering down.' That evening Lande again came across Barnard in the cafeteria brooding heavily over the loss. 'He felt so guilty. He said the boy's death was his fault. If he had been quicker he could have prevented it. His sorrow was obvious and all he could say was, "I was responsible."'

Barnard had gone into Lillehei's office after the operation. Still shaken, he told his mentor he was quitting heart surgery. 'I am the cause of that boy's death. It's no use saying I'm sorry because it won't bring that child back,' he said. Lillehei simply told him he had learned another vital lesson – you can use your finger to stop a bleeding hole to give yourself time to think about the next step. It was a mistake everyone made once. The next day he must open the patient just the same. 'That was the greatness of him,' Barnard told G Wayne Miller later. 'The next day was a new day with new challenges and new hopes.'

Lillehei was to defy the gloomy prognosis he had received from Wangensteen. He would not die until 1999, aged 80. In an interview to mark the 25th anniversary of the first heart transplant, he gave a graphic account of Barnard as he saw him then in Minneapolis. His memory, for one thing, astounded him: 'We had a large number of patients, at least 35, sometimes 40, and we used to make rounds. The residents would make rounds twice a day, and I would make afternoon rounds ... We would see all these patients. All of my senior residents before and after Barnard carried a pocket-sized notebook, and took down all the blood tests and x-rays I suggested should be done. On the first day that Chris was with me, I noticed that he never took down a single note, but I didn't comment on it. On the second day, probably, I did mention it. I said, "Chris, get a notebook and take down these things. It's important." He said, "Yes." The next day he still didn't have a notebook, so I was kind of sharp to him and said, "Get a notebook." He said, "Listen, Dr Lillehei ..." – he was always very polite, of course. As a matter of fact I never got him to call me by my first name even to this day. "Dr Lillehei, have I to date forgotten anything you have suggested?" He hadn't, so I said "No." He said, "Well, I can remember these things." And he did. I thought it very unusual since there were dozens of shopping-list type things to be done. He had a superb memory for detail as well as excellent intellectual ability.'

Barnard's fellow surgical residents in Minneapolis were some of the brightest and best of their generation – they included Norman Shumway, who would go on to develop the heart transplant technique on which the groundbreaking Washkansky operation was based; and Christian Cabrol, who would perform France's first heart transplant. But for Lillehei, Barnard stood out. 'Younger surgeons were attracted to Minneapolis like a magnet. I didn't know it at the time, but some of the best brains in the world came here. At that time they seemed like ordinary surgical residents – the 'John Hunter type', loud and profane, addicted to drink and low company, especially female – but as you look back in the records, they were outstanding individuals. All we did was to give them the opportunity and encouragement. In that high-level group the outstanding thing most of us noticed about Chris was his intensity and seriousness.' (Hunter, known as the 'founder of scientific surgery', was an 18th-century Scotsman famous for his wild socialising and lack of interest in books, but also his genius as a surgeon and anatomist. Having suffered angina for most of his life he eventually died of a heart attack.)

Even then Barnard's brash confidence could easily cause friction. 'He could be very charming but, on the other hand, he could provoke a rather intense dislike among some people, colleagues and staff, because he was always outspoken and often had unconventional ideas,' recalled Lillehei. 'He had a somewhat abrasive personality, very self-confident.' He felt there was no time to waste, as John Perry recalled: 'He was very impatient ... He knew that he had to accomplish something noteworthy with which to return home before the support from his government was exhausted, or return empty-handed.'

Wangensteen had set Barnard the task of finding a way to repair faulty heart valves. He was given a grant from the National Institutes of Health in Washington – Wangensteen was famous for his ability to secure grants – and began work. He decided to try to devise an artificial valve with plastic materials to replace the aortic valve, the valve that passes oxygenated blood to the body from the left ventricle, the heart's main pumping chamber. He had started this project before Louwtjie left Minneapolis, and was delighted to discover that one of the men making the valves for him in his garage lived two streets away from Sharon Jorgensen. It gave him the perfect excuse to stop off in the area on the way home.

When Barnard succeeded in making his first working valve he bounded out of his basement laboratory, up five flights of stairs and into Wangensteen's office. 'He grabbed my arm, pulled me from my desk, out the door, into the hall and then asked me where there was a faucet,' says Leontine Day. 'I said there was one in the janitor's broom closet, so we went in, he put the valve on the faucet, turned on the water, and then said, "Look!" I did, and the valve pulsed. Then I congratulated him and he went back down to the lab. He was intensive in his research. He would let nothing interfere and stuck to it until he could see it through.'

But the valves did not work so well when inserted into a dog's heart. The dogs died within two weeks. In the end Barnard was forced to accept he could not build an entirely new valve. He was able, though, to design one that could be used to assist an ailing valve, if not replace it. It was a compromise, but at least it worked. He wrote a thesis on the problems of making and testing an artificial aortic valve for which he was given his Master of Science degree.

Minneapolis was a leading surgical and research centre, but it was by no means the only one where far-sighted surgeons were making telling advances. At weekends Barnard and several others often drove two hours south to the Mayo Clinic at Rochester to watch John Kirklin operate. 'We considered him exceptionally brilliant,' wrote Barnard later. Kirklin had devised a heart-lung machine that was rather more complicated than the DeWall-Lillehei bubble oxygenator. From Kirklin Barnard picked up 'many safeguards and shortcuts'. He also learned to close a ventricular septal defect, one of the most difficult holes in the heart to repair, without damaging the heart's intricate web of invisible nerves. If these nerves were cut it disrupted the heart's electrical conduction system, causing heart block, where the heart would slow down and sometimes arrest. (One of Lillehei's great innovations was the pacemaker, a device that could eventually be inserted into the chest to give low-voltage charges to keep the heart regular until damaged nerves had recovered.)

Wangensteen also sent Barnard to Houston where Denton Cooley and Michael DeBakey were operating. DeBakey, known for his short temper, soon got rid of the overeager Barnard. Cooley welcomed him, and they would remain good friends. Cooley's speed, confidence and grace with a scalpel astonished Barnard. 'It was the most beautiful surgery I had ever seen in my life. Every movement had a purpose and achieved its aim. Where most surgeons would take three hours he could do the same operation in one hour.' Cooley later recalled Barnard's 'intelligent personality and his honest approach to surgical technique' from this first meeting. He felt 'an immediate warmth' between them.

Barnard was officially due to leave Minneapolis in June 1958. In fact he left a few weeks earlier, driving to New York in a Chevrolet he had bought with a bank loan and putting it on a ship for Cape Town before catching a plane. He missed Deirdre and André and South Africa. He felt a duty to Louwtjie, who had held the family together while he advanced his career. Despite all the warnings that he had taken on too much, he had accomplished everything he had told Wangensteen he would, and had been duly awarded his PhD in surgery. When he walked into Wangensteen's office to confirm he was leaving, the man he had once felt reminded him of his father had good news for him: a generous grant from Washington to help him get open-heart surgery off the ground in South Africa. There would be money to pay for the latest heart-lung machine to be shipped back to Cape Town, plus $2 000 a year for three years.

Barnard must have sought some kind of financial help towards what he hoped to do in Cape Town, for he would always look back on this as the day he learned never to be afraid to ask for something. But still he could barely believe it. He later wrote of how every pioneer 'carries others in his heart' and in his was written the name, among others, of Owen Harding Wangensteen – 'father, teacher, friend'.

More than a year had passed since Louwtjie and the children

had returned to Cape Town. Letters between them had dwindled. Barnard knew he had to go back, but he was racked with doubts. His love affair with Sharon Jorgensen was still going strong, and she begged him not to leave. 'He was a very loyal man when it came to his children,' she says. 'That's why he went back. I wanted him to stay. I pleaded with him, in tears. I would have married him. I was heartbroken for a long time afterwards. Apart from the man I later married, Chris was the love of my life.'

6

Ambition

Barnard was welcomed back to Groote Schuur like a triumphant king returning from a crusade. He had worked with the great pioneers of open-heart surgery and could boast the latest know-how. As importantly, he brought the means to put it into action: the heart-lung machine given to him by Wangensteen. All open-heart surgery had been stopped at the hospital some months earlier, after a disastrous operation in which a man died on the table. We must wait for Barnard, Jannie Louw had ordered.

It was 1958, an election year in which the Nationalists strengthened their hold on the country in the face of a gathering storm of anti-apartheid protest. While Barnard had been away South Africa had seen a series of laws introduced that further entrenched the segregation of races. The prime minister, Hans Strijdom, had pledged 'white supremacy with justice for all' and he had done his best to ensure the first part, at least. He would soon die and be replaced by the terrifying figure of Hendrik Verwoerd, a Dutchman who had studied in Nazi Germany and was seen as the architect of grand apartheid. The landscape looked bleak. As Barnard stepped off the plane in Cape Town and felt the autumn chill, he could not help but think about the spring warmth he had left behind in Minneapolis. Nor could he put Sharon Jorgensen out of his mind. He had not seen Louwtjie and the children for 14 months.

Barnard's version of his reception at the airport portrays Louwtjie as a cold, angry woman interested only in scolding him for not writing often enough and for not bringing presents for the children. As they drove towards a flat in Pinelands Louwtjie had rented she complained of how he 'dumped' the family in her lap. He wondered if, in coming back, he had not made the 'most terrible mistake of my life'.

Louwtjie, however, recalls the nervousness she felt about seeing her husband for the first time in over a year, sensing he had changed – and her suspicions of another woman, which he confirmed to her two days later when she confronted him. 'He said that the strangeness between us was very natural. He asked for time to sort out his feelings. Only when I pressed the matter consistently did he speak the truth. His words came like thunder to my ears. I did not want to believe it when he said: "Look, Louwtjie, you are quite right. I am in love with a woman in Minneapolis. She is wonderful. You can't expect me to turn my love on and off like a tap. I will love her as long as I want to and at the moment you can't do anything about it." He stood there like a judge, pleased that it was all over. He had passed the death sentence.'

Louwtjie's bewilderment and hurt deepened when she learned that Barnard had told friends the strain in their relationship was the result of *her* having affairs while he was in America, working hard. Yet she decided once more that her pain must come second to the needs of Deirdre, now eight, and André. The months that followed were turbulent, with Louwtjie leaving home at least once.

Yet the domestic turmoil did not seem to affect Barnard's mission: to master open-heart surgery. Within a fortnight of his return the heart-lung machine had also arrived from America, in boxes. So too had his showy left-hand-drive Chevrolet.

He was now feted as the rising star of the Groote Schuur cardiac unit. He delivered a 'very exciting, first rate' lecture to young doctors on what he had learned in America, recalls Stuart Saunders, then a registrar and later to become vice-chancellor of UCT. But there was one setback. On his return from America Barnard had expected to be made an associate professor of UCT, something which would not happen for a further four years. Jannie Louw said: 'He was bitterly disappointed … and he blamed me for it … He then turned his wrath on the university authorities and never forgave them for it.'

Barnard continued the research he had started in Minneapolis into the development of an artificial heart valve; he was also performing open-heart surgery on dogs using the heart-lung machine, preparing for the first such successful operation to be carried out on a person on the African continent. (A dog's heart is similar to a human's, and dogs were cheap and easy to come by.) It would be a medical milestone and inadvertently, for the apartheid regime at a time when world loathing was growing, a small propaganda coup, a foretaste of what was to come less than a decade later. The government's efforts to destroy the rising anti-apartheid movement were again attracting world focus in the midst of the long-running Treason Trial hearings, involving 91 defendants including Nelson Mandela, which were about to move to Pretoria Supreme Court for the trial proper. It was set to be the 'most significant mass trial in South African history', said the newspapers. Anything positive, such as a medical first, boosted the country's image.

But as Barnard prepared for his historic operation, the death of his father, Adam, intervened. He was 83 and had been diagnosed with bowel cancer several weeks earlier. Barnard failed to make it to Knysna – where Adam and Maria had been living with relatives for some years – in time to see his father before he died. He helped carry the coffin, but he had refused to see the body before burial. There was something in the appearance of death in a loved one that Barnard never did come to terms with. He preferred to remember his father as he had been when alive. In later life Barnard always spoke of his sadness that his father had not lived to see his success as a cardiac surgeon.

A number of coloured families from Beaufort West attended the funeral, hearing from the minister in the pulpit how the saintly Adam Barnard had continued observance of the Biblical tithe for the poor until the day he died: one-tenth of his monthly pension of £11 went on groceries and medicine for the needy. 'They stared at me without smiling,' Barnard said in *One Life*. 'A few of the older men nodded, and some of the women had handkerchiefs in their hands. The preacher would soon talk about my father, but nothing he could say would ever equal this – the mute presence of these Coloured people who had come two hundred miles to see the burial of a White minister who had loved them as he had loved his own family.'

In his autobiography Barnard has the minister reading from a moving letter sent to him by Adam several months before he died. Whether the letter had remained in someone's safekeeping in the ten or so years between the funeral and the book being written is not clear, but the quotes are precise: 'Of some things I am proud, especially my sons. Christiaan has just won new degrees of honour in America and will soon be coming back to see us. This will be a source of joy, and I confess that I can hardly wait for the day of his return … Christiaan has honoured me. He labours in God's name against pain and sorrow. He told me that in Ceres he had found a parish of human life …'

Although Chris and Marius, as successful doctors, were their mother's favourites, Adam had a soft spot for Dodsley, who had had a more troublesome upbringing, and had gone to war. Yet Dodsley was not at the funeral, an absence that caused a rift between him and Chris. Dodsley's second wife, Kay Veldman, says, 'We'd been away and our phone was cut off. We got a telegram a week after Adam had died. Dodsley was devastated, and wrote to Chris explaining what had happened, but Chris was very hard about it. He was bitter. That was the start of the problems between the two of them.' In his will Adam, fiercely anti-Catholic, left £100 to Dodsley's daughter from his first marriage, on condition that she attended a Protestant school.

Adam's death brought Barnard and Louwtjie closer together, if only for a while. She loyally provided the love and support he needed, and their relationship settled down again. Maria began to stay with them occasionally, until she went to what was then Salisbury (now Harare) where Marius was working as a GP, but Louwtjie confessed she felt little love for her. She was older and more frail, but she remained cold, distant and domineering.

On 28 July 1958, ten days after his father's death, Barnard was in the operating theatre at Groote Schuur where a 15-year-old girl, Joan Pick, was to become the first patient to undergo successful open-heart surgery in Africa. The girl had a relatively simple congenital defect – a narrowing of one of the heart valves – and she had been deliberately chosen as the first to be operated on using the heart-lung bypass machine to reduce the risk of failure. The machine did not come ready-made: Barnard, who had not slept during the night because he was so worked up about the operation, had arrived at 6 am to help assemble the contraption, a DeWall-Lillehei bubble oxygenator, with the chief technician, Carl Goosen.

Barnard's account of the operation tells of a race to complete it against a rapidly dropping blood supply from the heart-lung machine. He would discover afterwards that a clamp had slipped from a major blood vessel connected to the oxygenator, allowing blood to seep onto the floor unnoticed. The continual danger with the bypass machine was that if air instead of blood got into the supply line to the body, it could either kill the patient or cause severe brain damage. Nothing of this incident featured in the dramatic report of the operation carried two days later in the *Cape Times*: 'Miracle Operation on Girl in City'. The story spoke of a 'seven-and-a-half-hour operation' during which the team of surgeons had 'worked continuously under considerable strain' and had neither eaten nor drunk. 'They were exhausted when the operation was over.' Inevitably, it was pointed out that the girl was coloured.

Joan Pick was recovering well, the hospital superintendent told the newspaper. The operation had been a complete success, and meant patients needing open-heart surgery would no longer have to travel outside South Africa. The publicity thrilled Barnard: 'We wanted to make a name for ourselves,' he said later. 'I never slept the night before. I kept on going through the different moves and procedures in my mind. I was terribly nervous.'

Barnard was not identified in the *Cape Times* report; neither was the surgeon who assisted him but who was actually his superior, Walter Phillips. It had been Phillips, the older, much respected but rather staid head of the cardiothoracic unit, who had been involved in the earlier disaster that led to the patient's death. Barnard's return from America, brimming with confidence and zeal and loaded with up-to-the-minute technical knowledge, had put Phillips in the shade. Barnard was also the clear favourite of Jannie Louw, his mentor, who ran the surgical division, and Schrire. Barnard made no secret of his ambition, nor of his impatience with Phillips. 'He showed an ill-disguised contempt for Phillips,' says André Swanepoel, a physician in the unit. 'Chris had a clear determination to get to the top,' says Rodney Hewitson, already then a respected thoracic surgeon at Groote Schuur. 'He used people and he stepped on toes. Phillips couldn't compete.' Barnard and Phillips clashed often. There could only be one loser: Phillips gave way to the younger man, and later resigned.

Barnard's impetuous temper in and out of theatre was gaining notoriety. Many nurses were afraid of working with him in case they made a mistake, or were too slow, and became the victim of a thrown instrument, a stream of abuse or even a sharp kick. He worked slowly, thoroughly, generating enormous tension during an operation. For some it had the effect of an electric charge that kept them alert. For others, it created unbearable pressure. Many would avoid working with him altogether or eventually left for jobs elsewhere. He sought and expected perfection from the people around him. Those who failed to make the grade suffered abuse.

His short fuse could prove disastrous, as in the case of a patient who was operated on to repair a heart valve. What should have been a simple operation turned horribly wrong when oxygen bubbles entered the bloodstream and stopped the patient's heart. Barnard exploded. A technician helping on the bypass machine recalls how Barnard tore off his surgical gloves, hurled them into the patient's open chest and stormed out screaming, 'You've killed the patient!' A young registrar who was assisting on the operation says, 'We pumped the patient's heart until all the bubbles were out. We were taken aback that a surgeon could simply walk out on a patient. Another surgeon who was present at the time laid a strong complaint against Barnard, but it was all covered up.' The patient survived but was left partly disabled.

Barnard's marriage may have strengthened after the death of his father, but it was not long before he was behaving again as if he did not care whether it lasted or not. Ernette du Toit was a fifth-year medical student who caught his eye. 'When he discovered I lived near him in Pinelands he would offer me lifts. He made a pass at me but I turned him down because he was married. Once he told me he wanted to meet my mother and he came into the house and played the piano for us. I came from a strong DRC background and this wasn't at all the way a married man behaved in those days. Even then he had an eye for young girls.'

Raoul de Villiers, whose then fiancée Sunet was often the target of Barnard's unwelcome interest, tells of one night at a club when Barnard spent the evening dancing with an attractive, dark-haired nurse while Louwtjie sat watching. 'We were very embarrassed for Louwtjie. We felt sorry for her,' says De Villiers. 'Chris had spoken to me about wanting to get a divorce.'

Bill Piller recalls a dinner party given by the Barnards at their Pinelands home for members of the cardiac unit to celebrate the first 100 open-heart operations at Groote Schuur. One of Barnard's favourite songs, *Personality*, was played repeatedly. 'A good time was being had by all when Chris, who had to work the following day, announced to all at 10.30: "Louwtjie, we must go to bed now, these people want to go home!"' Piller also remembers being rather embarrassed by his host's openly sexual behaviour with one of the nurses at the party. 'He sat with the girl on his lap, fondling her breast.'

But at work Barnard continued to achieve remarkable results. He also started a successful programme of surgery on children with congenital heart defects at the Red Cross Children's Hospital. 'As a heart surgeon he had almost unequalled range; there was no operation he could not perform,' wrote David Cooper, who later worked with him at Groote Schuur.

As director of surgical research at Groote Schuur he was able to explore new ideas, and the transplanting of organs was beginning to grip his imagination. It would lead him to perform a controversial experiment for which he was mostly condemned – the creation of a two-headed dog. The grafting of one dog's head onto the chest of another horrified most of Barnard's colleagues, especially 'Val' Schrire and Jannie Louw. Barnard made a film of the monster lapping up milk with both heads, which he planned to show during a forthcoming trip to Russia, where the experiment had also been carried out. When he published a paper on the subject the story got into the newspapers, and Barnard found himself at the centre of his first media controversy. He argued that the experiment was valid and would help test rejection – others said the work had no scientific value and had been a stunt.

Louw believed Barnard had called the press in to take pictures. 'This disturbed me considerably, to such an extent that I had a placard placed in the laboratory which read, "Do not toy with the Delilah of the press." Needless to say, the placard disappeared overnight. Chris felt chagrined and would not speak to me for some time.' After this, Barnard found it harder to obtain funding for his research work.

Early in 1960 Barnard was awarded an Oppenheimer bursary to travel overseas. He wanted to visit Russia where a highly innovative surgeon, Vladimir Demikhov, had been responsible for a series of experimental grafts, including the two-headed dog. Barnard also planned to return to Minneapolis and apprise himself of the latest developments there. London was on the list too, where Russell Brock was in the forefront of transplant thinking and research. Barnard was clearly determined to stay up with the pack. In March he wrote to the director of the Russian Ministry of Health: 'I plan to visit the USSR from May 18-29 and would be very grateful if you would arrange for me to visit your research centres in Moscow, where they are working in the fields of cardiac surgery and the transplantation of tissues. If there are research centres elsewhere in the Soviet Union which you feel I should visit, I would be happy to do so, as I would like to meet as many of your best surgeons and research workers as possible.' At the start of the letter Barnard tells the director of his unit's 'very good results' in open-heart surgery, and adds: 'In addition, I am engaged in surgical research work and we are particularly interested in the field of cardiac surgery and the transplantation of organs.'

As a cardiac specialist the only organ Barnard was interested in transplanting was, of course, the heart. In America he knew Norman Shumway and Richard Lower were already transplanting the hearts of dogs; they had published a medical paper on their work together. A human heart transplant was the goal of their research, but the hurdles were daunting. Unlike the kidney and the liver – which would be transplanted for the first time in 1963 – the heart held a special, almost mystical place in the human psyche. To Barnard it remained a simple pump. But its absolute power to dictate the quality of a person's life fascinated him.

Before travelling to Moscow, Barnard returned to Minneapolis. He caught up with the state of cardiac research at the university and looked up old friends. He told people there that he had been working on a book for 18 months about the 'surgical anatomy of the human heart'. He also sought out Sharon Jorgensen, telling her he was 'confused' and wanted to resume their relationship. She told him it would not work. 'When he first went back to Cape Town he would write two or three love letters to me every week. But by the time he came back I wanted to move on,' she says. 'It wasn't there for me in the same way any more.' They arranged to meet up later that year in Europe, but it never happened. She would see him once more, the following year, when he revisited Minneapolis to give a lecture and he had dinner with her and her fiancé, a student who would later become a diplomat, and her mother. When she married in August 1961, Barnard sent her a congratulatory telegram which she still has.

Rebuffed by Sharon on that first trip back to Minneapolis, Barnard must have suffered an attack of guilt. Knowing nothing of his attempted reunion with his former love, Louwtjie recalled: 'While he was (in Minneapolis) I received the most beautiful letter I had ever had from Chris. He told me that I was a wonderful woman and a very good mother and wife, and that he loved me deeply, that he was truly sorry about all the sadness and heartbreak he had caused me. On his return he sent me two dozen red roses. The little card read: "Thank you. I will always love you – Chris." I am sure he was sincere and meant it then … Perhaps it was his clever way of playing with me, like a puppet on a string.'

Louwtjie had by now spent many evenings dutifully helping with her husband's cardiac work. She had always made her own clothes, and those of the children. Now she turned her hand to sewing the cloth around the metal rings of the artificial heart valves that Barnard and Carl Goosen had developed. The cloth gave the surgeons material to stitch through to fix the valve in place. The rings were made, with the help of Johannes Barnard, in a South African Railways engineering workshop. Goosen constructed the valves in the garage of his home. Louwtjie covered more than eight hundred of these valves, proof of her dedication to Barnard's work despite the pain he had caused her.

The trip to America, Europe and Russia gave Barnard new impetus in his drive to improve his skills and knowledge. It confirmed to him that America led the field in standards of cardiac and vascular surgery. Yet his open-heart surgery results, especially with children at the Red Cross Children's Hospital, were among the best in the world. When Walter Phillips finally left Groote Schuur, Barnard took his place as head of the cardiothoracic unit. In 1962 he was made an associate professor by UCT and delivered a memorable inaugural lecture which demonstrated his natural ability as a showman and communicator. 'It was the most impressive lecture I've ever attended,' says Joe de Nobrega, then a medical student, who would later work under Barnard. 'At exactly

8 pm the lights went out. The hall was packed – there were students sitting on the stairs. We thought there had been a power cut. All of a sudden over the loudspeaker system came a tape recording … boom-boom-boom-boom it went in the dark … Then the lights came on and Chris Barnard made his entry, like a gladiator, onto the stage and said, "The heart is just a pump." The impact was immense – if Marlon Brando had done it, it couldn't have been more impressive.'

Barnard was performing intricate operations, often on children's hearts as tiny as they were sick, and having to stand for long hours. But at this stage there was no sign of his rheumatoid arthritis interfering with his work. What was increasingly noticeable was his tremor. His hand wavered slightly as it held an instrument and closed in to perform a delicate manoeuvre. It was not uncommon for a surgeon, but there were many others whose hands were steady, and a tremor never looked good. De Nobrega, who assisted Barnard on a large number of operations, says: 'His tremor would somehow stop when it came to the point, say, of putting the stitch in. He never put in anything less than a perfect stitch.'

In the early 1960s one operation was relayed live from the Red Cross Children's Hospital to an audience of surgeons and students at UCT. Rodney Hewitson, who would be a rock-like presence as Barnard's assistant during the early heart transplants, says, 'When the camera closed in you could see on the big screen Chris's hand clearly shaking. Technically he wasn't top class, but he was thorough and he wouldn't accept anything second-rate. When Val Schrire was pushing him to do more operations because the waiting list was growing, Chris told him he would rather do 100 cases with 100 per cent success than many more and lose some. He was a perfectionist and he had a remarkable three-dimensional mind – he seemed to know from a difficult perspective exactly where the anatomy led. He could see it in his mind's eye.'

Walt Lillehei was following Barnard's progress. He had received dozens of letters from him since his departure from Minneapolis. 'All of them were about the patients he was seeing and operating on,' said Lillehei. 'He asked questions about various types of surgical techniques. I was well aware that he was making superb progress, and that was confirmed later by the excellent results he obtained in difficult cases. In particular, he took on some very sick babies early in his career, which was difficult surgery. He was making a name for himself, and not solely because he was the first surgeon to do successful open-heart surgery on the African continent.'

In the laboratory Barnard was working towards his first heart transplant with dogs.

But he was feeling cut off from the mainstream, complaining to Lillehei that medical journals with the latest papers took months to reach him. Now he came close to leaving South Africa for America, where he would undoubtedly have realised his boyhood dream of earning a huge salary. For more than a year he had been in talks with a teaching hospital in New York about setting up its cardiac unit. The basic salary would be $20 000 a year, with at least that again to come from private work. He would have complete freedom to appoint staff and get the unit going from scratch. The hospital, at the Albert Einstein College of Medicine, had written to Barnard with the offer after hearing from one of his mentors at Minneapolis, Richard Varco, that he was concerned about his future in South Africa.

No wonder: these were volcanic times politically, with South Africa's international isolation being sealed by the United Nations and the Commonwealth. The Sharpeville massacre of March 1960, in which 69 unarmed blacks died after being gunned down by police, had brought world outrage and condemnation. In the aftermath the ANC and PAC had been banned and the rigid battle lines drawn which would remain for decades. In the following months hundreds of people died and 18 000 were detained. The ANC, now forced underground, abandoned its passive resistance policy and founded its military wing, uMkhonto weSizwe (Spear of the Nation), under the leadership of Nelson Mandela; its first efforts at sabotaging vital installations began at the end of 1961.

Verwoerd, described by British prime minister Harold Macmillan as 'granite-like', survived an assassination attempt in the weeks after Sharpeville. (His escape and recovery – two bullets had been fired into him at close range – were hailed by Afrikaners as 'the work of God'.) The colonial era was crumbling: Macmillan, during a visit to Cape Town, had warned of the 'wind of change' sweeping through Africa, making it clear that Britain was in favour of black majority rule in South Africa. A string of African countries had gained or were gaining independence. Horrific stories of murder, rape and arson erupting in the Congo in particular after the departure of the Belgians terrified white South Africans. In mid-1961, after a referendum, South Africa proclaimed itself a republic. (There is no record of which way Barnard voted, if he did, but perhaps his views can be gleaned from a comment made much later: 'I'm an Afrikaner who has been a royalist since birth – like my parents before me.' He also said Britain was probably the only nation that would have 'taken the trouble to drag us into the 20th century'.) Withdrawal from the Commonwealth followed.

In such a volatile climate, with his country now becoming the pariah of the world, it was natural for Barnard to worry about the future. He wondered whether he could really make his mark from Cape Town.

The New York offer was highly tempting. His reply in September 1961 shows that any notion that he was transformed overnight by the first heart transplant from a country bumpkin into a jet-setting world traveller is ill-founded: 'I am very interested in seeing your department as I have never had the pleasure of visiting the Albert Einstein College of Medicine. Unfortunately, I am leaving for a tightly scheduled tour of Europe on October 3, and I am not sure whether I will be able to fit in the journey to New York. Arrangements have already been made and confirmed for me to lecture in England, Sweden, France and Israel, and being a lecturer and examiner here at the University, I must be back in Cape Town in time for the final year students' examinations at the end of November.'

Having lived in America Barnard knew the wealth he could acquire by working there. The Albert Einstein College promised him a large salary and huge resources, far greater than anything he could dream of in Cape Town. (At his appointment to associate professor his annual salary was increased to R5 800.) At about the same time – no doubt also as a result of his complaints to Varco – Barnard was offered a post in Richmond, Virginia, by David Hume, one of the world's leading kidney surgeons.

He did visit the Albert Einstein College, and Hume in Virginia, and returned to Cape Town to agonise. He seems almost to have reached a decision to go to New York. But he then talked it over with Schrire and Louw. According to the letter he finally sent to the Albert Einstein College, in February 1963, both men had persuaded him that his future lay in Cape Town. 'I am sure you realise that the question of whether or not to move to New York has been one of the most important and difficult decisions I have ever had to make,' he wrote. 'When you telephoned last week I was still undecided, although fairly sure that the correct decision would be to join you in New York.' His family, he said, were 'looking forward' to the move.

Had he followed his instincts and gone the course of medical history would have been different. What changed Barnard's mind? In the letter he tells of his meeting with Louw and Schrire, which led him to decide to stay in South Africa. He then goes into great detail about the problems of starting a cardiac unit and getting it up to the level of experience and research he had in Cape Town. He thought it would take three years. At Groote Schuur, he wrote, 'We have grown up together, as it were, and have gained most of our experience together. Now that we have reached a point of mutual trust and respect, I cannot lightly consider withdrawing.' Louw and Schrire could not possibly match the financial rewards being offered across the Atlantic. They could, however, pledge unwavering support for his advanced research programme, and he was a man in a hurry. His mother's maxim – Be First – had never been forgotten.

Politically things were beginning to look as if they would settle down too. Mandela had been imprisoned for leaving the country illegally – the Rivonia Trial after which he would be jailed for life was still some way off – and the protest movement was being crushed by the jackboots and guns of the apartheid regime. Barnard was thinking hard about turning his hand more to private practice – he had had some experience of this assisting Louw – with the aim of combining it with his work at Groote Schuur, and the quality of life for a white professional earning good money in South Africa was better than anything he could achieve elsewhere.

He must also have been aware that in South Africa he would face fewer legal obstacles to performing a human heart transplant.

America was a far more sophisticated country in terms of personal litigation. While kidney grafts on the whole had not yet raised the ethical and moral dilemmas of removing organs from cadavers – and therefore the critical definition of when a person was truly dead – the transplanting of unpaired organs like the liver and the heart could not avoid them. A donor of these organs had to be dead. An accident such as the one that led Barnard to hurl his gloves into a patient's chest and walk out would have almost certainly resulted in a lawsuit in America.

There was another more personal motive for deciding to stay in Cape Town: Deirdre was showing great promise as a waterskier and Barnard, with characteristic overdrive, had set his sights on making her a world champion. The facilities available to help achieve this dream would not be there in New York.

Within a few weeks of rejecting the American job Barnard had performed his first heart transplant on a dog. 'It was easier than I expected. As soon as I released the aortic clamp the transplanted heart began to beat.' The dog lived no more than a few hours. Barnard made a film of the operation and showed it during a lecture to medical students at the University of Pretoria in which he declared that rejection of the new organ rather than the operation itself was the main stumbling block to a human heart transplant.

Barnard's travels and contacts helped him keep up with the latest developments in transplant surgery around the world. The pioneering cardiac work of Lillehei, and the kidney transplants being performed by Hume, Thomas Starzl and the Briton Roy Calne in America, were attracting publicity outside medicine. New anti-rejection drugs had recently been used which seemed to give hope that kidney transplants could work with non-related donors – even cadavers – and recipients. Most of the successful kidney grafts until this time had been performed using a kidney from a twin or close relative, which reduced the risk of rejection. In May 1963, *Time* magazine's cover story was devoted to surgical advances since World War II and predictions for the future. Organ transplantation was seen as the key development, and the area where the most exciting advances were likely to be made. The story appeared at about the same time Starzl carried out the first transplant of a human liver, although the patient did not survive.

Three further attempts at liver transplantation failed, and Starzl halted the programme for several years.

Later that year Barnard embarked on a ten-week trip to Europe. He attended medical congresses in Italy and Ireland and visited the 'very active cardiac surgical centres' in what was then West Germany, where he was deeply impressed. He returned from this extensive tour even more resolved to push on with his research work. Frederick Snyders – known as 'Boots' – was one of Barnard's black assistants in the animal house. He recalled the difference in Barnard after this trip: 'I felt his whole character had changed. He appeared more unfriendly and moody, and more determined to achieve what he wanted.'

Barnard was still in touch with the Albert Einstein College in New York because he had offered to provide any help he could in setting up its cardiac unit. Soon after returning from his trip to Europe he wrote to David State, head of surgery there, explaining that he planned to spend 'at least three or four months' in America 'visiting all the most advanced centres'. The trip could not take place until 1965, however, as he needed to try to obtain funding – perhaps a travel grant from the Carnegie Corporation. State wrote to him: 'It was good to hear from you once again. It would appear that you have learned the secret of the full-time surgeon, namely, that you are away full-time.'

Another reason for the lengthy visit to Europe was Deirdre's involvement in international waterskiing competitions in France and Spain. She was now 13 and had been waterskiing intensively for three years. At 12 she had won the South African senior girls' title and was awarded her Springbok colours. In Spain she had competed in the junior European championships – with her father as team manager – coming second; in France, at the world championships, she had been outclassed by older competitors. But it was clear she would go much further.

From the moment he saw her potential as a ten-year-old girl waterskiing on the lagoon at Knysna during a holiday, Barnard had been infatuated with the prospect of making her a world beater, at any price. In 1960 he had acquired a small powerboat at cost from a boatmaking friend. He called it 'Louwtjie'. Later bigger, more powerful boats followed, until a grateful wealthy patient gave him an 18-feet, 225-hp craft which he called 'Pacemaker'.

Soon after this – and with the help of a loan from Louwtjie's father – he bought a lakeside house at Zeekoevlei, near Cape Town, so that the boat could be moored at the end of the garden and Deirdre could practise every spare moment.

Barnard's ruthless obsession with Deirdre's waterskiing, and the hurt he would cause by brutally abandoning her when injuries stopped her reaching the top, would leave bitter, lasting scars. For years, too, André, a sensitive boy, but who appeared to his father to excel at nothing, was virtually ignored by Barnard as he pursued his ambition for Deirdre. 'In the mornings and afternoons after he came home from work he'd hook the boat on to a trailer, drive to a lake and I'd ski back and forth,' recalled Deirdre of her early days waterskiing. 'He was quite strict. He'd keep going even if there was a gale. If I didn't ski well and fell in, he'd make me swim ashore. Some days I'd pray for heavy rain so I wouldn't have to train ... Many a time I came home howling and sobbing.'

Yet Louwtjie would remember these years as some of the happiest of her married life. The focus on Deirdre's waterskiing had bonded the family. 'André, although almost completely ignored by Chris most of the time, was never jealous of his sister's place in her father's heart,' she wrote in *Heartbreak*. 'He, too, was grateful that the tension had left our lives to be replaced by this shared happiness.'

The need for fame – even if it came by proxy – was by now entrenched in Barnard. At one point he told a colleague, while pointing at a newspaper picture of a Springbok sportsman: 'I want to be as famous as he is.' Much later he confessed that he felt at this time that his ambitions were 'going nowhere' and that he saw Deirdre as his passport to fame. Certainly reports of her waterskiing exploits appeared regularly in South African newspapers, sometimes referring to her as 'the daughter of Prof. Chris Barnard of Pinelands'.

Bob Frater had first come across Barnard in the early 1950s when as a student he attended a lecture Barnard gave on TB meningitis: 'His energy, enthusiasm and vitality were obvious. We didn't know quite what to make of him, but we knew he was remarkable.' Two years after returning from America, Barnard invited Frater to work in the cardiac clinic at Groote Schuur. He found the atmosphere to be 'one of great excitement'. Barnard was using innovative techniques to repair complex congenital heart defects such as tetralogy of Fallot – a condition often known as 'hole in the heart' where the blood has too little oxygen, producing 'blue babies'; transposition of the great vessels; and Ebstein's anomaly, a misplaced valve which restricts the amount of blood being pumped to the lungs. His excellent results with these, among the most difficult problems a heart surgeon could face, were being noted by some of the world's leading cardiac specialists.

But Barnard was anxious to achieve fame beyond medical circles. After one particularly novel valve replacement performed by Frater he was surprised to find full details of the operation, hailed as a 'world first', on the front page of the newspapers the next day. 'I asked Chris where the information had come from, and he said he had no idea. However, by the manner of his answering the question, I suspected that he in fact knew very well and had been responsible for providing the information.'

This episode, for Frater, proved the 'consuming hunger for recognition' he believed to be part of Barnard's make-up. 'He understood what he had to do to gain that recognition. He had a very clear idea of his own value. He would not lecture to students without a large attendance. He sought overseas engagements and, in fact, travelled a lot.' If there was no outside grant travel costs were covered by the provincial authorities, but the surgeon was expected to pay it back at the rate of 1/36 of the amount owed per month. 'Chris had soon accumulated enough travel that he was in hock to the province for years to come,' said Frater.

Frater had been lured to Cape Town from the Mayo Clinic in America with the promise that he would eventually share the workload with Barnard in what was becoming a renowned cardiac unit. But he found Barnard unwilling to give up his supremacy. Even when Barnard fell seriously ill and was off work for two months with hepatitis he wanted to retain his hold. He confessed to colleagues he was worried about Frater's expertise – even jealous. 'He was very sick,' said Frater, 'and from his hospital bed he announced there would be no more cardiac surgery until he had recovered. Val Schrire went to him and said, "That's nonsense! You asked Frater to come back to join you from the Mayo Clinic – he has been trained at the best centre for cardiac surgery in the world – and we are not stopping operating because you are sick. And there is nothing you can do about it anyhow since you are too sick to argue!"' Indeed Barnard was often delirious during this illness, probably the result of the drugs he was being given. He hallucinated and later claimed that the ghost of a patient who had died in the ward had tried to strangle him. By the time Barnard had recovered Frater had seized his chance to stake his claim to a regular slot in the operating schedule. He did not leave for two years – and then to take the job at the Albert Einstein College that Barnard had turned down. Barnard had put his name forward with a strong recommendation.

Frater remained on good terms with Barnard, later describing him as a 'truly remarkable physician-scientist'. But he was not, for him, a 'natural surgeon': 'The technical manipulations standard to surgery did not come easily to him and when he operated there was clearly both a significant effort of will to perform manoeuvres successfully and a significant element of anxiety while doing so. To counter this, there was a high level of determination, tenacity and resilience. There was no question of not achieving the tasks at the best possible level of surgical execution.'

Frater was not the only talented figure who found that Barnard disliked being upstaged. John Terblanche worked with him on the early dog heart transplants and had set up a successful research programme on kidney transplants. They clashed after Terblanche performed particularly well in Fellowship examinations for the South African College of Medicine. 'It led to serious conflict between us,' said Terblanche. Barnard unfairly accused him of failing to devote enough time to his laboratory work. Barnard was a fierce enemy, and Terblanche found himself back on the wards. He left the hospital the following year without making his peace, although returned later and eventually became head of the department of surgery – above Barnard.

Surgeons who worked closely with Barnard often said he seemed to have an uncanny 'sixth sense' which, coupled with an extraordinarily quick brain, enabled him to 'think on his feet' during operations. It gave him the ability to overcome unexpected problems that might have stumped less mentally nimble surgeons. Frater called it 'functioning by instinct'. 'He would say, "The heart doesn't look right." When asked what he meant, he could give no explanation, but the subsequent behaviour of the heart generally bore him out.' This instinct carried through to the care of the patient after the operation. 'It was notable that he would often arrive at a patient's bedside, without being called, at precisely the moment when the patient's condition changed for the worse,' said Frater.

South Africa would not have television until well into the 1970s. But during a medical congress in New Zealand Barnard gave an accomplished television interview that again showed a flair for the media. Other surgeons watching were impressed and assumed he had had plenty of experience, but in fact it was probably his first appearance in front of a television camera.

Early in 1964 a medical event took place that showed both how advanced America was in the field of heart transplant research, and how hampered its surgeons were by fear of litigation and public opinion. A few months earlier James Hardy had carried out the world's first lung transplant, attracting wide publicity. Now he planned to perform the world's first human heart transplant at the Mississippi Medical Center, Jackson. The donor was to be a young man who had suffered irrecoverable brain damage, and the recipient a 68-year-old man with advanced heart disease who was being kept alive with the help of a heart-lung machine. But the donor clung to life, while the older man's heart suddenly failed. Hardy boldly decided to use a chimpanzee's heart instead, but it was too small to cope, and the man died after 90 minutes. Hardy had shown that the operation could be done, at least. But he was also heavily criticised, and the public's hostile reaction – Hardy was made to feel like a pariah who was dabbling in witchcraft – deterred others in America from trying a human heart transplant until Barnard had broken through the legal and ethical barriers.

In Cape Town Barnard and his team took careful note of Hardy's operation. He carried on with occasional heart transplants in dogs and baboons in the laboratory, concentrating on the technique needed to perfect the operation itself rather than worrying about controlling rejection. He was also keen to suggest to Stuart Saunders, then specialising in liver failure, that he should try cross-circulating a patient with a baboon filled with compatible human blood to relieve the ailing liver. 'It was a very unusual idea,' says Saunders. 'We had to wash out the baboon's blood first. I had never heard of it being done. We had to carry the baboon into the hospital hidden in a laundry basket to avoid complaints.'

During the operation Barnard inevitably appeared in theatre. 'It was 4 am. We were having trouble with the perfusion, but Barnard looked at it and in five minutes solved the problems.' The patient lived for several more weeks before dying from pneumonia.

Outside work Barnard was spending every possible moment pushing Deirdre to train, even getting involved in the running of waterskiing events. His drive to make her a world champion was almost inhuman. Friends began to worry about Deirdre's well-being. Dene Friedmann, also a waterskier and Deirdre's closest friend, says, 'It was very tough on her. She was just a young girl and she didn't get the chance to go out with friends like a normal teenager.' After the family moved to Zeekoevlei the pace grew relentless. Barnard would have Deirdre out on the lake at 6 am, then again for three more hours after school. 'She used to pray for bad weather so she wouldn't have to do it. It was often terribly cold. She and Chris would fight if she told him she didn't want to train.'

André, on the other hand, hardly merited his attention and grew ever closer to his mother. Barnard rarely went to watch him play rugby for SACS (South African College School, a leading school for boys) because he wasn't in the first team. Worse, family friends witnessed what can only be described as mental abuse being inflicted on him by his father. 'André had a puppy called Sixpence which had been rescued from the animal house,' says one. 'We'd been out one evening and when we returned to Chris and Louwtjie's house, Chris beckoned us upstairs to where André was sound asleep with the puppy curled up next to him. All of a sudden Chris let out a huge scream and André woke up in a great fright. He was hysterical. Chris thought it was terribly funny, and went downstairs laughing while we stayed with André trying to calm him down. He was only ten or so. We were dumbstruck. We couldn't believe what we had seen.' Another family friend, Joan Steyn, says, 'André was a very mixed up boy. Louwtjie always complained to Chris that he wasn't paying him enough attention.'

Despite the pressures on his time and energy, Barnard's sexual antics were showing no sign of slowing down. Ernette du Toit, who had gone on to join the pathology department at Groote Schuur, recalls stories of him stalking the corridors with pairs of silk stockings in his coat pocket, hoping to entice one of the young nurses into a laundry room. On one occasion he was caught making love to a nurse in a VW Beetle in the hospital car park. 'The girl was British. She was hauled over the coals and then sent back to London. Nothing happened to Barnard at all,' says Bill Piller.

He had also started taking flying lessons, which would have been expensive and were presumably another gift from a patient. Barnard would sometimes arrive home in his suit in the evening and tell Louwtjie he had to go out 'for flying lessons', according to Fritz Brink, a close friend who had first got to know Barnard when he sold him medical equipment in Ceres. 'It was clearly absurd,' said Brink.

Bennie Shapiro, a Cape Town doctor who hosted lively parties, recalls meeting Barnard at a medical congress in Johannesburg. They were staying at the same hotel. Barnard asked him if he 'knew any dames' in the city and when Shapiro mentioned two attractive English nurses, Barnard insisted he call them up and invite them over to the hotel 'for a party'. Barnard became a regular unaccompanied guest at Shapiro's parties at his seafront house in Clifton. Donald Ross, a South African who had been at medical school with Barnard and was now at Britain's National Heart Hospital, says, 'Chris used to come once a year to attend a congress but mainly because we had a big group of beautiful girls. The nurses there were his chief interest. He'd come officially to visit me and exchange chats and talk about surgery and watch me operating for a little while, and then he'd take the girls out. He had an eye for the girls.'

Barnard's reckless behaviour baffled friends. 'In those days there was a different approach to marriage – you didn't just jump into bed with other people,' says Marlene Cywes, wife of Syd, who had worked closely with Barnard as his 'scrub' nurse. 'But Chris went against all that. With someone who loved him as much as Louwtjie did he should have been happy.'

Marius Barnard had decided he had had enough of general practice in what was then Rhodesia and had arrived at Groote Schuur to become a surgeon. This gave Barnard fresh impetus, if any was needed. Marius was eager to specialise in cardiac surgery and shared his brother's fascination with research. After spending a year in the research laboratory performing many of the animal heart transplants and working on his Master of Surgery degree thesis, he needed practical experience abroad. In 1966 Barnard wrote to various contacts in America: 'Marius is a hard worker and has proved his sense of duty and dedication in these last few years. He is anxious to learn and is an enthusiastic experimental surgeon.' Marius would eventually secure a position in Houston for a year, under Denton Cooley, one of the most adventurous cardiac surgeons and certainly the fastest. What he learned under Cooley would be invaluable to his brother when he returned to Groote Schuur a few weeks before the first heart transplant was carried out.

Barnard by now felt he needed to learn much more about rejection. 'The big battle in a heart transplant was not going to be in placing a new heart in a human being, but getting it to stay there,' he wrote later. 'Unless we could control this immunological rejection there was no basis for attempting a heart transplant.' According to Gil Campbell, Barnard first contacted Norman Shumway to discuss whether he might spend time with him in Palo Alto studying heart transplants. 'Norm told him he should go to Richmond where his old partner Richard Lower was still doing this work, and he could also see what David Hume was doing in renal transplantation.' Barnard organised a three-month trip to America. In Richmond, Virginia, he would work under Hume, who was at the forefront of work on kidney transplants. He let Hume believe he was planning to set up a renal unit at Groote Schuur, which was only partly true. His main goal, as he admitted in *One Life* some years later, was to learn how to successfully transplant a kidney, and control its rejection, as a practice run for the heart. 'The kidney had become a stepping-stone to the heart. Its transplant would be a run-through for a heart transfer,' he said.

In Richmond Barnard assisted on kidney transplants and learned how to manage the intensive care of patients after the operation. He studied anti-rejection drugs and seemed to revel in the dynamism of the place: 'Prodded by Dr Hume we never slept, and the drama never ceased.' Richard Lower's work with Shumway on more than 300 heart transplants in dogs at Stanford University in California had blazed the trail. Barnard did not miss the opportunity in Richmond to examine Lower's methods.

He also visited Starzl in Denver. In his autobiography, *The Puzzle People*, Starzl writes: 'How I met Barnard is worth explaining because apparently he was secretly planning a heart transplantation long before he performed this historic operation in Cape Town ... I was one of the necessary steps in his preparation although I did not know it.'

When Barnard arrived in Denver he was especially keen to know more about a new and effective anti-rejection drug Starzl was using. 'This was no casual visitor ... Lower and Dave Hume told me later that Barnard had seemed interested mainly in learning how to treat rejection. They assumed that he was going to start a kidney program in Cape Town and so did I. I told him candidly that we were planning to go ahead with heart transplantation in Denver, but not until we were successful with the liver. A chest surgeon named George Pappas had been recruited ... with the promise that heart transplantation would be the next item on our agenda. If Barnard had any such plans of his own, he did not mention them.'

He did, however, confide in others at Hume's centre in Richmond. He told them he was going back to Cape Town to do a human heart transplant.

7

Transplant

Back from America, Barnard freely began admitting his goal: to transplant a human heart as soon as possible. What he had seen in Richmond and Denver showed him he was some way behind others. He was yet to perform his first human kidney transplant. The research work in the laboratory intensified.

He also kept in touch with Marius, who would remain in Houston until the following year. Denton Cooley and another Houston surgeon, Michael DeBakey, were the pioneers of artificial hearts. DeBakey transplanted the first such device, of a kind – it was more a simple mechanical pump to assist the patient's ailing heart – in 1966. Marius was in a perfect position to keep watch on the developments in heart transplant surgery in the US.

While Barnard had been in America Verwoerd had been assassinated – stabbed to death in parliament by a deranged man employed as a messenger – and a new prime minister installed, John Vorster. As minister for justice, Vorster, a 51-year-old attorney, had been ruthless in cracking down on the resistance movements. Mandela was serving life imprisonment on Robben Island; Robert Sobukwe, leader of the Pan-Africanist Congress, was also detained there. International pressure was growing, with UN arms embargoes and economic sanctions in place, yet South Africa was going through a boom period.

Vorster was no less hardline than his predecessor. But he adopted a far more outgoing approach towards the rest of the world, especially Africa. He was determined to improve the image of his country. Barnard would get to know Vorster extremely well in the coming years. The surgeon's pioneering drive was in harmony with Vorster's view of what South Africans should be doing. 'The time demands of us that we must tell the world what we have achieved,' said Vorster.

The first casualty of Barnard's single-minded propulsion towards his goal was Deirdre. Her progress towards the top of the world's waterskiing elite was being marred by persistent injury, although she managed second place in the world championships in Australia that year. She lacked the killer instinct, thought Barnard. When she lost she smiled and shrugged her shoulders. She was not distraught, as he believed she should be. During the months he had been in America, Deirdre's training had slackened. She tended not to go out on the lake at 6 am. Even before the trip, he had told her he would no longer be involved in training her: 'All the years of training, all the tears in Zeekoevlei, all the trials and medals and victory cups came down to this: I had failed to transplant into her my own hunger for victory,' was how he put it in *One Life*. In an interview in 1987, he said: 'When she passed her peak and stopped winning I began to lose interest in the game. I could see I couldn't make a champion out of her, so I decided to make a champion of myself. I diverted all my energy into my profession and an attempt to achieve something great.'

After such an intense father-daughter relationship over many years, it was a callous ending. Deirdre continued to compete in international competitions, but she began a slow decline. Eventually she would be admitted to hospital with depression and she would suffer weight problems for several years. At her worst she would turn up barefoot and ragged at her father's office, desperately seeking his attention. In the same 1987 interview, Barnard admitted that his relationship with Deirdre in her teenage years had been abnormally close: 'I think in her subconscious mind I was more than a father; I was virtually a boyfriend. I mean, we were everything in each other's lives because I didn't find all that satisfaction in my married life. We were always together then, even at parties.'

Deirdre, responding in the same London *Sunday Times Magazine* article, was candid too: 'He suddenly became non-existent. Before that we had been so close and we were so fond of each other – he was everything to me – that being dropped like a hot potato felt ten times worse. It hurt me terribly.' Her father showed no sympathy: 'He never took any blame for my problems. He said it was me who wasn't strong enough to survive being dropped like that.'

André too was suffering. Neglected by his father, there were sure signs that he was struggling in Deirdre's shadow. Some close friends in Pretoria, the Franzots, offered to put André up so that he could attend Pretoria High School for Boys for two years, the run-up to matriculation, and escape the problems of home.

Barnard's mother, wheelchair-bound from a stroke, was now living in a nursing home in Cape Town. Repelled by the sight of his strong-willed mother rendered helpless by the stroke and by old age, Barnard rarely visited her. (After Adam's death, Maria had spent years with Marius in the then Rhodesia – now Zimbabwe – and later lived for long periods with Barnard and Louwtjie who nursed her. Maria would remain in the nursing home until her death in 1977.) His time was in any case almost entirely devoted to preparing for his first kidney transplant.

Edith Black was a 36-year-old white housewife with serious kidney failure. It had taken a year since his return from America, but Barnard was finally ready to perform a kidney transplant. Mrs Black's diseased kidneys were removed and she was connected to a dialysis machine, or artificial kidney, to await a suitable donor. After several were rejected as incompatible, a coloured youth was brought in after a road accident and his red blood cells were found to be a good match for Mrs Black's. The operation to transplant one of his kidneys into Mrs Black went with 'surprising ease', said Barnard. (She would live for more than twenty years.) It gave him the encouragement he was hoping for.

'From then on it was all stations go for a heart transplant,' says Francois Hitchcock, a young registrar who assisted at the kidney operation. 'After we had completed the operation someone said, "Now you can do the heart transplant." The name of Washkansky came up. Chris said, "But are we ready? Are we sure?"' Martinus 'MC' Botha, the pathologist, said later: 'The success achieved in the case of Mrs Black gave everyone concerned encouragement to go on and take up the next great challenge facing us and the rest of the world – the transplanting of a human heart.' Botha himself had recently returned from a three-month overseas trip in which he had visited laboratories in Holland, France and America to study the most advanced work being done on tissue-typing. It had been established that the closer the match between the donor's and recipient's white blood cells – the cells that fight infection – the less risk there was of rejection of the transplanted organ.

After the Edith Black success Barnard pestered Schrire 'day and night' to give him a suitable patient. It had to be someone for whom nothing more could be done in a conventional sense; someone with terminal heart disease whose death could otherwise not be avoided.

Barnard later said that once a reluctant Schrire had accepted that he was serious about doing a heart transplant, he had eventually 'offered' him Louis Washkansky as a candidate. But Schrire remained sceptical, believing the cost of a single heart transplant would cover a host of other vital operations. He made the point that none of the dozens of dogs who had received new hearts from Barnard and his research team had lived more than a few hours. His scepticism – 'He thought it was nonsense, and he had the job of persuading the patient to agree to it,' says one former colleague – would later grow into antagonism and become a source of great bitterness between the two men.

In *The Beat of My Heart*, the first outline of his autobiography, Barnard recalled: 'I told my brother Marius, "We must transplant a heart too." After a Sunday in solitude in my home in Zeekoevlei – it is a Sunday I will remember all my life – I went to Dr Schrire and told him that I had decided to act. It was at the beginning of November. "Okay," he replied. "We'll look for a patient."' On 11 November – the day after he had discussed the idea of a transplant with that patient, Washkansky – Barnard addressed a group of young doctors, telling them: '"In the near future I can see that we will ask people to give us their kidneys, their heart, their liver and even their lungs. We will ask for organs such as the heart because *someone* very soon will carry out a transplant of this organ." That *someone* was me.' The emphasis was Barnard's – and he was clearly saying that on the day he gave this lecture he had the fixed aim of being the first to perform a human heart transplant.

Later Barnard would always deny that he had been determined to win 'a race' to do the first heart transplant. In 1987 he said in an interview with David Cooper, a former colleague in the cardiac unit who later compiled a book of testimonials to Barnard to mark the 25th anniversary of the first heart transplant: 'It may be hard to believe, but at no time before the operation did it ever occur to me that I was planning to do something that would so capture the public's imagination. To me, it was just one more new operation in the long list of procedures made possible by the development of the heart-lung machine. Furthermore, at no time did I ever consider that I was involved in a race to perform the first heart transplant. There was no sense of urgency in our planning; everything was organised methodically and without hurry.'

Yet, in *One Life*, he admitted that the 'delay and subsequent anxiety' in being handed a patient who would be the first recipient of another's heart caused an 'alarming flare-up' in his arthritis. 'Both hands and feet began to swell, and with such pain I feared it would prevent me from operating when Professor Schrire finally decided to release a patient.' Why, if there was no race and Barnard was not desperate to win it, was he suffering such anxiety? Why not take the wait in his stride?

In later years he knew that any confirmation of such a race would play into the hands of critics – some of them undoubtedly jealous of his success and fame. He didn't want to go down in medical history as a glory-seeking opportunist. But others at the time had little doubt of his competitive driving force, without suggesting necessarily he was ill-prepared. He made a point of informing close colleagues of his plans, urging them not to tell anyone else. He didn't want the pressure of publicity on his back ahead of the transplant, although a story was published in the *Cape Times* on 21 November saying that surgeons were on standby at Groote Schuur to perform a heart transplant; Barnard was named as the man who would 'probably' lead the team. Barnard was acutely aware that cardiac surgeons in America and elsewhere were close to performing a human heart transplant, including Shumway and Lower at Stanford. They too had announced, on 20 November, that they were ready, and needed only a suitable donor. According to Desmond Stoffberg, a civil servant who would later be assigned to assist Barnard after the eruption of publicity following the first heart transplant, Louwtjie had been expected to keep track of any announcements on the radio news.

Francois Hitchcock was on duty at Groote Schuur one evening in November when Barnard called. 'He asked if I'd heard the news on the radio. He said he had just caught the end of it, and it had said that at Stanford they were ready to do a heart transplant, or they had done one. He wasn't sure. He said, "You better go out

Right: The missionary church in Beaufort West where Barnard's father Adam, a Dutch Reformed reverend preached to coloured people. Barnard's mother, Maria, often played the organ here with Christiaan pumping the bellows. *(Shaun Harris/PictureNet Africa)*

Below: The rectory, the Barnard family home next to the mission church in Beaufort West. Christiaan was born and grew up here until at 18 he left for medical school in Cape Town. *(Shaun Harris/PictureNet Africa)*

Above: Swimming group: Barnard *(second row, far right)* aged around 12 with other members of the Otters, the Beaufort West swimming club, and their instructors. *(Andrew Brown)*

Right: Barnard as a young man, around 1940. He wore hand-me-down clothes that rarely fitted properly. The soldier next to him was one of more than 300 000 volunteers of all races who formed the South African forces that fought on the side of the Allies in World War II.

Right: Christiaan and Louwtjie on their wedding day in November, 1948. They were married at the Groote Kerk in Cape Town. Barnard was then working as a general practitioner in Ceres.
(Sunday Times Archives)

Bottom left: Ningi, or Katherine Stevens, the art student Barnard fell in love with before going to the medical school at the University of Cape Town.
(Private Collection)

Above: Sharon Jorgensen, who had a long-lasting affair with Barnard while he was training as a cardiac surgeon in Minneapolis in the late 1950s. She pleaded with him not to return to South Africa.
(Cliff Lundstrom)

Barnard operating. He expected his staff to match his standards of perfection and did not hesitate to scream at them if they failed.
(Groote Schuur Hospital Museum Archives)

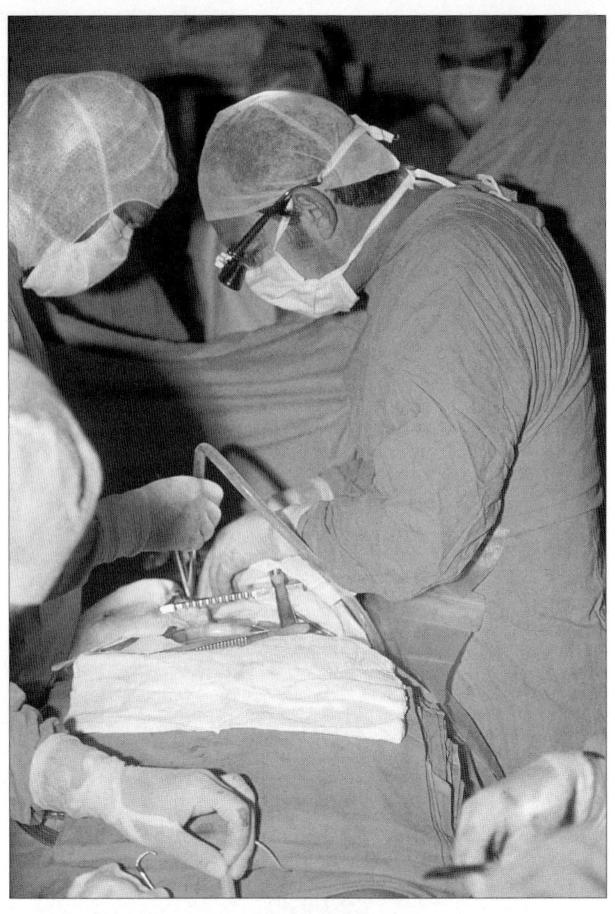

Louis Washkansky, who would become the first man to be given a new heart, with his wife Ann. He insisted on enjoying a busy social life despite suffering a series of heart attacks.
(Andrew Brown)

kenwood demonstration

Stuttafords

THE CAPE TIMES

LATE FINAL

MONDAY, DECEMBER 4, 1967

table lamps

Stuttafords

WORLD'S FIRST HEART TRANSPLANT

Groote Schuur doctors make history

LIFE BEATS ANEW FOR CITY MAN

UNIQUE DOUBLE OPERATION

TEAM WAITED FOUR WEEKS

SHOCK SET HEART GOING

HEART DONOR HAD STOPPED TO SHOP

Denise Ann Darvall, 25-year-old accounting-machine operator at a Cape Town bank, whose heart was used in the operation.

His will to live inspired doctors, says wife

'Phone the Cape Times

41-0661

INSIDE

Dick Stent on Davis Cup chances —PAGE 15

HEART OP. NEWS

A gift made to order Exclusively For You

Only at the Charles of the Ritz Beauty Bar

Stuttafords

The front page of the *Cape Times* on 4 December 1967, the day after Barnard had performed the world's first human heart transplant. Denise Darvall, the young woman whose heart was given to Louis Washkansky, is pictured in the centre of the page. Her father, Edward Darvall, is shown on the right, and at the top is the first picture taken of the surgical team involved in the historic operation. (*PictureNet Africa*)

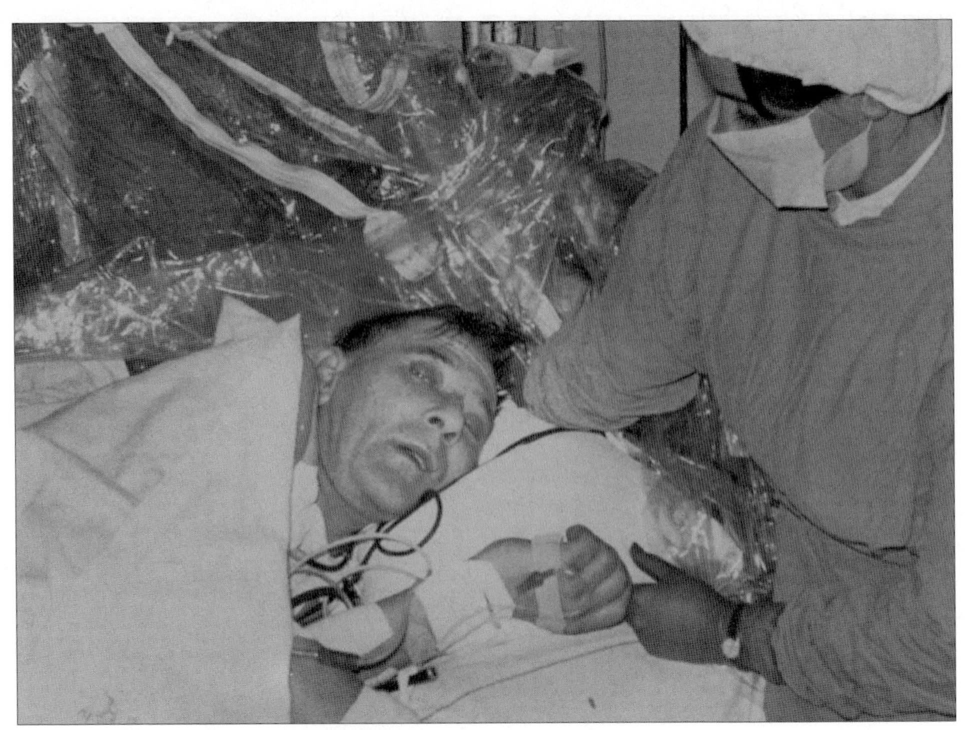

Top: Louis Washkansky, the first man to be given a new heart, receives constant nursing care as he recovers 36 hours after the transplant.
(Sunday Times Archives)

Right: Barnard with Louwtjie, daughter Deirdre and son André, enjoying a rare family day together in the days shortly after the first heart transplant.
(Sunday Times Archives)

Top: Receiving an honorary Doctor of Science degree, its highest honour, from the University of Cape Town, two weeks after the first heart transplant.
(Groote Schuur Hospital Museum Archives)

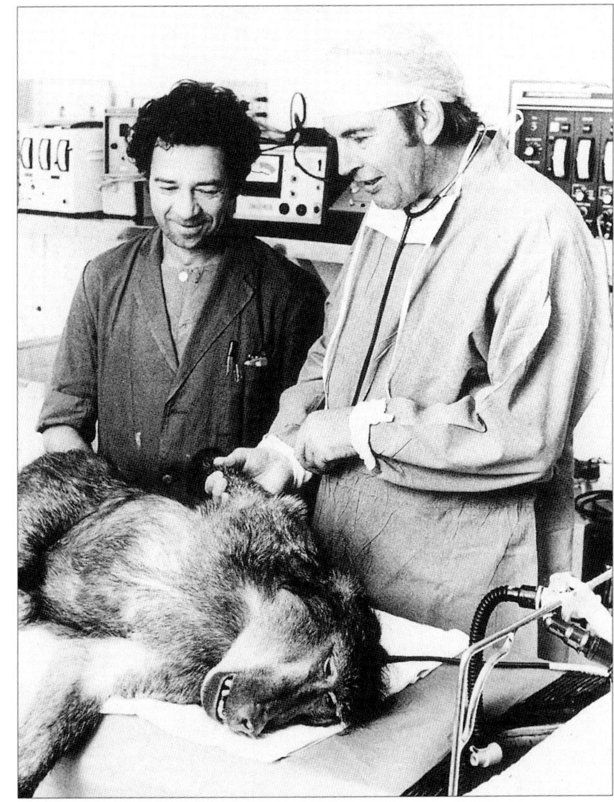

Right: Baboons were used for much of the laboratory research work. On one controversial occasion Barnard used the heart of a baboon to aid the failing heart of a transplant patient when no human donor was available. The operation was unsuccessful and Barnard abandoned the idea after outrage from animal welfare groups.
(Groote Schuur Hospital Museum Archives)

Top: Barnard arrives in London during what would become known as 'Professor Barnard's Tour of Europe' in January, 1968. On the left is MC Botha, the pathologist whose advanced tissue-matching work helped ensure the first heart transplant could go ahead. Behind Botha can be seen Bertie Bosman, who would be responsible for the intensive care of Washkansky and later transplant patients. The woman in the foreground was immediately linked to Barnard by the press but was in fact a friend of another member of the party. *(Sunday Times Archives)*

Right: Barnard is given an audience with Pope Paul VI at the Vatican. To Barnard's relief the Pontiff did not criticise his work but offered to pray for him. Although he had been brought up by his father to fear Roman Catholicism, Barnard always described this as the most impressive meeting of his life. *(Sunday Times Archives)*

Above: Barnard arrives back in South Africa after another trip to Europe. In the 12 months after the first heart transplant he was said to have travelled more than 300 000 miles.
(Sunday Times)

Above: Barnard is welcomed back by Louwtjie after his first trip to Europe in January 1968, during which he was fêted as a celebrity and faced criticism from his peers. The broad smiles masked a strain, which would soon surface, and spell the beginning of the end of their marriage.
(Sunday Times Archives)

Right: The 'Tailor of Rome', Angelo Litrico, made suits for Barnard free of charge for 17 years from the time of his visit to Italy to meet the Pope in January, 1968. In return Barnard would examine sick children during his visits to Italy and refer some of them to Groote Schuur hospital for heart operations.
(Ivan Kroschenko/BMC Studios, Rome)

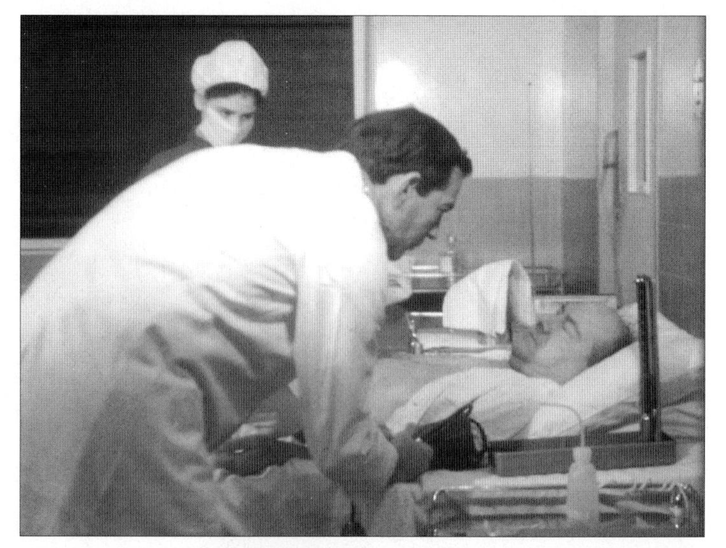

Right: Barnard examines Philip Blaiberg, his second heart transplant patient, who was to live for 19 months after the procedure.
(Groote Schuur Hospital Museum Archives)

Above: Barnard with his son André, then 16 and studying for his matriculation in Pretoria. André would also become a doctor but died at 32 as a result of what Barnard believed was a suicide. Barnard blamed himself for the tragedy, saying he had failed to spend enough time with his son.
(Sunday Times Archives)

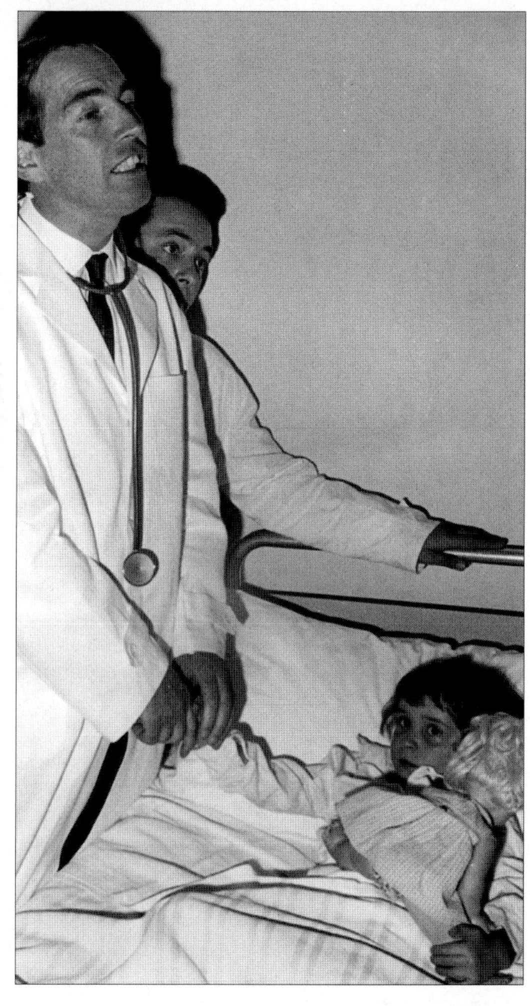

Right: Barnard examines a four-year-old girl, Silvana Cavallini, at a clinic near Rome at the request of Sophia Loren. The actress had hosted a lavish party in Barnard's honour when he visited Rome soon after the first heart transplant.
(Gianni Foggia/AP Photo)

With Gina Lollobrigida in early 1968. They had a brief fling which became highly public when Louwtjie discovered love letters to Barnard from the Italian actress.
(Daily Mail Archives, London)

In March, 1968, Philip Blaiberg became the world's first heart transplant patient to leave hospital. Hundreds of journalists, photographers and well-wishers were gathered outside Groote Schuur hospital to witness the event.
(Groote Schuur Hospital Museum Archives)

Barnard receives the Freedom of the City of Cape Town, 3 May 1968.
(Groote Schuur Hospital Museum Archives)

Barnard dances with one of the world's most glamorous women, Princess Grace of Monaco, after opening the Red Cross Ball in 1968. Pictures like this convinced Louwtjie, who had been left behind in Cape Town, that her marriage was over.
(Sunday Times Archives)

Top: Barnard with Denton Cooley *(centre)* and Spanish cardiac surgeon Cristobal Martinez-Bordiu, the Marques de Villaverde and Franco's son-in-law, at a 1969 press conference in Houston, Texas, where Cooley was based. Both men became great friends of Barnard. Cooley was renowned for his skill and speed as a surgeon.
(Sunday Times Archives)

Bottom right: The commemorative stamp issued in South Africa in 1969.
(Daily Mail Archives, London)

Top: With the self-exiled King Constantine of Greece at the Italian Open Tennis Championships in Rome, 1969. Barnard was a schoolboy tennis champion.
(Sunday Times Archives)

Right: Barnard leaves La Perla restaurant in Cape Town with a 19-year-old hairdresser. The picture, taken in 1969 only days before Barnard's divorce case was due to be dealt with at the Cape Supreme Court, was to cost the photographer, Terry Shean, his job.
(Terry Shean/Sunday Times)

Despite the 28-year age gap, Barnard and his second wife Barbara were as close and romantic as any newly-in-love couple. Here they dance at their engagement party just months after Barnard's divorce from Louwtjie. (*Sunday Times Archives*)

With his second wife Barbara on their wedding night. He was 47, she was 19. The couple were married at the home of Barbara's parents Fred and Ulli Zoellner in Johannesburg on Valentine's Day, 1970. Press photographers were allowed in for a few minutes and pandemonium broke out, hence Barnard's strained expression. (*Terry Shean/Sunday Times*)

Right: With eight-year-old Mirella Candiotto, an Italian girl with a heart defect that her mother hoped Barnard would cure. Barnard always said his greatest joy came when he successfully repaired the hearts of children.
(Sunday Times)

Bottom: This picture was flashed around the world and suggested Barnard was flirting alone with Sophia Loren, who had thrown a party in his honour at her home near Rome in early 1968. In fact Loren's husband Carlo Ponti was sitting next to the actress but he had been cut out of the picture.
(Daily Mail Archives, London)

Right: Barnard's elder brother Johannes, or Barney, who worked as a highly-inventive engineer for South African Railways. When Barnard lived in Cape Town as a medical student in the 1940s he lodged with Johannes and his wife Joyce.
(Terry Shean/Sunday Times)

Above: Barnard flanked by his two greatest heart transplant successes: Dorothy Fisher, given a new heart in 1969 and who lived for more than 12 years and Dirk van Zyl, who was to live for 23 years after his transplant in 1971. Such long survival periods were remarkable and more so for being achieved before the advent of the immuno-suppressive 'wonderdrug' cyclosporin in the early 1980s. *(Sunday Times Archives)*

Above: Barnard with daughter Deirdre on her wedding day in 1978. He had lavished attention on Deirdre as she grew up while neglecting his son André, whose wedding in Britain in the same year he failed to attend.
(Sunday Times)

Right: Barbara in 1981, regarded by renowned photographer Patrick Lichfield as one of the most beautiful women in the world.
(Sunday Times)

Right: Barbara arrives at Deirdre's wedding with sons Frederick *(left)*, seven, and Christiaan, aged four.
(Sunday Times)

Bottom: Barnard at a dinner in Rome with American actress Norma Jordan *(far right)* and Angelo Litrico in 1981. Italian newspapers said Barnard had 'lost his head' over Jordan, an affair that would then have been illegal in South Africa under the apartheid laws. It was one of the betrayals of Barbara that would lead to her divorcing him a few months later.
(Private collection)

Top: A radiant and clearly relieved Barbara leaving the Cape Supreme Court in January 1982, after her uncontested divorce from Barnard. Her husband's inability to stay faithful had finally persuaded her to give up on their 12-year marriage.
(Sunday Times)

Right: Once retired from surgery Barnard embarked on a full-time career in books, lecture tours and consultative work. Here he promotes his 1984 collection of *Cape Times* columns, *The Best of Barnard.*
(Terry Shean/Sunday Times)

people
Vol. 1 No. 1
MAY 27, 1987
ONLY 98c + GST
WIN A WEEK AT THE WILD COAST SUN

BARNARD BOMBSHELL

Beer and wine are good for you
NEW HOPE FOR HEADACHE SUFFERERS
Bizarre secrets of Charles' & Di's marriage
NEW PROOF UFO'S ARE REAL
Mr T turns lawyer
CHRIS, 62, TO WED KAREN, 22
I WAS EATEN ALIVE AND SURVIVED
Higgins falls for "Murder She Wrote" sleuth

Not long after his second divorce, Barnard met another beautiful 19-year-old, part-time model Karin Setzkorn. His devastation at his loss of Barbara made him cautious about taking the plunge for a third time and the couple did not marry until 1988.
(*Sunday Times Archives*)

Deirdre, now in her thirties, had grown used to seeing her father with girls far younger than her. She and Karin *(right)*, who was to become her stepmother, became friends but their relationship over the following years fluctuated.
(*Terry Shean/Sunday Times*)

Right: With Karin at their wedding party at La Vita, Barnard's restaurant in Newlands, Cape Town, in January 1988. Despite her early misgivings about a relationship with a man 41 years her senior, Karin found herself in love and keen to have children with Barnard.
(Sunday Times Archives)

Bottom: With Armin, his fifth child and first by Karin. Armin was born in 1989 when Barnard was 66.
(Sunday Times)

Above: With Diana, Princess of Wales, at an awards dinner in Italy in 1996. Diana, who would die in a car crash in Paris the following year, asked Barnard to try to find a job in Cape Town for her then boyfriend, heart surgeon Hasnat Khan, because she wanted to leave Britain. Newspapers labelled this picture, 'The King and Queen of Hearts'.
(Daily Mail Archives, London)

Right: Past bitterness forgotten, Barnard with Karin, Barbara and Barbara's second husband Joe Silva at the *Sunday Times* Best Dressed Women Awards in 1991.
(Horace Potter/Sunday Times)

Barnard, a boxing fan, with three-times world heavyweight champion Muhammad Ali, a Parkinson's Disease sufferer, at the World Sports Award of the Century Gala in Vienna in 1999.
(Ronald Zak/AP Photo)

At a press conference in Vienna in November 2000. During his lifetime Barnard received hundreds of awards and accolades. Here he is given the Men's World Award. Vienna, where he had set up the Christiaan Barnard Foundation, was now his second home.
(Martin Gnedt/AP Photo)

Above: With Karin and their second child, Lara, born in 1997. It would not be long before strains in the marriage would begin to surface.
(Andrew Brown)

Right: The last picture taken of Barnard before he left Cape Town in 2001 to go on an overseas trip which ended with his death in Cyprus on 2 September. On the wall are portraits of his youngest children, Armin and Lara, who was born in 1997 when Barnard was 74.
(Sunday Times)

Hamilton Naki, who was awarded an honorary Masters degree in Medicine by the University of Cape Town in 2003 for his life's work in the university research laboratories. Once a gardener, Naki was one of several research staff who played a key role in the experimental animal heart transplants at Groote Schuur hospital in the 1960s which led to the first human heart transplant.
(Fanie Jason)

Barnard's first wife Louwtjie arrives at Barnard's funeral. They were divorced in 1969 after 21 years of marriage.
(Roger Sedres/Die Burger)

Deirdre and Armin at their father's funeral. Armin is carrying a casket containing his father's ashes.
(Roger Sedres/Die Burger)

Marius Barnard, who was a member of the team that performed the first human heart transplant, arrives at the church in Beaufort West for the funeral of his brother, with his wife Inez.
(Roger Sedres/Die Burger)

Above: Karin, Barnard's third wife, with son Armin and daughter Lara at the City Hall memorial service.
(Roger Sedres/Die Burger)

Right: Barnard's sons, Frederick *(left)* and Christiaan from his second marriage, to Barbara, after the Cape Town City Hall memorial service on 11 September, 2001.
(Roger Sedres/Die Burger)

now and find a donor!"' Barnard was serious. For Hitchcock, who would assist at all the early transplants, there was no doubt Barnard was in a race and seemed worried he might be beaten. 'It was a case of, I have now decided I am going to do a heart transplant, and I'm going to do it first. I think when he had taken the final decision that once we had permission to do the heart transplant and Washkansky had been told and had agreed, we should be the first.'

In an interview in 1970 Louwtjie confirmed: 'Chris was determined to be the first surgeon in the history of medicine to carry out a heart transplant. A small incident a few days before 2 December revealed the extent of his determination. We had been entertaining a few guests and the radio was on as a sort of background noise. Nobody really listened to the news. Suddenly Chris sat up as if struck by horror and rushed to the radio. "Have you heard? They spoke of a heart transplant." He was most excited. He grabbed the telephone and called up the state broadcasting office to get the details. There were some long and anxious minutes of waiting. Finally, it turned out there was no heart transplant operation – only a report about the plans of some British surgeons. Chris was enormously relieved.'

MC Botha later said, 'We had prepared well, we were ready, and had a patient waiting who unquestionably needed such an operation, when Shumway made his announcement. Then Donald Longmore in London let it be known that he considered himself likewise ready. In the ordinary, healthy spirit of rivalry … we did hope to be at the forefront. But we did nothing to unnecessarily risk a patient in reckless haste.'

Louis Washkansky was by nature a fighter and a gambler. Born in Lithuania, to Jewish parents, he was now 55, according to his brother-in-law Solly Sklar. Others said he was 53, and some said 56. Brought to South Africa at nine by his parents, Washkansky had grown into a stocky, powerfully built man who, in his younger days, had enjoyed amateur boxing and working out at the gym. He ran a successful retail grocery business. He loved to drink, smoke heavily and party, and regularly took his wife Ann ballroom dancing. Whenever Ann tried to slow him down, persuade him to drink a little less, he would tell her: 'Stick around kid, I'll make you famous.' He was a hugely popular figure in Cape

Town's Jewish community, and, until the last of his four heart attacks forced him to quit, had been a police reservist. In the war he had served with the South African Engineering Corps in North Africa and Italy, his love of life and mischief making him popular with the other 'sappers', who called him Washy. He was a rebel. Throughout his service he refused to wear army-issue boots, claiming medical reasons. Instead he wore knee-high leather cowboy boots of his own, in homage to the Western novels and films he adored. After the war he successfully claimed a refund from the army for 'using one's own leather' – and with the proceeds of 9d for each day's service went on a mammoth drinking spree with friends.

In 1955 he had been diagnosed a diabetic, and four years later coronary artery disease brought on his first heart attack. Others followed in 1960 and, the biggest, in 1965. At that stage his own doctor gave him just a few months to live. Still he kept working, kept dancing and drinking when he could, telling Ann he was 'on top of the world', although he was forced to take a number of pills every day to control his condition. In February 1967, after another attack, he was admitted to Groote Schuur with massive heart failure. By July he was still deteriorating and he was referred to Barnard to see if there was anything surgical that could be done. Barnard, not yet ready to consider a heart transplant, had said no, he was beyond help. Washkansky was sent home. He had been left with such a swollen, diseased heart – perhaps only a third of it in working order – that doctors were truly amazed he was still alive.

In September he was readmitted to Groote Schuur. On the day Washkansky went into hospital again he appeared to be dying. He was pale and weak, with his legs grotesquely swollen by excess body fluid. The doctors warned Ann he would be 'lucky' to last more than a few hours. Somehow his spirit pulled him through this immediate crisis. For several days and nights he had to sit in a chair while the surplus liquid was drained through holes drilled in his legs.

'On the fifth day of this treatment I went to see him,' said Ann. 'You know, his colour was so grey it was almost black.' Washkansky slipped into a diabetic coma, and out again. He suffered a minor stroke. Ann was told there was no hope of recovery, and that her husband would be moved to a nursing home. When she told him where the home was – opposite the Jewish cemetery – he flickered a smile. 'At least I won't have far to go.'

His physician, Barry Kaplan, said, 'Everyone had given him up. The physicians had given him up. The cardiac clinic had given him up, because there was nothing else they could do. Yet this man refused to die.'

Kaplan was asked by Schrire to put it to Washkansky that he could have a heart transplant. 'I'd never heard of such a thought, but since Schrire looked rather nonchalant, I decided to look nonchalant too – although I was a bit staggered by this,' recalled Kaplan. 'There was no point in waiting, so I began to walk from the clinic to the ward. Louis was sitting up with his swollen legs dangling outside the bed, smoking a cigarette. I said to him, "Louis, something may be able to be done for you, but it entails a tremendous gamble ... Such a gamble that you may not come out of it alive."' When Kaplan told him they might be able to transplant another person's heart into him, Washkansky replied immediately: 'If that's the only chance I'll take it.'

Kaplan pressed him to think it over and to discuss it with Ann. But Washkansky was adamant: 'There's nothing to think about. I can't go on living like this. The way I am now is not living. I'll take the chance as soon as possible.' Later, to another doctor, MC Botha, he said: 'I've been a gambling man all my life, doc. I'm not going to give up a gamble on my life at this stage.'

Kaplan informed Schrire and Barnard that Washkansky was prepared to go ahead. Barnard himself now visited Washkansky in Ward A1. He found him quietly reading a Western novel. After introducing himself and telling him he would be transferred to his ward, Barnard went on to explain the reasoning behind the decision to offer him a transplant. Washkansky simply told him he was ready to get on with it. 'Washkansky was a brave man – a hero,' wrote Barnard in *One Life*. 'But he was not brave or a hero because he grabbed at a chance for life. Rather more, his special glory is because he struggled to live long enough to be there when we arrived. The man with a heart like a ruined battlefield had refused to surrender – fighting on and on, until the moment came when I walked in to say he had a chance to live with a heart transplant.'

When Washkansky broke the news to Ann that he was going to

get a 'brand new heart' she thought he was delirious. She and other members of the family tried to tell him, gently, he must be confused. It might be a new valve, they said. Or a pacemaker. 'Poor chap, he was so weak, he could hardly speak,' said Ann. 'We all agreed with him that he was having a brand new heart, just to pacify him.' But two days later he had been moved to a room in Barnard's ward, and Ann met the man – the 'big noise' as he put it – her husband had been telling her about. His youthful looks shocked her. 'I was quite horrified. I saw this young boy. You know, I thought he was about 25. Then I had a look and thought he must be a little older and he started telling me what he was going to do.' Barnard said he had an 80 per cent chance of surviving if he had the operation. Without it he would soon be dead. The odds appealed to Washkansky.

According to the Washkanskys' adopted son Michael, who was 14 at the time of the transplant, Ann had not fully grasped what Barnard told her that day. She tried at first to persuade her husband not to go ahead with it. She was convinced that his own heart would somehow stay in place, while a new one was put in. What hit her forcefully, and upset her, was that, for her husband to live, someone else had to die. 'That was hard enough to accept. But I didn't want to know who it was.'

Barnard had a patient, finally. The problem he now had was to find a suitable donor. When Edith Black, a white woman, had received a kidney from a coloured youth, newspapers focused on the inevitable apartheid angle. Yet it hadn't caused uproar. Schrire felt the heart was different. He told Barnard he must find a white donor. He did not want the hospital accused of stealing the hearts of black people to save the lives of whites. The heart held a special, mystical power for blacks and coloureds which the kidney did not.

But Schrire's instruction, which must have frustrated Barnard, led to a donor being rejected ten days before the operation eventually took place. Whatever the motives, it was an astonishing risk to take, since Washkansky's condition was worsening and Barnard had already expressed his fear that he might not last until a donor was found. In fact Washkansky's impatience at having to wait for a donor was causing its own problems. He was in pain from his legs, struggling to breathe and anxious to get on with the transplant.

On the night of 22 November Ann was called by the hospital to be told her husband was being prepared for the transplant. By the time she reached Groote Schuur it had been called off. She found Washkansky back in his bed, his chest shaved. He was fuming. To try to make amends, he was offered his favourite meal of steak with an egg on top. It was a false alarm which left Washkansky 'livid', said Ann. 'He was really despondent.' In his autobiography Barnard stuck to the official line given at the time, that the heart of the potential donor – a coloured youth who had fallen off a truck – had suffered damage while they spent hours trying to locate the family to obtain permission to remove it. Later he admitted the decision to deny Washkansky a new heart earlier had been made on racial grounds alone.

According to Fritz Brink's wife Maureen, other potential donors were also rejected because of their colour. 'He told me he had several black hearts but he wouldn't use them because the outside world would turn against him. There was more than one case of a black heart being available. He was worried about being accused of switching off the machine to take the heart.'

According to one estimate there were more than twenty cardiac teams around the world ready to perform the first heart transplant. Some of them had carried out far more experimental animal heart transplants than Barnard. Some had done more research into the effects of anti-rejection drugs which killed the patient's ability to fight off infections. This was the crucial, dark area. Anti-rejection drugs worked by suppressing the body's natural instincts to attack 'alien' invaders. Normally this would mean disease and infection. But the body had no way of telling the difference between a harmful disease and a foreign organ, such as a new heart. How to balance the use of such drugs with protecting the patient from deadly infection was the dilemma. 'It's like deliberately giving a person AIDS,' was how Joe de Nobrega put it many years later.

What Barnard had that many of his peers elsewhere lacked was a boldness and self-confidence that allowed him to follow his instincts. He also enjoyed a cosy relationship with the attorney general of the Cape, as he would show later when faced with the need to remove a donor's heart while relatives' permission had not been obtained. Cape Town was (and still is) a small city, and the white Afrikaans elite who ran the hospitals, the police, the courts and the provincial administration departments were sympathetic to one another. The decision as to when a person was dead enough to have their vital organs removed was something best left to the doctors themselves. It was generally accepted that a person was dead when the heart stopped beating and the lungs stopped breathing. In a few countries, however, they already felt that if a person's brain showed no sign of activity they were legally dead. Yet in America surgeons in some states had been told that if they removed the live heart of a person who was brain-dead they would be charged with murder, even if that person was being kept alive only by a ventilator. Barnard had no such warnings echoing in his ears.

Denise Darvall was a quiet girl. Her friends thought her reserved. She worked as a bank clerk and lived at home with her parents, Edward and Myrtle, and her brothers Keith, 14, and Stephen, 17, in the Tamboerskloof area of Cape Town, close to the city centre. Edward was 63 and had been forced to retire through ill-health after a career in men's clothing. Myrtle was 53. She and Denise were close. They both had dark eyes. Denise loved classical music and ballet, and played the piano. She had never had a serious boyfriend. She had recently bought a car, a green Ford Anglia, and on Wednesday afternoons when the bank was closed she often took friends for a drive. The Darvalls were a solid, respectable family. Denise and Myrtle were the main breadwinners.

On the afternoon of Saturday 2 December, a sunny summer's day, hot but with the hint of a breeze, the Darvalls decided to go for a drive in Denise's new car. They planned to visit friends, and wanted to arrive with cakes. Along the way Denise and Keith, sitting in front, sang 'that Dr Zhivago song', *Lara's Theme*, said Edward Darvall. In Main Road, Observatory, a busy through route, Denise parked the car close to the Wrensch Town Bakery, which stood on the corner of a four-way intersection. Leaving Edward and Keith sitting in the car, Denise and Myrtle got out and crossed the road at the traffic lights. In the shop they bought a caramel cake, then stepped out to return to the car.

Friedrich Prins, 36, a police reservist, had been drinking. As he approached the intersection in his powerful Ford Zephyr he was speeding. He didn't see the red light, or the two women, until it was too late. He had no time even to brake. The force of the impact killed Myrtle instantly. Denise was hurled into the air and, as she landed, struck her head on the wheel of a parked car. She was barely alive; she was unconscious and bleeding from her ears, nose and mouth. It was 3.40 pm. When the ambulance arrived they found a doctor, who lived nearby, already attending to the women.

Groote Schuur hospital was less than a kilometre away. Ann Washkansky had been visiting her husband, trying to keep his spirits up. He had been angry. Some of the doctors had come to say goodbye because they were off fishing for the weekend. 'I could not pacify him. He said, "They can go to hell, because I'm getting out of here."' Ann, with her sister-in-law, left the hospital and drove along Main Road. They saw a crowd of people. 'It must have happened about three minutes before. We saw two women lying in the street where they had been knocked down by a car and the ambulance had not yet arrived. I turned my head. I can't stand sights like that. We drove quickly past.'

Barnard had gone home after his usual Saturday morning ward rounds. Before leaving the hospital he had assured Washkansky that the doctors who had gone fishing were on alert and could be easily contacted. Deirdre was taking part in a waterskiing event at Ceres. It was a beautiful day, perfect for waterskiing. He overcame his fears that it might be too far away and, from his office at the medical school, called Louwtjie. She was out shopping, so he drove home to Zeekoevlei. When Louwtjie returned she told him it was too late to go to Ceres, and, according to Barnard's account, then locked herself in André's room, peeved that he had arrived home late. By now, of course, André was living in Pretoria with the Franzots.

Barnard put on an Ink Spots record, trying to relax as he listened to the dreamy close harmonies, then took to his bed for a nap. But he kept waking, working through in his mind the mechanics of the transplant operation. He decided on a small change to the technique he had been using in dogs for so long. It meant he would not have to cut the septum dividing the atria in the donor heart, reducing the risk of further damage. He would not rigidly follow the methods of Shumway and Lower.

Barnard later characterised the run-up to the first heart transplant as his 'longest mile'. It was the mile-race against Daantjie

Rabie all over again, this time for bigger stakes: a race that simply had to be won. Now, just after 8 pm, the telephone went. It was a registrar, Coert Venter, to tell him he thought they had a donor for Washkansky. Barnard asked if she was coloured, and Venter's puzzlement at the question showed that Schrire's decree was not public knowledge. It was a woman who had suffered serious brain damage in a road accident. The neurosurgeons were examining her, said Venter, to establish whether any activity could still be detected in her brain. He would call back when they had finished. For Barnard, this was the final, 'untouched ten yards' of the race.

When Venter called again to confirm that the donor, kept 'alive' solely by a ventilator, was now in the cardiac ward and that her blood group, O Rhesus negative, was compatible with Washkansky's A Rhesus positive, Barnard knew it was time to head to the hospital.

At Groote Schuur Edward Darvall had collapsed when told his wife was dead. They had to stretcher him into the hospital. He was in a state of shock. Denise was still moaning, and he thought they might save her. Later he sat in a doctor's office with his sons Keith and Stephen, who had now joined them. Two registrars, Bertie Bosman and Venter, entered and sat down with the Darvalls. The two boys went outside.

Bosman and Venter gently explained to Edward Darvall that his daughter's injuries were so bad that nothing could be done to save her. She was being kept alive by a ventilator. There was a man in the hospital, however, whose life might be saved if he would allow them to remove Denise's heart. It was a question no father had been asked before.

'It took me about four minutes to make up my mind,' Darvall told Bill Pepper, who wrote *One Life*. 'I thought of what I would do if he hadn't asked me that question, and realised I didn't know what I was going to do with my daughter. You see, my wife always said ... that if anything happened to her she wanted to be cremated. My daughter never said anything, but now I had to decide for her about that – and about her heart as well.' He recalled Denise's giving nature – a birthday cake she had made for him once, a bathrobe she had bought for him with her first week's salary. She was always giving things to people. So he decided that if Denise had been able to answer the question herself, she would have said yes. Bosman, a sensitive man who from now on would always be trusted with the task of approaching relatives for permission, also told Darvall that they wanted to take Denise's kidneys to try to save the life of a small boy. 'He was sad because my daughter was dying and he could do nothing for her ... If they could take my daughter's heart or kidney and put it into someone else, it was better to do that than to let it die with her and then bury it or burn it up into a pile of ashes. So I told him: "Well, doctor, if you can't save my daughter, try and save this man."' The doctors, he had even said at the time, had been 'very decent' to ask his permission.

Neurosurgeons had confirmed to Barnard that Denise Darvall was brain-dead, and her body was alive only because a ventilator was breathing for her. There had been no movement in the pupils of her eyes for several hours. For some time there had been no reflexes or reaction to stimuli at all in her body. The electronic machine which monitored her brain (EEG) showed no sign of activity. Permission to remove her organs had been granted by the family. Val Schrire had examined Denise and confirmed that her heart had not been damaged. She would be kept on the ventilator until the time was right, to preserve the condition of her heart. The one obstacle left was the tissue-typing, which would show whether the donor's white blood cells – the ones which fought off infection – were compatible with Washkansky's. Only if they were, thereby reducing the risk of rejection of the new heart, could the transplant definitely go ahead. That would take time, and MC Botha was busy working on it.

Barnard visited Washkansky, who was being shaved for the operation. According to Barnard, Washkansky told him he felt 'kind of shaky'. It was 'like going into the ring when you don't know what you're up against'. He asked how the odds looked now. Getting better, said Barnard.

Next Barnard called Ann Washkansky, who was waiting for news at home. At first she thought he was calling to say her husband was dead. She was told it wasn't necessary to come into the hospital; she would be called as soon as it was over. Her son Michael recalls: 'We weren't expecting the donor to be a woman. That came as a terrible shock. It had never crossed our minds that a woman could be the donor. We thought they would have to use another's man's heart.'

Just after 11 pm Botha called Bertie Bosman to say that the tissue match was 'not ideal' but was close enough. 'Look, Bossie, so far as I'm concerned this thing can start rolling,' he told him. Calls went out to the surgical team who were dotted all over Cape Town. Many were in bed, but three theatre nurses had gone to a fancy-dress party that evening. When the call came they hastily jumped into a car and drove to the hospital. On the way two of them, Tollie Lambrechts and Amelia Rautenbach, managed to change from their 1920s bathing costumes. The other, Sannie Rossouw, rushed into theatre barefoot and with just a raincoat covering her costume. No-one seemed to notice. Alastair Hope, a heart-lung machine technician, was on his way in when his car broke down. He ran the rest of the way, about a kilometre. In all more than thirty members of the team, who had been on standby for this moment for three weeks, arrived at Groote Schuur to prepare for the transplant.

Barnard was facing the most critical few hours of his career. He had long wanted to be famous. His ego demanded it. His hunger to be first, and a compulsion to explore common to all pioneers, had pushed him towards the frontier he was about to cross, while others stood back and agonised. The magnitude of what he was about to do did not escape him. For the first time he would perform an operation in which he would take a living patient and remove an organ essential to life. The patient's diseased heart might be failing but it was keeping him alive. If he removed it and replaced it with a transplanted heart, and it did not work, he had killed the patient. He would be playing God. He mulled over the consequences of what he was about to embark on as he sat, then kneeled, in the surgeons' dressing room wearing nothing but a pair of checked underpants. Peggy Jordaan, a senior theatre sister who led the A nursing team, walked in on him. 'He was kneeling. He looked as if he was praying,' she says.

Denise Darvall, to all intents and purposes dead, but breathing through a ventilator connected to her lungs through a tube down her windpipe, was wheeled into B Theatre in Ward C2. A few minutes later Louis Washkansky, listening to the reassuring words of the anaesthetist Joe Ozinsky, was brought into the adjacent A Theatre. Soon he would be 'put under'. When he woke, he would have a new heart.

Barnard continued to prepare himself for the transplant. He had parted company with unquestioning faith in his father's God when he became a medical student. Darwin and the theory of evolution were much more appealing to his scientific mind. But he retained a superstitious belief in a higher power and he often prayed silently before an operation. Now, under the shower, he would later recall, he prayed. According to *One Life,* it was a noble, lyrical prayer, 13 lines long, which asked God to help him succeed for the sake of the patient, others like him and the rest of his surgical team. But in the version given in the earlier draft, *The Beat of My Heart,* written before Pepper got involved, the prayer was rather more prosaic and to the point: 'God, don't let me make any mistakes. Make me do the best I can. Let me be your favourite son, just for a little while. Give me a hand!'

Rodney Hewitson had now arrived and was 'scrubbing up'. He had assisted Barnard at countless operations. He was a more skilled surgeon, according to his peers. He was also fiercely Christian, and objected to the way Barnard swore and blasphemed during operations. Hewitson did not think Barnard was 'technically one of the best'. But he admired many other qualities in him. Famously taciturn, Hewitson balanced Barnard's histrionics. The two made a good team.

Yet on this night Hewitson was truly sailing into the unknown. He had played no part in the dog heart transplants in the laboratory, which had been mainly carried out by Marius. The fact that Barnard's number two in such a vital operation had had no experience of the technique involved in transplanting a heart was not publicised at the time. Afterwards Hewitson gave no interviews and kept his views to himself. Had it been known, those who accused Barnard of rushing ahead with the transplant to beat the rest of the world would have had more ammunition. 'I was never part of the laboratory team. Chris has given the wrong impression that the whole team had been through it all together in the laboratory and knew exactly what had to be done. But I was not involved in the dog heart transplants,' says Hewitson now.

Timing was all. To prevent damage to Denise Darvall's heart, the ventilator could not be switched off until the last moment. Now began the most extraordinary battle of a remarkable night. Barnard knew that once the ventilator was turned off, Denise

Darvall's organs would begin to degenerate. Until the body could be cooled by connection to a heart-lung bypass machine, every second lost risked damage to the heart which was to be transplanted. At that time the accepted definition of death in South Africa was the moment the heart stopped beating and the lungs ceased. Now that Denise had been declared brain-dead, it was within the power of the doctors to decide when to switch off the ventilator and bring about her 'legal' death. That decision alone carried enormous responsibility: doctors could be struck off for doing it.

Under Denton Cooley in America Marius had studied the use of potassium to arrest the heart. Potassium is a mineral essential to the well-being of the body: it helps maintain the heart's normal rhythm, and keeps the nerves and muscles working properly. But a highly concentrated dose of potassium is fatal. Infused into the circulation, it paralyses the heart. Today it is common practice to use this method to stop a heart beating or fibrillating either to allow open-heart surgery or to remove a donor's heart for a transplant as soon as the donor has been declared brain-dead. Towards the end of the 1960s it was being used increasingly, as part of an ultra-cold cardioplegic solution, to give surgeons working on the heart a still, bloodless field. Before the Washkansky operation it was being commonly used in dog heart transplants. There were no ethical problems involved in stopping the heart of a donor dog to improve the chances of a successful transplant.

With Washkansky now anaesthetised on the table in A Theatre and waiting to be opened and hooked up to a bypass machine, Barnard went into B Theatre. He turned off the ventilator, and watched the electrocardiograph (ECG) machine which monitored electrical activity in Denise Darvall's heart. Marius was in this theatre, with Terry O'Donovan, a South African who had trained abroad and had been invited back to Groote Schuur by Barnard himself. Marius, by his own admission, had been eager to open Denise's chest and begin removing the heart, presumably after an injection of a cold high potassium solution to arrest it. O'Donovan's widow Jenny says Barnard had also been keen to do this, contrary to what he would later claim. The mineral, easily flushed away by perfusion (saturation) of blood, would not damage the heart. But O'Donovan refused to allow it. 'I said to Chris I would not pick up that knife until the ECG was flat,' he wrote years later. 'He said, "Well, okay then," understanding that obviously everyone has moral codes which they adhere to and that he would accept my decision not to make the skin incision until the heart had actually stopped beating.' Joe Ozinsky, who was moving between both theatres, says, 'It's better if you do stop the heart with an injection of potassium. It gives you a heart in perfect shape. It was being done then with dogs in the laboratory, but to have done it with a human donor could have been seen as murder.'

'Chris just wanted to get on and remove the heart without waiting for it to stop,' says Jenny O'Donovan. 'But Terry felt it was morally wrong. He also told them that if it ever got out that they had taken out a beating heart it would create a very bad impression.' Marius said of the argument soon afterwards: 'My feelings before the operation were that we should take this heart in the best condition possible. Our responsibility was to the patient into whom we were going to transplant – not this girl who, although her heart was beating, was dead. But my brother insisted that this heart must stop before we operated. If I had had my way, we would have gone ahead before it stopped.' He now accepted his brother had been right.

But in the same interview Marius did not mention Terry O'Donovan's role in the argument about whether to remove the beating heart. O'Donovan's account makes it clear that Barnard had wanted to stop the heart. Marius, speaking very soon after the event, was perhaps conscious of the potential damage to his brother's reputation, as well as that of the transplant museum as a whole. Barnard was certainly ruthless enough in the pursuit of a goal not to want what he might describe as a technicality to increase the risk of failure. To others it was about the massive moral and legal dilemma of when to accept a person's death. According to the Hippocratic Oath doctors were obliged 'to do no harm' to a patient. Barnard was well aware that in some American states the threat of a murder charge had deterred cardiac surgeons from pursuing their hopes of performing a human heart transplant. Later it would become an accepted practice, but at the moment Denise Darvall's body lay in front of Barnard the act of hastening the arrest of her heart to remove it sooner would have been seen by some, as Ozinsky says, as murder.

In *One Life* the only reference to potassium at this point is when

Barnard orders a further dose to be given to Denise Darvall to replace the amount being lost in fluids, vital to keep the heart and kidneys in good condition. He describes the anxious wait after the ventilator is switched off, with the girl's heart seemingly 'refusing to die' and Marius commenting, 'What a shame, we're killing a heart.' Marius was expressing his fear that by not removing it now they would seriously damage the heart. 'No-one answered this, but I knew he was right,' wrote Barnard. 'To provide a donor heart in the best condition we should act now – cutting it out while it was still beating. What intermingling of mythology and ritual prevented us from touching a beating heart in a body which had been declared clinically dead? If this was forbidden we should not even be making the transplant.' O'Donovan then insists he won't remove the heart until the ECG line is flat, and Barnard nods. Marius asks, 'What do you say, Chris?' and he replies, 'No, we must wait until it stops.'

But his account is strangely vague about the time it took for the heart to stop beating. By the time *One Life* was being written, a chronology of the operation – approved by Barnard – had been published in a special edition of the *South African Medical Journal*. Joe Ozinsky, who compiled it, says the ventilator was switched off at 2.20 am. Cardiac arrest occurred at 2.32 am, 12 minutes later (about the time a heart might take to stop naturally from hypoxia, or lack of oxygen in the blood, once the lungs had ceased). The first incision was then made in Denise Darvall's chest. Yet in *One Life* Barnard writes curiously: 'So we waited, while the heart struggled on – five, ten, fifteen minutes. Finally it began to go into its last phases ...' Even when the ECG line was flat, Barnard says he then insisted on waiting a further three minutes to make sure 'there is no heartbeat coming back'.

Marius said they waited even longer, five minutes, to make sure there could be no mistake, a figure often used in later medical papers. But the official internal record of the transplant, written for the hospital files shortly afterwards, gives yet another version. It says of Denise Darvall: 'She was taken to the operating theatre on supportive therapy. The anterior chest wall was prepared and the usual sterile drapes were applied. When there had been no activity on the electrocardiogram, absence of breathing and absence of all reflexes for seven minutes, she was declared dead.

The heart was rapidly exposed through a median sternotomy.' There is no mention here of the ventilator being switched off or the 12 minutes it then took for cardiac arrest to occur. This report was initialled 'CNB'.

A sign of the huge sensitivity surrounding removal of the heart and the 'moment of death' issue at the time can be seen in an article published soon afterwards by *Newsweek*, the international news magazine: 'The surgeons will not say whether they took Miss Darvall off the respirator before her heart stopped. "That's an impertinent question," one of the surgeons told *Newsweek* correspondent John Barnes. "We took full resuscitative measures until the time of death." But, reports Barnes, he did say they had not tried to revive her after the heart had stopped.' By the time the *South African Medical Journal* special edition appeared on 30 December there were clearly no qualms about stating that the heart had stopped only after the ventilator had been switched off.

Whatever the truth of what happened in B Theatre that night, it seems astonishing that after weeks of preparation to perform the transplant, the timing of when to start removing the donor's heart had not apparently been decided on earlier. Here they were, with Denise Darvall's body laid out before them and the clock ticking, and the Barnard brothers and O'Donovan were arguing over what was then the most crucial point of all. To some this is further evidence of a lack of planning, an unseemly haste to do the first human heart transplant.

When the green ECG line finally lay flat and still, O'Donovan and Marius began opening Denise Darvall's chest to expose the heart. They connected it to the bypass machine which began perfusing it with cooled, oxygenated blood. Only now could they be certain it had not been damaged, visibly at least, in the accident. At the same time in the next theatre, Washkansky – his chest now open – was linked to a bypass machine and his body started to cool. Barnard began clamping the major blood vessels. At one point a nurse clamped a line to the heart-lung machine too soon, before the machine had been turned off, causing a connection to blow from the pressure. Washkansky's blood spilled over the floor.

Once Denise Darvall's heart had been cooled enough – the lower temperature preserved the organ better – O'Donovan cut it from its moorings and placed it in a stainless-steel dish filled with a cold solution. He then walked through the connecting scrub-room into A Theatre. 'I thought, whatever you do, don't drop it,' says Peggy Jordaan. The heart was connected to a small pump attached to the bypass machine so that it could be perfused by Washkansky's circulating blood. It sat in the dish, pulsating. 'It started to beat. What a strange sight it was to see this heart beating by itself in the dish,' says Francois Hitchcock, who was standing next to Barnard as second assistant.

Denise Darvall's kidneys were also removed before her body was wheeled away. They were to be packed in ice and rushed to another hospital for a life-saving operation on a ten-year-old boy. At Groote Schuur the B Theatre team now filed into the gallery of A Theatre. There were already people there, hospital staff who had heard what was going on and others. One was Bennie Shapiro, a specialist physician who had tended Washkansky. He had arrived home from a party in the early hours to find the telephone ringing. When he answered, his emergency service operator told him she had a message she didn't understand: 'History is now being made at Groote Schuur and you still have time to get there.' Knowing what it meant, Shapiro wasted no time. Now, like every other observer, he was mesmerised by the scene in front of him. 'It was like Columbus must have felt when he sailed to America,' he said. 'We were all very much aware of the magnitude of it and we just didn't know what was going to happen next.'

As Barnard removed Washkansky's swollen, decayed heart, the theatre was filled with a monumental, silent tension. 'Chris looked so grim. You could feel the determination flooding from him. Everybody was very tense, very quiet,' said Shapiro. After placing the heart in a dish, Barnard stared back at the emptiness of Washkansky's chest. Now he could not turn back. It was, he said later, his 'moment of truth – the moment when the magnitude of it all really hit me … I looked down and saw this empty space … the realisation that there was a man lying in front of me without a heart but still alive was, I think, the most awe-inspiring moment of all.'

Hitchcock recalls, 'Chris always said how struck he was by the empty chest of Washkansky after his heart was taken out, but that didn't impress me that much. What I remember more vividly, as I was standing so close, is watching Chris's neck pulsating twice as fast as normal. He was extremely tense and excited. There was a lot of adrenalin around. His pulse was racing.'

Barnard would follow the plan he had devised while lying on his bed the afternoon before. Rather than risk damage to the conduction system (the heart's 'nerves' which carry the electrical impulses vital to a healthy rhythm) by removing the entire atrial 'lid' of the donor heart, he had left the lid intact but cut two holes, one for the two main blood vessels, the venae cavae, and one for the four pulmonary veins. These holes would be fashioned to fit the 'lid' of the old heart which had been left in place. Now Barnard began to sew Denise Darvall's heart into the empty chest of Louis Washkansky. Hewitson, standing opposite, finished the stitching. At 5.43 am the transplant was completed. They began to perfuse the heart with warming blood. At 5.52 am an electric shock was used to defibrillate the heart so that it would take up its natural pumping rhythm. The charge was powerful enough to jolt Washkansky's body upward.

Now began the test: could the transplanted heart bear the load of maintaining Washkansky's circulation? Or had it, after all, suffered some unseen damage in the violent impact that had ended Denise Darvall's life? Once, briefly, then a second time, for longer, the heart-lung machine was turned on to aid the struggling organ, then turned off. At 6.13 am bypass was switched off for a third time. No-one gazing down from the packed gallery dared speak. They hardly breathed. Hope swelled as the seconds went by. This time the heart seemed to be holding its rhythm. Washkansky's blood pressure was steady. Barnard knew he had succeeded. From behind his green mask the words he shouted, 'Jesus, dit gaan werk!' could not have pleased Hewitson. But relief swept through the theatre. One of the nurses hugged Barnard. 'I felt so excited I didn't know whether to laugh or cry,' said Amelia Rautenbach, another nurse who had been in B Theatre. 'Professor Barnard's face was a picture of excitement, of great achievement.' An intern who was in the gallery said: 'The atmosphere was fantastic. It was as though the tension had been cut with a knife when everyone knew it was going to be all right. I felt slightly hysterical. We were all almost tangibly aware that this was medical history in the making. There was terrific tension. I hardly dared to breathe.' The intern, a young doctor, thought he saw tears in Barnard's smiling eyes when it was over.

Another sensation, however, hit Barnard. All through the transplant operation he had had the curious feeling that the brightly lit theatre was in darkness. Now the darkness was gone, as if a powerful light had come on. He left Hewitson and Hitchcock to 'close up', slipped off his mask and special thin rubber gloves – the usual heavier gloves aggravated the pain from his arthritis, he said – and headed for the tearoom.

Barnard nibbled at the avocado sandwiches laid out for the surgical team, and reflected on the five-hour operation. He relaxed with a cigarette – he had long smoked, usually other people's cigarettes – and chatted with Bosman, Botha and the others about what to do next. Marius, who had been so moved that he had 'wanted to cry' when the transplant was over, checked his brother's pulse. It was 140. Barnard called the hospital medical superintendent, JG Burger, and Lapa Munnik, member of the Executive Council for Health on the Cape provincial administration. Shortly after Munnik was informed, the prime minister, John Vorster, was called by Nico Malan, the administrator of the Cape, who had heard from Munnik. 'The sudden importance of this unique operation is shown by the fact that the prime minister of the country was informed within about thirty minutes of Chris Barnard telephoning me,' said Munnik. 'Chris Barnard had put South Africa and its medical standards on the world map.' As he sat in the tearoom at Groote Schuur, smoking and eating sandwiches, Barnard could have had little idea of the size of the storm that was about to break.

8

Aftermath

Officials at Groote Schuur were initially wary of claiming a world first. But the *Cape Times* medical correspondent, John Scott, could see how big the story was. He was being deluged with calls from foreign newspaper, television and radio reporters: 'I found myself giving interviews to foreign correspondents before they jumped into aircraft headed for South Africa.' One of Scott's colleagues found Edward Darvall still in deep shock, and said: 'So far as the heart transplant was concerned, he did not yet seem to fully appreciate the significance of what had been achieved at the hospital. He was still too stunned by his double loss.' Confirmation that the transplant had taken place came in a statement from JG Burger, which did not name any member of the surgical team.

Barnard's first personal call that morning had been to Louwtjie. After leaving the hospital he drove straight to the nursing home to tell his mother. She had always told him he must be first. Nothing less was good enough. Now he could tell her he was.

On his way home he heard the noon radio news bulletin announcing the transplant. He craved recognition for what he knew was a pioneering operation, but the rules of his profession forbade any form of personal advertising. For the time being he would play the humility game in public, at least. He made a spoof call to his close friend Fritz Brink, pretending to be a BBC reporter from London interested in Christiaan Barnard. But when John Scott called him at home that afternoon, he told him he did not want his name mentioned in the story, or any photographs taken of himself. Later, at the hospital, Scott approached Barnard about having a picture taken. Barnard insisted it must be of the whole team. Calls went out to all of them. Most responded for what was a unique event in their careers. Never before had they been asked to pose for a photograph after an operation, and nor would they again. Marius Barnard preferred instead to attend his usual Sunday evening church service. The photograph was published on the front page of the *Cape Times* the next day, and was immediately syndicated around the world. Chris Barnard, standing in the centre, had the biggest smile. Val Schrire, next to him, looked rather bemused. Most of the world's major newspapers carried the story on their front pages. It led the television and radio news bulletins everywhere. According to Barnard, one of the first calls he had received at home on the Sunday had been from a London newspaper wanting to know if the donor heart had come from a white person. 'Val Schrire had been right – so right,' he decided.

As the world's media descended on Cape Town that Sunday evening, Louis Washkansky lay in the recovery room in Ward C2, still hooked up to a ventilator. He had no idea that he was already being talked about as some sort of 'miracle man' in homes across the globe. He had told Ann to stick around, he would make her famous. Neither of them could have guessed it would be for something like this. Relatives of the Washkanskys had gathered at Ann's flat in Sea Point, a Jewish stronghold in Cape Town. There was a party atmosphere – Louis had been expected to die within a few days without the transplant. Now there was hope. The telephone rang, and it was a Reuters reporter wanting a statement. 'Until then we had no idea what Reuters was,' said a niece. 'Professor Barnard had told us that the transplant was the first in South Africa but we didn't realise it was the first in the world.'

Acclaim poured in for what was widely seen as a major medical breakthrough. Barnard stressed that the biggest battle they now faced was the threat of rejection. It would be a few days before they might start to see signs of this as Washkansky's bodily defences rallied in the face of the 'foreign' invader, his new heart. The immunosuppressive drugs were designed to thwart this. But by doing what they were supposed to do – suppress the immune system – these drugs would also render useless his ability to ward off infection. They were treading through a minefield in the dark, since no human had been given another's heart before. But at some stage, Barnard would argue repeatedly, you had to move on from animals: you had to shift from the laboratory to the operating theatre.

Marius said his brother should get the Nobel Prize. 'We don't always agree but there are some things that we share that we don't share with other people. I know how much he wanted this operation and how he put his ideas into this and how he felt about this.'

While euphoria coursed through the corridors of Groote Schuur, Edward Darvall and his sons were at home, consumed with grief. They had lost two members of the family in sudden and cruel circumstances, yet the world was talking of their loss purely as a contribution to medical history, something to be proud of. Once he had taken part in the group photograph, Bertie Bosman and his wife Annette set out to warn the Darvalls of the impending press onslaught. 'We went to their home,' says Annette. 'We felt we had to warn them that if they didn't find somewhere else to stay for a few days their lives would be hell. They were all so traumatised they couldn't think straight. Bertie phoned a niece of Mr Darvall's to come and fetch them.'

A number of surgeons had been ready to perform the first heart transplant, waiting for the right combination of events. In America both the fear of legal action and the belief that not enough was known about rejection was holding back the likes of Norman Shumway and Richard Lower. Barnard's achievement took everyone by surprise. Shumway, in fact, had the grace to say it was 'pretty exciting': 'It sounds to me like a damn fine job.' Denton Cooley later said of all the cardiac surgeons in the world standing around the pool, Barnard had been the one who dared to 'jump first' into the cold water. Michael DeBakey called it a 'great achievement'. 'This breaks the ice – it's a real breakthrough.' He added: 'The only question remains the ability to prevent the rejection phenomenon, the major factor that has so far prevented the application of this method.' Adrian Kantrowitz was particularly intrigued when he heard the news. He had been on the verge of performing a heart transplant on a baby in New York, which would in fact go ahead three days after the Washkansky operation. (The baby died within hours.)

In London, a fulcrum of the international anti-apartheid movement, the view was mixed. There was excitement, but more scepticism than in many other countries too. Donald Ross, still at the National Heart Hospital, remembers being 'not as gripped by it as the media'. 'We thought it was very interesting, but it wasn't a new breakthrough. It was the first patient to have a heart transplant. Transplantation had been done in Russia, in dogs and so on, for many years and we were actively doing it in the lab like lots of people were throughout the world.' But he was surprised: 'I had gone to South Africa that year to give a lecture, and as I was coming down the stairs of the plane there was a reporter asking me, "When do you think the first heart transplant will be?" And I said, "Within the next five years." Chris did it the next month. Everyone in the world was playing around with it. He had the courage to do it in a patient.' Ross would perform Britain's first heart transplant within six months.

The London *Times* reported the day after the Washkansky transplant: 'Professor Barnard is well known to his British colleagues as a dynamic leader and able surgeon. The feeling last night was that if he has been in charge the chances of success must be rated as high as in any pioneer operation.' The London *Daily Sketch* declared: 'Dr. Chris Barnard is a slight, dynamic figure. His achievement in successfully transplanting a human heart assures him of a place in medical history.' The *Sketch*'s medical correspondent, John Stevenson, had interviewed Barnard by telephone. He asked him whether he had been 'jubilant' at 'pipping both American and British surgeons at the post?' Barnard told him: 'The truth is that, from a research point of view, we are all at the same stage in this work. It was a classic case of who got the first set of right circumstances.'

Reaction from behind the Iron Curtain was especially telling in view of South Africa's stance on communism. In Moscow, *Pravda* put the story on its front page. In an editorial which must have delighted the apartheid regime, eager as it was to overcome growing isolation, it said: 'In spite of South Africa's backward place in the community of nations, positive, creative forces seem to thrive there, as proven by the immense feat of Dr Christiaan Barnard ... his achievement is to be saluted over and above any barriers that may otherwise exist.' Russia's leading heart surgeon said Barnard's achievement was of 'unprecedented importance'. Hungary's most prestigious daily newspaper said: 'Even if the precarious health of the diabetic, Washkansky, will not yield 100 per cent success, though we do hope it will, the mere fact that Dr Barnard performed this unique feat, proves there are forces in South Africa entirely overlooked or deliberately ignored by prejudiced political reporting, no matter how justified the political point of view may be. It is these human elements that force second thoughts ... perhaps it is time to take a closer, unjaundiced look at the other side of the South African coin. Let us begin by congratulating Dr Barnard and his staff.'

In the immediate triumphant aftermath of the transplant there was little if anything made of the fact that the photograph of the smiling surgical team contained not a single black or coloured face. The role of the black research workers in the laboratory, such as Victor Pick and Hamilton Naki, would not emerge for several days. Schrire had indeed been right. The success of the transplant operation on Washkansky was in no way clouded by the race issue, as the second transplant involving Philip Blaiberg – who would receive the heart of a coloured man – was destined to be a month later.

Yet there was one aspect of the whole startling affair which, as the frenzy rolled on day by day, aroused more controversy than any other: Barnard's personality. As his good looks and telegenic charm flashed around the world, his apparent appetite for publicity and ease in dealing with the media upset his more staid colleagues in the medical fraternity. Many condemned his approach. Some complained to the South African Medical and Dental Council that he had breached the 'no advertising' rule. Here was a profession steeped in protective mystery and science whose practitioners were not used to answering questions about their work in public. Confidentiality, often an excuse for secrecy, was a shibboleth. Yet now Barnard and his team from, of all places, apartheid South Africa, appeared at press conferences beaming and delivering as much information about Washkansky's condition as they could manage. Until this time 'serious' doctors simply hadn't behaved like this.

South Africa did not then have television. But in America and Britain there was an immensely popular soap series, *Dr Kildare*, featuring a dashingly handsome hospital doctor played by Richard Chamberlain. Newspaper profiles compared Barnard to Kildare; even, in America especially, to a young John F Kennedy. Barnard's looks were not as smooth as Kildare's, and his high-pitched voice with its distinct Afrikaans accent sometimes jarred, but he was boyish, lean and energetic, and his mischievous sense of humour, combined with a candour that surprised and delighted experienced news correspondents, made him a compelling and entertaining speaker. His charisma and self-confidence were captivating. Had he not possessed these qualities, the impact of the Washkansky transplant would no doubt have been equally huge for a day or two. But faced with the traditional stonewalling from surgeons unused to the glare, would the media interest have lasted so long? As Barnard himself said later, with some exaggeration, 'If I had been fat, bald and wore glasses no-one would have batted an eyelid.'

Instead, from the moment news of the transplant emerged, Louis Washkansky became the most famous patient in history, and Barnard rapidly became the most famous surgeon in history. He still is. Washkansky's first words the day after the operation were reported globally as if they were fragments of a newly discovered work by Shakespeare: 'I'm much better. What kind of operation did I have? You promised me a new heart.' His first meal, a boiled egg, attracted equal fascination. His blood pressure readings and pulse rate were the subject of lengthy analysis at press briefings. On the day after the operation, a meeting at Groote Schuur between Ann Washkansky and Edward Darvall produced another poignant photograph and story for the world. 'You are a man in a million. I am so terribly grateful to you,' Ann was reported as saying to Darvall. 'I wish you all the luck in the world. I hope your husband lives and I wish you happiness,' responded Darvall.

The chance to address dozens of foreign correspondents daily, to face the television cameras, enthralled Barnard. He expanded on his answers at press conferences by drawing illustrations on a board. He was a natural communicator, and he treated the journalists attending the briefings like hungry young medical students. They simply lapped it up. Benjamin Pogrund, who was covering the story for the London *Sunday Times*, recalls one press conference where Marius was anxious to bring things to a close. 'Chris was in front of the journos and the cameras and he was loving it. I was standing at the back talking to Marius, who said to me that Chris was tired and the press conference should end. He asked me to do what they do at US presidential press conferences – to bring it to an end by thanking Chris. I refused. I said everyone was having a great time and my colleagues would lynch me if I tried to stop the conference. So instead, Marius called out, "Telephone call for you, Professor Barnard." To which Chris responded, "Ag, Marius, take a message for me," and went on answering the journos' questions. He was revelling in the publicity. To us it seemed boyish and endearing.'

Peter Hawthorne, who was working for *Time* magazine, wrote in his book *The Transplanted Heart*, completed within five weeks of the transplant: 'Professor Barnard's early press conferences were mostly impromptu, quite uninhibited and a joy particularly to the overseas press. Barnard would usually begin by saying, "Well, I don't think there's anything I can tell you," and would end by holding the whole room in awe as he lectured to his audience, drawing diagrammatic explanations on the blackboard, about some aspect of Washkansky's case. The first question invariably was, "How's the patient?" "How's the patient?" Prof. Barnard would repeat as if not sure he had heard correctly. Then he would give a detailed breakdown of the patient's condition, leaving no doubt about the fact that the man was progressing satisfactorily in every way, and usually concluding with some surprising titbit of information that would give the journalists their lead-in for the day … such as, "I have no doubt that if the patient's condition continues to progress in this way, I'll have him home in three weeks."'

John Scott saw things rather differently. 'My impression was that everyone, including Barnard, was taken aback by the impact the transplant had. But the moment Barnard realised it had knocked us all sideways, he exploited it to the full. He became so high and mighty that within a few days he would only give press conferences to everyone at large or private interviews to foreign television teams and newspapers. He wasn't interested in being interviewed by little old local newspapers any more.' Scott developed other contacts within the transplant team, including Marius and Bertie Bosman. 'In my view there was sibling rivalry between Marius and Chris. It seemed to me that Marius's nose was clearly put out of joint by the adulation focused on his brother. So when you went to Marius for help he flowed freely with information.'

Photographers took pictures of Washkansky from the doorway of his room. Reporters were found on the balcony to the room and had to be ejected from the hospital. Barnard's saintly status in the public's eye was assured when, on the fourth day after the operation, Washkansky gave his first interview. Bosman went into his room with a sterilised radio microphone on behalf of the South African Broadcasting Corporation. Washkansky was still doing well – there was no sign of rejection, and the effects of heart disease were visibly wearing off – and he had moved on to a diet of minced chicken and mashed potato. That day he had been wheeled out of his room to be given a cobalt 'bomb', a highly concentrated dose of radiation to aid the anti-rejection drugs. He had also seen his wife Ann for the first time, for four minutes, and she had emerged saying he had 'looked too beautiful'. Washkansky was even cracking jokes with the nurses caring for him, often laced with sexual innuendo. He had been 'terribly upset' to learn the identity of the donor, said Ann. But now he asked if he would grow breasts, and whether in future he should stand or sit when urinating. 'I'm the new Frankenstein,' he said, making the classic mistake of giving the name of the fictional doctor to the monster he created. In the interview, which was broadcast around the world, Washkansky told Bosman that he was 'feeling quite fine'. Asked how it felt to be famous, he answered: 'I am not famous. The doctor is famous – the man with the golden hands.'

Those hands had already become the focus of another moving angle to the story for the media. It had become known that Barnard suffered from rheumatoid arthritis. Asked at a press conference if this was true, Barnard said: 'Yes. In long operations when there is a lot of sewing up to do there is constant pain, but on Sunday there was no time to notice that.' The disease was slowly crippling his fingers and he may even have to give up surgery, he told the reporters. Marius, asked for a comment on his brother's condition later, said he, too, suffered from rheumatoid arthritis. It ran in the family, and it didn't bother him.

Time put Barnard on its front cover and declared the heart transplant to be 'the surgical equivalent' of the ascent of Everest. Barnard and his team now faced 'the medical equivalent of the problem of how to get down – in other words, how to keep the patient and transplant alive'. *Newsweek* hailed the 'miracle in Cape Town', and, playing up Washkansky's Frankenstein joke, said: 'The gallows humor of the remark was appropriate: the sturdy, 170-pound Washkansky had been on the edge of death – indeed over the line – and had been brought back to life by perhaps the most remarkable bit of surgical virtuosity in the history of medicine … Lurid fiction had become scientific fact and the distinctions between life and death had become blurred and rearranged.'

Condemnation also came, much of it from people hostile to the concept of removing a person's heart at all. If the heart could be used to save another person, it must still be alive, they argued. Barnard had forced the world to confront the question: When was a person truly dead? For many, brain-death was not enough to allow the plundering of a person's organs. What Barnard had done was to kill Denise Darvall to save Louis Washkansky. It was the same outrage which had greeted the first unsuccessful kidney transplants by Richard Lawler in the early 1950s in America; the same disgust which had rained down on the head of James Hardy in 1964 when he transplanted the heart of a chimp into a dying man. But Barnard had gone a step further: he had dared to transplant a heart, to many people the very soul of a human being, the powerhouse of the emotions, the nucleus of identity even. Religious leaders of most faiths, however, applauded the transplant, or at least did not condemn it: they drew a distinction which many laymen did not between the physical heart and the soul, and welcomed sincere efforts to save life.

Some of Barnard's critics were undoubtedly motivated by professional jealousy. They appeared to resent his 'upstart' success. They ignored his recognised work in the field of congenital heart defects. His results in this field had been among the best in the world for some years. Yet now he was accused of being an opportunist – he had stolen Shumway's ideas and ruthlessly used Washkansky as a guinea pig to achieve fame. They said he was poorly prepared and did not know enough about rejection to have carried out the operation. Much of this criticism came from America, which had been expecting Shumway or another of its leading cardiac surgeons to perform the first human heart transplant.

The explosion of publicity and fame that hit Barnard in the days following that 3 December was bound to leave casualties. Louwtjie had welcomed him home on the morning of the transplant with a cup of tea. But her husband's life would be transformed from that day, and it was to spell the end of any pretence to a normal marriage. Later, she confessed bitterly: 'These words, "heart transplant", I would like to wipe out like my country would like to erase the word "apartheid". To me, personally, heart transplant spells disaster. Its effects are engraved as deeply on my heart as its impact on medical history.' Her husband, she said, had 'rocked the world' with his operation, capturing the imagination of millions and bringing new hope to many sick people. 'After this outstanding medical achievement, South Africa and the world claimed Chris as theirs, but in the shadows stood three people who admired him too, and loved him ... Telegrams poured in from all over the world, filled with praise, admiration and condemnation ... Our private life had vanished overnight ... We were left to the vultures of the world. Before I could think, the whirlwind developed into a storm and the storm became a hurricane which destroyed everything in its path.'

Michael Washkansky, just a young boy, deeply resented the way his father's desperate fight for survival was turned into what he saw as the centrepiece of a circus act. It seemed to him that the world had come to gawp at his father lying in a hospital bed, inside an oxygen tent, as if he was a freak. Some newspapers tried to make something of the fact that Louis Washkansky, a Jew, had been given the heart of a Gentile. Ann Washkansky dismissed such efforts with contempt. 'My husband's life had been hanging by a thread,' she said. 'He knew that the operation provided his only chance of living longer. I was petrified but my husband had so much confidence in the medical men that he even inspired me.'

Edward Darvall mostly tried to stay out of the way. He was a frail man who had undergone major stomach surgery. Yet he maintained a strength and dignity in grief which earned him many admirers. Before the joint funeral of his wife and daughter, which Barnard did not attend, he asked for donations to be sent to the Groote Schuur cardiac unit. Within days of the transplant a public fund was set up to raise money to help the Darvalls survive financially. Donations to the Darvall fund poured in. It was soon clear that there would be more than enough money to help the family, and the appeal was renamed the 'Chris Barnard Fund', with the aim of raising money for research.

Remarkably, when Friedrich Prins appeared in court to face a charge of culpable homicide, Edward Darvall put on his best suit, left the sanctuary of his home and turned up to lend support to the man who had killed Denise and Myrtle. After Prins had been found guilty, Darvall made a statement, read out by an attorney, asking the magistrate to show the 'greatest possible clemency'. The attorney said Darvall, who was sitting in court, would have preferred to have addressed the magistrate personally, but he was not 'emotionally equipped to do so'. Two months on, he was still grief-stricken. His statement said: 'Tragic as it might have been the death of Miss Darvall has not been entirely pointless. It set in motion a train of events which have proved to be of very material benefit to humanity as a whole ... Mr Darvall's feeling is that the personal tragedy caused to him by the death of his daughter and Prins's responsibility have been offset by the fact that such a death contributed to medical science and to humanity as a whole.'

This unprecedented plea for leniency worked. Despite evidence that Prins had been drinking on the day of the accident, and that he had been speeding, the magistrate sentenced him to just two years' jail, with one year suspended for three years. In legal circles, and in the press, there was astonishment that such a plea in mitigation had been made on behalf of a drunken driver who had destroyed two lives. But Darvall's noble gesture was a measure of the extraordinary emotional drama of that first heart transplant. What was one man's grief for his dead wife and daughter when mankind stood to gain so much? Under photographs of Denise Darvall in the newspapers the captions had read: 'She gave her heart for humanity.'

Edward Darvall would die in 1970, after enduring several years of publicity as the first father to give his child's heart to save the life of another person. He never once expressed regret for what he had done. His sons, Stephen and Keith, reportedly disagreed at the time with his decision to allow Denise's heart to be taken – they said he had been too shocked to consider it properly – and have always kept their distance from celebratory events surrounding the first heart transplant. It was for them, after all, the time they lost a cherished mother and sister. They do not criticise their father now. 'As brothers we were too dumbstruck to take in what was going on,' says Stephen, now a traffic policeman. 'We had no feelings, we were too devastated. It was like a dream. It was my father's decision, and he believed he was doing a service.

Afterwards there was chaos everywhere, with television cameras here from every country in the world, and my father was in a state of shock. He couldn't sleep. He stayed on tranquillisers until he died. He had lost his wife and daughter, and he never recovered. I think it's what killed my father in the end.'

The grief and despair of the Darvall household could not have been further removed from the upbeat mood at Groote Schuur. Washkansky told Barnard that as soon as he woke from his operation he had wondered why he felt different. 'Then I realised that I was breathing. I could breathe again. I was not gasping for air.' For ten days his condition slowly improved, except for occasional scares over raised pulse rates or irritability which Barnard feared might be a sign that something was wrong. He even began to talk about being home by Christmas. He was monitored closely every second of the day and night. His anti-rejection drugs were constantly reassessed. Sister Georgie Hall, who had nursed Princess Anne in London when she broke her nose in a riding accident, had appeared in all the post-operative photographs of Washkansky. Now, in the second week of his recovery, she spoke of her special patient's healthy appetite and sense of humour: 'He's eating like a horse.' He had wanted steak and mushrooms, but got steak and eggs. 'He's delightful – full of fun and nonsense, and with an answer for everything.'

With Washkansky doing well – he had taken his first few steps and had even sat out sunbathing on his balcony – it was announced that a book would be written telling the story of the world's first heart transplant, and the team behind it. The proceeds would go to the Chris Barnard Research Fund to promote vital work on heart disease. But as the publicity around Barnard the personality snowballed, the idea was dropped. American television had already put together documentaries on the transplant, including extensive interviews with Barnard. Naturally the reporters wanted to know about his upbringing and what drove him. He spoke of how he had been the son of a poor missionary and had gone barefoot because his parents couldn't afford to buy him shoes. He had grown up determined to succeed and had changed the face of medicine. It was a compelling human interest story. His mother may have dismissed the notion that he was forced to go barefoot – she said, 'There were shoes for those who wanted them' – but the romantic mould was set. The book became a planned autobiography by Barnard, to be published by a Cape Town company, again with proceeds to the Fund. The hunt began for a ghost writer.

The need to keep infection away was paramount, yet Washkansky had become such an object of fascination that foreign television crews and photographers gained access to the ward. They were even allowed to set up powerful television lights and sound equipment in his room while relatives filed in to see him, and to film their meetings. Less than a fortnight after his operation Washkansky was getting grumpy again and began to complain of abdominal pains. He asked for more privacy. Barnard agreed. 'We had agreed that today he could be seen by a cabinet minister, his wife and family, as well as being photographed by *Stern,* interviewed by the BBC, and televised by CBS. I decided to honour these but restrict their time and allow no more until he felt better.' It was truly the modern-day equivalent of the Victorian freak show. There was no attempt to manage the media interest by a public relations officer as there would be today. It was left to Barnard and his team to handle as they might.

The world had been following Washkansky's progress daily, almost hourly. So far it had been a story of unequalled daring, drama and high emotion. It had hope and tragedy entwined as never before. It had the same sense of a vast adventure beyond the known boundaries as the 'space race': America and Russia vying to be the first to put astronauts on the Moon. Heart disease was in many countries the biggest killer. If Washkansky lived, had Man found a way to conquer it?

Over the next few days the drama was to intensify, and take a turn which many had predicted, especially Barnard's critics. Washkansky was ailing. By 16 December there was a loss of appetite. X-rays had shown a tiny shadow on the lung. Washkansky had a temperature. Barnard's immediate fear was rejection, and he stepped up the immuno-suppressive drugs. It could also be a blood clot on the lung, and they began treating Washkansky for this too. But it turned out to be neither. It was double pneumonia, and by the time they began giving Washkansky penicillin to combat it, it had taken hold. The increased anti-rejection drugs had in fact further weakened Washkansky's ability to fight off the infection, as Barnard acknowledged later.

News of the ominous slide in Washkansky's condition provoked as much worldwide interest as had the transplant itself. Pictures of Barnard and his team, now looking drawn and haggard, appeared on front pages again. The television cameras were there to capture the frantic comings and goings at Groote Schuur. Ann Washkansky was now huddled into the hospital through side doors to avoid reporters. The battle to save Washkansky's life went on for several days, with every nuance in the drama being played out under the world's gaze. It ended at 6.45 am on 21 December. The post-mortem a few hours later, attended by a grim-faced Barnard, confirmed that the new heart had been working perfectly.

At the moment of his greatest sadness – his greatest loneliness, too, he would recall later – Barnard did not hide away. He faced the same news correspondents he had charmed and entertained for the 18 days Washkansky had lived. He looked deeply shaken. The findings of the post-mortem only served to enforce his frustration that Washkansky's death had been avoidable. There had been no rejection of the transplanted heart. He denied the transplant had been 'an experiment'. It was 'a treatment for a sick person'. No, he would not give up on heart transplants. The *Cape Times* noted of Barnard's performance: 'Though fatigued and strained, deeply disappointed, and sometimes frowning into the blaze of lights, he made a powerful impact with the honesty, sincerity and the directness with which he answered all questions.'

Marius had spoken to his brother that morning. He told him: 'Well, we climbed Everest. Next time we'll know how to get down.' For Edward Darvall, Washkansky's death meant a final ending to his daughter's life. 'There was at least part of my daughter still alive in Mr Washkansky. But now she is completely dead.'

International reaction was mostly positive. The London *Daily Mail* said: 'The past 18 days has seen a succession of big news stories … but one above all has appealed to the deepest emotions of men and women everywhere. It is that of Louis Washkansky. Now it is over. Louis Washkansky is dead – and the news was received yesterday in millions of homes with a sense of personal bereavement. He did not pull through. Nevertheless the case of Louis Washkansky is an outstanding triumph in the history of medicine and surgery.' The London *Daily Mirror* commented: 'Millions will be saddened that the human story of this man's brave fight for life could not have a happy ending. Mr Washkansky's death does not diminish the medical breakthrough achieved by South Africa's brilliant team of surgeons.' The *Wall Street Journal* said: 'Louis Washkansky left his mark on the world. His was a great adventure and he was a brave man.'

Adrian Kantrowitz, who had performed the world's second heart transplant, summed up the feelings of many of his peers. He said the Washkansky transplant had been 'a great step forward', adding, 'This is the way progress is made. Man takes one step forward and then falls down. I'm sure this procedure will prove successful.' Yet Washkansky's death sparked another round of fierce argument about whether or not the operation should have taken place. Again, there seemed to be no agreement among equally eminent cardiac surgeons. To most, it had been a triumph. A man who was doomed to imminent death had been given 18 more days of life. More importantly for medicine, the transplant had broken through the barriers holding surgeons back. To a few, Barnard had simply failed. He had put Washkansky and his family through unimaginable torment for, at best, a gamble; at worst, for the sake of achieving a medical first.

A week before Washkansky died, a 58-year-old dentist, Philip Blaiberg, had been admitted to Groote Schuur, already earmarked by Schrire as Barnard's next heart transplant candidate. Blaiberg later said of his first encounter with Barnard: 'Though our conversation was brief and he stayed only a few minutes, I was immediately impressed with the stature of the man and his air of buoyant optimism. He inspired me with the greatest confidence ... Here was a man to whom I would willingly entrust my life.'

Now that Washkansky was gone Barnard went to see Blaiberg to ask if he had changed his mind. Blaiberg had been feeling too ill that morning to ask after Washkansky's condition. He had no idea he was dead. When Barnard appeared in his room he was unusually agitated and clearly distressed. 'I feel like a pilot who has just crashed,' he told a baffled Blaiberg. 'Now I want you, Dr Blaiberg, to help me by taking up another plane as soon as possible to get back my confidence.' Once Blaiberg had learned of Washkansky's fate, he assured Barnard: 'I want to go through with it now more than ever.' His transplant, the world's third, would not take place until early the following month.

The day after Washkansky died he was buried, without his new heart, at Cape Town's Jewish Cemetery. The heart had been removed for further examination. The funeral was shown on television screens across the world, and reported on the front pages the next day. As Ann Washkansky sobbed, the Chief Rabbi of the Cape, Israel Abrahams, spoke of the 'tremendous, epic struggle' waged in a hospital room for her husband's life. He told mourners: 'The great heart's rhythm to which the whole world listened is now stilled. In a deep, true sense, all mankind stands at this moment at the graveside of Louis Washkansky … Without his will to live, the operation could never have been performed. It will endure as an example of the individuality of the human spirit.'

Marius and MC Botha were pallbearers. They wore skullcaps, and, clearly moved, looked tearful. Other members of the transplant team were also there. Barnard was not. That night he and Louwtjie would fly to America, where Barnard had been invited to appear on a prime-time CBS show, *Face the Nation.*

The transformation in Barnard's life which had begun on the day of the heart transplant was to be set by this trip. He had been feted at home – Vorster and the cabinet had congratulated him, he had been awarded an honorary Doctor of Science degree by UCT, its highest honour; and on the night of Washkansky's death it had been announced that he would be granted the Freedom of the City of Cape Town.

But Barnard could never resist the opportunity to travel, even before Washkansky.

Later he said he agonised over whether to go to America. Others at Groote Schuur encouraged him to get away and take the break. By not going he would be admitting that Washkansky's death was a defeat, he felt. He didn't want his critics to get the better of him. Yet his decision to go surprised some of his colleagues. Philip Blaiberg was awaiting a donor. With the experience he had had in the run-up to the Washkansky transplant, Barnard was fully aware of how crucial timing was. The trip to America had to be made via London, which meant Barnard faced a journey of some twenty-four hours. A suitable donor could be kept 'alive' on a ventilator to await Barnard's return, but that was hardly desirable. Regardless, Barnard went, he and Louwtjie chauffeured to Cape Town airport accompanied by CBS executives – Louwtjie wearing newly bought clothes – and travelling in the aircraft's first-class section for the first time in his life. Never again would Barnard, the son of a lowly missionary, sit in an aeroplane in anything other than a first-class seat.

Louwtjie had seen the hysteria surrounding her husband. She had been besieged by reporters and photographers at home, and had given interviews to foreign television teams. But she was taken aback by what she experienced now. At Heathrow Airport, she said, 'there seemed to be a million cameras waiting to "welcome" us. Slowly I walked down the gangplank, but before I reached the bottom I became blinded and deafened by flashing cameras and a screaming mob of reporters. The next moment we were literally swept off our feet, pushed into a car and taken to a waiting plane.' It was a melodramatic account. Contemporary newspaper stories of their brief appearance between planes said there were no reporters on the tarmac at Heathrow because Barnard had asked for there not to be. Only photographers and television cameras were there. On arrival in America, said Louwtjie, they were 'treated like kings' with 'everyone at our beck and call, our every wish was their command'. Sitting in the television studio audience, seeing her husband perform seamlessly in the face of tough questioning on a show watched by millions, she put aside all the years of pain. 'I thanked God for the privilege of being married to this brilliant man.'

Returning to America as a 'star' was especially poignant for Barnard. It was the home of his old mentors, Owen Wangensteen, Walt Lillehei, Richard Varco. It was also the country of those he had 'pipped at the post': Kantrowitz and Shumway. Kantrowitz and Michael DeBakey were also special guests on the *Face the Nation* show and put some tough questions to Barnard, dealt with confidently.

But the trip sealed the fate of the Barnards' already-rocky marriage. Louwtjie felt uncomfortable with what she called the 'charade' going on around them – the luxury hotels, chauffeur-driven limousines, no expense spared. It was 'film-star' treatment. On Christmas Day they were in New York and she felt homesick. She missed the children. 'We don't really belong here,' she thought. An omen of the future came when one reporter, noting the fascination for the world-famous surgeon women seemed to be showing, and his obvious interest in them, asked her: 'Are you jealous of all the beautiful women running after him now?' Things turned sour when a rival network, NBC, tried to muscle in on the Barnard visit. CBS had paid $3 000 to the research fund to secure Barnard, and would have none of it.

Barnard was, of course, wallowing in the attention. He had enjoyed the *Face the Nation* show, feeling it had gone far more smoothly than he had expected. He had also been interviewed on television by Walter Kronkite and by the *New York Times.* He had successfully dismissed accusations of 'stealing' Shumway's ideas to perform the heart transplant, pointing out that the Stanford surgeon had published his results with dogs in medical journals so that others could learn from them. But it was a theme that would always haunt Barnard in America. Despite the praise lavished on him by the likes of Cooley and DeBakey, who recognised his courage, he would always be seen as the man who 'stole Shumway's ideas'. To Barnard it was nothing more than simple sour grapes.

Next, the Barnards were flown by CBS to meet the US president, Lyndon B Johnson, at his ranch in Texas. Barnard caused a minor diplomatic crisis afterwards when he told a reporter he thought Johnson had looked 'tired'. It did not go down well with Johnson.

Looking back on this trip 25 years later, Barnard claimed that he had hoped it would bond him and Louwtjie together. Instead, he found his marriage falling apart. Summing up their diverging personalities, he wrote in *The Second Life*, the sequel to his autobiography: 'Unfortunately, Louwtjie never had much of a sense of humour. She was a happy person generally, with a quick smile – but serious. And such a severe outlook on life can become excruciatingly dull. After years of study and hard work I needed some fun. My life was missing that spark, that extra something that makes living a joy. That's the reason I started looking at other girls – a long time before the transplant. Louwtjie wasn't to blame but nor was I when I think about it. We just sort of drifted. I'd grown with my career and she was still married to the medical student. The first few sips of success were so sweet and I wanted to enjoy every last drop – but that very success and publicity we were now enjoying in America had every prospect of bringing our marriage to a very painful end. She knew it and I knew it.'

Walt Lillehei later recalled meeting Barnard in New York during this visit. He accompanied him to the South African consulate for an appointment with Pik Botha, then consul, who would become a household name in the coming years as the country's hardline foreign minister. Lillehei vividly remembered Botha's words to Barnard that day. 'He had not previously met Chris. He said, "Dr Barnard, you have done a great thing for South Africa. Most of the people in this country and around the world think South Africans live in mud huts and wear grass skirts – a very primitive society. I encourage you. Talk to many people, meet many people and spread the message not only of the heart transplant but of the cosmopolitan society in our country." Chris was listening, of course, nodding his head, and I must say in later years he took that very literally.' Barnard later told Lillehei that the South African government paid some of his subsequent travel expenses.

News that Blaiberg had suffered a setback interrupted the trip. Before the Washkansky operation there had been no pressure from the media because no-one had known it was happening. No pictures or film had been taken of the Washkansky transplant. Now the world's focus was on Barnard as he prepared to carry out his second heart transplant. The failure of Kantrowitz's effort soon after Washkansky had been given a new heart, followed by the death of Washkansky, had been proof to detractors that the technique was experimental and should be put on hold until more was known about rejection and fighting off infection. On the way back to Cape Town Barnard was questioned by reporters at Heathrow. Exuding confidence, he was adamant he would go ahead with Blaiberg. He vowed he would be ready to perform the transplant as soon as he returned to Cape Town, if a suitable donor was found, shrugging off suggestions that he would be too tired after his trans-Atlantic flight. The dash by jet from America to South Africa via London had added to the drama. It had all the ingredients of a Hollywood screenplay.

Within a few hours of touching down in Cape Town, the call came. Clive Haupt was a newly married 24-year-old man who had suffered a brain haemorrhage while playing football on a beach. His blood tissue appeared to be a good match for Blaiberg. There was one problem: Haupt was coloured. The scenario feared by Schrire before Washkansky loomed again. He and Barnard discussed it, and decided to go ahead, as long as Blaiberg agreed; he did, without hesitation. Barnard later said that because the transplants were 'the only positive news coming out of South Africa' the government could hardly criticise them. Haupt's heart was strong, too, which gave them a better chance of success.

When Barnard arrived at Groote Schuur he was greeted by hordes of reporters, photographers and television teams. Inside, he found there was a snag. Bill Hoffenberg was the consultant physician who had been asked to examine Haupt, who was being kept 'alive' solely by ventilator, and declare him dead so that his heart could be removed. Hoffenberg was a well-known anti-government activist who was under a banning order due to come into force the next day. His was a case which, months before Barnard had triumphed with the Washkansky transplant, had made headlines around the world. Under the order Hoffenberg would not be allowed into any educational institution (he taught in medical school, and Groote Schuur was a teaching hospital) and, unable to work, he planned to leave the country. When he examined Haupt – the last patient Hoffenberg would be allowed to see at Groote Schuur – he detected some reflexes. He was aware that because of his political profile he could be accused of trying to 'undermine the prestige Barnard's exploit had conferred upon the country'. But he stood his ground, and went home without confirming death. Several hours later he returned to the hospital. With the transplant team waiting to get the go-ahead, he again said he could detect reflexes and refused to pronounce Haupt dead. At this point an exasperated Jannie Louw, head of the department of surgery, said: 'God, Bill. What kind of heart are you going to give us?' Barnard was also in the room but, says Hoffenberg, 'said nothing except to snort'. Finally, a few hours later, he re-examined Haupt and found no reflexes. The transplant could go ahead.

Hoffenberg's role in the Blaiberg transplant did not emerge until after Barnard's death. But his name was often thrown at Barnard during overseas press conferences at that time. He refused to get involved. Hoffenberg says now, 'The South African government seized on the transplants with great alacrity and joy. They were getting a lot of flak internally and overseas, and this provided welcome relief. The focus of the news shifted from me to Barnard in a big way. The strong implication was that this sort of thing was possible if doctors concentrated on their work and kept out of politics.' Hoffenberg's family were so angry with Barnard for failing to speak up on his behalf when he became famous overnight that his mother-in-law wrote to him. 'She got a rude letter back telling her to mind her own business. In retrospect, I think he could have said something. Almost every other doctor at Groote Schuur did come out publicly on my behalf. Marius came to see me regularly and seemed genuinely upset.'

According to Barnard's account in *The Second Life* there was no argument this time about whether or not to take Haupt's heart while it was beating. He thought waiting for the heart to stop was unnecessary. The debates sparked by the Washkansky transplant had strengthened his belief that brain-death was enough to permit the removal of the heart. But in an interview given a few weeks after the Blaiberg operation to the *Kerkbode*, the DRC journal, he was asked whether he would ever consider removing a heart that was still beating. He replied: 'I have considered this, but have not yet done it out of respect for public opinion.' Either, aware of the sensitivity surrounding the issue, he was lying then; or his memory failed him when he recalled it nearly 25 years later. In 1969 both he and Marius separately stated that they had waited for the donor heart to stop beating in the first three transplants.

Blaiberg's transplant on 2 January may have been Barnard's second, but it was no less dramatic and controversial than Washkansky's. The American television network NBC had signed a deal with the Blaibergs (he had a wife, Eileen, and a daughter, Jill) for $50 000 for exclusive rights to film the operation and for interviews. Photographers were now well aware of the commercial value of any pictures taken, especially in view of the NBC 'buy-up'. MC Botha spotted a man in a white hospital coat taking pictures from the gallery and ejected him from the theatre. Another was caught trying to take photographs through the window of the theatre door. NBC would later launch a high court action to stop a photographer it believed had taken pictures from selling them. The case was thrown out when the photographer provided an affidavit denying he had been responsible. But the publicity added to the controversy.

As Barnard – struggling, he said later, from a flare-up in his arthritis – put in the final stitch to Blaiberg's new heart the hospital was hit by a power cut. The heart-lung machine, the only thing keeping Blaiberg alive, had to be pumped by hand. While the lights were still out, and not knowing how long they would be without power until the hospital's emergency generator came on, Barnard decided to allow blood into Blaiberg's heart in the hope that it would take over circulation. Unlike Washkansky's new heart, which had needed to be shocked and weaned off the bypass machine so painstakingly, Blaiberg's heart began fibrillating as soon as the blood flowed through it. It then began to beat spontaneously. The lights came back on, and the heart-lung machine pumps restarted, helping the new heart with its load. After a few minutes the bypass machine was off, and Blaiberg's heart continued to pump strongly.

The 'coloured-heart-in-white-man's-body' line was a godsend to the foreign media, who had struggled to find ways of working up the apartheid angle after the Washkansky transplant. Now they could combine the two stories for which South Africa was famous – racism and heart transplants.

Peter Younghusband's story in the London *Daily Mail* typified the tone: 'Clive Haupt's heart broke the race barrier today. South African doctors removed it from his dusky-skinned body and transplanted it into the body of a white man. But what remained of 24-year-old Clive Haupt, a Cape Coloured factory worker, didn't make it. His body will be buried in a segregated cemetery – in the "non-white" section, according to South Africa's racial laws. If it is any consolation to his widow – only three months married – Clive's heart will one day lie in a white man's grave. But that is the nearest he will ever have achieved to becoming a first-class citizen. Here we have the irony and the pathos of life in South Africa under the official policy of apartheid.' (Haupt's heart would never in fact lie in a white man's grave; it would eventually be preserved in a jar of formalin at Groote Schuur.)

Younghusband went on to list the many areas where Haupt and Blaiberg, the man whose life he had saved, would have been forbidden to stand or sit side by side: restaurants, buses, post office queues, clubs, dances, football, rugby and cricket matches ... Their children would not have been able to attend the same school, nor would any member of the Haupt family have been allowed to marry or have sex with any member of Blaiberg's. Younghusband did not point out, though he might have done, that Haupt's body had been taken initially into the wards reserved for 'non-European' people at Groote Schuur, while Blaiberg's room was in a ward for whites. A mixed intensive care unit for heart patients would not be set up for at least a year, and then only after Barnard, among others, had put huge pressure on the hospital authorities and their political masters. The demands of such a unit made it impossible to run two separately. The wards at Groote Schuur would remain segregated under apartheid, although the operating theatres were used for all.

In France Barnard was named 'Man of the Year'. But here there was also fierce criticism of the Blaiberg transplant from the anti-apartheid movement. Breyten Breytenbach, the Afrikaans poet, who would later be jailed in South Africa, was then living in exile in Paris. He said, 'I'm sorry so much publicity is given to the heart transplants in South Africa because medical progress there is not reflected in politics or in the general morals of everyday life.' Surgeons were fighting to save the life of Blaiberg, a white man, while South Africa had one of the highest infant mortality rates in the world, he said.

Barnard appeared unabashed by efforts to turn the Blaiberg operation into a political event. He stood tieless outside the hospital, his white shirt collar open over his jacket, looking confident and dashing as he told reporters Blaiberg was doing well. He could not have looked less like a surgeon.

When he attended Clive Haupt's funeral he was mobbed. Thousands turned out, and many tried to touch him, even kiss his hands, or talk to him. Hundreds of letters, telegrams and cards were flooding into Groote Schuur every day with congratulations, most from overseas. Some were abusive, calling him the new 'Dr Frankenstein'. After his impressive performance on American television, which had made news bulletins everywhere, Barnard was desperately being sought for televised interviews in other countries, especially by the BBC in London.

Four days after the Blaiberg operation, Norman Shumway performed his first, and the world's fourth, heart transplant on a 54-year-old man. After Kantrowitz's failure and Washkansky's death, Barnard truly set the transplant bandwagon rolling with Blaiberg. It would gather pace at an alarming rate. Cardiac surgeons came under enormous pressure to show that they, too, could do a heart transplant. It became a matter of national pride, with Britain's first heart transplant team even appearing at their first post-operative press conference brandishing a Union flag. Within a year of Washkansky's operation, around 80 heart transplants had been performed in 15 countries.

Barnard said he would not go abroad again until he was satisfied Blaiberg's condition was safe enough; he was taking no chances. Access was far more strictly controlled than it had been to Washkansky. He was placed in a specially-devised sterile unit. The critical rejection period passed, and so did the 18th-day mark which Barnard had feared, superstitiously, after Washkansky. Blaiberg seemed to be making excellent progress. Shumway's patient died after 15 days.

The prime minister, John Vorster, invited Barnard and other members of the transplant team to a private dinner to show his appreciation of what they had done for the country. When the *South African Medical Journal* published a special heart transplant edition, containing the official report of the Washkansky operation by Barnard and others, the government ordered 10 000 extra copies to be printed, and bought them.

Reporters noted that Barnard's salary of a little over R600 a month was paltry compared to what he might receive outside South Africa. Asked why he didn't take up reported job offers from abroad, as well as tempting opportunities to 'sell his story', he said, 'I could walk out of here and become a millionaire, but I don't want to. Is it so odd that the only thing that interests me is my work?' But he was still doing a relentless round of interviews, mainly with foreign press and television stations. He made a long-playing record with members of the transplant team also giving talks on their role in the Washkansky drama. He had also begun work on his autobiography, although at first he said he wanted a biography written about him which would tell his story in a more objective way. He was persuaded otherwise. One ghost writer after another fell by the wayside, unable to pin Barnard down long enough to make real progress. One, Benjamin Bennett, a local journalist, wrote 18 000 words before giving up. After a newspaper photograph appeared of Barnard looking strained, questions were asked about whether he was overdoing it. But his ego, already large, had by now become addicted to the drug of publicity.

The transplants were also generating funds for Groote Schuur. A group of leading mining companies led by Anglo American and De Beers announced they were donating R1 million to build a new research centre at the medical school. With this kind of pull, Barnard's position was unassailable. Anything he did to promote himself had the effect of boosting funds for the research fund, even the hospital itself.

Three weeks after the operation, he left – without Louwtjie – for a fateful 'whirlwind' trip to Germany, Italy, Britain and France which generated almost as much publicity and hysteria as the Beatles might have done. It would be dubbed 'Professor Barnard's Tour of Europe'. At Rome airport he was mobbed by thousands of 'fans' who saw him as a miracle-worker. He was photographed dancing with beautiful models, partying with film stars Gina Lollobrigida and Sophia Loren, and meeting the Pope – an occasion he would always say was the most memorable of his life. By now, an Italian publisher, Giorgio Mondadori, had moved in on his autobiography. He was prepared to pay a vast sum to the research fund for the world rights. The day before going to the Vatican, Barnard got a call from the self-styled 'tailor of Rome', Angelo Litrico, who could barely speak English, but whose clients included Richard Burton and a number of heads of state. Mondadori had decided that if Barnard was going to be one of his properties, he must look the part.

Litrico visited Barnard at his hotel, measured him up and returned to his shop to start work. By the next morning Barnard, renowned for his lack of interest in clothes until now, was wearing the finest Italian suit he had ever seen. He also had a velvet-collared Litrico overcoat, four new shirts, four pairs of shoes and a dozen ties. It was the beginning of a remarkable friendship between the two men. For the next 20 years, while Litrico was alive, Barnard would not have to pay for a single suit or tie. Litrico, for his part, would refer Italian children in need of heart operations to Barnard.

Barnard's staunchly Calvinist father had preached passionately against the 'Roman danger' from his pulpit in Beaufort West. The Vatican had not criticised the heart transplants but had said it was disturbed by the emotion surrounding the operations. It was anxious for people to distinguish between the spiritual nature of the soul and the heart as a physical organ. Barnard was aware that the Pope's approval or condemnation could sway hundreds of millions of people. In fact he found, in Pope Paul VI, a sympathetic figure who congratulated him and said he would pray for him and his patients. Afterwards Barnard felt 'so moved that I couldn't face any food served in a restaurant. I still could not believe that Chris Barnard had had a private audience with the Pope.'

But it was his meeting with Gina Lollobrigida, then a big star, that was to have the most far-reaching consequences, although he didn't know it at the time. She invited him to a party at her house on the Via Appia but he arrived feeling tired and asked to go upstairs to lie down. 'She took me up to her bedroom which was dominated by a large double bed,' he recalled in *The Second Life*. 'I took off my shoes and jacket, loosened my tie and lay down on the bed and fell asleep. I woke up when I heard Gina coming into the room. She was carrying a bottle of champagne and two glasses. Huskily she murmured, "Now we're going to be alone," as she sat on the bed next to me and slowly ran her fingers down the side of my cheek ... We celebrated with champagne several times during the night and I left early next morning. She drove me back to my hotel in her Jaguar – absolutely naked inside a mink coat.' Barnard found Lollobrigida to be an 'extremely vibrant and sexually uninhibited woman'. 'Had I known the trauma which would follow I would have kept well clear of the Via Appia that night,' he said.

Later Sophia Loren and her husband Carlo Ponti held a reception for him at their country home near Rome. The press pictures showed a smiling Barnard leaning across a cross-legged Loren, her stocking tops clearly visible. One London newspaper headlined it: 'Together in Rome, two experts in the art of manipulating men's hearts.'

Barnard, with MC Botha and Bertie Bosman, who had met up with him in Rome, and were also on the official trip, then went on to London. The backlash against Barnard's endless appetite for publicity had already begun in Britain. He posed for a picture in Trafalgar Square, and a pigeon landed on his head. When the photograph appeared the next day, coupled with a sarcastic caption, it made him look foolish. Another member of the Barnard party on this trip was Don Mackenzie, who had established himself as the 'official' photographer for the research fund. Fast-talking and sharp-witted, Mackenzie had known Barnard for some years and had been involved in early negotiations over his book. He was aware of the commercial value of getting exclusive access to Barnard's activities, and the two men struck a deal. 'Chris's expenses were being covered by the television stations but I had to pay my own way,' he says. 'Chris told me he would make sure I got some good exclusive pictures which we could sell. "You pay a fee," he said to me.' From now on he would never be far from Barnard's side.

The BBC arranged a special programme, *Barnard Faces His Critics*, in which eminent surgeons, scientists and commentators were invited to put questions to Barnard and Botha. Some of Britain's leading surgeons had attacked Barnard in the pages of the *British Medical Journal* and the *New Scientist*, accusing him of shamelessly seeking publicity and 'jumping the gun' on heart transplants before enough was known about immuno-suppression. Barnard infuriated them further by saying, 'I don't believe in arguing in medical journals.' On the BBC show Barnard's performance was again assured, confident and even witty. He also appeared to be disarmingly honest. He dealt with a barrage of criticism about how the publicity had been handled, especially the identifying of donors and recipients. Barnard stressed the hospital had played no part in this and that the media interest had been unstoppable. Malcolm Muggeridge, a well-known moralistic journalist and broadcaster, asked whether the first heart transplant had been done in South Africa because the 'vile doctrine of apartheid' meant life was 'held cheaper' there. Barnard refused the bait, and simply said the operation had been done to save a dying man. Notable surgeons in the audience, including Russell Brock, a former president of the Royal College of Surgeons who had co-published a paper on heart transplantation in 1959, a year ahead of Shumway and Lower, spoke up for Barnard. But the show hit its lowest note for most when the man who would be Britain's first heart transplant patient, Frederick West, was brought on in a wheelchair, unidentified, to ask questions and to plead his own desperate case for a new heart. This 'stunt', as it was branded, was none of Barnard's doing. Yet because West was inevitably in favour of heart transplants it helped to consolidate Barnard's reputation as a publicity-seeker, with tabloids condemning it as 'The Chris Barnard Show'.

In France there were more television interviews and meetings with leading surgeons eager to confront and question the 'wonder-boy' from Cape Town. There was also a highly publicised scuffle outside a nightclub with photographers, confirming Barnard's celebrity status.

Before returning to South Africa, Barnard stopped off again in Italy to meet Giorgio Mondadori at his country house in Verona. He would later claim that Mondadori warned him off seeing more of Gina Lollobrigida – though he felt they might have had 'a future together' – because the publicity would harm the sale of the book and his reputation. Gianfranco Cantini, the Mondadori representative who fixed the deal with Barnard, says, 'We told him he shouldn't get involved with Gina and the rest, that he was a scientist, not a movie star. But he was a complex personality. He loved a social life. He had spent all his young life in the desert, and when he was at medical school and in the US he was poor. When he achieved glory he went crazy for all that jet-set society.'

The Mondadori deal was huge – Cantini says they paid $100 000 to the Chris Barnard Fund for the world rights to the book. (Later Barnard saved the life of Mondadori's young son Paolo with a successful operation to repair a complicated heart defect.) They soon had over a million dollars' worth of orders. All Barnard's royalties would go to the fund, although he would retain film rights. Cantini says he also gave Barnard 'around $30 000' in cash over the following 18 months while the book was being written. A film was already being talked about in the press, with Gregory Peck or Paul Newman as Barnard. In Milan, on the way back to South Africa, Barnard met film-maker Alfredo Bini and, according to his own account, spent the night with one of his girlfriends.

While he gallivanted round Europe, Louwtjie was being humiliated almost daily with newspaper stories and pictures of her husband's antics: dancing with a vivacious model in Germany (he said years later he had spent the night with her), flirting with Sophia Loren and Gina Lollobrigida in Rome, brawling with paparazzi outside the Crazy Horse Saloon in Paris. At home she confronted him bitterly, and he blamed the press for sensationalising what he claimed were innocent incidents. But Louwtjie was soon disturbed by the change in her husband: 'Clothes had now become an important factor in his life. Chris had always had a complete disregard for clothes and his appearance was always bordering on the shabby ... Now he preened in front of the mirror. He glared at his reflection ... His image – the one he had suddenly acquired – had to be constantly nourished and pampered. Now, most of his faithful clothes were cast to one side, in the same way he had cast us, his family, aside.'

Some of Barnard's colleagues were also angry at the lurid publicity he was getting. For them it simply wasn't the way a respected surgeon should conduct himself. They felt it brought Groote Schuur into disrepute. They weren't bowled over either by his new Italian shoes.

9

Divorce

Barnard's behaviour had also infuriated the country's politicians. Desmond Stoffberg, a civil servant with the Cape provincial administration, was gardening one weekend when he was called to an urgent meeting with Nico Malan and Lapa Munnik. Had he heard the reports of Barnard 'shooting his mouth off' abroad? Stoffberg was told he would be seconded to 'manage' Barnard in the face of overwhelming media interest. He would have to report to Malan and to the Department of Foreign Affairs every time Barnard went abroad, giving them detailed itineraries in advance, so that South Africa's embassies could be alerted. Malan was a personal friend of the Barnards. Louwtjie had also spoken to him about the need to exert some control over her errant husband.

Blaiberg continued to do well. On the 43rd day after his transplant he was pictured on his feet, shaving himself. Then came what was, to Barnard, an irresistible stunt: 'He walked into my room, masked and dressed in his usual sterile outfit, carrying a transparent plastic box,' said Blaiberg. 'In it was my old heart in a preservative solution ... Professor Barnard and I sat on my bed and examined my heart with cool professional interest.' Barnard told Blaiberg he was the first man in history to gaze at his own heart. Don Mackenzie snapped away from behind a glass panel, and again the pictures went round the world. With other transplant surgeons failing to match Barnard's apparent success, every positive news item and picture of Blaiberg seemed to confirm him as the 'man with the golden hands'.

Another foreign trip loomed, to Portugal, Italy, Puerto Rico and America. This time Louwtjie would go for the latter half too. Malan and Munnik both felt her presence would help keep her husband in line, and had told her so. Whether she went for this reason is not certain. Barnard, according to his own account, left for a brief stop in Lisbon to sort out arrangements for a later visit to the university; he then planned to fly on to Milan to see Giorgio Mondadori and the man who would write his autobiography, Curtis Bill Pepper. Louwtjie was to meet her husband in Rome to take the flight to Puerto Rico.

At his hotel in the Portuguese capital Barnard received a love letter from Gina Lollobrigida, urging him to travel to Italy for a few days where she was filming. (The girl who delivered it to his room was rather attractive, and Barnard took her to bed for good measure, believing 'You should always tip the postman,' he claimed in *The Second Life*.) He read Lollobrigida's letter and put it in his briefcase.

At first he disliked Pepper, an American former *Newsweek* journalist who lived in Rome with his sculptress wife and who had written a successful book about the friendship between a sculptor and a pope. His long hair and scruffy appearance suggested to Barnard a liberal who wanted to change the world, 'but didn't know how'. 'Perhaps it was my ingrained Afrikaner conservatism,' he said later. In fact he quickly forgot his first impressions and grew to like and respect Pepper. Over the next 18 months they would become close and produce a worldwide bestseller.

In America Barnard was to address cardiac specialists in San Francisco and, in Washington, a Congressional committee investigating the viability of heart transplants – the ethics, legality and costs involved. He left Louwtjie to settle into their room on the 23rd floor of their San Francisco hotel while he went down to prepare the lecture he was to give. He was missing some slides, he recalled later, so he telephoned her in the room and asked her to check his briefcase. She found the love letter from Lollobrigida, describing her intimate feelings for her husband. 'Shattered and terribly alone I decided I must give Chris his freedom,' she wrote dramatically in *Heartbreak*. She walked to the window, opened it and peered down to the street below. She felt dazed enough to consider jumping. 'A gentle hand on my shoulder restrained me. I had not heard anyone enter our suite. I turned round. There was no-one there. From a picture frame on the dressing table, the two radiant faces of my children smiled at me. That was what saved me from taking my own life.' In another account Louwtjie said it had been 'a vision' of Deirdre which had persuaded her not to throw herself from the window. Barnard said later he had gone back to the room to find her sitting on the ledge in front of the open window. When she waved the love letter at him, saying their marriage was over and she planned to return home, he pleaded with her not to do anything that would embarrass him.

Downstairs he had a room full of America's most eminent heart surgeons waiting to listen to his lecture, many critical of him. He could not afford the scandal of a marital drama. Not for the first time, he pledged his love and promised to change. She relented, reluctantly, and he went back to deliver the lecture. Afterwards he and Louwtjie rowed again. She told him he was trying to satisfy his 'huge ego' by proving that every woman in the world would sleep with him. 'Here's one woman who won't satisfy your male ego any more,' she said. For the rest of the trip she froze him out in bed. 'Louwtjie had always been a good lover. She was the first girl I had ever gone to bed with and I'm sure I was the first man in her life,' Barnard said later.

That night, at a banquet in his honour, Barnard sat among the other VIPs and celebrities on the top table while Louwtjie, feeling neglected, was left to sit at a lower table. 'His promise was already forgotten ... His social and personal image excluded everything else. He was a man obsessed,' she said.

Barnard's appearance before the Congressional committee, headed by the Democrat Walter Mondale, generated huge publicity. The Americans had never forgiven him for stealing their glory, and never would. Shumway had not attended the San Francisco gathering despite being based an hour's drive away. Mondale, recalled Barnard, seemed intent on establishing that the medical profession should not be left alone to make decisions about whether heart transplants were acceptable. He asked Barnard who paid for the operations, suggesting taxpayers and their political representatives had a right to make the rules. One of Barnard's greatest assets, both in and outside the operating theatre, was the ability to 'think on his feet'. It saved many operations from disaster when unexpected obstacles arose, and it equipped him to cope supremely well during live debates. The Vietnam war was now at its height, and Barnard pointed out that the taxpayer was funding the American war effort. Did that mean, he asked Mondale, that every time a US general wanted to launch an attack he had to ask the taxpayer?

Before going to Washington Barnard made an emotional return to the place where his dreams of becoming a cardiac surgeon had been born – the University of Minnesota Hospital in Minneapolis, where his greatest mentor, Owen Wangensteen, welcomed him warmly. He did not feel such warmth from his lecture audience. In fact, he sensed a certain resentment as he spoke of his experiences during the first two transplants.

Blaiberg was now ready to leave hospital but he wanted to wait for Barnard to return from America. He was a walking, talking testimony to the skill of Barnard and the Groote Schuur cardiac team. While he was doing well no-one could seriously claim that Barnard had raced ahead prematurely. The loss of Washkansky was, for now, all but forgotten, but even he had lived longer than Shumway's and Kantrowitz's patients.

When Blaiberg emerged into the sunlight on 16 March 1968 he was met by a wall of reporters, photographers and television crews. He was the world's first heart transplant patient to leave hospital, 74 days after his operation. 'Hey, doc! What's it like to breathe contaminated air again?' shouted one reporter, perched on the shoulders of another. Blaiberg had declined a wheelchair, insisting that he wanted to walk as he left Groote Schuur. As he and his wife Eileen were driven away to their home, he kept saying: 'This is Chris Barnard's day really, not mine.'

Barnard had clearly decided it was Blaiberg's day. After shaking hands with him briefly outside Groote Schuur, he vanished back inside. (Years later he claimed he had been more interested in chatting to a French singer, Francoise Hardy, who had turned up to meet him.) He and Louwtjie had arrived home the day before. At Cape Town airport police held back crowds of 'admirers'. The photograph on the front page of the *Cape Times* shows Louwtjie walking in front of her husband, looking relaxed and smiling. Perhaps she was just glad to be back. But she does not look like a woman who had been driven to the brink of suicide or who wanted to shrink from the attention. She had reached a decision, as she said later: 'If I can't beat them, I will join them.' In the following weeks she found herself trying to embrace the new lifestyle. The Afrikaner girl who made her own clothes and read the Bible spent increasing amounts of money on new outfits and cosmetics. The 'fame and glory' had taken hold. 'In this brief but wild fling I was hoping that by copying Chris in his new image I might come closer to him. But it didn't work.' According to Stoffberg, Louwtjie even went as far as having a face-lift: 'What would a woman do in her circumstances – she wasn't a spring chicken at that stage and there were young girls chasing Chris around the world. It was her idea. She was trying to maintain an image.'

It says something for the love she must have felt for Barnard that she was prepared to go to such lengths to keep him, despite his self-confessed infidelity over many years. Perhaps it was her strong sense of duty towards Deirdre and André. Or was it simply pride – coming from such a rigidly Afrikaner family was she prepared to try everything possible to ward off the inevitable 'shame' of divorce? On taking up his new job Stoffberg had been told by close friends of the couple: 'You must at all costs avoid a divorce.'

Barnard was soon off on another marathon tour, back to the US and on to Brazil – where surgeons called for him to be given the Nobel Prize – and Peru, giving lectures and receiving honorary degrees. In Cape Town he was presented with the Freedom of the City. Then came the Hendrik Verwoerd Award, worth R10 000, for 'outstanding service to the country' and, later, the South African Medical Association's highest award, a gold medal 'for meritorious service to science and humanity'. The accolades and honorary degrees were never-ending.

Louwtjie accompanied him on an exotic trip to Iran, where he met the Shah. In Tehran, during a melee with photographers, Barnard turned, recalled Louwtjie, and in Afrikaans told her: 'You will have to get used to the fact that people are interested in me and not in you.' They went on to Majorca and Spain where they were feted everywhere and treated to sumptuous hospitality by a wealthy industrialist, Eduardo Barreiros. They also met General Franco's son-in-law, the Marques de Villaverde, a cardiac surgeon who would soon perform the country's first heart transplant. The two men would become friends.

Hostility towards the globetrotting Barnard had firmly set in by now at Groote Schuur. Jannie Louw, a revered figure, and Schrire, urbane, serious and recognised as one of the world's leading cardiologists, were appalled by Barnard's behaviour, but were powerless to stop it. Barnard had an open line to Vorster, among others. His colleagues, such as Hewitson, Hitchcock and

O'Donovan, were increasingly convinced that a wonderful opportunity to establish the Groote Schuur cardiac unit as one of the best in the world was being squandered.

Friction between departments was growing. Despite the large number of casualties brought in there were few identified as potential heart donors. Barnard suspected resistance, and he was right. The neurosurgeons resented the way the transplant team 'stalked the wards' looking for possible donors. They decried the notion that one patient might get preferential treatment over another because he or she might have a suitable heart or kidney for transplant and needed to be kept in the best condition. The ventilator of one brain-dead patient was disconnected before the transplant team could consider him as a possible donor. 'We disconnected the respirator because we felt this patient was unsuitable as a donor,' says Kay de Villiers, a neurosurgeon who was one of Barnard's staunchest opponents. 'I would not countenance the fact that people prepared as transplant donors were receiving better care than those patients who were going to live. They had no business wandering round the wards looking for potential donors.'

It wasn't purely a personal dislike of Barnard and his playboy image that was behind the animosity, although this accounted for much of it. In some quarters there were serious concerns – still expressed today – that people whose brains registered no apparent activity on the EEG for several minutes might eventually recover consciousness. There were medical papers containing evidence from studies that suggested this could happen. Some neurosurgeons accused the transplant team of being too eager to have a person declared dead so that they could 'raid' the body for its organs. There were stand-up rows in the corridors of Groote Schuur. When, during a conference, Barnard publicly challenged the neurosurgeons to explain themselves, one of his strongest adversaries, Frances Ames, later to head the UCT neurology department, rose and said bluntly: 'It's because we don't trust you.' Ames, who was also a psychiatrist, was not, on this occasion, directing her mistrust at Barnard alone but at transplant surgeons in general. (While she respected his ability, Ames remained scathing of Barnard's personality, witheringly describing him as a 'talented psychopath' and a man 'in a state of perpetual adolescence'.)

Barnard's prolonged absences placed a heavy strain on those left behind. Bertie Bosman, a registrar charged with supervising post-operative care, had grown close first to Washkansky and then to Blaiberg. He had worked seven days a week and had often spent the night at the hospital to keep a more watchful eye on his patients. (He would commit suicide in 1976 after a bout of depression – he had had few holidays since the Washkansky transplant despite requests to Barnard to be allowed to take them.) Bosman's wife Annette would take him coffee, sandwiches and clean clothes. 'He had to look after the patients while Chris danced around the world,' says Ernette du Toit. 'Chris ran him into the dust,' says Kay De Villiers.

Bosman's workload increased again with news that Blaiberg, after two months at home, had begun to show worrying signs of tiredness. Shortly after his 59th birthday he was readmitted to Groote Schuur with hepatitis. He deteriorated rapidly, and his wife was told he might die. He rallied, relapsed, then recovered again, and once more the world prayed for Barnard's patient and waited for news from the scores of foreign journalists who arrived to cover the story. (Even while Blaiberg languished, Barnard and Bill Pepper managed to spend a few days hunting in Botswana.)

After a month Blaiberg seemed to have beaten the hepatitis, only for pneumonia to set in. Barnard considered giving him a second new heart, an idea which 'stunned' Eileen Blaiberg, she said. The drama was being played out again in the pages of newspapers and on television screens. The London *Daily Mirror* noted, with amusing irony: 'Heart transplant operations themselves are still highly controversial. They are made more controversial when they are associated, as in this particular case, with a constant bombardment of publicity, rumour and speculation.'

Blaiberg finally began to pull round, thanks to an anti-rejection serum flown in from Germany, although it would be some weeks before he was strong enough to return home. His improvement was a relief for Barnard. A few days later, more than a dozen international cardiac specialists arrived in Cape Town for the first world symposium of heart transplant surgeons. Shumway had been invited but did not attend. The conference lasted four days and produced many stories about the 'moment of death' debate, brain-death and the availability of heart donors. What didn't make the news was the wild party Barnard threw at the home of a friend, Emiliano Sandri, who was abroad. Louwtjie was conveniently away – in Spain, at the invitation of Barreiros (Barnard had also been invited). The apartment overlooked the Atlantic and the food and drink were laid on by Sandri's Italian restaurant. 'Don Mackenzie, being a fashion photographer, also ensured that the most beautiful Cape Town models came to keep the surgeons up-to-date on female anatomy,' said Barnard later. Stoffberg left early but recalled seeing the surgeons the next morning, 'bleary-eyed and unshaven'. Several, including Barnard, had been studying hard.

Nico Malan gave a lunch for the surgeons and, during his speech, recited the words of a poem which so impressed Barnard that he adopted it as a summary of his own philosophy. From then on he often read out the verse during speeches and lectures. Written by an American poet, RL Sharpe, it was called *A Bag of Tools*. It read:

Isn't it strange
That princes and kings,
And clowns that caper
In sawdust rings,
And common people
Like you and me
Are builders for eternity?
Each is given a bag of tools,
A shapeless mass,
A book of rules;
And each must make –
Ere life is flown –
A stumbling block
Or a stepping stone.

Hardly great art, but these simple words held a serious resonance for Barnard. With his ability to tug the heartstrings of his audience they usually helped blur the eyes, his own included, at the right time. Throughout his life he had turned every potential obstacle into a 'stepping stone' to further his own cause. He could be highly manipulative. 'I surround myself with good people and I use them,' he would tell friends unashamedly. At a memorial service after his death his son Frederick recited the poem as his epitaph.

Louwtjie returned from Spain with a gift from Barreiros – a brand-new silver GSM Dart car. Deirdre had suffered a bad accident while waterskiing in England but Barnard had decided not to fly to London to visit her in hospital. 'I'd lost interest in my family and old friends,' he admitted later. Now he told Louwtjie he had been invited to the Red Cross Ball in Monaco hosted by Princess Grace and her husband Prince Rainier. She wanted to go with him, but he told her she was not invited. She threatened to end the marriage if he went, according to Barnard. He went, and Louwtjie saw the result on the front page of her newspaper: her husband, wearing a new Litrico smoking jacket, dancing intimately with the beautiful Grace Kelly. At the ball, a lavish open-air affair packed with celebrities and European aristocrats, Barnard bumped into the father of a Cape Town doctor. They joked about why they were there without their wives. 'I never take a sandwich to a banquet,' said the doctor's father. Barnard agreed.

With Blaiberg continuing to improve after his setback, Barnard was keen to do another heart transplant. After all the criticism thrown at him for performing the first two transplants too soon he was able to point out that his results were the best in the world. Denton Cooley in Houston had now carried out more heart transplants than anyone else but not all had survived. Pieter Smith, a 52-year-old former miner, was to become Barnard's third, and the world's 42nd, heart transplant patient. The operation would provoke the biggest controversy of them all.

Evelyn Jacobs was a 38-year-old black woman who lived in the township of Guguletu. After falling in the street near her employer's home in a 'white' suburb she suffered a massive brain haemorrhage. Passers-by recognised her and drove her to her employer's home. There a paramedic attached a note to her clothing with her name and address and she was taken by ambulance to Groote Schuur. According to the hospital authorities, the note was lost and no-one could identify Jacobs when she was declared dead. Her blood tissue was a close match for Smith's. But without an identity, how could relatives be asked permission for her heart to be taken? It was midnight on Friday. The true circumstances surrounding the decision to use Jacobs's heart were never made clear.

Barnard, in *The Second Life*, claimed her identity was known and that police were sent to find relatives but failed. Barnard said Smith had been in so much pain he had tried to kill himself a few days earlier, and with the shortage of donors getting worse the opportunity could not be passed up. Several heart patients had already died waiting for donors. He could get no decision from the hospital medical superintendent or from the district surgeon who were legally empowered to give permission. Both were wary of causing a scandal because the donor was black. Barnard called the attorney general of the Cape, WM van den Berg, whom he knew, and asked if he could give permission. Van den Berg told him, according to Barnard, that he could not give permission but he would promise not to prosecute. That was enough, and the transplant went ahead.

Legislation was being drafted by the government that would outlaw the naming of donors and recipients in transplants. Although it was not yet in force, Barnard now refused to give the name of the donor whose heart had been used to save Smith. He knew her family would be furious. After four days of searching for his missing sister, Evelyn Jacobs's brother found her body at the UCT Medical School. The story erupted. The family said they would not have given permission if approached, and Barnard and his team were accused of stealing black hearts to save white men. Reporters went to Guguletu to prove how quickly her relatives could have been found. The allegation was that no attempt at all had been made to contact the family of Evelyn Jacobs – and that, had she been white, her heart would not have been touched without permission. Again, Barnard was the subject of headlines around the world for the wrong reasons.

Smith was in fact doing extremely well, better than Washkansky and Blaiberg had done in the early days. But the controversy clouded the success and caused enormous, lasting damage. Fears spread around the townships that if you were taken to Groote Schuur the doctors, like vultures, would rip out your heart. Trust in Barnard and the transplant programme among these communities would not recover quickly. It exacerbated the donor shortage. Barnard received threatening letters. When he stopped at a petrol station – in a gold Mercedes given to him by the German magazine *Stern*, which had replaced the old green Fiat he had driven for years – he was told by the coloured attendants that they would rather resort to witchcraft than go to Groote Schuur for treatment.

Smith's transplant again highlighted the nonsense of the apartheid system for many people. An international sports boycott had seen South Africa left out of that year's Mexico Olympics. The anti-apartheid movement was now focused on a planned tour by the England cricket team. Basil D'Oliveira was a coloured player who had been born in South Africa but who now played in, and for, England. Before the team was selected the South African government had suggested that a team which included D'Oliveira would not be acceptable. Initially the England selectors left him out, enraging opponents of South Africa. Then, after another player was injured, he was put in the side. Vorster had in fact tried to adopt a more practical policy towards foreign sports teams, arguing that South Africa could not dictate to other countries who should be in their national sides. But the right-wing of the National Party disagreed, and Vorster backed down. Now he accused England of selecting D'Oliveira to pander to South Africa's political enemies and announced the England team would not be welcome. The tour was called off.

At some point before D'Oliveira's inclusion as a player in the team, it had been suggested in Britain that he might cover the tour as a journalist. Even this upset many NP supporters. On his travels Barnard had argued against a sports boycott, although he would later change his mind. His attitude to the absurdity of apartheid in a country where he was allowed to transplant hearts across the racial divide was mirrored by the *Hogarth* column in the Johannesburg *Sunday Times*: 'We do have a curious set of values in South Africa. Dr Blaiberg walks about with the heart of a Coloured man; Mr Pieter Smith's life has been saved by the heart of an African woman. But the thought of Basil D'Oliveira sitting in a press box with white journalists represents some kind of affront to society.'

Whether it was the pressure over the Smith transplant, the strain of yet another foreign trip – to Brazil and Portugal – or even the tensions of a dying marriage, Barnard ended up in hospital being treated for a suspected bleeding ulcer. At one point it was thought he might need a blood transfusion. It was time for another successful picture stunt: Blaiberg came in to examine Barnard with a stethoscope. Get-well cards poured in. A bouquet of red roses arrived from Gina Lollobrigida. Stoffberg quickly dispensed with her card and pretended they had come from someone else. The bleeding cleared up and Barnard was found not to have an ulcer. His illness was put down to the fact that, as a poor eater, he had been taking anti-inflammatory tablets on an empty stomach for years to control his arthritis. Louwtjie had tried to warn him: 'He is living on his nerves. But he won't listen. He's so stubborn.'

Others blamed the strain on Barnard's obsessive interest in the well-being of his patients, despite his frequent travels. He often arrived on the ward in a dinner jacket after a function to check on his patients. One doctor said his concern for his patients was greater than he had seen in any other surgeon. Another, a member of Britain's first heart transplant team, pointed out that Barnard 'is not the bluff, hearty surgeon who would dispose of one case and then call for the next', adding, 'In trying to break the barriers that lie ahead of you, you run the risk of breaking yourself.' Even a minor health problem was being turned into a heroic drama.

After five days Barnard was out, and preparing for a trip to London, Edinburgh and Dublin. In the year after the Washkansky transplant, it was estimated, he travelled 300 000 miles. If even half the racy episodes he recounted in *The Second Life* were true – his prime motive for writing the book in the early 1990s was to earn money and, as such, he played up the sexual antics he claimed to have got up to – he had also bedded a stream of women. (Three succumbed to his charm in less than a day in London, including Francoise Hardy, according to Barnard.)

Somehow he found time to perform a series of highly-publicised operations on children from foreign countries, Italy especially. Angelo Litrico and, to a much lesser degree, Sophia Loren asked him to help a number of children whose parents had been told there was no hope. On flying visits to Rome, usually en route somewhere else, he would hold impromptu clinics in Litrico's shop to examine a line of sickly, doomed children. They and their parents would form queues outside when they heard Barnard was coming. Barnard accepted the cases he felt needed his help, and arrangements were made through Litrico to have the child flown to Cape Town. In virtually every case Barnard and his team at the Red Cross Children's Hospital sent the children home with some sort of future, their hearts repaired. However brief his stay, Barnard never forgot to leave Rome with at least one newly made Litrico suit.

Barnard was faced with one of the toughest challenges of his life by a seven-year-old Irish girl, Aileen Brassil. When he opened her chest he discovered a heart that should not have been working at all. Instead of four chambers it had only two, poorly separated, leaving him baffled as to how she had survived so long. He had to rebuild it there and then, devising an artificial septum with plastic and repairing the faulty valves. Afterwards Barnard said the six-hour operation was the most difficult of his career, including the transplants. It was one of his most moving successes, too. The girl left Groote Schuur to return home smiling, and lived for a further seven years. Barnard was captivated by Aileen's positive personality, declaring he had 'fallen in love' with her. Desperate parents the world over saw him as a miracle-worker. Foreign newspapers ran stories about communities raising funds to send children to Barnard, to the chagrin of their country's finest heart surgeons. One exasperated British doctor's comment came to be used to describe any congenital heart defect deemed impossible to fix: 'Even Barnard couldn't do it.' (Often, he did.)

A brief pause in the downward spiral of the Barnards' marriage came with an unexpectedly successful summer holiday at Buffels Bay, near Knysna. André, who had matriculated and was about to start a year's national service with the navy at Simonstown, was there. So too was Deirdre, whose waterskiing career had stalled and who was due to begin a degree course at Stellenbosch University. Barnard and Louwtjie seemed to get on well, though she had a gloomy sense that these were to be the last 'happy' days of family life. At one stage they took a romantic drive together and Barnard pointed to a piece of land he wanted to buy. He told Louwtjie they could build a cottage there for holidays, perhaps retirement. Louwtjie's intuition was right – he would buy the land, but the cottage would be built for himself and his second wife, Barbara.

Within weeks of the holiday, while Barnard was abroad, Louwtjie learned from a friend that her husband was having at least one affair, possibly more. There was a girl in his department and other girls he was supposed to be entertaining at a friend's flat. There was also talk of a young girl from Johannesburg, the daughter of wealthy parents. Two love letters arrived for him from different women, one describing a meeting with him in Germany. When Barnard returned, Louwtjie met him at the airport and, once again, confronted him with his betrayals. As she drove him away she turned and slapped him furiously across the face. Witnesses saw the car swerve. Barnard 'laughed loudly', said Louwtjie. He told her the world thought she was 'jealous and selfish' for not giving him the freedom to enjoy 'this new and exciting life' he had worked for.

Barnard was soon away again, but when he returned he was met at the airport by Stoffberg. In the boot of the car were his clothes. A flat had been arranged. Louwtjie was going to divorce him.

Barnard was now completely free to pursue women. Terry Shean, a young photographer with the *Cape Times,* was about to go home one evening when the paper got a tip that Barnard was entertaining a woman at a restaurant. Shean already knew through a friend that Barnard was seeing a 19-year-old hairdresser. When he and a reporter, Bob Molloy, got to the restaurant Barnard and his party were on their way out. Sure enough, says Shean, it was the hairdresser. He fired off a few shots, and pandemonium broke out as Barnard grappled with him for the camera. Molloy pacified Barnard, suggesting he call the duty editor at the paper. When they got back to the office the duty editor spiked the story. Barnard was assured it would not be used. Shean was told he could sell the picture to a foreign agency for publication overseas, but a fortnight later it appeared in South African papers via the agency. Furious, Barnard called executives at the newspaper demanding Shean be sacked. Eventually Shean agreed to leave. 'I saw Barnard afterwards and told him I had lost my job,' says Shean. 'He looked at me straight in the eye and swore he had not called anyone.'

On the day of the divorce hearing at the Supreme Court in Cape Town, 23 May 1969, Barnard was out of the country. Louwtjie went to court and claimed divorce on the grounds of desertion. She told the judge her husband had not lived at home for two months. The consent paper stated that Barnard had agreed to pay Louwtjie R300 a month in maintenance – his state salary was now around R1 200 a month – and to pay for the children's education. Louwtjie would continue to live at their family home, The Moorings, which was in her name. Barnard would cover all the running costs of the house. The planned cottage at Swartvlei, near Buffels Bay, was also mentioned. Louwtjie was to have use of the cottage free of charge, except when her husband was there. Louwtjie was given custody of the children, although both were away from home now, with Barnard allowed reasonable access. The judge formally gave Barnard two months to 'restore conjugal rights' before a final decree would be issued.

Both Deirdre and André were devastated by the divorce. 'It was very traumatic. I went out roaming the streets in Stellenbosch, all night. No-one had told me anything,' says Deirdre. 'My mother got a call from the navy to say André was in a terrible state.' Deirdre was in for an even greater shock. She would soon learn from a newspaper billboard that her father planned to marry a girl younger than she was.

Barnard had left a few days before the divorce hearing on a marathon expedition that would take him to 14 countries. It was believed to be the longest air ticket ever issued in South Africa – press photographs showed staff from the travel company holding it stretched out like a snake. It wasn't all work: he enjoyed a break on the island of Ischia, off the Naples coast, waterskiing and swimming with Barbara Zoellner, only 18, and her parents, Fred and Ulli. Barbara's mother was especially impressed by Barnard and was keen for him and her daughter to get together. He had now done five transplants, his fourth being 63-year-old William Killops, and the fifth his first coloured transplant patient, Dorothy Fisher, who would turn out to be one of his most successful. Blaiberg was progressing so well that he had even published a book. Pieter Smith was doing even better, playing tennis and announcing his determination to work again. In other countries where patients were dying calls were being made to halt heart transplants until more was known about rejection. Barnard's results confounded the trend.

Fred, or Friedrich, Zoellner was rather more sceptical of Barnard than his wife. An attorney by profession, he had been a German army officer during World War 2. He had arrived in South Africa in the post-war years and built up a vast fortune in the steel industry. Unsurprisingly perhaps, in view of his background, he was an intensely private man. He was stylish, highly cultivated, and enjoyed his wealth, owning a fabulous art collection and a cellarful of vintage wines. By coincidence, as a young man he had spent a year at the same Cambridge University college, Gonville and Caius, once attended by William Harvey, the 17th-century physician who had revolutionised medicine by establishing how the heart pumped blood round the body.

His daughter's involvement with one of the most famous men on earth now threatened the low profile Zoellner had always cherished. In the years after World War 2 a number of Nazis were thought to have arrived in South Africa to start new lives, although there is no evidence that Zoellner was anything other than a regular army officer. (What there is of his war record, held in Berlin, does not reveal anything controversial.) Some of the leading architects of apartheid, such as Verwoerd, had studied in pre-war Germany. Zoellner became a strong supporter of the National Party. He warned Barnard, who was only ten years his junior, that he did not want his only child mistreated. He made it clear he was against the relationship, at least in the beginning.

Ulli, short for Ursula, was said to have come from an aristocratic German family and to be wealthy in her own right. According to those who knew her well she had been married to Fred's best friend, also a German army officer, who was killed in the war. They had adopted Barbara soon after her birth in Bonn, Germany, in 1950. It was Ulli who engineered the first meeting between Barnard and Barbara, through her husband's doctor, Solly Marks. Marks knew Barnard well and had treated him for his suspected ulcer. 'When I told Chris Barbara came from a wealthy family he was very interested in the bank balance,' says Marks. 'He said, "How much?" Fred was almost congenitally well-connected. He knew all the captains of industry in South Africa extremely well.'

On the face of it Barbara could not have chosen a more dangerous man to fall for than Barnard. She had grown up racked with insecurity about her parents' volatile marriage. The Zoellners rowed fiercely, and sometimes violently. Barbara's nose had been broken once when Fred threw a heavy doorstop at Ulli and missed, hitting Barbara instead. Her father had a long-running affair with a secretary and even invited other mistresses to visit their home. Barbara called them his 'stray cats', and despised them. She grew up with a deep scepticism of men and a fear of having her trust betrayed. But Ulli was adamant that the 47-year-old surgeon was a great improvement on the brainless young playboys with whom Barbara would almost certainly end up. He would introduce her to a new world of doctors and scientists. Barnard himself, conscious of the age difference, told Fred: 'I believe even if we have ten years of happiness it will be worth it.'

Fred Zoellner, keen to drive a wedge between his daughter and Barnard, sent Barbara to Paris to study art. But they arranged to meet up again in Rome, and the romance took hold. They had dinner with Bill Pepper and his wife Beverly. Barbara came across 'as a sort of child', says Pepper. 'She had strange tastes. If someone comes to Italy and puts ketchup on their spaghetti, well ...' According to Barnard in *The Second Life* he may have been interested in Barbara, but he was far from committed. He had flings with an American blonde in Madrid and a German girl on Ischia – while he was staying in the same hotel as the Zoellners. He found it hard to understand why Barbara would fall in love with 'a man more than twice her age and of a different social and economic background'. He decided she needed security, hardly a gift within his power to give. But, he confessed many years later, the concept of romantic love baffled him, then and always. He could accept a mother and father's love for their children. But he had never been able to understand how two 'unrelated individuals' could 'love' each other. It was an extraordinary admission for a man who had, by then, married three women.

In love or not, Barnard must have felt invincible. Three of the world's surviving heart transplant patients were his. He was on good terms with the prime minister and other powerful politicians. (A trip to Gabon to visit Albert Schweitzer's jungle hospital had produced another small propaganda coup when the president promised Barnard his country would never condone attacks on South Africa.) A commemorative stamp was to be issued in South Africa with Barnard's face towering over a picture of Groote Schuur hospital and the date 3.12.67. NASA was even said to have asked him to carry out some gravity-related experiments on organs for its space programme. He believed, as he told Louwtjie, he could have 'any girl in the world'.

Now he took on the South African press. The explosion of publicity around the first heart transplants had brought matters to a head, and a special conference was held to sort out problems between medicine and the media. But all it did was to pour oil on the flames. Barnard clashed with the editor of *Die Burger*, Piet Cillie, telling the conference that the South African coverage of the first heart transplants had been 'irresponsible and immature'. Cillie hit back by saying that 'for an exhibition of sheer virtuoso sensationalism there is nothing to beat Prof. Chris Barnard's performance this morning.' Cillie added: 'Your mistakes are buried under six feet of earth – but ours appear in 72-point type.'

Barnard's relationship with the media would veer from infatuation to loathing, and back. He complained that reporters who did not specialise in medicine were sent to cover medical stories. Yet he spent his life after the early heart transplants offering his opinion in the press and on television on a range of non-medical subjects. He objected to the 'invasion' of his privacy – yet he would call up news editors to offer his views on a story, unsolicited. He relished the excitement and attention the life of a playboy brought him but threatened to sue when newspapers called him one.

Philip Blaiberg's survival had done more than anything else to establish transplantation as a viable means of treating terminally ill heart patients, and to cement Barnard's reputation. Barnard, for all the accusations that he was an arrogant showman who had jumped the gun, was realistic about the significance of what he had achieved. In a letter, he wrote: 'It has always been my philosophy that one comes to a point in one's experimental work when one must pass on to clinical material, and from there build up as one's knowledge grows. Aviation started with a small propeller plane, but with experience it grew into a supersonic jet. I feel that heart transplantation is perhaps today at the stage of the propeller plane, but in years to come, with a responsible clinical approach, we will reach the supersonic jet age of transplantation.' It was an apt image – Charles Lindbergh's solo flight across the Atlantic in 1927 was perhaps the only other pioneering event of the 20th century that focused such sudden excitement and attention on one person. Lindbergh received some 3,5 million fan letters, still a record.

In August 1969 Blaiberg suffered another relapse and died,

some nineteen months after his operation. It was a massive blow to Barnard, professionally and personally. 'You can't help getting emotionally involved sometimes. He was a tremendous man,' he said on the day. Blaiberg's heart showed acute rejection. Killops had not lived for long, but Smith and Fisher were still improving. Other countries were moving towards a moratorium on heart transplants, especially Britain. (In America Richard Lower, Shumway's partner, was facing a wrongful death lawsuit from the family of a donor whose heart had been used without their permission, a case which would drag on for four years and end in his acquittal after a week-long trial in 1972.) There were some at Groote Schuur who wanted to suspend them too. Barnard vowed to continue his programme, but in fact no more heart transplants would take place in Cape Town for nearly two years.

So often had Barnard spoken up for South Africa abroad that he was being dubbed the country's 'roving ambassador', just as Pik Botha had urged him to be. He'd become an official trustee of the South Africa Foundation, an organisation supported by philanthropic businessmen like Harry Oppenheimer with an openly expressed aim of improving the country's image abroad. But he liked nothing better than to turn things on their heads. He would sometimes defend an idea simply because others were attacking it, and vice versa. His relationship with his fellow Afrikaners had always been ambivalent. He had never forgotten the treatment his family had received in Beaufort West. He had already upset the establishment by calling for equal pay for coloured and white doctors. Now he was invited to be guest speaker at a meeting of the Afrikaanse Sakekamer, the Afrikaans chamber of commerce in Cape Town. He was introduced, he recalled later, as 'one of the greatest Afrikaners this country has produced' and he felt, that day, 'extremely proud' of his heritage. He might easily have used the occasion to win favour, speaking entertainingly about transplants or any other non-political matter. Instead he showed he had no need of approval from his own kind. He sliced into the jugular.

Barnard asked the businessmen to help him answer three questions that were often put to him during his overseas travels: How is it that black maids looked after white children in their homes but only whites could care for them in hospitals? Why had a Chinese woman and a white man been charged under the

Immorality Act when they had been living together for 30 years? Why were Indians treated as second-class citizens? (As the years passed Barnard changed his recollection of these questions to include sports discrimination and non-equal pay for doctors of different races). Uproar from the audience, and the backlash quickly followed. Cabinet ministers accused him of 'not being a true patriot'. Afrikaans newspapers warned him to steer clear of politics if he wanted to retain the respect of the South African public. In response Barnard claimed it was his duty to speak out against a sickness he regarded as worse than a man with a hole in the heart: 'What right do we have in South Africa to say this person is a first-class citizen and that person is a second-class citizen? What right do we have to say a Japanese is white and a Chinese is coloured? On what basis do we decide these things?'

One leading Afrikaaans daily defied the Nationalist outcry, if only to use Barnard's questions as an example of what had to be confronted if they were to maintain political superiority. *Die Beeld* said Barnard had certainly 'brought a storm about his head' ... 'Still, we felt that a point must be made. In the South African situation, where South Africans talk with one another, difficult questions must continually be asked – questions that must of necessity give sharp offence here and there. Only in such a continual debate with ourselves can we South Africans sharpen our strategy and our tactics for the problems that we must deal with.' The newspaper could not bring itself to repeat Barnard's questions.

Barnard later followed up with even more direct attacks, often comparing the Nationalists to Nazis. According to his account in *The Second Life* this stance ended his friendship with Nico Malan. It also brought a call from Nico Diederichs, then finance minister, who told him he could no longer defend him in cabinet meetings. Malan summoned him to his office, said Barnard, who was, of course, an employee of the Cape provincial administration: 'I will never forget that meeting because it almost reduced me to tears. From the moment I walked into his office he slated me for my un-Christian-like behaviour and political ignorance.' The two men never spoke again, said Barnard. He also found all the VIP privileges he had enjoyed since the first heart transplant – he would be waved through passport control and customs at South African airports, for instance – suddenly taken away.

The Second Life was written at a time – the early 1990s – when South Africa's political landscape was being transformed. Mandela had been released and the movement towards a new, democratic South Africa was well under way. Understandably, Barnard, still remembered for his ambassadorial role under Vorster, was now keen to stress his earlier efforts to embarrass the apartheid regime. His controversial remarks certainly had a big impact at the time. Over the following three years he would keep up the attacks on the Nationalist government and its apartheid policy, even vowing to stand for parliament for the opposition United Party at one stage.

But beneath these verbal assaults on the government was there a seam of self-interest? Undoubtedly they brought foreign correspondents running to his door. He was a man brazenly dedicated to his own ego. Even he admitted that much of his sadness at the loss of a patient was attributable to a sense of failure, his bruised pride. He loved nothing more than to leave a mark. If Afrikaners were trying to embrace him as one of theirs – something they had not done when he was a boy – he would give them a kicking and show he was bigger than they were. Stuart Saunders recalls that when, after the early heart transplants, he was standing with a world-famous violinist outside Groote Schuur, Barnard emerged and walked towards his Mercedes. When Saunders introduced the great violinist, who was clearly awestruck by the great surgeon, Barnard, seeing his effect on the man, seized the moment: 'And do you play professionally?' he asked, and walked on, leaving the violinist humbled.

Nevertheless, asking those three questions and comparing Nationalists to Nazis was a deliberately risky stand to make for someone with Barnard's high profile. More so in view of his personal circumstances: he had become engaged to Barbara and, by the time he began speaking derisively of Nationalists and Nazis in the same breath, they had married. Fred Zoellner, who had fought for the Nazis, supported the NP and had made his fortune in an industry as notorious as any for exploiting its black workforce, was now his father-in-law.

10

Barbara

Little more than three months had passed between the divorce from Louwtjie and the engagement to Barbara. To his critics Barnard appeared driven by vanity, a middle-aged man prepared to desert his wife and family for the flattering attentions of an awestruck teenage girl. Others believed the turmoil in his private life was the inevitable fallout of the sudden onset of fame. But, as he and Louwtjie knew, and we have seen, the breakdown of their 21-year marriage had begun long before the first heart transplant. In view of Louwtjie's early awareness of her husband's infidelity, it was remarkable that their union had lasted so long.

Barbara's interest, though cool at first, fanned the blazing ego of a man already at a dangerous stage: mid-forties, children grown up, wife ageing. She was one of a series of younger women who came within Barnard's grasp now that he was famous. Barbara was, though, younger than the rest – and more beautiful than most. Even if Barnard was at first attracted by her wealth, there can be little doubt that his interest soon grew into love.

His passion for Barbara after their engagement was clear to Bill Aragon, who saw him at a gathering of some of America's leading cardiac surgeons in San Francisco. In a letter written years later, after meeting Barbara for the first time, Aragon recalled: 'Chris, meeting Barbara brought back to my mind that evening in San Francisco in 1969 when for the first time you advised me that you contemplated marrying this wonderful girl you had recently met, and that you loved her to the point that you considered that if you had even five years by her side, your whole life would have been fulfilled.'

Louwtjie, Deirdre and André were left to pick up the pieces. Deirdre was devastated that her father was now involved with a girl so young, and seemed to have forgotten her. Later she recalled:

'It was a horrible time of my life. I got all sorts of hang-ups. I became extremely fat and had to go into hospital. My dad sent me a weight-losing chart, but he didn't bother much apart from that because he was so busy and famous and had become so involved with himself ... When I walked out of hospital I saw this model of a girlfriend of his, wearing a Hermes dress. She was about my age and I thought, "I've never seen such a beautiful girl in all my life." Later on ... I saw a newspaper headline saying he was engaged to her and it killed me.'

On one occasion, recalled Louwtjie in a magazine interview, Deirdre became hysterical and locked herself in her bedroom, screaming, 'This can't be! My father cannot start something with a girl of my own age!' Louwtjie called Barnard to come over and see for himself 'what he was doing to our own children'. When he arrived and tried to talk to Deirdre, André intervened, brandishing a magazine at him which contained pictures of his father with Barbara. 'You are my father, but how can I respect you when I have to see pictures like this of you?' he demanded. 'What would you have said if your father had behaved like this?' Louwtjie recalled: 'The arrow struck. Chris worshipped his father as if he was a saint. He went pale at André's words. He became terribly angry. He worked himself up to discipline André. I stepped between them.'

As she pored over newspaper stories and pictures about the glamorous new girl in her former husband's life, Louwtjie's emotions were seared by another assault: the publication of *One Life*. She was mortified by what she saw as a grossly twisted portrait of her character. '*One Life* is indeed a very interesting and amusing story, and an excellent account of the first heart transplant. But the contents relating to me were cruelly distorted,' she said in *Heartbreak*. She claimed that some of the scenes in the book had been rewritten after the divorce, at Barnard's request, to put her in an even worse light. She had been shown an earlier draft but found the published version 'a different matter altogether ... I read through it with increasing horror.' Bill Pepper, she said, went as far as to apologise to her 'with tears in his eyes', saying it had been beyond his control.

Pepper is appalled by such suggestions, which he learned of only when interviewed for this biography. 'It's a total fabrication,' he says. 'I went to see Louwtjie to interview her when I was working on the book – Chris had agreed I should. I told her I needed to make it as accurate as possible. She looked at me and said, "You're writing a book about this man who has treated me badly, and I'm not going to do anything about it, goodbye." She sent me away. She never said one word to me about anything.' He denies rewriting any part of the book at Barnard's request. 'I had 80 or 90 tapes of interviews with Chris and as I wrote the chapters at home in Italy I sent them to him. He may have corrected medical terms but that's all. I had nothing to apologise to Louwtjie for.'

Barnard's close friend at medical school, Harry Webber, featured heavily in the book as Harry Kahn, the student who introduced him to communism. At the time *One Life* was published Webber was working in London, but he still had family under his original name of Aufrichtig living in South Africa. He was concerned that he might be identified, and his relatives penalised on suspicion of being communists. Under the *Suppression of Communism Act* they could be detained for months without charge. Barnard's baffling apparent naivety in his handling of some issues outside the realms of medicine surfaced here in a way that was nothing short of astonishing. Webber says, 'I told Chris about my anxieties and he said I would have no problem. He had already called up Vorster and asked his advice! He had discussed my situation directly with the prime minister.'

The book was a phenomenal success in South Africa and a bestseller in many other countries, including, of course, Italy. It got generally favourable reviews, although Barnard's ultra-cynical adversary Malcolm Muggeridge suggested his importance was more fleeting than permanent, noting wryly in the London *Observer* that he was 'in his way a highly significant figure. The Zeitgeist picked him up and used him for a minute. He will have a place in all the social histories of our time, assuming there are any.'

Sales of *One Life* brought in hundreds of thousands of rands for the Chris Barnard Fund. It spawned serialisations around the world and gave Barnard another reason to travel. He was in great demand for interviews. His life story had been turned into a sweeping, dramatic epic: a boy born into poverty grows up to realise his destiny as a medical pioneer dedicated to the saving of human life. Ironically it was published just as various countries were starting to halt their heart transplant programmes in the face of intense criticism. Most would not resume them until the development of an anti-rejection 'wonderdrug', cyclosporin, more than a decade later.

Powerfully written, if at times it reads like a melodramatic Hollywood screenplay, *One Life* (the title, according to Gianfranco Cantini, who said he had suggested it, referred to Barnard's mission to save Washkansky's life) presented Barnard as a man driven to succeed but racked with disarming self-doubt. The South African edition, published by Howard Timmins, contained a dedication to Louis Washkansky and Denise Darvall. This was missing from foreign editions. There is a strong current of Biblical reference and plenty of deliberately grand imagery to conjure up the magnitude of what Barnard had achieved with that first heart transplant. But, inevitably, it was not only Louwtjie who complained. Marius scoffed at the highly romanticised version of his brother's life. Others felt the book failed to recognise Marius's contribution. 'He had far more to do with the pioneering than he was given credit for,' says one of his close friends.

Barnard's childhood friend Fanie Bekker, who features strongly in the early chapters, had stayed in touch with Barnard in adult life and helped him reconstruct many of the boyhood events in Beaufort West. But once the book was published he found himself sidelined. 'Fanie told me he felt like a ticket you buy on the bus and then screw up and throw away afterwards,' says Don Mackenzie, who also helped out on research and photographs.

Louwtjie's fury over the contents of *One Life* led to her giving a series of detailed interviews to a German magazine. These formed the basis of her book *Heartbreak*. In them she revealed the contents of Gina Lollobrigida's letter to her husband, a move that brought the wrath of the Italian actress on her head. Lollobrigida threatened to sue anyone who published the letter. Barnard had also told a journalist he had slept with about his encounter with Lollobrigida; she wrote the story and Barnard was also threatened with legal action. Lollobrigida's letter, according to published accounts at the time, said: 'Hallo Chris. I think I am mad … I cannot work any more, eat any more, sleep any more. I need you as a man and as a heart doctor. Write that you will come, that you have not forgotten me. I need you more than anything else in the world.'

Lollobrigida issued an angry statement admitting that she had fallen for Barnard: 'I cannot blame myself for having had a sincere feeling for a man the whole world loved and admired at the time.' She said he had told her he loved her and even asked her to marry him. She now realised he was 'an idiot, a man seeking unlimited publicity at any cost'. The proposed marriage was 'a project of alliance between a renowned actress and a famous surgeon'. Even now, well over thirty years after the fling turned so publicly sour, Lollobrigida can hardly bear to hear Barnard's name. 'I hate that man,' she spat down the line when asked to give an interview for this biography.

Barnard had always been interested in money. Now he would boast to friends that he didn't even need to carry cash when he travelled. Everything was laid on for him. He was always able to combine trips to medical congresses with interviews and appearances on television, and now that *One Life* was being published in a number of countries the pace increased again. There were promotional tours to do, with the justification being, if one was needed, that all his royalties went to the research fund. He told some colleagues that he had opened a Swiss bank account, perhaps with the encouragement of Fred Zoellner. He was no doubt receiving fees from foreign magazines for exclusive interviews and pictures – the Mercedes from *Stern* had been a 'thank you' gift – although much of this would go to the research fund. Desmond Stoffberg later admitted that while Barnard did not charge a fee for overseas lectures, there was often a surplus of 'expenses' since several organisations in one country might cover the same air ticket. The extra went into Barnard's account.

As Louwtjie said, 'After he became famous he developed a great interest in financial matters. I remember how impressed he was when we were invited to meet Paul Getty. Chris never tired of enthusing about this man's riches, as if riches were the most important thing in the world. Money, prestige, fame – even clothing: all this became suddenly important for him.' He had never been overly generous, but now he became mean. Once, when Barnard returned from Italy with four new Litrico suits, André had asked if he could have one. His father refused.

Now that her marriage to him was over, Louwtjie rationalised the way she had put up with his unfaithfulness: 'In the end I got accustomed to closing my eyes, to pushing my head in the sand and persuading myself that it was all a bad dream. At times, I even believed it. When Chris came back to me, lovable, charming, sincere; when he simply laughed away my questions and doubts and denied everything – I believed him. I let myself be carried away time and again by his fascinating personality, his radiance, his quick intelligence – and believed what he said. I also knew that Chris needed me, that he loved me in quite a different way from all the other women in his life. Those women did not mean more to him than prey means to a big-game hunter. As soon as one fell for him he was no longer interested. He turned around and went after the next prey.'

Louwtjie's damning insights did not emerge until Barnard had married Barbara just after midnight on Valentine's Day, 1970, after a four-month engagement. (Louwtjie's birthday was on 13 February, the day before.) Despite Barbara's age and her father's misgivings about the relationship, they had been sleeping together for months. When in Cape Town Ulli would pick Barbara up in the morning from Barnard's flat.

Solly Marks and his wife, friends of both the Barnards and the Zoellners, had counselled against the marriage. Marks had treated Fred Zoellner for high cholesterol for some years, and knew him well. He had, of course, helped bring Barbara and Barnard together. 'Fred, Ulli and Barbara would come to our house for drinks. I told them about Chris, and Ulli was enthusiastic. I had no idea things would get serious, and afterwards I felt guilty about introducing them. I said to Barbara that Chris wasn't immoral, he was amoral. I told Ulli we felt it would be a mistake for them to marry, that Barbara was a lamb being led to the slaughter.' Marks happily admitted later that his early fears had been wrong. The marriage would last far longer than he or anyone else expected – 12 years – and produce two children.

The affair between the 47-year-old heart surgeon and the 19-year-old virginal heiress brought a touch of glamour to the bleak South African scene for the foreign as well as national media. With its mixture of Barnard's fame and Barbara's family wealth the pairing had the Kennedy-Onassis appeal that guaranteed interest. It was billed as a 'fairytale romance'. Barbara had been educated at a top girls private school in Johannesburg and at finishing schools in Paris and Switzerland. She had never before had a serious boyfriend. She may have just qualified as the princess, but anything less like a chivalrous knight in shining armour than Barnard would have been hard to imagine.

Pictures of Barbara sporting a dazzling engagement ring had been appearing for several months. She had even given an interview in an effort to kill off the frenzied interest in which she insisted the age gap 'made no difference' and that her fiancé did not deserve his reputation as a playboy. They had first met at a dinner party at her parents' home in April, when she had been impressed by his charm, but it had not been until the holiday on Ischia that she started to see him as 'so much more than a friend'. Had she known what Louwtjie would soon be saying about the behaviour of her future husband the interview might have gone rather differently.

At about the same time Barbara was speaking so loyally of him, Barnard was busy reinforcing his playboy image in an interview in London: 'People often think that anyone who is absorbed with the interiors of bodies has no eye for beauty and charm. But I have, you know. Oh yes, I have. I work hard but I love living as well. I always have. It's not that I think I'm getting old and must catch up. I've always liked to have fun. I like wine. I like to smoke now and then. And, of course, I'm naturally and normally happy with women. And why the hell shouldn't I be? The only really odd thing is that women seem to be particularly attracted to doctors. I get hundreds of love letters from all kinds of women.'

The official engagement party at the Zoellners' home was a huge affair with 150 guests. Barbara began receiving abusive phone calls and threats – some from hoaxers claiming to be Deirdre – and the police were called in. Barnard would not confirm the date of the wedding in advance, but it leaked out. Again it would be held behind the high walls and iron gates of the Zoellners' lavish mansion in Johannesburg rather than in public. A church wedding was out of the question in any case – Barbara was a Catholic and Barnard was divorced. The guest list was to be highly selective, with only a dozen people invited who were not family members. Deirdre, who had clearly managed to overcome the shock she felt at her first sight of Barbara, sat beside her father. André, who was close to his mother, did not go. Nico Diederichs and his wife were there. Nico Malan was invited but did not attend. Solly Marks and his wife were not invited.

Reporters and photographers besieged the house and tried to find ways of gaining access. One photographer smuggled himself into the grounds inside a milk truck, another posed as a delivery man. After the ceremony, conducted by a magistrate, it was decided, on Bill Pepper's advice, to allow photographers and reporters in. Pandemonium broke out, with Barnard's temper fraying as he and his new bride found themselves hemmed into a corner. Armed security guards who worked for Zoellner had to persuade the photographers to return to the street.

Benjamin Pogrund was night editor on the *Rand Daily Mail* that night, seeing copy from reporters at the gate: 'I seem to remember that Barnard first turned nasty towards the press, publicly, on the day of his wedding to Barbara, when he realised that the media had to dance attendance on him.' Reports of the wedding, in fact, quoted Barnard addressing the journalists after inviting them in: 'The press has meant a lot to me and been responsible for much of my fame and for bringing to the public the progress of science.' It seems to have been when some photographers clambered over the Zoellners' expensive furniture to get better shots that things turned ugly. The same reports described Barbara as 'radiantly beautiful in a full-length white polo-necked double crepe wedding dress … her long, flowing, dark hair hung loosely around her shoulders.' Barnard wore a specially made Litrico dress suit.

Barnard's honeymoon with Louwtjie had been two weeks at the Wilderness which he later remembered chiefly for getting badly sunburnt. The day after his wedding to Barbara they set off on a six-week 'working' tour of Europe and America and the Middle East, starting with four days in Rome at Pepper's flat and a party attended by Sophia Loren and Carlo Ponti. Some fashion editors persuaded Barbara to pose for cover shots for *Vogue* and *Harper's Bazaar,* Barnard later recalled, and her modelling career was born. The paparazzi surrounded the apartment, snapping anyone who stepped out onto the balcony.

Desperate parents with heart-sick children queued outside. 'The line went halfway round the block,' says Pepper. 'There were people with children who had dark circles round their eyes. I hired a nurse to help, and the couples would come up so that Chris could examine the child. When he felt he could do something, operate on a boy or girl, he would arrange for them to fly at cost price on South African Airways, to Cape Town. I had a visiting room for them. I'll never forget one man going to the elevator and he was clutching all the money he had and he said, "We want to leave this for the doctor," and I said, "It's free." They had come with their money to pay him and he wanted nothing.'

When they returned from their extended honeymoon they moved into an apartment in Clifton, an upmarket suburb on Cape Town's Atlantic seaboard. It was in the same block as the flat he had been living in since separating from Louwtjie. Barbara was unable to cook – it was the first time she had even had to think about it – but she soon began to learn.

Barnard found his new life invigorating. He told friends his arthritis, which had previously been so bad at times that he could not do up his shirt buttons, was now barely noticeable. He also confided that Barbara was demanding in bed, and at times he struggled to meet her needs, a failure which bothered him immensely. But he felt refreshed, and from now on he always advised that if a man wants to feel young again he need only take up with a younger woman. He was to follow his own advice more avidly than anyone. 'He used to compare the way he got out of bed towards the end of his marriage to Louwtjie, hobbling like an old man crippled with arthritis, with the way he sprung out energetically after a night with Barbara,' says one close friend. 'He was amazed that Barbara would walk around in front of him naked. Louwtjie never did.'

At Groote Schuur the transplant programme was stalling. There was to be a further setback when Pieter Smith died, 622 days after his operation, from stomach cancer. Dorothy Fisher was still going strong. But, it seemed to Barnard, the cardiologists at Groote Schuur were not referring potential transplant patients to him. His relationship with Val Schrire had become extremely strained. Barnard was incensed by rumours that Schrire was publicly denigrating his recent surgical results. But Schrire was dying from cancer. Wally Beck, who would succeed him, says, 'Val Schrire blamed his pancreatic cancer on Barnard at the start when he began to suffer. Barnard would burst into his office at any time and demand things in front of other doctors and patients and Val couldn't stand this.' In 1972, before he left his office for the last time to take up a bed in Groote Schuur, he called his staff in one by one to say goodbye. He told one colleague: 'When I'm gone I don't want you to work for Barnard. He's evil.' Bennie Shapiro visited Schrire in hospital shortly before his death. 'He unleashed a torrent of abuse about Barnard which went on for some time,' says Shapiro.

Barnard was being drawn increasingly into political debates at home and abroad. He was also clashing with the hospital authorities over his non-conformist attitudes towards the mixing of races in intensive care wards, and the use of coloured nurses to care for white children at the Red Cross Children's Hospital. His high profile made it impossible for the authorities to act against him for fear of stirring up bad publicity. Other doctors may have campaigned more vigorously for change in the system of segregation on the wards, but Barnard never shirked when confronted by the bullies of the apartheid regime. To him it was simply impractical nonsense to suggest that children of different races could not be cared for in the same ward, and by good nurses of whatever colour.

Bill Piller, a cardiac unit technician at Groote Schuur, recorded in his official history, *The Cardiac Clinic – The Schrire Years* how the cardiologist in charge of a new four-bed coronary care unit meant for whites only, Brian Kennelly, and Stuart Saunders, then head of the department of medicine, enlisted Barnard's help to fight segregation. 'Knowing that "coloured" patients were not permitted in a white ICU these two physicians eventually approached Professor Chris Barnard to discuss the tremendous difficulties that were being experienced in treating the increasing number of "non-white" patients with coronary heart disease, with only four available beds. The overflow of many of these critically ill patients had to be located in general medical wards that had no facilities for their specialised care. Prof. Barnard was sympathetic and proceeded to use his clout and reputation to break down the barriers that perpetuated compulsory segregation of patients, nursing and medical staff that was common in all hospitals throughout the country. After the world publicity his heart transplant operation provoked, it was too embarrassing for the authorities should his request be ignored. The cardiac clinic's CCU was the first integrated intensive care unit in the country.'

In November 1970, in the BBC television show *The Question Why*, Barnard faced up to two of the fiercest critics of the South African government, Peter Hain and David Sheppard, then Bishop of Woolwich and a former England cricketer. Hain, who had been born in Kenya and had grown up in South Africa (he would later become a Labour government minister in Britain), were leading voices in the anti-apartheid movement's sports boycott campaign. Agreeing to go on the show was typically bold of Barnard since its host was Malcolm Muggeridge, the broadcaster whose hostile opinion of his heart transplant work was well known.

On the programme Barnard argued forcefully that while he was against apartheid he believed isolating South Africa through boycotts would only harm the people who needed help most. He deployed shock tactics by showing slides of civilian victims of an MK bomb in Johannesburg. In *The Second Life*, however, he admitted: 'In the years to come it became obvious to me that isolation in the field of sport contributed significantly to stimulate the reform process. I've never been afraid to admit my mistakes and, whenever the opportunity arose, I've said publicly in South Africa that when we are eventually accepted back into international sport, we should erect a monument to Peter Hain.'

Why did Barnard so often choose to make himself unpopular internationally by opposing those who were against apartheid? The truth was he was arrogant: he didn't care what people thought of him. He was passionately patriotic, but so too were those who supported moves to isolate South Africa as a means of destroying apartheid. Under attack, Barnard's Afrikaner blood rose. He would defend his country against all comers. To the outside world, it meant he must support apartheid, something he always denied. At home he occasionally attacked the system and his controversial statements always made news abroad. But when it came to foreign arenas where he might be asked for an equally forthright indictment of his government, he reared up and kicked back, claiming 'double standards' were being applied to his country. He was still an employee of the provincial administration but this had not stopped him being a law unto himself. His dual approach was a riddle which those closest to him – and perhaps even he – found hard to explain.

Barnard's position on apartheid at this time was similar perhaps to that of another famous Afrikaner, Laurens van der Post: 'He detested, and publicly reviled, apartheid. But he would never agree that the outside world should take action,' wrote JDF Jones in his biography of the writer, *Storytelle*r, adding, 'Laurens opposed apartheid: his only reservation was that he preferred not to lash out publicly against his native land from abroad ... When in South Africa he was happy to lash out at the Government in his many interviews and speeches.'

Over the coming years Barnard would confuse matters further by first flirting with the United Party, the official opposition, and then by aligning himself with the NP, the party his father had detested: he would be cultivated by Connie Mulder, the minister of information who had ambitions to become prime minister, and nurture aims of his own to go into politics at a high level. Some believed he was seduced by the unimaginably wealthy world he had married into and his closeness, after the initial friction, to Fred Zoellner.

Whatever the wrongs of his country's system Barnard, unlike Van der Post, was certainly happy to stay in South Africa. A few months before the first heart transplant, in a fit of frustration, he had applied for a job at the National Heart Hospital in Britain, but his application had apparently arrived too late to be considered. For a short time after the Blaiberg transplant he flirted with the idea of setting up a clinic in Italy but the plan came to nothing. Apart from this he had not thought about leaving South Africa since the early 1960s, despite the deepening mire it was sinking into.

Dirk van Zyl became Barnard's sixth heart transplant patient in May 1971. He had apparently read about the shortage of recipients and contacted Barnard directly. He was a young man – just 37 – and Barnard was confident it would work well. But while the anaesthetist Joe Ozinsky was putting him under, Van Zyl's heart arrested and began to fibrillate. Thirty minutes of frantic drama followed while Barnard and his team tried to restart the heart with electric shocks. They almost gave up, but finally it began to beat again. The worry now was whether Van Zyl had suffered brain damage. He hadn't. After the transplant, Van Zyl's recovery was smoother than that of any of Barnard's previous patients. He was discharged a month later and returned to work shortly afterwards. He would live for 23 years, making him the world's most successful heart transplant patient before the advent of cyclosporin.

Later the same year Barnard performed his first – and only – heart and lungs transplant. Barbara had watched the operation, defying her husband's prediction that she would faint or leave early. It was the third heart-lung transplant in the world, with the first two patients living for just a few hours. Barnard's patient, Adrian Herbert, survived 23 days.

Barnard was now 49. He was about to become a father again. Showing the same kind of vulnerability to irrational fears that his mother had displayed, he had been growing anxious that he was unable to make Barbara pregnant. Now that she was, he worried that because of his age – another illogical anxiety – the baby would not be normal. Barbara endured a complicated labour lasting 18 hours before the doctors at the Mowbray Maternity Hospital, detecting signs of foetal distress, decided to deliver the baby by Caesarian section. Although he had delivered many babies as a student and young doctor, Barnard waited outside while his son, Frederick Christiaan Zoellner Barnard, was born on 10 December 1971. Not for the last time, he wondered if he would live long enough to see his new son become a man.

Barnard was never one to waste time: earlier in the day, while Barbara was in the early stages of labour, he attended a court hearing to stand as a character witness for a friend's son who had become involved in an illicit diamond-buying operation. He later drew on the experience: a diamond-dealing story would pop up in his novel, *The Unwanted.*

In 1972 Barnard was promoted to professor in the division of surgery by UCT, and he took the title Professor of Surgical Science, a position he had held in honorary capacity for three years. This did not mean a pay rise – the official letter telling him of the promotion pointed out that he was already earning the salary of a professor – but it did give him a seat on the university senate, one he would rarely occupy. He abhorred bureaucracy and administration and was, in any case, absent too often to be useful. Later medical students often complained that one of the attractions of the course had been the chance to attend lectures by Barnard. His momentous achievement in 1967 had inspired many youngsters in South Africa and elsewhere to become surgeons. But he was virtually never there to give those lectures.

The Clifton flat had been furnished by Zoellner money and

Barbara received a generous monthly allowance from her father. Barnard was irked by his lack of earning power. If he went into private practice he would be seriously restricted. Only a large state teaching hospital could fund a heart transplant programme and the kind of research needed to back it. He began to look towards building a livelihood outside medicine. Encouraged by the success of *One Life,* he considered books. Since his autobiography he had published, in 1971, *Heart Attack – All You Have To Know About It* (foreign editions were given the snappier title of *Heart Attack –You Don't Have to Die*) which he had written with the help of Eugene Dowdle, now Professor of Clinical Science at UCT.

Heart Attack is a dry work but it sold reasonably well in several countries. It paved the way for a series of books by Barnard – all co-produced with writers – that sought to make medicine accessible to the ordinary reader. Publishers knew the Barnard name would sell a medical book to the layman, and he always had a knack for communicating complex ideas in a popular way. His books over the next 30 years would cover all aspects of medicine, including arthritis – the fact that his expertise was in the field of cardiac surgery did not seem to matter.

In the early 1970s Barnard was also keen to buy a farm, an ambition he had held for years. He had retained from his Karoo boyhood a love for open space. An old friend from medical school, Piet Willers, had bought a farm near Malmesbury, an hour's drive from Cape Town, which he wanted to turn into a wine estate. He needed capital and offered Barnard a half share. Whether or not Fred Zoellner financed the deal – Barnard certainly took Zoellner to see the farm early on – it was to end, like many of Barnard's business ventures to come, in acrimony.

Barnard had visions of spending his days in a magnificent white pillared farmhouse, something that would remind him of the home of his boyhood friend Michel Rossouw where he had played. But the farm was slow in getting started and had irrigation problems. It constantly demanded more capital. Barnard would proudly drive Barbara out to see the land but she, hoping for something more like the glorious established wine estates of the Franschhoek valley, was less than impressed. Barnard was put out when Willers employed his son to manage the farm, and eventually Willers paid back Barnard's investment. The experience did not deter Barnard from his dreams of becoming a farmer.

The brutality of the regime that enforced apartheid was never far away, but it was about to take on a shamelessly brazen form. UCT students mounted a campaign for 'Free Education for All Races'. The police met their peaceful protests outside St George's Cathedral in Cape Town with merciless violence. In the words of Gerald Shaw in his history of the *Cape Times:* 'In his twenty-three years as a newsman the *Cape Times* chief reporter, Roger Williams, had never seen anything that appalled, dismayed and sickened him as much as the police assault on protesting students on the steps of St George's Cathedral in Cape Town, on Friday 2 June 1972. There was no shooting and no-one was killed. Yet what happened finally removed any doubt that might have remained about the essential nature of the Vorster government ... The sheer savagery of the police operation on that day sent a clear message to South Africa and the world that the Vorster government was ready to use any means to crush dissent in the country. The police assault on university students on the steps of St George's Cathedral was a watershed event of the same order as Sharpeville in 1960, in spite of the fact that there was no loss of life. It marked a new phase of ruthless repression and foreshadowed the nation-wide rebellion of black youth in the mid-1970s and 1980s.'

Dramatic pictures of police, many in plain clothes, smashing their hard-rubber truncheons on the heads of unarmed students, and beating and kicking others, in 'sheer, unprovoked brutality which was carried through from the steps of the Cathedral to the high altar, under the figure of Christ', as Williams reported, horrified the world. Days of confrontation outside the Cathedral followed, with more arrests and police violence against students defying court orders to stop demonstrations. On the night of 6 June several thousand students crammed into the City Hall to hear prominent speakers attack the government's crackdown on the right to protest. One of those speakers was Marius Barnard. He had been warned by the Groote Schuur authorities that if he addressed the meeting he could be sacked. He told the students that the time had come 'for us to do something in spite of the government'. Barnard did not attend the gathering, but said: 'If they sack Marius, I'll close up shop and leave with him.' Nothing more was heard of the threat to fire Marius.

Barnard was soon being linked to the UP, whose spokesman on health, Lionel Murray, had been in charge of the Chris Barnard Research Fund from its start. Barnard even said he was thinking of standing as a UP candidate in the next election. If he was serious about becoming an MP he would have to leave state medicine. Nevertheless, he began casting around for someone to act as his political adviser.

The idea came under attack from an unexpected quarter – Louwtjie. She publicly vowed to 'stand against Chris in whichever constituency he tries to get elected … I'll do it to stop him going into politics. He is a surgeon and he should stick to surgery.' The prospect of the embittered ex-wife competing for votes against the glamour-boy surgeon appealed greatly to the media. The London *Daily Mail*'s South Africa correspondent, Peter Younghusband, noted that Louwtjie was an NP supporter, a niece of the late Eric Louw, a former foreign minister, and on first-name terms with most of the cabinet. 'She is also a woman of considerable intelligence who has a quick and biting tongue.'

Barnard later killed off any hopes of standing for the UP by saying he objected to being told what he could say by party leaders: 'They haven't invented a party for me yet,' he said. It was just as well – the UP was approaching its death throes and would finally dissolve in 1977. Donald Woods, the outspoken editor of the East London *Daily Dispatch*, had said: 'Voting for the UP is like taking a sleeping pill.'

At Groote Schuur Barnard was struggling to find South Africans who would work with him. Hewitson had taken over the thoracic surgery unit – his son John, himself now a cardiac surgeon at the Red Cross Children's Hospital, says his father stopped working with Barnard 'because of their fighting' – and Terry O'Donovan had left to go into private practice. Many of the staff under Barnard came from other countries, and the unit was always short of people. His patients here and at the Red Cross Children's Hospital often came from overseas – Italy and Rumania in particular.

It is generally recognised in the medical profession that a surgeon should not operate on a friend: the emotional ties might blur the judgement. But Barnard ignored this unwritten rule, as he ignored most rules. Martin Franzot, who had become a second father to André, was seriously ill with heart failure. Barnard had performed vein grafts on him and replaced a defective heart valve some years before, but none of this was the problem. Franzot had blocked arteries, leading to perished heart muscle, and doctors in Pretoria believed nothing could be done to save him. André appealed to his father to help. Groote Schuur had a new rule that no-one over 50 could have a heart transplant. Franzot was 53, but Barnard arranged for a bed and prepared to do the transplant once a suitable donor appeared.

The operation on Franzot in August 1972 went well enough until it came to weaning the new heart off the heart-lung machine. André, who had given up ambitions of becoming a veterinary surgeon and was now at UCT Medical School, was waiting outside the theatre. Barnard tried and tried again to get the new heart to take over the circulation. Each time, it failed. After several hours of turning the pump on and off, Barnard was forced to accept that his close friend was not going to make it. He instructed the technicians to switch off the heart-lung machine – it was the first time one of his transplant patients had died on the table – and walked out to face André.

In tears, André demanded to know why his father had taken out a heart which was, at least, keeping Franzot alive. Two years later, the memory of André's response to this bitter failure would combine with the suggestion of a colleague, Wally Beck, to produce another world first for Barnard: the 'piggy-back' heart transplant. Instead of replacing the ailing heart he would leave it in to work alongside the new heart as a backup.

Barnard's public criticisms of the apartheid regime angered many NP hardliners who accused him of being a traitor to the Afrikaner cause. Abusive letters, some containing clear threats to his life, arrived almost daily at Groote Schuur. One evening, after a meal in an Italian restaurant in Sea Point, Barnard and Barbara were returning to their car when they were hit in the road by a van. It was a rainy night and the couple had crossed to the middle of the busy road to wait for a gap in the traffic. Barnard was knocked into Barbara, who was flung upwards and landed on the back of a car going in the other direction. If she had hit the front of the car she might well have died.

Barnard had eight broken ribs, two fractured vertebrae and a collapsed lung. Barbara broke her collar bone, her nose and some neck vertebrae, and she suffered a badly injured left shoulder that would cause her trouble for years to come. She spent a month in hospital. A man described as 'an African' was charged with reckless driving and appeared in court, but he was eventually acquitted for lack of evidence that he had been driving the van that hit the Barnards.

Barnard was convinced it had been an attempt to kill him, and the line certainly made it a more dramatic story for the press. It had happened three days after a well-publicised announcement that Groote Schuur authorities were looking into Barnard's 'political activities' and his decision to join the UP. He had also stirred up considerable animosity among hardliners by coming out publicly against hanging: 'They hang as many people in Pretoria in a year as I save with heart operations, about 150. Most civilised countries have abolished the death penalty. I suppose we have our traditional way of life to thank for retaining it,' he said.

The car involved in the incident had Beaufort West number plates, adding to the paranoia. Barnard had said he would never return to Beaufort West, claiming its residents regarded him as 'a traitor to Afrikanerdom' and because of the conversion of his father's church into a badminton hall. The police, however, said at the time they could find no evidence that it was anything other than an accident caused by a hit-and-run driver. Marius's view, as he no doubt told his brother, was: 'If you stand in the middle of the road at night you may well be hit by a car.' But until his death Barnard remained adamant that someone had tried to kill him that night.

His stay as a patient in Groote Schuur was predictably fraught. At first he insisted on running his own treatment but eventually had to allow Stuart Saunders to take over. As well as goodwill cards from around the world, politically-based hate mail was pouring into the hospital at a rate of 50 letters a day. Marius told reporters: 'Given the circumstances, and the fact that he is reasonably sedated, I find him more pleasant to deal with than at any time in his life before.' Barnard's enforced three-month absence from the operating room did give him the time, though, to think about what would be his first novel, *The Unwanted*.

He was not content to produce medical books alone, knowing

they would never make real money. A bestselling novel, however, might. He began writing a novel, but quickly realised it was beyond him. He needed to work with a successful novelist. His first choice was an award-winning Afrikaans writer, Chris Barnard. Barnard the surgeon thought it would be highly amusing to link up with a writer of the same name. Barnard the writer didn't think so, telling Barnard the surgeon that he did not feel he could write well enough in English. Instead, he recommended Siegfried Stander.

Stander was 37 and had published six novels in South Africa and Britain by the time he met Barnard. He had twice won the prestigious CNA literary award for fiction. He had given up his job as a journalist on the *Cape Argus* to write fiction full-time, partly because he wanted to devote his energies to his novels – but mostly because he had had two heart attacks and had been told he needed to avoid stress. Stander and Barnard got on well – the writer came from a village in the Karoo not far from Beaufort West. They would produce three novels. After each heart attack Stander had been a patient in Groote Schuur but Barnard had had no reason to see him, or be aware of him, since he did not have surgery. In 1988 Stander would die of a heart attack. Remarkably, it appears that at no stage did Stander discuss his condition with Barnard, the world's most famous heart surgeon.

Despite his heart condition Stander was a yachtsman and angler and looked solid and sturdy. He was also fiercely private and stubborn. 'He was in absolute denial about his heart trouble, which ran in the family,' says his widow, Jo Heydenreich. 'He wouldn't go for regular check-ups and he wouldn't talk about it. He carried on enjoying his whisky and smoking. I'm certain that in all the years he worked with Chris they never discussed Siegfried's condition. Siegfried would have been worried that Chris would insist he went in for a bypass operation or even a transplant. Siegfried was terrified of surgery.'

Barnard wanted their first novel to expose the absurdities of the apartheid system. It would feature a white heart surgeon working at a big state hospital, whose half-brother is a coloured genetic specialist. Barnard had been friendly towards the few coloured medical students at UCT in the 1940s. But to get more up-to-date information he now sought out coloured students and doctors who could talk to him about their experiences. 'Siegfried was very excited about the idea because his earlier work had pushed the notion that men are equal whatever their colour,' says Jo. 'He wasn't an activist by any means, but he was a liberal-minded man.' He was also short of cash, and saw the collaboration with Barnard as a sure-fire way to generate income that might balance less commercially successful work.

Stander worked at his simple stone cottage on Lookout Beach in Plettenberg Bay, an Indian Ocean resort beyond Knysna on the Garden Route. Once he and Barnard had worked out the central idea of the novel, Stander devised a more detailed storyline and developed the characters. He would dictate the words onto tape which he then sent to Barnard at his office in Cape Town. There the tapes were transcribed, usually by Dene Friedmann, who was devoted to Barnard and was regularly seen typing away furiously until late into the night. Barbara also helped type the manuscript. Barnard would make notes suggesting changes and additions and send it back to Stander to redraft. Every now and then Stander would fly to Cape Town and spend two days with Barnard, often sitting in on operations to absorb the atmosphere and observe detail. The two men would discuss the progress of the book for hours on end. 'They got on extremely well,' says Jo. 'I don't think they ever had a serious argument.'

Stander later vividly described one visit to watch Barnard operate which established their relationship: 'It was open-heart surgery with all the elaborate and very impressive equipment that goes with it. The operation went perfectly. But then, at a relatively critical stage, the first assistant, busy putting a clamp on to, or taking it off, one of the major blood vessels, allowed the clamp to slip. A great gout of blood spattered over everyone, over the lamps, the heart-lung machine, the anaesthetic machine, surgical trays, everything. Chris absolutely riveted his assistant with one single searing word which I won't even repeat here. Up in my gallery I was probably as shocked – although still not fully aware of what had happened – as any of the others. But then I saw that the bleeding had stopped as dramatically as it had started. Chris had reacted in a split second. Even while pinning his assistant back by the ears it was his hands that found that severed artery and his fingers that closed it off. And then I realised that here I was dealing with a true professional – a great and courageous surgeon perhaps – but above all a professional. I had seen a flash of the famous Barnard temper, but I had also seen a professional in action. The only way to deal with people like that is to be coldly professional yourself. He was in a foul mood when we met in the dressing room afterwards. I gathered my courage and said, "That accident you had, it goes in the book." He glowered at me and said "NO!" I said, "It goes in the book." And then I explained the reasons ... He heard me out and eventually saw it my way.'

Stander's Karoo background – he came from Rietbron, about 100 kilometres from Beaufort West – was an asset. The main character in *The Unwanted,* Dion van der Riet, also comes from Beaufort West and some of the book's themes appear to be autobiographical. Van der Riet is a dashing and successful heart surgeon with a weakness for women who refuses to toe the line. Like Barnard, he always runs up the stairs of the hospital where he works rather than wait for the lifts. A love affair with a young art student, a character no doubt in part based on Ningi, haunts him when she returns to his life. Van der Riet had insisted the girl have an abortion when they were young lovers. (Ningi, of course, says they did not even have sex, and she certainly did not return to haunt Barnard, so the narrative is entirely fictional.)

Stander was to be paid an advance by Barnard of R300 a month for 12 months while he worked on the book, to be paid back from his share of the royalties when it was published. Stander reluctantly agreed to a split in Barnard's favour of 80-20 per cent of the royalties from worldwide sales. He would get a third of any fee for film rights. Stander, naturally, wanted equal billing on the front cover. The South African edition had 'Christiaan Barnard in collaboration with Siegfried Stander' above the title, Barnard's name in larger type. They may have got on well, but Stander would have to fight every inch of the way in the coming years to secure what he felt was a fair deal on royalties and credit for the novels they produced. On foreign editions his name was frequently missing from the front cover, although this may have been down to publishers who knew it was the Barnard name that would sell the book. Stander complained to Barnard that in a television interview about the book he had not even mentioned him.

For their next novel, *In the Night Season*, which would give vent to Barnard's provocative views on euthanasia, Stander would secure a 40 per cent share of royalties, but only after much wrangling. In one letter to Barnard's attorney Noel Tunbridge (a former neighbour from Zeekoevlei) Stander, then being offered 20 per cent again, wrote: 'You must understand one thing: I am not demanding more than my share. I am asking for an equal division, which seems to me eminently reasonable, for the fact is that my contribution towards the creation of the work and therefore to its eventual success will be considerably more than 50 per cent. Chris will undoubtedly contribute a great deal, but I will write the book. It's as simple as that. Frankly the notion of receiving a very minor share of the proceeds of a book based on one of my original ideas and on which I have done most of the work seems to me so unjust as to be almost absurd. *The Unwanted* has brought me no more than a reasonably successful book of my own would have done. If this situation is to be perpetuated there is obviously no advantage in another collaboration. I might as well continue with my own work.'

Similar letters flew back and forth between Plettenberg Bay and Cape Town when it came to the contract for the third novel, *The Faith.* The title is the name of a hospital ship that ventures upriver into guerrilla-infested border country to tackle a deadly virus threatening a black homeland. A hostage drama develops, and the thrust of the message seems to be that ordinary whites, coloureds and blacks trying to live normal lives were being used by political extremists on both sides – in Pretoria and in the bush. In May 1978 Barnard told Stander he wanted to 'bring into our new novel a bit about the destruction of game in the newly developed African countries.' A passage is duly included giving some startling statistics for the number of elephants and zebra being killed by poachers in some countries. The novel's main character, a white male doctor, falls in love with a coloured woman doctor, a relationship then illegal in South Africa under the *Immorality Act*.

The Faith would not be published until 1984, seven years after it was conceived, and the delay seems to have been caused at least partly by the wrangling over joint credit and equal royalties for Stander. Eventually Stander would win a 50 per cent share of royalties (although, as with *In the Night Season,* Barnard would be paid a 10 per cent commission for his promotional work) and his name would appear on the cover under Barnard's. 'What it boils down to really is a question of identity,' Stander had written to Barnard in April 1977. 'I feel that my part in what is after all a joint project is again in danger of being relegated to insignificance. It's an undeniable fact that the book will be based on a theme and plot that were my conceptions. During the coming months I will be faced with the hard slog of creating a living, breathing world from nothing but what is in my mind. I don't want to start with a feeling of resentment at being forced to sit below the salt at my own table.'

Unfortunately for Stander, although he doggedly succeeded in raising his share of royalties from the second and third novels, it was the first, *The Unwanted*, that proved far and away the most successful. It topped the bestseller list in France for three weeks, with its first edition of 25 000 copies selling out almost immediately. In Britain it reached number three in the bestseller list. An American publisher paid a $40 000 advance for the book. In 1987, some thirteen years after the novel's first publication in South Africa, Stander received a cheque for nearly R2 000 as his 20 per cent share of a rights sale to the Soviet Union and Latvia. The later novels got nowhere near this level of success although they were both praised for the quality of Stander's writing and the content.

But in the early days of the partnership there were high hopes of seriously big money and lucrative film deals which did not materialise. In another letter in early 1977, Stander asks Barnard if he had 'got any further with the question of us establishing a company in Liechtenstein or Switzerland? I think it's essential, if we don't want to pay our arses off in tax.' There is no record of Barnard's response, or further clue as to whether any such company was set up. Both men already had Swiss bank accounts.

Despite Stander's deep and continuous rancour over royalties and billing he enjoyed working with Barnard, and Barnard often commented in letters to Stander that he was looking forward to teaming up with him again 'as routine cardiac surgery has become so dreary'. Stander never made the money he dreamed of from the collaboration – he was constantly complaining of having to 'live on the generosity of my bank manager'. But one memorable day he returned from a trip to Cape Town carrying a bag stuffed with R5 000 in notes. 'Chris had paid him his royalties in cash for some reason,' says Jo. 'Siegfried went out and bought a Jeep, which my son still has. We call it the "family heirloom."'

Barnard and Barbara sometimes flew down to Plettenberg Bay to stay at the Beacon Isle Hotel, which stands on the beach. Jo recalls, 'While we had dinner Barbara and I used to sit and listen to Chris and Siegfried discussing their books. But I remember quite vividly one function we all went to in the hotel. There was a woman there who was disabled in some way. She had a lame foot and no-one was asking her to dance. She obviously wanted to be part of things and she looked miserable. Chris saw how she was feeling, went up to her and invited her out for a few dances, and she lit up. It made her evening. He was capable of doing wonderful things like that.'

It was Barbara, over dinner at the Beacon Isle Hotel one evening, who came up with the title *The Unwanted.* It was meant to describe society's attitude to coloureds and blacks, sick children and old people: all depicted in the book as outcasts. (In France, Barnard's publisher Pierre Belfond refused to use the title, saying it was too downbeat to attract buyers. There it was called *Men Never Die.* In view of its huge success there Belfond was clearly right.)

As an indictment of apartheid – Barnard had let it be known he was working on a novel that would cause a stir – *The Unwanted* is fairly tame. It highlights the ridiculous rules of segregation in hospitals, restaurants, living areas and so on. It calls for an acceptance of 'shared humanity' regardless of race, and in the story of two half-brothers of different colour there is a running condemnation of racism. It is finely written and full of fascinating medical detail and drama. But it confines itself to the question of whites and coloureds not living as equals; it doesn't touch on the plight of black people, then officially known as Bantus, in a white-run South Africa. *The Unwanted* certainly doesn't urge revolutionary political change. When it was published in South Africa in 1974, by Tafelberg, in English and Afrikaans, its racial theme was conveniently ignored by some reviewers. It was a mark of the distorted climate of the time that a lengthy review in the *Pretoria News*, which described it as 'an absorbing novel', failed to even mention what the dust-jacket blurb trumpets as the hero's fight against 'prejudice and blind mores'.

Reviews abroad were mixed, but Graham Lord of the London

Sunday Express praised it as 'an absolutely convincing portrayal of what it must be like to be a doctor in South Africa today, where only too often medicine and common humanity are challenged by the sad idiocies of apartheid'. Lord's review was so positive that it was published in some South African newspapers.

Although Stander wrote the words, Barnard was clearly the source of the novel's insights into the surgeon's mind. Barnard was often described by friends and enemies alike as a 'child' by nature, or a '*naturkind*', as Mark Horwitz put it, and it was a description that seemed to appeal to him. In the final pages of *The Unwanted,* Van der Riet reflects: 'Perhaps I, too, have always been an essentially simple man. My ambitions and strivings have never been particularly complex. I haven't thought very far or about any particularly troubling subjects. Perhaps I am guilty of that. Guilty of innocence.' But as Stander and others found, Barnard's apparent simplicity masked a complex and creative mind. 'Chris was very good at dramatising stories about himself,' says Jo.

In the Night Season is a far better novel than *The Unwanted,* and was partly based on a true story Stander had been aware of as a journalist in Port Elizabeth: a woman dying of cancer sues her doctor for not telling her she was terminally ill. The case against Charles de la Porte is eventually dropped, and the woman's husband asks him to end her agony by switching off her ventilator. Barnard had resisted the views of some publishers that a novel about euthanasia and a woman dying of cancer would not appeal. The book condemns the determination of modern medicine to sustain life at all costs. As De la Porte says, 'Medicine has managed to rephrase the old adage that where there's life there's hope. Often there is life without hope.'

Stander's death was reported in South African newspapers. Yet, despite their long and fruitful working partnership, Barnard did not so much as send a card of condolence to Jo. 'Siegfried died a poor man,' she says. 'His career never really went anywhere after Barnard. He really believed at the start that they would make a lot of money. But, in hindsight, collaborating was the biggest mistake he could have made.'

Barbara had given birth, by elective Caesarian, to another healthy baby boy on 18 January 1974, named Christiaan Alexander. After what had been allowed to happen to his father's mission church in Beaufort West – it had been gutted, its pulpit smashed, and at one stage it had been turned into a sports hall – Barnard had no qualms about deserting the DRC. He had been taught by his father to believe that Catholicism, the 'Roman danger', was almost Satanic. Barbara had been brought up a Catholic but her lonely childhood and her parents' volatile and unconventional marriage had soured her view of the faith. The Catholic church where she had expected Frederick to be christened refused because Barnard was divorced. So Frederick was baptised an Anglican. When the time came for Christiaan to be baptised the Anglican church told Barbara she would have to convert. They turned instead to a Roman Catholic priest, Father Tom Nicholson, who was a friend of Barnard's, through Dene Friedmann's family; he agreed to baptise Christiaan. Frederick would also soon become a Catholic.

Barnard was growing increasingly bored with what he called 'routine heart surgery'. South Africa was one of only four countries where heart transplants were still being carried out. Norman Shumway continued to perform them at Stanford. But Britain and most other cardiac centres in America had imposed a moratorium until more was known about rejection. Barnard's great achievement of 1967 had started a stampede, but now there seemed little left but dust. He wanted a new challenge, and the case of a 47-year-old man with severe heart failure was to trigger one.

The right side of Leonard Goss's heart, which pumped blood from the ventricle to the lungs to pick up oxygen, and received 'used' or de-oxygenated blood back from the body into its atrium, was working perfectly well. But the left ventricle which pumped the oxygenated blood round the body was badly diseased. It was Wally Beck, who had taken over from Schrire, who suggested to Barnard that it might be possible to leave much of the patient's own heart in place while transplanting a new heart to aid circulation. Surgeons in other countries had tried just such a technique with animals years earlier. Barnard would later claim in *The Second Life* that he had thought of the idea immediately after the Franzot failure because of André's emotional response, which may well have been the case. But in an interview he gave to Siegfried Stander in 1975 intended for foreign syndication, he admitted that 'time passes and one forgets' and that it was not until Beck made his suggestion that he began to seriously conceive a way of carrying out what would come to be known as the heterotopic or 'piggy-back' heart transplant. Beck says, 'Barnard was very bad at giving credit to other people. It was me who suggested he try the 'piggy-back' transplant when we were having tea one day. I suggested transplanting a whole heart to help the working half of the patient's own heart. In medical papers it's written, but in his own accounts he gave me no credit at all.'

Much of the laboratory work for this new operation was done by a young Belgian surgeon, Jacques Losman. He and Barnard used baboons to find the best method of placing the new heart in the chest cavity alongside the old one. It still seems an incredible concept, but it worked. In fact, Goss would become the second patient to undergo this new operation. Another man, Ivan Taylor, who was 58, was put forward as a more urgent case and, once it had been explained to him, accepted Barnard's plan to make him the first person in the world to have two hearts. He was even rather relieved that his own heart would not be removed. Barnard told him to think of a horse pulling a load up a hill and growing tired; either you replace the horse with a fresh one which then has to take on the entire load, or you hitch a new horse up and leave the old one there to help pull some of the burden.

The operation on Taylor in November 1974 was given worldwide publicity. Barnard was again seen as a daring surgical pioneer. The medical world was not so convinced, and the apparent success of Taylor's operation (he would survive 19 weeks) and then of the one on Goss a month later did nothing to lift doubts about dealing with rejection. Barnard, however, would never again do a single, or orthotopic, heart transplant. In 1977 he would arouse fierce controversy again by using first a baboon's heart, and then a chimpanzee's heart, in two 'piggy-back' operations after patients could not be weaned off the heart-lung machine following heart surgery. The first patient, a woman, died within hours and the second, a man, died after four days. Barnard, infuriated by the outcry, mainly from animal welfare groups, said he would never again use animal hearts in humans.

Soon after Christiaan's birth Barnard and Barbara had moved from their Clifton flat to a ranch-style mansion in Constantia, Cape Town's most expensive suburb. Barnard could not have hoped to have afforded such a place – it was bought for them by the

Zoellners. Shortly before they moved in there was a gruesome double murder nearby and Barnard was so nervous of sleeping in the house, surrounded as it was by a large, leafy garden, that he hired a security guard to patrol the grounds at night.

Barbara was a notoriously shy person. Yet she often posed for fashion shoots for magazines. One, *Fair Lady*, developed a special relationship with her. Barbara would be photographed at home modelling a designer's new creation and sometimes give interviews. By arrangement with the magazine's editor, Jane Raphaely, Barbara had a right of veto over anything in the article. The pictures were often syndicated abroad and Barbara's fame as a model spread. Patrick Lichfield, the society photographer, described her as one of the ten most beautiful women in the world.

Several maids kept the house clean, and they also employed a full-time gardener, a standard lifestyle for Constantia's wealthy whites in apartheid South Africa, as it is now. From the back lawn the view swept down to False Bay and beyond to the blue Hottentots Holland mountains. In front of the house the pine-covered slopes of the back of Table Mountain formed the view. There was a kidney-shaped swimming pool. Barnard began collecting exotic birds and had an aviary built to house them. Many of the letters his secretaries typed at Groote Schuur at this time concerned his efforts to import one multi-coloured bird or another from South America.

They had thought about building a luxurious new house overlooking the sea at Clifton but had decided against it because of the cost. Estate agents had then trailed them round one unsuitable property after another. 'I wished people would realise that what we really wanted was a family home. I'm sick of houses that look like Hollywood sets,' said Barbara. 'This house has more privacy than any other house we've seen.'

Barnard quickly settled into the lifestyle that went with such a house. He built up a cellar of vintage wines. Roger Williams, the chief reporter of the *Cape Times*, recalls a conciliatory phone call from Barnard the day after they had had one of many doorstep rows: 'He congratulated me on the picture we had run that morning of Barbara with a portrait of her commissioned by her father, which is why we had gone to the house the day before. Then he said it had been a pity we left so soon because he had wanted to show us round the house. In particular, he said, he wanted to show me his wine cellar, in which he now had "well over a thousand" bottles of the best wines, from South Africa and from prestigious wineries abroad. He sounded very proud of his cellar, the contents of which he had labelled and recorded.' This turnaround in Barnard was typical of the way he swung back and forth with the press depending on his mood. 'One day he would heatedly tell me he would never again speak to the press and the next day he'd phone to tell me something that had cropped up which might interest me,' says Williams.

The Zoellners made sure the house was expensively and tastefully furnished. Barnard told friends it upset him that his Groote Schuur salary was 'barely enough to pay for the maids and the gardener'. The only way he could hope to earn good money was through his books and his lecture tours – sometimes he was invited to lecture on cruises – although he was still insisting he 'never charged a fee' for these.

He had by now adopted another poem which he read out to adoring lay audiences, called *It's All in the State of the Mind:*

If you think you are beaten, you are;
If you think you dare not, you don't.
If you'd like to win, but think you can't
It's almost a cinch you won't.
If you think you'll lose, you've lost
For out in the world you'll find
Success begins with a fellow's will
It's all in the state of the mind.
For many a race is lost
Ere even a race is run
And many a coward fails
Ere ever his work's begun.
Think big and your deeds will grow
Think small and you'll fall behind
Think that you can and you will
It's all in the state of the mind.
If you think you're outclassed you are
You've got to think hard to rise
You've got to be sure of yourself

Before you can win a prize.
Life's battles don't always go
To the stronger or faster man,
But sooner or later the man who wins
Is the fellow who thinks he can.

Barnard felt the poem, by Walter D Wintle, neatly summed up what lay behind his success: an extraordinary determination and will which had driven him since a boy.

Another of his favourite 'party pieces' on lecture tours, which he used until he died, was his infamous chauffeur story. Most of his social occasion speeches were based on little more than a few scribbled notes. He was a skilled raconteur. The chauffeur story was utterly implausible but was guaranteed to break the ice. In the early days after the first heart transplant, so the story went, he had needed a chauffeur to drive him to engagements so that he could rest in the back of the car. His chauffeur, named Van der Merwe (a common all-purpose surname in South African jokes), always sat in on his lectures. Arriving one evening in a small town Barnard is so exhausted that he asks the chauffeur to take the lecture (the town is so remote that they rarely see newspapers, a dig at Afrikaner insularity). Barnard finds the chauffeur's lecture so interesting that instead of sleeping at the back of the hall he sits and listens. Everything goes well until the question-and-answer session. At that point a famous heart surgeon, Michael DeBakey, stands up, introduces himself and asks a difficult question. Barnard freezes, sure that the game is up. The chauffeur pauses, gazes down at his papers, and then looks up. 'Professor DeBakey, I'm very surprised that a heart surgeon as intelligent as you should ask such a stupid question. And to prove how stupid it is, I'm going to ask my chauffeur at the back of the hall to answer it for me.'

He also liked to joke about the wealthy white American who, he claimed, had begged him not to give him a black heart. Gordon Hersman was a young registrar at Groote Schuur for four years in the 1970s. He recalls Barnard bawling out down the corridors of the cardiac clinic, in his best southern US drawl: 'I don't want no black heart!' regardless of who was around. Hersman says three consultants quit in one day after deciding they had had enough of

Barnard's rudeness and foul-mouthed tantrums. His obsession with his own sexual prowess could be embarrassing: 'A group of overseas visitors had joined us on a ward visit,' recalls Hersman. 'When we reached the female ward, Barnard saw one of his patients reading a magazine that had his second wife, Barbara, on the cover. He grabbed it and held up a full-page photograph of a famous model, showing off the latest in brassieres. "See that," he announced, to everyone's intense embarrassment. "I've screwed her several times."'

Barnard's compulsive travelling inevitably, again, took its toll on the marriage. Barbara often went with him but much preferred to stay at home with her two young sons. When she was at home she worried about what her husband was up to, with good reason. She insisted that before each trip a detailed itinerary was drawn up so that she knew precisely where he was supposed to be at any one time. His trips often took in several countries. In the latter years of their marriage especially, her anxiety about his behaviour away from home, coupled with the cruel pressure he put her under to stay slim, left her tortured by jealousy and insecurity. She developed anorexia, and Barnard was less than sympathetic. 'Chris liked thin women, but then he had the nerve to moan to me that Barbara had become too thin for his tastes,' says one friend. Pierre Belfond, his French publisher, says, 'When Chris and Barbara came to France to promote his books and we went out to dinner he would never allow her to eat anything other than salad.' One of Barbara's closest friends, Bertha Ludolphi, her business partner in a successful fashion boutique, recalls, 'After having children Barbara put on a little bit of weight and Chris told her she was fat. She was this tall, elegant, beautiful creature, with long, slender fingers and long legs, and he would keep telling her she was fat. When I first met her she was anorexic.' Tony Ingala, who was and still is Bertha's boyfriend, and who became Barnard's restaurant business partner, says, 'At times when Barbara lost weight she was just a bag of bones and Chris didn't like that either. He would tell her to her face she was too skinny for him.'

André, now qualified and pursuing post-graduate work as a paediatrician, was living in England with his wife Gail, a British nurse he had met at the Red Cross Children's Hospital in Cape Town. Citing other commitments Barnard had not gone to the wedding, in February 1978, nor sent a present, giving Louwtjie a perfect opportunity to vent her anger once more: 'He didn't give André a cent,' she told a newspaper. 'He merely sent a telegram of congratulations, from "Chris, Barbara, Frederick and Christiaan." I later noticed that André had scratched out the name "Chris" and written in "Dad" instead. He looked sad and heartbroken. I burst into tears. Where there's no publicity involved Chris has no interest.' Barnard later wrote to André saying he had arranged for £200 to be sent to him as a wedding gift. Of Barbara, who had thrown a lavish engagement party for André and Gail at the Constantia house a few months earlier, he wrote: 'Unfortunately Barbara has not gained any weight yet although she is really trying very hard. I do not quite know what is wrong with her nor can the doctors find out the cause of this colossal weight loss.' Only years later would he admit, in private, that his behaviour was the likely trigger for Barbara's eating disorder.

Despite her health problems, Barbara strove hard to make their home an attractive place to be for her husband. She learned to cook well and became an accomplished dinner-party hostess. She would bath and change into something stylish for the evening before Barnard returned home. She never drank before six pm. Then out would come a tray of wine, Grappa, aperitifs, and she would light up her first cigarette of the day. She drank to help her sleep, according to friends. The unpredictable demands on Barnard as a surgeon meant he could not guarantee being home at a set time each evening. He believed she failed to understand this, causing friction. Regardless, he was addicted to travelling. 'He needed the attention he got abroad,' says Ingala.

Barnard was away in 1975 when his older brother Dodsley was killed in a car crash. He did not go to the funeral. They had not spoken for several years, according to Dodsley's wife Kay. Two years later Barnard lost his mother Maria, aged 92, who had suffered several strokes. Barnard, who had visited her rarely, said he and Marius, seeing the helpless distress their crippled mother was in, had asked doctors to let her die. He also let it be known that he and his brother had a 'death pact'; if the circumstances arose each would make sure the other was allowed to die with dignity rather than be kept alive artificially. Both brothers believed in euthanasia.

In between these two family deaths came the suicide, from a

barbiturates overdose, of Bertie Bosman. 'Bossie' had played a vital role in the intensive aftercare of heart transplant patients, becoming emotionally entangled with people sometimes psychotic from anti-rejection drugs. As a surgeon he also carried out some kidney transplants. From the start, with Edward Darvall, he had been given the harrowing task of asking traumatised relatives for permission to use organs for transplant. He was sensitive and conscientious to a fault. When he was admitted to Groote Schuur in a coma, from which he would not surface, Barnard paid numerous visits to his bedside. Some of Barnard's colleagues blamed his 'slave-driving' for Bosman's death. At one stage Bosman's wife Annette complained to Jannie Louw that the treatment of her husband was 'inhumane'. But when he died she wrote to Barnard, saying the years her husband had worked with him 'may have been stressful but they were possibly the happiest and most stimulating years of his entire medical career.' At his death Bosman was 46 and a father of four sons. Annette says now, 'I don't blame Chris for Bertie's death, although everyone did at the time. Chris was a hard taskmaster and being away a lot placed a heavy burden on others. But Bertie was a strong man and he loved his work. If he hadn't have wanted to do it he wouldn't have. He found it hard to turn his back and walk away from a patient.'

A vain man, Barnard, now well into his fifties, and married to a girl nearly thirty years younger, grew ever more fearful of ageing. 'Getting old is one of life's greatest tragedies,' he said once. He told friends he occasionally had face-lifts, although he always publicly denied he had. Soon after meeting Barbara, and feeling self-conscious about sitting with her on the beach, he had tried to persuade a plastic surgeon friend in Cape Town to correct what he felt were his unsightly, deformed toes – caused, he claimed, by wearing hand-me-down shoes that were too tight as a boy. The plastic surgeon told him it was not worth doing. Barnard openly believed that cosmetic surgery was a good thing: 'A person who is deeply unhappy with some aspect of their bodies can suffer more than a person with a hole in the heart because they know others can see the problem,' he would argue oddly. Barnard had become a friend of Ivo Pitanguy, the world's most famous plastic surgeon, who counted a number of Hollywood stars among his clients. Barnard was often seen at his clinic in Rio de Janeiro and at his home in Switzerland. Pitanguy also visited South Africa. He will not confirm that Barnard was a client, but says, 'We became very good friends. I admired him and he liked my work.'

Barnard would certainly recommend Pitanguy to some of the wealthy people he mixed with. Sources close to Pitanguy believe the two had the kind of deal Barnard sought wherever possible: he secured services, accommodation, flights, meals in exchange for what he believed was his value as a public relations asset. Throughout the 1970s and 1980s he took parties of foreign surgeons and dignitaries to hunt springbok at the farm of his friend George van Wyk near Beaufort West. Barnard and his groups never paid. He saw it as a public relations boon for which Van Wyk should be grateful. It was a side to Barnard that irritated friends. 'He believed the world owed him,' says Van Wyk. Like others, Van Wyk says he was always led to believe he would get what was due to him in Barnard's will.

Barnard's first known attack of the disease that had dogged his father and that would eventually claim his own life – asthma – came at the end of 1976. During a strenuous lecture tour of Switzerland and Germany he had to cancel some engagements and call in a doctor. Shortness of breath left him hardly able to walk at one stage. One attack was so severe he thought his 'end had come'. When he returned to South Africa he needed a fortnight off work.

His arthritis flared up painfully on occasion, and he spoke of being forced to give up surgery. (As a six-year-old Frederick was so concerned about his father's health that when his teacher asked the class to nominate subjects for prayer, he stood up and said he wanted to pray for his 'Daddy's hands'.) Bored with routine surgery, and frustrated by the time it took to earn money from books, Barnard looked for other outlets. He was developing a cattle farm near Knysna (on land he had bought cheaply from a friend) and would soon branch out into the restaurant business.

Professionally he had achieved everything he had set out to do. But his star was tainted. His uncompromising personality left no-one confused: they either adored or despised him. The medical establishment, especially in his own country, remained wary of him. A surgeon wasn't supposed to be a playboy, entertain audiences, take part in political debates on television, 'write' novels.

His more staid peers, particularly in America, were often mean-spirited towards him. In October 1975 some 500 of the world's leading heart surgeons and cardiologists had gathered in Detroit for what was billed as the most prestigious symposium on cardiac surgery in 20 years. Two of the biggest names were missing – Barnard and one of his great mentors from Minneapolis, Walt Lillehei. Lillehei was in disgrace after being convicted of tax evasion. Barnard was snubbed out of spite: the organising committee still believed he had plagiarised the work of Shumway and Lower.

11

Info

In 1978 South Africa was hit by a political earthquake that would have serious consequences for Barnard. A flamboyant character by the name of Eschel Rhoodie, head of the recently disbanded Department of Information, had been accused of using public funds to set up a newspaper, *The Citizen,* as part of a government-bankrolled secret international propaganda war. The prime minister, John Vorster, had resigned 'for health reasons' and his place had been taken by the 'Great Crocodile', PW Botha. Connie Mulder, the information and interior minister, in a lie that would bring about his downfall, had initially denied the allegations. Up to this point there had been no official confirmation of the extent of what would soon become known as the Information scandal. Now a judge, Anton Mostert, who had been appointed by the government to investigate 'financial irregularities' in Rhoodie's department, blew the whole affair wide open: he called a press conference to reveal evidence he had heard from leading figures in the clandestine operation.

Despite Botha's efforts to stop publication of the details the next day's newspapers screamed: 'It's all true'. Some R12 million of public money had been used to set up *The Citizen* to present a pro-government line at a time when South Africa was facing mounting isolation and world criticism over apartheid. Mulder, who before this had been expected to succeed Vorster, resigned from the cabinet in disgrace. Vorster himself would later have to step down as state president when his own role was confirmed.

But there was more. Many more millions of rands had been channelled illegally through the budgets of several other departments, especially Defence, to provide Rhoodie with an enormous slush fund. What was to emerge in the coming months was truly staggering: for years Rhoodie had been running a massive network of front companies which had stakes in businesses across the world ranging from newspapers to television companies to publishing houses. In America efforts had been made to buy a major newspaper, the *Washington Star*. In Britain Rhoodie had tried to acquire the publishers Morgan Grampian through two South African businessmen, who managed to buy a large number of shares; but their moves to gain a controlling interest were thwarted.

The 'Info' fund, amounting to some R64 million and hidden in secret Swiss bank accounts, had financed an extraordinary lifestyle for Rhoodie and all who worked closely with him. Private jets, the best hotels, the most beautiful women were available to buy the loyalty of anyone thought to be an asset in Pretoria's war against what was called the 'psychological and propaganda onslaughts' being targeted at South Africa by the rest of the world – all, it turned out, with the knowledge and approval of Vorster, Mulder and other senior cabinet figures, and the sinister help of the head of the Bureau of State Security, General Hendrik van den Bergh. Indeed, Mulder and Rhoodie were using the clandestine propaganda machine to bolster Mulder's international image ahead of his expected takeover from Vorster, whose health was failing. The scandal and the attempted cover-up was South Africa's Watergate – and was, inevitably, dubbed 'Muldergate'.

The downfall of Rhoodie and Mulder would spell the end of Barnard's political ambitions, although his role as roving ambassador and informant in the pay of Rhoodie would not be revealed until many months later. Key details of their relationship have not emerged until now.

*

In *The Second Life*, published in 1993, Barnard wrote of his involvement with the Information scandal: 'During the previous year the Department of Information had asked me to appear on television shows and make contact with politicians and ambassadors in various parts of the world. I never asked to be paid for this work – but they covered my expenses. These payments were also made in a very unusual way. I was never asked to submit an expense account or give statements and receipts. Eschel would just give me, every now and then, an envelope with cash – which I signed for. I asked him several times whether I had to declare this income, but he was non-committal. This worried me to such an extent that I even went to see Owen Horwood, who was minister of finance at the time. He was also not sure how to handle the matter and told me they hadn't decided about it yet. I'm eternally grateful to my accountant, Mr Lotter, as he insisted I declare the money on my income tax return. When the Information Scandal rocked the South African government later, I had nothing to hide – I'd made it known to the receiver of revenue that I'd received expenses from the government and, while I thought the method of payment odd, it had all been above board as far as I was concerned.'

Rhoodie, a suave, shrewd and sophisticated man some eleven years younger than Barnard, must have been astonished by the world-travelled heart surgeon's apparent naivety. Few people offered envelopes stuffed with cash would ask if they should declare it on their income tax form. They may agonise over the ethical dilemma, but they would hardly raise the question with the person handing over the money. But then the 'naivety' of the 'poor country boy' was precisely the facade that Barnard liked to present.

He did write to the secretary for inland revenue, Mr HN van der Walt, but not until nearly a year after Mulder's resignation, and then, as he told him, because 'there has been a lot of discussion in the press about my association with the South African Government and the fact that I have received monies from the South African Government to cover some of my expenses'. He felt it was now necessary 'to give you some breakdown of the monies received and the monies spent'. Then he lists all his expenses and income from 17 September 1976 until the day after Mulder's resignation, 8 November 1978.

This period began, went the letter, 'more or less from the time that I became involved in this project after my discussion with the then Prime Minister, Mr Vorster. The monies received are from overseas sources, from the Provincial Administration and from the South African Government. The payments made are for overseas and local travels, paying for guests invited to South Africa and for certain television programmes.' He adds, 'I have made a rough estimate of my out of pocket expenses for tips, taxis, hotels, etc which I paid from honorariums given to me by various hosts.'

Barnard declares three payments 'for travel expenses' from the 'SA Government' in this period: one of R12 000, one of R10 000 and another of R5 270. A documentary he made for French television to counteract anti-South African media coverage had cost him a total of R12 000 in 1977.

In an official statement the government said that records left behind by Rhoodie had shown that Barnard had received 'around R20 000'.

Yet this letter from Barnard had landed on Rhoodie's desk in Pretoria in March 1978, several months before the Information bubble was to burst:

Dear Eschel
I have made arrangements to obtain an American Express credit card and I have also filled in Form A to obtain foreign exchange facilities. I wonder whether the sum of 30 000 American dollars would be in order.

Again, a man like Rhoodie, who preferred shadowy deals with cash-filled envelopes, and as little trace left behind as possible, must have been taken aback by such a blatant letter. There is no record of his response – it would almost certainly have been made in a telephone call – but the sum mentioned by Barnard was small compared to the vast amounts being wired across the world almost daily by Rhoodie at that stage. Whether Barnard was asking for this money as a one-off payment for a special job, or whether it was to 'cover travel expenses' for a series of missions, is unclear. Long before this he had set up an account at the Union Bank of Switzerland in Zurich – out of reach of the South African tax authorities – which was the same bank that held the government's secret Information funds. In October 1977 he submitted expenses totalling $9 823,42 to a French television channel for the documentary *The Open Heart of South Africa* and instructed them to pay the amount into this account. There is no mention in the letter to Van der Walt nearly two years later of these expenses being reimbursed.

It is unlikely that Barnard would have been able or willing to draw out such a large sum from his South African bank account to cover the running costs of making the documentary. Rhoodie, who would later tell a court that he kept up to R60 000 in cash in a safe at home to fund ad hoc payments, almost certainly provided the day-to-day funds for what was an extremely high-profile project involving interviews with the likes of Jimmy Kruger, Breyten Breytenbach and Helen Suzman. This is all the more likely in view of evidence given by Rhoodie in camera to the Erasmus Commission – set up to investigate the Information scandal after Mr Justice Mostert was removed for his dramatic stand – on 17 November 1978.

Rhoodie, who had been 'retired' from his civil servant's job when the Department of Information was closed down in June of that year, told the commission that Barnard's services were 'worth around R100 000 a year' to the Department. 'In the case of Professor Barnard we sit with a man who has entree to the rulers of the world like no other person. I don't mean rulers of the Western world only, but the East and the Middle East and elsewhere. It's easy for him to get access to certain oil potentates. Such a man, who has an enormous reputation in the world, for him to stick out his neck ... I think he really gave a lot from his side and if I take everything into consideration, then I say to myself that I must at least pay Chris Barnard's expenses. Consider what he is paid for a big operation that he takes part in – R3 000, R4 000 – then you easily get to a figure of R10 000 a year he gets as an honorarium.'

Rhoodie explained that with certain prominent people like Barnard the payments had to match their lifestyle. 'He told me that he had enormous expenses with his travels, board and lodging, people he saw and entertained and if I could help him in that respect ... In his case we decided on a more clear-cut arrangement, namely that he would provide his services and that we would cover his basic expenses plus an honorarium.'

Rhoodie's evidence was not made public until the thousands of pages of transcripts of the Erasmus Commission hearings were made available 18 months later – and, of course, there was never any mention of the American Express card and the $30 000, nor Barnard's Swiss bank account.

The first details of Barnard's close friendship with the mastermind behind the Information scandal did not emerge until March 1979, when Barnard said in a newspaper interview that he knew him 'extremely well'. Rhoodie had been reported as saying that

Barnard had worked hard to improve South Africa's image abroad, but he had gone no further. Barnard, however, described Rhoodie as 'a genius'. 'He and I are much the same,' said Barnard. 'We're impulsive, want immediate action – want something done yesterday. And I think that's where we both made mistakes. Maybe the whole machinery of government doesn't work that fast.' Still there was no evidence to link Barnard with the slush fund.

In August of that year, while Rhoodie was awaiting extradition in France to face charges of stealing public money in South Africa, Barnard went out on a limb again to speak up for the man he called 'my friend'. Little did he know that Rhoodie was about to reveal something of the scope of his work for the Department of Information in a foreign magazine interview. On 6 August, in the weekly column that he was now writing for the *Rand Daily Mail*, Barnard took a typically bullish stand: 'He laughed a lot. He worked hard. He played hard. He was my friend. Today he is being pilloried for the first three attributes. I have no doubt that when I mention his name there will be many who would put me in the dock for the fourth.' Nothing less than a witch-hunt was under way, and Rhoodie was a scapegoat, he wrote.

'I knew Eschel Rhoodie socially, at first only a nodding acquaintanceship. To me he was a senior civil servant appointed to serve a government whose policies I had opposed since the day it first came to power more than thirty years ago. We were both Afrikaners from a similar background and era, yet his policies were poles apart from mine … We saw each other seldom, mainly when our paths crossed socially. When we did, we agreed on one single political reality – the need for stable government in southern Africa to be able to tackle the problems of the region. Where we differed was in the composition and direction of that government … We both knew that our country was at war … I fought my war by telling the truth where it hurt most – in public, to the offender's face … What he was doing to fight his war later became public knowledge, but in such a smeared and twisted fashion that the doing of it was downgraded to some cheap cloak-and-dagger routine … I too believed that for the truth to triumph it was only necessary to tell the truth. Today I am not so sure that I am right … Eschel always said there were two ways to fight a war –

with money or blood. If you didn't like losing money, do you think you'll be more amenable to giving blood?'

It was a declaration of loyalty that no-one had asked for, least of all Rhoodie, sitting in a French jail cell. Barnard had already said he would go to France to speak for Rhoodie, although what he could have said to prevent his extradition is hard to imagine. But what was Barnard thinking when he decided to write this column? He must have realised that sooner or later details would start to come out about his work for the Department of Information, yet here he was drawing more attention to his friendship with Rhoodie. The only explanation is that he believed such a public statement of support might persuade Rhoodie and anyone else in the Department who knew of his involvement to keep quiet about it out of a sense of mutual loyalty.

He knew any suggestion that he had been travelling the world partly on behalf of the apartheid regime would seriously damage his reputation. The day before the article appeared, Barnard had claimed that the editors of the various newspapers that syndicated his column had refused to publish it. On the contrary, said Allister Sparks, editor of the *Rand Daily Mail* which had been engaged in a lengthy investigation into Muldergate, it would appear 'tomorrow'.

There had been a delay, but the real reason was that the journalist who ghost-wrote the columns for Barnard, Bob Molloy, had grave misgivings about the wisdom of such a piece. He wanted a more thorough discussion with Barnard. Molloy, a writer on the *Cape Times* and a graduate in clinical psychology, had been collaborating on these columns with Barnard since the early part of 1978. He thought he had come to know Barnard well, but the 'Rhoodie column' was to be a shock for him. He recalls: 'This was a very formative moment in my relationship with Barnard. Until then I had been more or less doing a job, earning a dollar and keeping my views to myself … I held no brief for Rhoodie, who was one of that first generation of Afrikaner beneficiaries of the apartheid regime living high on the hog and loving it. My concern was for my meal-ticket, who wanted to go off on a major rant about his friend regardless of the political ramifications. The first draft of the column was an appalling piece of self-servery and special pleading. I gave up on it and substituted it for some other topic that week.

'We then spent much of the following Sunday debating the issue at his Constantia home, while Barbara tried to keep the peace with offerings of good Cape white and platters of edibles. My position was that I didn't want him blundering into some untenable position in which he supported a man who might ultimately become a convicted criminal. It was to be an eye-opener for me in that Barnard stuck to his guns. His bottom line was that he wished to publicly state his support for his friend, despite the fact that anyone who had the slightest connection with the affair – and that included members of the cabinet and the prime minister – was keeping his head down. I pumped him for any special knowledge he might have had of Rhoodie's shenanigans but he had no inkling of the real issues at stake. His stance was simply that Eschel must be feeling damn lonely and exposed and needed somebody to pipe up for him. In the end I was forced to agree that support of a friend come hell or high water was a laudable position to take.

'I came away from the Barnard home that day feeling I had a better grasp of the man. He had become less of a cardboard cut-out from the Karoo who mouthed farm-boy platitudes and was turning out to be a very complex character. Indeed in the years to come I was reminded time and time again that I was dealing with a many-layered personality.'

Molloy put it to Barnard during this heated discussion that he had 'pushed the government view on occasion at Rhoodie's request'. Barnard, however, denied this and challenged him to give examples. All he would admit to Molloy was attending some of Rhoodie's foreign press parties but, realising he was being used as an example of a success under apartheid, he had confronted Rhoodie and refused to go to more functions.

Molloy did succeed in persuading Barnard to include an outline of the allegations against Rhoodie in the column, and a paragraph stating that if these were true they should be tested in open court. If found guilty, Rhoodie should be punished according to the law. But Barnard added: 'Whatever the outcome I shall always remember that he is my friend – present tense.'

If Barnard's real hope was that by such a remarkable display of loyalty he might save his own skin, he was very much mistaken. Just a day after this column appeared the international wire services began running details of an interview Rhoodie had already given a Dutch magazine, *Elseviers,* presumably before Barnard's column was published. Rhoodie revealed more shattering evidence of the enormity of what had gone on during the Information years, including a little of what Barnard had done. Rhoodie said Barnard's contribution had proved 'immeasurable' in building and improving contacts in Africa, the Middle East and the Far East. Barnard, he said, had undertaken numerous journeys 'on our behalf' to the Philippines, Saudi Arabia, India, Kenya and the United States. Barnard 'often made his journeys under the worst possible conditions, in between operations, and at his own expense ... until he allowed me to pay for his travels and expenses'. The 'at his own expense' comment was something that anyone who knew Barnard would have doubted. The rest seemed to make sense as in the previous two years Barnard had spent little time doing his job as a cardiac surgeon at Groote Schuur.

Barnard was furious, not least because several of the trips referred to by Rhoodie had been made at the invitation of foreign health organisations or, in the case of the Philippines, President Marcos and his wife Imelda. Others, especially to the United States, had combined promotional book tours and lectures with attendance at conferences organised by – as the world was now beginning to learn – front organisations for the Department of Information such as the Foreign Affairs Association and the Institute for the Study of Plural Societies run by Rhoodie's brother Nic. But that, for Eschel Rhoodie, was the beauty of Barnard. He could move in the highest circles around the globe, mixing with political leaders in some of the most sensitive areas like the Middle East, and publicly speak out against the vilification of South Africa in any number of print and television interviews, all the while claiming to do so as an individual who denounced apartheid. He had the perfect cover and clearly enjoyed the sense of being part of a high-powered, clandestine operation that placed him at the very heart of South African politics. Now that cover was blown, and some groups began calling for him to be refused visas to their countries.

Since the first heart transplant in December 1967 he had enjoyed the privilege of being granted 'special leave' from his duties at Groote Schuur at very short notice so that he could travel abroad extensively, leaving the running of the cardiac unit to his brother

Marius or Joe de Nobrega. Official UCT leave documents – he was on the joint staff of the university and Groote Schuur – often noted that the trip had been 'approved by the Cabinet' and his expenses 'funded by the Department of External Affairs'. Now that life was about to collapse around him. In September 1979 the minister of the interior, Alwyn Schlebuch, announced that Barnard's 'special leave' privileges would be withdrawn and from now on he would be 'treated like anyone else'.

After hearing of Rhoodie's magazine revelations, Barnard told the South African Press Association he had worked 'always for South Africa'. He 'deplored' what his friend had said, and added: 'It will close many doors. It is a pity that Dr Rhoodie had to mention this. I don't know what he meant when he said I undertook the journeys in his name. All projects which involved Government money took place with the full approval of the Government and in consultation with the then Prime Minister, Mr Vorster, as well as Dr Connie Mulder. I made two conditions: That I did not have to speak well of or defend certain aspects of the Government I do not agree with – like apartheid – and that I would be compensated in full for any costs I had to bear.' He failed to add that he had laid down one further condition – that Barbara should be able to accompany him on trips abroad.

The truth was that Barnard had been an enthusiastic ally of Eschel Rhoodie – although there is no evidence to suggest he was aware of the full range of his activities – and a willing tool of the apartheid regime. He had long chafed at the fact that his salary as a state hospital surgeon barely covered the running expenses of his Constantia mansion. By now he had made money from books, although not as much as he would have done if he had not donated his estimated R500 000 royalties from *One Life* to the heart research fund. He also received ad hoc payments for lectures abroad – when asked how much he charged, he preferred to call it an honorarium. But he was married to an heiress whose father was said to be the second richest man in South Africa, after Harry Oppenheimer, and he was utterly seduced by the trappings of wealth. Now his role close to the seat of power gave him money, political prestige, and yet another excuse to spend his time travelling, meeting the wealthy and glamorous people he adored.

In his book *The Real Information Scandal*, Rhoodie writes of how

Barnard's high-powered connections helped Mulder plan a sensitive trip to the Middle East, which was later cancelled by Vorster: 'A special visit (to Egypt) was planned for Mulder in January 1978 to mend fences, which would also have taken him to Israel, Jordan and Morocco. Professor Chris Barnard's friendship with the Moroccan and Jordanian kings had facilitated matters.'

*

But how and when did Barnard first become involved in what was to become South Africa's biggest single political scandal? Eschel Rhoodie, a ruthless operator, had made it clear to Mulder and others in the cabinet that he considered no-one and nothing beyond reach in the pursuit of his goal: 'Our approach is that we will use any individual, any organisation, any method, anything, and that we will employ and apply them if we can thereby help to promote our country's interests abroad,' he had said.

In an unofficial way Barnard found himself putting South Africa's case – while always stressing his opposition to apartheid – during his trips overseas in the weeks following the first heart transplant. At a time when UN arms embargoes and international sports boycotts were isolating South Africa it would have been impossible to avoid politics and apartheid, even if he had wanted to. He did not forget Pik Botha's 'call to arms' in New York. On a trip to Paris in early 1968 he sought advice from Denys Rhoodie, Eschel's older brother, who was in charge of press affairs at the South African embassy, and who would later play an important role in the Information scandal. They got on well, and to avoid the incessant media interest Barnard stayed with Rhoodie rather than at a hotel. They formed a close bond. Barnard stayed with Rhoodie on several more occasions when the civil servant was transferred to London. At this stage Eschel Rhoodie was running press affairs at the South African embassy in The Hague. His widow, Katy, believes he met Barnard at least once at that time, which would have been expected of Rhoodie in view of his job. Certainly Barnard was on the mailing list in 1972 for the first issue of *To the Point*, the propaganda magazine funded by the Department of Information and co-edited by Eschel Rhoodie.

In 1972 Denys Rhoodie returned to Pretoria as head of the British and Commonwealth desk at the Department of Information.

He says he was approached by Connie Mulder, who wanted to launch a worldwide propaganda campaign to counter the anti-South Africa crusade. 'I told him the man he needed was Eschel. He was dynamic, full of energy and ideas.' Mulder took his advice and brought Eschel back to Pretoria, appointing him secretary of information. By early 1974, Denys Rhoodie, now deputy-secretary of information, says he became involved in the more 'covert, confidential work' his brother was engaged in. 'We were approaching all sorts of people we thought might help. At some stage we went to see Chris Barnard at his office. He was enthusiastic. He felt very strongly about South Africa. He had a real passion.' He could not pinpoint the exact date of this meeting, but it must have taken place around early 1975. Barnard had for some time been on the 'guest programme' list of the Department of Information – he would have dinner with prominent visitors to South Africa to help them form a more favourable opinion of the country.

But Barnard was anxious to get more involved, perhaps unwittingly encouraged by Donald Woods, the newspaper editor who would later be banned and forced to flee South Africa. In September 1974 Woods told Barnard by letter: 'You may recall that my wife and I called on you a couple of years ago when I said (as I still believe today) that you have a tremendous role to play in our country's future politically but that you should stay out of the party structures for the time being until the final groupings have shaken into place.' Woods, of course, would not have dreamed of encouraging Barnard to put his skills to good use on behalf of the apartheid regime; he assumed he would work against it.

Two months later Barnard wrote to his friend Nico Diederichs, then minister of finance, who was one of the chief architects of apartheid, and was aware of Rhoodie's schemes: 'You will remember the very pleasant afternoon we spent together at my home recently. I told you about my wish to help South Africa wherever I can. I also told you that I had mentioned this to the Secretary of Foreign Affairs. From the lack of interest he has shown, I can only assume that they feel I can do very little.'

Barnard's letter had some effect. The Rhoodie brothers arrived at his office and outlined what they envisaged for him. In what was probably Barnard's first trip in his semi-official political role, in March 1975, he and Barbara were invited to the Philippines by President Marcos and his wife Imelda to attend the opening of a heart clinic. They were then whisked off to Nepal for the coronation of the king – where Barnard met Prince Charles and wasted no time in talking to him about South Africa, even inviting him for a visit. Barbara's presence ensured maximum publicity. She danced with Prince Charles.

In October 1975 Barnard went to the United States to promote his first novel, *The Unwanted*, and to give a series of lectures. To prepare himself properly he asked the Department of Information to supply him with material on the economies of South Africa and other African countries. The tour in America went well. It included a high-profile lunch at UN headquarters in New York hosted by South Africa's then ambassador to the UN, Pik Botha, which attracted the attention of the foreign correspondents based there. Both men lashed a recent address to the UN by Idi Amin, the Ugandan leader, who was, they said, nothing more than 'a common murderer'. Barnard, whose attendance generated huge interest, told reporters apartheid was like a 'disease', a simile which vexed Botha. But Barnard added: 'The UN could do with a heart transplant. We in South Africa are trying hard to change and we recognise that we are not perfect.'

But during this trip old friends in Minneapolis were alarmed by what they saw as a marked hardening of his political views from the 1950s. Then he had been known for his more virulent opposition to apartheid. 'Your apparent transformation of your strong apartheid stand from some years ago when we talked about it at Diamond Jim's ... leaves me at a loss,' wrote one friend.

When he got back to Cape Town Barnard wrote to Eschel Rhoodie to tell him he had found the 'various books and pamphlets of great help' and to ask his opinion of the success of his 'progress through the United States'. Eschel Rhoodie replied by congratulating him on the 'very good publicity for South Africa' he had achieved in America, and went on: 'I am a firm believer in face-to-face contact. These travels of a person with your status and name are of great value to us ... By the way, when are you going to write a book about your view of the social-political issues of this country, especially regarding the relationship between the races? If you were interested I would gladly "ghost" such a manuscript for you. You can then just go through the manuscript and approve or scrap what you don't like. The book will mainly be for foreign consumption. Think about it. Naturally, the relationship between us will be treated as a secret.'

Barnard had already published several books, including his autobiography, *One Life*, and *The Unwanted*. The idea of writing, or at least putting his name to, a political book appealed to him: 'I am very interested in your suggestion about the book and would very much like to receive more details from you about it. It will certainly be a great pleasure for me to write this with a ghost writer,' he told Rhoodie.

The result would be *South Africa: Sharp Dissection*, published in February 1977, a political tract that relentlessly complains about the 'politics of hypocrisy' and the 'double standards' shown by the rest of the world in its dealings with South Africa. On the cover is the perfect picture: Barnard, wearing a deeply caring expression, cradling a black child in his arms. 'It is because of my concern with the recognised injustices in my own country and the unrecognised human suffering in many other countries, that I have decided to write this book,' he says in the introduction. Unlike most of Barnard's other books, before and since, there was no mention of a collaborator, nor were there acknowledgements to colleagues who may have helped. A quarter of the book is given over to a fierce attack on the media, warning that the abuse of freedom of the press could lead to the need for controls, a common theme of government threats; and blaming 'sensational reporting' for fanning the Soweto uprising. In 1969 Eschel Rhoodie had published a book called *The Paper Curtain*, regarded as the blueprint for the propaganda war he would later launch. It too attacked the media for its 'distorted' coverage of South Africa; it too accused a wide range of governments and organisations like the United Nations of 'double standards' by demonising South Africa over apartheid, yet turning a blind eye to human rights abuses elsewhere. The hand of Rhoodie in *Sharp Dissection* is clear now, but at the time no-one had any reason to suspect.

Rhoodie may have driven the project, but *Sharp Dissection* undoubtedly contains Barnard's beliefs at that time. Speaking as a 'White African', he says South Africa was being pilloried for being 'too honest'. Many other countries were plagued with racism, he says, but they had not made South Africa's 'mistake' and enshrined such racism in law. Freedom was a privilege to be earned, not a right. He calls for the immediate abolition of 'institutionalised petty apartheid', such as segregated beaches and theatres. All racial discrimination must be phased out 'at a steady and orderly pace'. It sounds like the old 'liberal' Barnard. But what does he want in place of institutionalised apartheid? He suggests 'the right of the individual to discriminate', a meritocracy where the country would be ruled by the most able, regardless of colour, but at the same time he wants to see the encouragement of black homelands. No mention of the obvious fact that the majority of the population had been denied access to the kind of education and facilities that might have enabled them to be included among the most able. And, more significantly, he rejects the notion of majority rule or one man, one vote. It would be 'committing national suicide': 'One man, one vote is a perfectly acceptable democratic system of governing a country where all the population groups have the same standards and the same code, but in a plural society such as that of South Africa one man, one vote would mean a massive degeneration into bloodshed and chaos, if we are to go by the experience of many countries, not only in Africa but around the world.'

Vorster, Mulder and Rhoodie must have rubbed their hands with glee. South Africa's most famous personality was giving many of their reviled policies the most human of faces – that of a doctor, a carer, a man associated in the minds of many with medical miracles and humanitarianism. And at the most critical time for South Africa. The Black Consciousness movement under Steve Biko was gaining ground. Riots had erupted across the country after the police violence at Soweto the year before, which itself had brought worldwide condemnation as powerful as anything seen after Sharpeville.

*

In January 1976 Barnard had travelled to India as the guest of several medical organisations. Naturally he met the prime minister, Indira Gandhi. It was just weeks after Angola had secured its independence, and the international row over South Africa's military intervention on behalf of Unita was still raging. In *Sharp*

Dissection Barnard writes: 'In the 1940s, before the ascendancy at the United Nations of the emergent African nations, India led the attack on South Africa at the UN on the issue of human dignity and freedom. Under the circumstances, I expected to find that Mrs Gandhi would be eager to learn more about South Africa from one of her own people – a non-politician and non-supporter of the South African Government at that. It was for this reason that, as soon as the formalities of introductions were completed and the hordes of photographers and television teams had left her office, I told her I was not going to discuss heart transplantation or heart disease, because she had probably read enough about this in the papers. What I was interested in talking to her about was the problems of a White African.'

Finding Mrs Gandhi unsympathetic, Barnard accused her of 'hypocrisy' and suggested she visit South Africa with a delegation. She declined.

Indian newspapers devoted much space to Barnard's visit, and he wasted no time in putting the case for the 'white African', insisting that apartheid had come about only because of the white man's fear of being wiped out by the black majority. He claimed segregation was 'on its way out' in South Africa.

With Angola and Mozambique by now in the hands of left-wing regimes, the crisis mounting in South West Africa and pressure growing on the white rulers of then Rhodesia, the apartheid government of South Africa was in a state of paranoia about its survival. *Sharp Dissection* ends with a chilling – and astonishing – warning from Barnard that 'Those who wish to push South Africa to the brink must not be surprised if their extremist threat to the very existence of the South African society evokes the ultimate defence as made possible by its nuclear capacity.' It is a clear statement that South Africa would use nuclear weapons against its enemies.

The book brought a tidal wave of hostile criticism against Barnard. While Eschel Rhoodie sat in his office in Pretoria, Barnard faced intense questioning at one press conference after another. Of course, he thoroughly enjoyed the notoriety and, typically, backtracked rapidly on any suggestion that he had threatened some sort of nuclear attack, a line which had generated enormous international publicity. He was also accused of supporting the apartheid regime by endorsing the policy of black homelands. Again, he denied this, although on what evidence was not clear. Apart from South Africa, the book was published in Germany, France, Belgium and the United States, in some cases no doubt with help from Rhoodie. Many of the larger foreign publishing houses who had published his previous books refused to touch it.

Pierre Belfond, the French publisher who had taken on *The Unwanted*, and enjoyed its success as a best-seller, was one of the few who did. As a known 'left-wing' publisher he risked alienating many of his peers and readers by backing the book. He did not know, of course, that it had been commissioned by the Department of Information and would have turned it down flat if he had. He had become very fond of Barnard but always rejected his repeated invitations to visit South Africa because he did not want to sanction the regime. 'I published the political book because of the loyalty I felt towards Chris after the success of his novel. I like to stick by my authors. But it was a flop. No-one wanted to invite Chris on their shows for interviews. I had to beg old friends. The book sold only a few thousand copies. Chris was very popular in France so the critics weren't savage – they just remained silent.' Belfond had tried to persuade Barnard to strengthen his anti-apartheid stand in *Sharp Dissection,* in vain. 'In the book he is very much against petty apartheid, but he said he couldn't go further because there were people in South Africa who would kill him. He told me about the car which had knocked him down. He did not mention the Department of Information. We never discussed them.'

Barnard had succeeded in causing a storm and, once again, his real views on apartheid were conveniently murky. He was the son of a missionary to coloured people, a doctor who did not hesitate to operate on black and coloured patients, and a man who publicly spoke out against apartheid. Surely he could not be a racist. Yet here he was working for the very apartheid regime he claimed to abhor, under the guise of 'patriotism'.

In April 1976, while he was gathering material for *Sharp Dissection,* Barnard wrote to the American secretary of state Henry Kissinger, who had been on a tour of Africa, criticising US policy towards South Africa and once again voicing fears for the 'white minority'. The letter begins in typically barbed fashion: 'I was extremely sorry that during your recent visit to Africa you did not include my country in your itinerary. Actually, during a visit to South Africa in the Fifties you stayed with my father- and mother-in-law, Dr and Mrs FA Zoellner, at their home in Johannesburg. Your signature in their guest book was shown to me with great pride as they are also of German origin. This was quite a few years ago and my present wife was then just a little girl. She has now grown up into a beautiful woman, as you can imagine, and was quite keen to meet you during our last visit to your country. Unfortunately, you were too busy to see us, even when we stayed at the same time at the Waldorf Towers in New York. I often think that you would probably have found the time if she was married to a black African doctor but, of course, that is ridiculous.' Two months later Barnard received a detailed rebuttal of his arguments from one of Kissinger's aides, without reference to the Zoellners.

*

By 1977 Barnard had been introduced to another of Rhoodie's close allies – Redvers, or 'Red', Metrowich, a former South African Broadcasting Corporation political journalist and publisher who was chairman of the Southern African Freedom Foundation, which at that time had not been exposed as one of the Information Department's front organisations. Metrowich began to advise Barnard on the political content of his speeches, and would even draft them for him.

Barnard, no doubt encouraged by Rhoodie with promises of what might be possible once Mulder succeeded Vorster, was clearly starting to look beyond surgery towards a high-profile role in politics. At a 'health care and human values' conference in Cincinnati he said he planned to retire from medicine and use his fame to promote his political beliefs. 'I see politics as a method I can use to continue the alleviation of human suffering. I sometimes feel my whole life is so futile when I've spent the whole day trying to save one person and I walk out of the operating room and read that ten persons have been executed.' He attacked US president Jimmy Carter and America's ambassador to the UN Andrew Young, and produced a remarkable comparison: 'They are pushing us to the brink of a horrible future because of their misunderstanding. People like Mr Carter and Mr Young have a terrible misconception about comparing South African blacks to

American blacks. It's much more correct to compare South African whites to American blacks.'

It would later emerge that Metrowich's salary was paid by the government. Few people knew this until the Information scandal broke, and it is highly unlikely that Rhoodie would have told Barnard exactly what the relationship was. But Barnard enthusiastically embraced the help offered by Metrowich, telling him, 'I always find it a great pleasure to be associated with you.' And later: 'Thank you very much for sending me a draft for my speech. As usual I have no complaints. It is excellent.'

In speeches made in America at this time Barnard called for the immediate abolition of 'social apartheid' rather than 'grand apartheid'. The homelands were a 'morally and honestly acceptable solution to a certain part of our problem' and should be 'consolidated'. He argued for a meritocracy, but not a democracy: 'Party politics cannot work here because the problem with party politics is that the party, especially in our country, make their laws and run the country for the good of the party. Just as the Nationalist government has never run this country for the good of the country; they've always run it for the good of the Nationalist party.' The insinuation was that majority rule in South Africa would lead to a similar government of self-interest by blacks and coloureds.

On a visit to France to promote *Sharp Dissection*, Barnard was placed on the spot during a live television discussion show that began by running a film claiming to show the brutal face of South Africa. He was furious about what he believed to be a trick, and pointed out many instances where he was certain the film had been doctored to show scenes of police violence that had not happened. Pierre Belfond had set up the interview through a close friend, the show's producer, and Barnard had been warned that a film would be shown. 'To try to make amends the producer offered Chris the use of a crew to make an hour-long documentary about South Africa as he saw it. It was very successful, not just when it was shown on the main Channel One in France, but in other countries too,' says Belfond.

During the making of this film Barnard interviewed Breyten Breytenbach, the exiled Afrikaner poet and anti-apartheid activist who had been jailed for nine years in 1975 for entering the country on a false passport, and who had been living in Paris. 'My heart went out to this deeply sensitive, fine man who was the victim of circumstances,' wrote Barnard later. 'I went to see John Vorster and begged him to release Breyten as he was no danger to South Africa or South African society. He refused.' (It wasn't the first time Barnard had appealed for the release of a jailed 'revolutionary' – in 1973 he was one of several prominent whites who asked John Vorster to release Bram Fischer, the advocate who had led the defence at the Rivonia trial and was serving a life sentence for sabotage; he was dying of cancer. Vorster told Barnard that he would stay out of the operating room if Barnard stayed out of politics.)

The interview with Breytenbach provoked allegations that Barnard had used the poet for his own political ends. Barnard strongly denied it, saying he had made the film after meeting some French writers in Nice who had told him Breytenbach was being tortured. 'It was not done for political reasons,' he insisted, lying.

Another man he desperately hoped would take part in this film was Robert Sobukwe, founder of the Pan-Africanist Congress whose anti-pass law campaign had led, in 1960, to the Sharpeville massacre and the banning of the PAC and ANC. Sobukwe was jailed for three years, but when his prison term expired he was put under house arrest on Robben Island for a further six years. As he had committed no crime, the government pushed through a special law to enable them to renew his detention annually. Eventually he was taken off Robben Island and sent to Kimberley under a banning order. He was kept under house arrest but allowed to practise as a lawyer. In September 1977 he was admitted to Groote Schuur suffering from the lung cancer that would kill him a few months later.

When Barnard heard Sobukwe was in his hospital he was very keen to meet him, says Joe de Nobrega. 'I introduced them and Chris immediately began talking to Sobukwe like an old friend. Then he looked round at the two security policemen in the ward and said, 'Who are you? Get out! I don't want you in my ward! This patient is recovering from major surgery and you're upsetting him. Out!' The policemen were shocked but they had to go and sit in their car outside. Sobukwe was not even Chris Barnard's patient.'

Sobukwe was recovering from an operation to remove a lung and had to remain in hospital for three more weeks before radiotherapy could begin. Barnard asked him if he could interview him for the French documentary. Sobukwe, smiling, declined. 'Chris tried to assure Sobukwe that the film was not political and that he just wanted to do a nice interview, but Sobukwe would have none of it,' says De Nobrega. 'He kept smiling and told Chris, "Good luck". In the end Chris snapped and told him he was being totally unreasonable.' Under the terms of the banning order, Sobukwe would not have been allowed to give the television interview. Either Barnard was confident he would not be prosecuted or, more likely, he had cleared the idea with Mulder and Rhoodie.

But Barnard did intervene on Sobukwe's behalf with the hard-line minister of justice, Jimmy Kruger. Sobukwe wanted to spend the three weeks resting at the home of a black Anglican bishop who lived in an official church house in the 'white' suburb of Newlands. He applied to Kruger for permission but heard nothing back. Finally he arranged to be driven to the house, where he was immediately arrested, placed in handcuffs and brought back to Groote Schuur. De Nobrega suggested making his home part of the ward and putting Sobukwe up there. 'Chris got on the phone and spoke to Kruger. It was astonishing. If he had been talking to his lowest registrar who had just done the worst thing to his patient he could not have been more extreme in his language,' says De Nobrega. 'He told him he was a nonsense politician who was getting in the way interfering with his patient. Kruger finally agreed to the idea.'

Later Barnard claimed to have spoken again to Kruger to try to get the banning order lifted, without success. 'He was suffering from a very severe disease and didn't have long to live. It is my duty as a doctor to alleviate suffering, and he was suffering under this order,' he said at the time.

But Sobukwe was to play another important part in Barnard's work for the Department of Information – and, according to Eschel Rhoodie, it was Barnard's most valuable role. At the time of Sobukwe's death in February 1978, American trade unionists, encouraged by Donald Woods, were threatening to launch a massive air and sea boycott of South Africa that would have cost the country countless millions. Barnard, then in Boston on another tour, was seen by Rhoodie as the ideal man to meet the union leader George Meany in Washington and persuade him of the folly of such a move. In return, Barnard told Rhoodie he wanted to be allowed to bring Sobukwe's children over from the US to attend their father's funeral. 'I arranged this with lightning speed,' said Rhoodie.

Rhoodie, in *The Real Information Scandal*, says, 'When I first heard that Woods had met with George Meany and that he had convinced him to lead a massive American labour union action against South African shipping and aircraft, we really had to move fast. I arranged first of all with the relevant State departments that there would be no obstacles in Chris Barnard's way if he wanted to bring the children of the PAC leader Robert Sobukwe to South Africa for the funeral of their father at Barnard's expense. Shortly afterwards Barnard went to the United States. We made certain the news of Barnard's action got to Meany and then, through Sydney Baron and other well-placed contacts, we hurriedly arranged for a meeting between Barnard and Meany. All in all it took us four days ... After a long meeting Barnard convinced Meany that instead of a boycott he should send a fact-finding team to South Africa. Meany agreed.' (Sydney Baron was head of a public relations firm in New York that had a lucrative contract with the Department of Information, and often set up US contacts for Barnard.)

According to Barnard, he had told Meany that in South Africa he would find 'that the whites are not all racists and that, generally speaking, all races work together and are changing things.' For whatever reason, the boycott did not go ahead.

Three of Sobukwe's children, who had been placed in the care of Andrew Young, did indeed fly to South Africa for their father's funeral – and the story duly emerged that Barnard had paid R4 000 for their air fares. Black people, deeply moved by his gesture on behalf of one of their heroes, sent him letters full of praise, and Barnard described Sobukwe as a 'very good friend'. It all helped to improve his image as a compassionate man whose political views were colour-blind. But, of course, the secret involvement of Rhoodie, with his briefcase stuffed with cash, is the key. Benjamin Pogrund, who wrote Sobukwe's biography and was a close friend, says, 'Chris Barnard was the man who paid for the tickets in name. But his brother Marius told me it must have been Info cash because Chris didn't have that sort of ready money. When I was working on the biography I wrote to Chris about it and I got a very polite reply, but he wouldn't tell me who had provided the funds. Perhaps the idea was to polish up South Africa's image.'

In the three weeks that Sobukwe spent at Joe de Nobrega's house, Barnard did not visit him once. A reply Barnard sent to one admirer, Mountain Mbengo, shortly after the Sobukwe funeral, cleverly avoided confirming that he had actually paid the air fares, but may well contain a typically cryptic admission: 'The least I could do for him was to make it possible for his children to attend his funeral. I always believe that one gets back more than one ever gives so actually I have not given but gained.'

Pogrund certainly admired the way Barnard dealt with Kruger on Sobukwe's behalf: 'Very few people would have dared to stand up to Kruger like that, but Barnard could and did. Bob and Chris Barnard were not friends as such. He used to talk to him in the ward and when he tried to persuade him to do the interview Bob was amused, even at the outburst.'

At the time Sobukwe was being treated at Groote Schuur, and Barnard was making his documentary for French television, Steve Biko met his brutal death at the hands of security police. As details of the way he had been beaten and left to die from head injuries began to emerge, riots erupted in the townships, followed by the inevitable police crackdown. As a professor at UCT, one of the country's leading 'liberal' institutions, Barnard was surrounded by colleagues and students who were incensed by Biko's death. Some of those he worked with were in the forefront of a legal campaign launched against the South African Medical and Dental Council for not taking action against the doctors who had witnessed Biko's dire condition before he died and had failed to act to save him.

Frances Ames was one of those involved in the legal action, which went all the way to the Supreme Court and would not run its successful course until eight years later. Ames asked him for a financial contribution to the cause. 'First of all he told me he had too many expenses to worry about so he couldn't afford to help,' she says. 'He said we could use his name if we liked, but that wasn't much good to us. Later he said he would contribute, then pulled out, citing poverty. I don't recall him ever speaking out about Biko.' In 1980 Barnard, on a book tour, told newspapers he did not intend to renew his subscription to the South African Medical Association in protest at its exoneration of the three doctors who had examined Biko, and urged others to do the same.

In *The Second Life* many years later Barnard talks of his 'country's shame' over Biko. But the strongest point he makes is about the Kruger interview in his French documentary, which took place just a few weeks before Biko died. He says he asked Kruger – a man who infamously remarked that Biko's death 'leaves me cold' – whether prisoners were being tortured and beaten by the police. Kruger, as one would expect, replied that prisoners were never beaten. Barnard, in *The Second Life*, professes dismay: 'Jimmy Kruger had looked straight into my eyes, filmed by a TV camera, and said, "I can assure you that prisoners are never beaten or tortured."'

When asked his opinion about Biko's fate, Barnard's response was usually to deplore it, but to point out that there were many prisoners who died in detention around the world.

In the highly charged and violent aftermath of Biko's death Vorster called a snap election. If there had been any confusion over Barnard's politics to date, since his ill-fated flirtation with the United Party in 1972, it was cleared up now. He used his formidable speaking powers to campaign actively for the National Party. True, he always insisted his aim was to 'change the system from within'. But nevertheless this son of a missionary who had once described the NP's victory in 1948 as 'a disaster for my family' was siding unashamedly with the party of apartheid. Colin Eglin, leader of the Progressive Federal Party, a liberal anti-apartheid party whose most prominent member was Helen Suzman, was seeking re-election as MP for the Sea Point constituency in Cape Town. He recalls: 'Barnard addressed a number of house meetings for the NP candidate standing against me. To have a personality like him helped to draw those key people of influence whose votes were doubtful. Then the word would spread.' Barnard's support for the NP did not stop Eglin doubling his majority in the seat.

At this stage the NP was proposing to set up a new system of government in which whites, coloureds and Indians would each have their own parliament and cabinet. The blacks would, of course, carry on in their separate homelands. Nationally the NP secured its biggest victory to date; Barnard was clearly pinning his hopes of high office on his friend Mulder becoming the next prime minister. But when Mulder's rising star plunged meteor-like into oblivion a year later, Barnard's own political ambitions vanished with it.

Many years later he wrote of Mulder and the NP: 'I was convinced that if he became prime minister he would get rid of apartheid very quickly. I used all my contacts and influence to get votes for him … At one stage in my life I thought it was possible to change the government's approach by gentle persuasion – which I continued doing for a long time. I was wrong. They'd been in power for so long and had become so arrogant and dictatorial, that such an approach would never work and I turned my back on the Nationalists forever.'

But that decision was not reached until the Info gravy train had slammed into the buffers. For now there was all to play for. In May 1978 Barnard went on a crucially important mission to Kenya. He was anxious, he said, to build up links between doctors in both countries and to help bring sick children to South Africa for heart surgery at a time when no other African country had the facilities or the surgeons to do such work. But there was another reason for the trip – he wanted to persuade the Kenyan government to send an athletics team to South Africa. Before leaving for Kenya he asked the chairman of the 'international liaison committee' of RSA Sport, which worked to defeat the sports boycott of South Africa, to provide him with useful information for his trip; he also accepted an offer to serve on the organisation's advisory board, and added: 'I hope that in some little way I will be able to contribute so that we will be readmitted to the international world of sport.'

The Kenya visit was a perfect example of the incalculable value of favourable media coverage generated whenever Barnard and his white medical team saved the lives of foreign black children at Groote Schuur. Before going to Kenya he had successfully repaired the heart of an eight-year-old girl from that country – in what he himself described as a fairly simple operation – and he was being hailed there as a 'miracle-worker'. Each such 'miracle' performed by Barnard highlighted the advanced state of civilisation in white South Africa as opposed to its black neighbours. Barnard himself, of course, found successfully operating on children of any colour to be his most rewarding work. Again, the dual nature of his role was wonderfully effective.

Barnard had been invited to Kenya by the attorney general Charles Njonjo, a long-standing friend and contact for whom he had arranged trips to South Africa. Barnard told RSA Sport that Njonjo 'plays a very important role in Sports Administration'.

Barnard's visit to Nairobi, bypassing Kenya's ban on people with South African passports, caused 'shock-waves' according to one of the country's newspapers. In various interviews he described how 'the apartheid of social separation is now being eliminated' in South Africa. 'It is being abolished all the time. There is a genuine wish among people of all races to stop discrimination.' Vorster was 'a very nice man' who would love to visit Kenya. Barnard repeatedly stressed the line then being taken in Pretoria: 'Our future will be in Africa and nowhere else. As Africans we should stay as friends.' He aired the suggestion that an athletics team should visit South Africa, although despite his friendship with Njonjo nothing seems to have materialised. He was being feted as 'a great man who loves all people', as one newspaper put it, when things suddenly turned sour. An unnamed Kenyan government spokesman said Barnard's 'apologies for the South African regime were detestable'. Still, most of the Kenyan media, clearly awed by the charisma and presence of Barnard, sprang to his defence: 'The bitter irony of the whole business is that when it came to the need to save the life of a Kenyan girl, Kenyans were glad and eager to send the girl to South Africa. Surely in exchange for the humanitarian gesture shown by Barnard in performing the heart operation, we Kenyans can afford to listen to what Dr Barnard has to say about politics ...' said one.

Another newspaper, *The Standard*, had taken the step even before Barnard arrived of publishing a speech he had made in Johannesburg strongly criticising apartheid. 'In fact he has been so outspoken in his disapproval of racial inequalities and indignities that he has never behaved like any of those other White South African political and theological blind mice who have been supporting racism in order not to be branded disloyal by its rabid architects and practitioners,' said *The Standard*.

With this kind of sympathetic attitude towards Barnard in one of black Africa's most powerful countries, Rhoodie's assessment of his 'immeasurable' worth to Pretoria can be easily understood. (A few years later, long after something of his earlier political role had been revealed, Barnard would find himself treated very differently by the Kenyan authorities, who refused him permission to leave a cruise ship and set foot in Mombasa.)

A month after the Kenya trip Barnard, no doubt with the help of Rhoodie, made another film, this time about the guerrilla war for independence for what would become Namibia being waged by the South West Africa People's Organisation. Barnard flew with a group of foreign correspondents to Ovamboland to show that the South African army was still in control, contrary to reports that SWAPO had overrun it. Barnard was filmed questioning SWAPO prisoners, who claimed that they had been abducted and forced to fight. Barnard had another agenda here – Siegfried Stander had asked if he could organise just such an expedition for him to gather material for *The Faith*. 'Could you use your influence to get a trip to the border arranged? The army might co-operate if we say we're planning a book about terrorists!' he wrote. Stander, however, did not make the media trip.

Some attempts by Barnard to promote his political beliefs backfired badly. He had already had two heated television confrontations with David Frost, considered one of the world's sharpest interviewers, and acquitted himself well. Some years earlier he had accused Frost of being a 'coward' and 'a conceited little man' for not giving him a chance to reply when he broadcast an investigation into the circumstances surrounding the use, without permission from relatives, of Evelyn Jacobs's heart in the Pieter Smith transplant. Frost now invited him to take part in another show, recorded in America, in which an anti-apartheid South African lawyer was also interviewed. According to Barnard, Eschel Rhoodie had heard about the lawyer's appearance and offered to dig up some 'background information' on him. At first Barnard pretended he did not know the lawyer during the show, but then he trotted out some of the 'dirt' Rhoodie had found. Barnard recalled in *The Second Life:* 'David Frost also has the killer instinct. He knew he had me and he slowly began twisting the knife with cutting sarcasm and ridicule. Then I did the worst thing possible – I lost my temper.' Barnard stormed off the show, but not before Frost had told him, 'You know, Professor Barnard, you had a good opportunity tonight to state South Africa's case and you goofed it.' That night, said Barnard, he could not sleep because he knew Frost had been right.

The Frost debacle had another spin-off. Barnard later recalled that Peter Sellers wrote to him: 'Dear Chris, I saw you on the Frost show and you made a real ass of yourself. It was not the way for a man of your intelligence to behave.' It was the last contact he had from Sellers, who had ignored his efforts to get him to agree to cardiac surgery at Groote Schuur and later died from a heart attack.

The Strini Moodley affair was another embarrassing episode. Amnesty International had written to Barnard asking him to investigate reports that Moodley, a political prisoner on Robben Island, was being kept in solitary confinement and was suffering from tuberculosis. Barnard looked into it and told Amnesty that far from being in poor condition, Moodley was 'in excellent health'. He was not a political prisoner, said Barnard – he had been jailed for 'terrorist activities'. 'He has been tried in an open court of law for terrorist activities and has been found guilty and sentenced to five years. This would be equivalent to a member of the Baader-Meinhof gang who were imprisoned in Germany for similar activities,' wrote Barnard. Moodley sued for libel, claiming R10 000. Barnard vowed to go to the Supreme Court to fight the case but, according to his own account, he was advised to settle, and in 1981 paid Moodley R3 000.

After the death of the state president Nico Diederichs in 1978, and months before his brother's involvement with Eschel Rhoodie would emerge, Marius Barnard – who would soon become an MP for the PFP – had said in his own newspaper column that Chris Barnard would be on his 'dream short-list' to be new president: 'It must be well known by now that my final nominee and myself have had many, many disagreements and that we seldom see eye to eye politically … Chris Barnard is well respected by both the government and the opposition parties. All race groups admire him greatly and even overseas he has no real enemies … I am sure he would be able to represent our country with statesmanship and stature.'

But just 18 months earlier, after the publication of *Sharp Dissection* and during a volatile period when squatters were being violently evicted from their makeshift homes near Cape Town, those political differences had surfaced at a poignant moment. Newspapers published an open letter from Marius to Chris Barnard in which he called on him to join him in 'pointing out human suffering and double standards in our own country'. Barnard responded fully several weeks later with a carefully argued piece packed with statistics and Information Department language, in which he stated that while he sympathised with the squatters, 'these were people who had broken the law and who had been given ample warning, but taken no notice'. But his more immediate, spontaneous response to the letter by Marius had been: 'I would like to ask Marius if he is prepared to tell me how much he is willing to spend on relieving the plight of the squatters. And in doing so I would remind him of the Latin motto of our old school in Beaufort West, which meant simply "Deeds, not words".'

The death of Diederichs had, in fact, indirectly led to Marius getting the chance to write a weekly column in the *Cape Times* in what was another clear example of the political differences between the Barnard brothers.

When Diederichs died, the Student Representative Council at UCT made a statement that was described as a 'gratuitous insult' to his family. Barnard threatened to resign from the UCT staff if an apology was not issued or disciplinary action not taken. The story was published in an Afrikaans newspaper and Barnard was contacted by the *Cape Times* for a comment. The *Cape Times* then ran an editorial criticising 'publicity seekers', a clear reference to Barnard: 'In public affairs, as in private concerns, there occur from time to time breaches of decent standards and taste in which the only appropriate response is to turn aside in disgust. This is not the province of newspapers – or of trouble-makers and publicity seekers, however celebrated – and can safely be left to the appropriate authorities.'

Barnard, incensed, called the *Cape Times* editor Tony Heard to point out that he had not instigated the story and that the editorial clearly referred to him. He demanded an apology, which was refused. Barnard then told Heard his column could not be published in his newspaper, although he would continue to run it in other papers in the group. 'The next day Marius called us up and offered to take over the column,' says Heard. 'I was tickled pink and, of course, I accepted. Marius's column ran for about a year, but it didn't have the same clout as his brother's.'

After the fall of Vorster, Mulder and the Rhoodie brothers, Barnard went to see the new prime minister, PW Botha. He was told he could continue being an unofficial ambassador for his country, but clearly things had changed. It was obvious that from now on there would be no envelopes of cash, although Botha claimed they did not discuss money. Barnard had by now grown disillusioned with politics. He would continue to speak out at every opportunity on political matters, but his days as a part-time aide to the government were over.

Was Barnard the manipulated or the manipulator in all this? Throughout his life he liked to play the innocent boy from the Karoo who was forever vulnerable to being used by those more sophisticated. After making a particularly sharp point in a letter he would often end by saying, 'But then, I'm just a poor country boy.' Bob Molloy, for one, found Barnard to be a far more complex man than he at first thought.

Denys Rhoodie insists that Barnard got involved with the Information Department activities 'with his eyes open'. He also believes Barnard's propaganda value to South Africa far outstripped that of the other big name linked to the Department, golfer Gary Player. 'Gary was restricted to sport, but Chris's appeal went much further. As a doctor he appealed to the wider interests of humanity. Whenever Chris came back from a trip overseas he would report to John Vorster, tell him what he had picked up. He said it was his duty to do this. It didn't matter to him who was prime minister. The treatment he got afterwards when Botha was in charge was very shabby. Chris never talked to me about party politics. But he knew what he was doing. He was very shrewd.'

Robert Schrire, head of UCT's political studies department, and the son of Val Schrire, sees it differently. He was approached by Barnard as early as 1971 to act as a 'political consultant' to him. He turned him down. He also knew Rhoodie, and says, 'They were very similar. Rhoodie was a likeable gangster. He was perhaps what Chris would have been if he had gone into politics earlier.' Rhoodie approached Schrire about getting favourable treatment for a PhD. 'He had one from an Afrikaans institution but he wanted the status of one from UCT. He indicated that if his work for such a PhD was looked upon favourably I would benefit. The

Department of Information had a lot of good contacts, there was a lot of travel, and there would be a lot of good spin-offs for me, and so on. Chris was tailor-made for this kind of approach because he had an overweening ego, great ambition and political naivety, and that's a wonderful combination for a smarty like Eschel Rhoodie to manipulate. Chris was waiting to be manipulated.'

Once extradited from France, Rhoodie was convicted on five counts of fraud and theft involving public money by a court in Pretoria. He told the judge that Vorster himself had approved the decision that 'no rules apply in the psychological and propaganda war' Rhoodie had launched. He was sentenced to 12 years' jail but would serve only six as the terms would run concurrently. The convictions were later overturned by the Court of Appeal in Bloemfontein. Rhoodie moved to America, settling in Atlanta. He died from a heart attack in 1993. His widow Katy says, 'Eschel and Chris got on very well. They were both go-getters. Eschel sometimes complained that some of the people he dealt with seemed to have very deep pockets, but didn't deliver the expected results. He never once said that about Chris Barnard.'

12

Divorce Again and Karin

Barbara had been a lonely, overprotected child. Her adoptive parents' violent rows and her father's blatant infidelity had left deep scars. She was distant and aloof until she got to know people and felt she could trust them. 'She told me her mother had never held her tight,' says Gloria Craig, one of her closest friends. In Barnard, Barbara had a husband who was easily bored and who saw women as trophies to satisfy his ego and libido. If loyalty was perhaps the most important thing in Barbara's life, she would not find it in her marriage. 'For Chris the challenge of Barbara was long gone. He had her. He needed new challenges,' says Tony Ingala, who would come to know him well.

In the late 1970s Barnard embarked on a series of new commercial ventures. He hoped to build an upmarket health centre on the Mediterranean island of Kos – birthplace of Hippocrates – with a Greek tycoon, Aris Argyriou. Years later, in 1993, he would be granted honorary Greek citizenship – Greece would not allow a non-citizen to practise as a doctor, and Barnard had often treated patients during his trips there. The Kos project never quite materialised as planned. In the end he lent his name to a health resort run by Argyriou and paid numerous (free) visits to his five-star hotel.

Barnard was also dabbling in stocks and shares and property. He and Barbara had kept on the Clifton flat they had lived in for the first four years of their marriage, and were presumably renting it out. In November 1977 Barnard wrote to his old accountants listing three companies whose books, he complained, had still not been transferred to his new accountants. They were: CN Barnard Properties, CN Barnard Investments, and La Corniche Estates. How small or large each company's portfolio was is not clear. Fritz Brink told friends he had introduced Barnard 'to quite a few deals he made damn good money out of'.

In 1978 Barnard persuaded his friend Emiliano Sandri to sell him the lease on his La Perla restaurant in Newlands, Cape Town. It opened with the same name under Barnard's direction. Soon it was struggling, and Barnard turned to Tony Ingala, a successful entrepreneur. Ingala and an associate, Aldo Novati, took over the lease from Barnard in return for a monthly payment. They changed the name to La Vita. Barnard was also allowed to eat and entertain guests on the house there, and acted as an informal public relations man. It was still 'Barnard's restaurant'. The business took off.

Barnard's book career was also flourishing, although sales of *In the Night Season* did not match those of *The Unwanted* and his partnership with Siegfried Stander had run out of steam. (Their final novel together, *The Faith* would, after years of lying dormant, emerge into the light only because of the tenacity of an editor at British publisher Hutchinson, who insisted on various rewrites to the original draft.)

Barnard had, however, published other books in the meantime – *South Africa: Sharp Dissection* was followed by *Good Life, Good Death*, a typically forthright look at euthanasia, suicide and the ageing process. Barnard was able to draw on the experience of seeing his stroke-afflicted mother living out her final years in an undignified twilight zone where she was unable to perform basic functions for herself. He had never doubted that quality of life was more important than the quantity of years a person lived. Euthanasia was an act of mercy, he argued, and should be legalised. Suicide was 'a basic human right'. In this book he outlined the 'euthanasia pact' he had with Marius, the result of both surgeons having to stand by and watch a patient at Groote Schuur slowly die from cancer years earlier. A collection of his popular columns from the *Cape Times* was also published.

A few years earlier Barnard had narrated a series of wildlife conservation films made by a South African, Paul Middleton, which had sold abroad. Now he was approached by a European-based company, Multimedia, to do a television series and book called *The Body Machine,* in collaboration with a gloriously named British medical writer, John Illman. (On the dust-jacket Barnard was grandly but inaccurately described as someone who had 'consistently championed the underprivileged in South Africa, regardless of creed or colour'.) The book was an impressive, large-format work with graphic illustrations that aimed to give the 'latest perspectives on body health, body maintenance and body repair'. The plan had been for Barnard to narrate the television programmes. But after a disastrous start – Barnard kept fluffing his lines – the producers decided to abandon the idea, and another narrator was brought in. Barnard, who was reduced to introducing each programme, explained the embarrassment by saying that he was much better when speaking without a script.

With La Vita thriving Barnard and Ingala opened another restaurant in nearby Claremont, La Vita Grill. Seeing the money rolling in from their first restaurant, Barnard this time went 50-50 with Ingala: half the costs and half the profits. They would go on to open a third restaurant together in Tokai; Barnard would open a fourth in Welgemoed with a chef he had employed, Chris Lesley, and a fifth in Bloubergstrand in a hotel owned by Fritz and Maureen Brink. Barnard furnished the restaurant, and the Brinks paid him a monthly fee to use his name.

Barnard was travelling extensively, as usual. Marius's departure from Groote Schuur to go into politics had removed what had become an anchor for his brother at the hospital. The advent of cyclosporin would soon make the single-heart transplant more viable again, both in South Africa and elsewhere. Yet the 'piggyback' operation would continue to play a small but vital role in many heart transplant programmes around the world. Barnard's interest in routine cardiac surgery was rapidly waning, and he complained increasingly of arthritic pain. With his burgeoning business interests to think of he began seriously looking ahead to early retirement from Groote Schuur.

In 1979 Barbara had gone into partnership with Ingala's girlfriend, Bertha Ludolphi, to open a boutique selling Italian clothes. It was called B&B. Barbara was South Africa's most famous and glamorous woman, appearing on magazine covers around the world. People went to B&B to see her in the flesh and ask for an autograph. She and Bertha made occasional trips to Italy to buy stock, although the fiercely protective Zoellners were terrified their daughter might be abducted by the Red Brigades, left-wing terrorists then engaged in a campaign of murder and kidnap. The danger of these trips to Italy, it turned out, would not come from machine-gun-wielding renegades; it would arise on Barbara's doorstep, in her bedroom even, while she was away.

In December 1980 the Barnards had given an interview to *Fair Lady* in which they spoke of their perfect marriage. 'Despite all the gloomy predictions, I never doubted that our marriage would last,' said Barbara. 'When you live with someone you learn to understand and compromise.' Within a year the marriage was finished.

The boutique had initially given Barbara a new confidence and independence. But it would not last. Barnard could see the money the shop was making and would eventually succeed in buying Ludolphi out. In 1981 Barbara was becoming dangerously thin again, and her husband's lifestyle only served to deepen her anxieties.

There were two attractive young waitresses at the Claremont La Vita. 'Bertha and Barbara went away to Italy and as soon as they were gone I organised a dinner at my house for the four of us,' says Ingala. 'There was music and dancing and things went on from there.' The girl Barnard had taken a fancy to, a student at UCT who was waitressing part-time, visited him several times at his home while Barbara was in Italy. They went to bed, and the maids spotted them from the garden. It was not until months later that the maids told Barbara what had happened.

That discovery coincided with more devastating evidence of her husband's infidelity. 'Barbara had heard a few rumours about the waitress,' says Ludolphi, 'but then she found out Chris was having an affair with the daughter of a very prominent Cape Town personality. The girl's mother was a good friend of Barbara's but she had known about the affair and it was a tremendous blow to the friendship. It was this that really prompted the divorce.' Barbara wasted no time in calling her father and telling him she had finally had enough. He was on the plane from Johannesburg later that day.

Barnard always swore nothing had happened with the waitress, even in his later memoirs. But Barbara told friends the maids had described how the girl had been sitting around the house giving them instructions as if she lived there and asking them if Barbara was a good mother. They had seen the girl on Barbara's bed with Barnard. Ingala says, 'Chris and the girl had a fling for a short while, there is no doubt about that. He told me he was sleeping with her.'

Barnard was in Los Angeles when he took a call from his attorney to say Barbara planned to divorce him. He refused to rush back to deal with the crisis in his marriage, not believing she was serious. He had freewheeled through the previous 12 months, behaving as if, once again, he was invincible. He was pictured with blondes in New York and a black American actress, Norma Jordan, in Rome. Angelo Litrico's brother Franco says, 'It was known in our circle that Chris and Norma had an affair. Barbara heard about that too. It was also one of the things that led to their divorce.' Under the *Immorality Act*, which banned sex across the colour bar, Barnard would have faced prosecution if he had embarked on such an affair in his own country. The story does not seem to have been carried by South African newspapers, perhaps mindful of his litigious nature. (It had not been long since he had won several defamation cases abroad against newspapers that reported ridiculous claims in a book that he had cut out the hearts of live baboons while they screamed.)

As with the end of his marriage to Louwtjie, Barnard had to agree not to return home when he arrived back from America. Barbara sent his clothes in suitcases to the airport and from there he went to the Brinks' hotel in Bloubergstrand. Barbara threw the marital bed out of the house. 'When Barbara made up her mind about anything that was it,' says Ludolphi. 'She didn't have to think about the divorce. She knew she had to do it.' Gloria Craig was staying with Barbara at the time: 'I begged her not to divorce Chris but she said she would never forgive him.'

Within a fortnight of her decision the divorce was in progress on the grounds of irretrievable breakdown. As we have seen, Barnard's relentless need to travel had undoubtedly been a strong factor in Barbara's increasing insecurity and failing health. Her natural jealous streak did the rest. The latest stories of her husband's unfaithful behaviour were enough to bring matters to a head. Under the *Divorce Act* details of the evidence given by Barbara to the Supreme Court in Cape Town on 13 January 1982 could not be published. The hearing lasted just five minutes and Barbara, elegantly dressed in a cream linen suit, 'appeared nervous', said reports. Barnard was not in court – he was on a 10-day trip to

Europe and the US. After the hearing Barbara continued to live for a while in the family home in Constantia with the two boys, now aged ten and seven. The house, a gift from her parents of course, was in her name. The couple also ended their partnership in the boutique, with Barnard selling Barbara his half-stake. The divorce made international headlines, and this time the interest lay not only with the famous heart surgeon. Barbara had become an icon of fashion and beauty written about in gossip columns across the world.

Indeed, she may have seemed nervous in the witness stand, but outside the court she appeared confident, a mature woman of 31 with an unmistakeable resolve. 'At least I won't have to diet any more,' she told friends. One newspaper noted that despite the trauma of her divorce she had been seen out enjoying herself in the weeks leading up to the hearing, as if relishing her new freedom from marriage to a man nearly thirty years older. On New Year's Eve she had danced the night away at a Sea Point nightclub, Charlie Parker's. One of the men who ran the club was a handsome Mozambique-born Portuguese by the name of Joe Silva. He was in his late twenties. Ironically Barbara had first met Silva when she was part of a group that went to the club to celebrate Barnard's 59th birthday. 'I introduced Joe to everyone including Barbara,' says Gloria Craig. There appeared to be an instant attraction.

Barnard's bravado at the news that he was to be divorced dissolved swiftly into devastation when reality dawned. His devastation turned to despair and jealousy-fuelled rage when he discovered that Barbara was seeing Silva. He dismissed his rival as 'a nightclub bouncer' and embarked on a very public campaign to win Barbara back, even publishing poems and an open love letter to her in a national newspaper. He pledged to give up all overseas travel 'and give her the family life she wants'. It was desperate self-delusion.

This was, as he often admitted later, the lowest point in his life to date. He was now living in a room in the Brinks' house in Bloubergstrand. Maureen and Fritz bore the brunt of his descent into what friends believed was a mental breakdown. 'He'd be lying in bed too depressed to eat, smoking away,' says Maureen. 'We had to plead with him to eat. He wept every day.' He went to work, but was unable to function usefully. The happier Barbara appeared to be with Silva the deeper Barnard's jealousy ran. When he dropped off the boys one day and saw Silva at the house – a 'young, bronzed, hunk of a guy' – it sent him into a downward spiral of bitterness and self-pity that lasted for months. 'I still went to my office every day – just to stare into space and plot how to get Barbara back,' he said.

Barnard was by now a grandfather – André and Gail had had a son, Adam, in 1979. Deirdre had got married in 1978, six months after her brother, to an Afrikaner, Kobus Visser (Barnard had made sure he was present to give his daughter away). In 1980 Deirdre gave birth to a girl, Karen. Yet Barnard was behaving with embarrassing disregard for his status, professional and social. He was occasionally seen around Cape Town in a dishevelled state. 'I contemplated suicide many times,' he said later. The Brinks took a number of calls from various parts of the world when an inebriated Barnard threatened to 'end it all'. At one point he hired a sangoma – a witch-doctor – to cast an evil spell on the maids who had told Barbara of his liaison with the waitress. They were supposed to contract a fatal disease, but somehow they survived unharmed.

Barbara's falling for another, much younger, man was a blow to his ego Barnard simply could not handle. Frances Ames's comment that Barnard was caught in 'perpetual adolescence' was never more apt. Emotionally, at least, he was.

But his manipulative skills had not deserted him. The Zoellners took a strong dislike to Barbara's new man, fearing him to be a gold-digger (unjustly – Barbara and Silva went on to have a lasting and successful marriage, producing a daughter), and Barnard exploited it to the full. He used the rows between Barbara and her parents over Silva to win back some of her confidence. He pleaded with the Zoellners to be less critical of their daughter. After the juvenile tantrums he had thrown at the start, his attitude now seemed to be the model of maturity. Barbara softened towards him. They were seen having dinner together at La Vita several times (Barnard would not have to pay), and then eight months after their divorce they flew to a friend's game reserve on the edge of the Kruger Park for what was widely seen as an attempt to patch things up. The newspapers, of course, were full of speculation that they would decide to remarry, just as Richard Burton and Elizabeth Taylor had done some years earlier during a trip to South Africa.

But on their return to Cape Town things fizzled out. Barbara took up again with Silva, and Barnard realised he had finally lost her. He sought solace, as usual, in the company of women. Fritz Brink remembered one week when he slept with four different girls at his house. He went on a nine-day trip round the Baltics on Tony Ingala's cabin cruiser. 'There were lots of girls. Chris seemed to have a different girl in his cabin every night,' says Ingala. An Australian, Karen Storay-Dowdle, pitched up in Cape Town seemingly on the rebound from a failed marriage. She was the sister of a girl, Victoria, Barnard had already met through contacts at Multimedia during a trip to Israel. Later he would insist Victoria was the one he would rather have bedded. But for several months Karen, who was 25, and a well-known horsewoman in her own country, managed to keep him occupied. She moved into the room he was living in at the Brinks'. By the time they parted, during a cruise on the QE2, he had stopped smoking.

Another woman Barnard dallied with at this time was an anaesthetist, Sheila Etoe. She was 32. 'When we started seeing each other he was still quite sad from his divorce from Barbara,' she says. 'But we had a ball, going to parties and dances. He waffled on about marriage but I never took him seriously, and I certainly wasn't interested. He was a philanderer. I could see how easily he broke hearts.'

One of the parties they went to was at the home of Maureen Brink's sister, Eileen le Roux. While he was dancing with Etoe he noticed a beautiful young girl in a yellow dress. He had seen her before when she waitressed for an evening at his Welgemoed restaurant. Her name was Karin Setzkorn. She was 19, a model, tall with blonde hair and marble-blue eyes. She was also an Afrikaner.

In fact, it was the third time he had seen her, as he would discover later. In late 1969, during a weekend trip to Buffels Bay, Karin's mother had approached him and asked if her daughter, then six, could sit on the famous doctor's knee while she took a picture.

When he talked to her at the party Karin found Barnard interesting but was understandably wary of a man of 60 who had twice been divorced. He even told her mother, 'You're my future mother-in-law,' which had everyone laughing, but would turn out to be true. Coincidentally Karin had once opted to do an oral examination at school on Barnard's career because she had been so enthralled by his autobiography, *One Life.* Barnard left the party with Karin's number, and called her the next day, Valentine's Day – the anniversary of his wedding to Barbara – to ask her out that evening. She agreed, and they dined at La Vita in Newlands where Barnard presented her with a bunch of red roses. It was extraordinary behaviour for a man of Barnard's age. But he seemed oblivious to ridicule. 'I felt sorry for him,' says Karin. 'He was very persuasive, but I was also intrigued. There I was out with the famous heart surgeon.'

Barnard would spend the coming weeks sailing the world on the QE2 with Karen Storay-Dowdle. At each port he would buy postcards and send them back to Karin telling her how much he missed her. She still has them. What she did not know was that he was sending similar postcards back to a 32-year-old woman, Sandy Gelb, whom he had been seeing for several months. But when Barnard returned to Cape Town it was Karin he chased. For the next few months the relationship developed, despite efforts by Karin's friends to persuade her to break things off. They told her the age gap of 41 years was ludicrous and she was wasting her life. 'They thought I was crazy to go out with an old man,' she says. At one stage she seemed to take their advice and did her best to cool things down. But Barnard persisted. It was the hunter and his prey once again. What better way to get back at Barbara than to date a much younger girl?

Karin began accompanying Barnard to various functions. They spent a few days on the farm at Sedgefield, then at Mala Mala, the game reserve owned by Barnard's friend Mike Rattray where he had tried to rekindle his relationship with Barbara. Karin's early misgivings were forgotten: 'I found myself falling madly in love with him. It wasn't like being with an old man at all. We had a lot of fun. One evening we went out with my friends and even they had to agree you forgot about the age difference with Chris.' Karin's father, rather like Fred Zoellner, was not so enthusiastic. But he warmed to Barnard in his presence and would always describe him as 'South Africa's greatest ambassador'.

In his final years at Groote Schuur Barnard showed little sign of mellowing. He was still infamous for bawling and bullying, although the young residents he verbally abused usually accepted it would make them better surgeons. A Russian surgeon, Dimitri Novitsky, who was doing ground-breaking work at Groote Schuur on the effects of brain-death on the heart, said that when he joined Barnard's unit in 1979 most of the junior staff consisted of doctors from other countries. Barnard's intuition made a strong impact on him. 'His presence in the ward or in meetings with cardiologists always dominated the picture due to his tremendous knowledge of congenital heart disease, his judgement, and his easy approach to extremely complex situations. His strong personality was respected by everyone on his team, and, even though sometimes his suggestions were initially totally unreasonable to me, they always turned out to be right.' Novitsky recalled that before Marius had left Groote Schuur, 'this sort of premonition ... was a big headache for his brother Marius, who at that time was Associate Professor of Cardiothoracic Surgery, putting him many times in difficult situations.'

His obsessive involvement whenever a friend needed an operation was renowned. He took responsibility head-on. When he performed a bypass operation on 'Bullet' Myers, a popular radiologist he had worked with for many years, the heart refused to restart on its own. 'My mother and I were getting very anxious, but Chris made a point of coming out of the operating theatre and explaining to us what was going on,' says Myers's son Martin. 'He told us, "I can't let Bullet die on the table", and then he went back in and worked at it until my father's heart restarted and he finished the operation successfully.' Myers lived for another four years.

But this zealous personal commitment to friends coupled with a conviction that he knew best could provoke deep resentment among colleagues. His belief in instinct and the intangible healing effects of a loved one's presence at a patient's bedside often caused friction among doctors charged with the care of that patient. His involvement was dreaded. 'If I'd known he was a friend of Barnard I'd have taken a holiday,' was a remark made more than once by senior consultants at Groote Schuur.

Barnard announced that he planned to retire from Groote Schuur at the end of the year, 1983. His department's most notable achievement at this time was another world first: the development of a new perfusion method of storing donor hearts for transplant for up to 17 hours – four hours had been the maximum acceptable time until then – by a young researcher, Winston Wicomb. But Barnard seemed distracted and often bored. Wicomb later recalled that when they began to use stored donor hearts in transplant patients and it made news around the world, Barnard objected to the attention he was getting. 'He said he was tired of seeing my name in the press and instructed me to refer all newspapers to him. Yet he knew little about heart storage, nor did he really want to know.'

To Wicomb Barnard seemed much more interested in sex, sometimes calling him into his office to discuss his latest 'romantic fantasy'. He even invited Wicomb, his wife and her sister for dinner at La Vita and then proposed the four of them return to his home for a sauna. They declined.

Barnard was officially going early because of his arthritis. He rarely operated. John Hewitson, son of Rodney, who was supposedly training under Barnard at this time, recalls: 'I hadn't seen him for about eighteen months, and then one day he came in to do a photoshoot for a newspaper that was doing a story about his last operation.' The article appeared in the London *Mail on Sunday* on 5 June 1983. It opened: 'Christiaan Barnard, undoubtedly the most famous surgeon in the world, picked up his delicate instruments and began probing into the living heart showing through the open chest of the patient before him. But it quickly became apparent that he could not go on. He left the operating table to his assistants, stood for a moment on the sidelines with his head in his hands, a hunched figure in green boots, surgical coat and trousers. This man, who when he first transplanted a human heart was so celebrated that he was actually offered £25 000 for the rubber gloves he threw away after that operation, stood up swiftly and walked out of the room.'

It was a bravura performance. Undoubtedly Barnard's arthritis was troublesome and could be painful, and for years he had been forced to take a variety of pills to keep it in check. But the only way he could retire from Groote Schuur early was to claim ill-health. Otherwise he had to work until he was 65. He had performed nine single-heart transplants, one heart-lung transplant, 43 'piggy-back' transplants and a kidney transplant, as well as hundreds of more routine open-heart operations in the 25 years he had worked in the

Groote Schuur cardiac unit. 'The truth was he'd lost the hunger for surgery,' says Karin. 'He needed challenges. Surgery had become too mundane for him. He also wanted to be able to exploit the commercial value of his name.' Barnard would later admit as much himself.

Two years earlier he had hinted at his growing disillusionment. In a *Cape Times* column he had described being on his way to deliver a paper in Israel in which he planned to talk about the success of the heart transplant programme at Groote Schuur: 57 patients, of whom 17 were still alive. But in preparing his paper en route he read World Health Organisation figures which said that in the same period of 14 years some 400 million children had died from malnutrition. He had always said the plumber, who maintains water supply and sanitation, saves more lives than the doctor, but the WHO figures staggered him: 'What do you do when you take a look back at your whole career and realise with a jolt that you have been barking up the wrong tree?' he wrote. It was a swipe at his government's racist policies that allowed rheumatic fever and malnutrition to flourish among poor shack-dwellers while expecting doctors to carry on dealing with the casualties. He urged his colleagues to 'read the political page with as much attention as the medical journal'.

Financially by now he was secure. His restaurants were doing well. So too was his stud farm at Sedgefield – stocked with 40 top-quality cattle imported from Germany. In an interview he said he was worth 'around R500 000', quite a sum in those days. His assets included a sports car given to him by Datsun. By the middle of 1983 he had aroused the anger of the South African Medical and Dental Council by signing up for a series of newspaper advertisements for an insurance company. He had also been approached by a businessman, Armin Mattli, who was prepared to pay him a lot of money to get involved in his rejuvenation treatment centre in Switzerland.

His imminent retirement must have come as some relief to the UCT and Groote Schuur authorities. An untouchable thorn in their sides, he had refused to conform. Through his weekly newspaper column he had an instant open channel to the outside world for any grievance that took his fancy. He complained publicly about the shortage of nurses, blaming apartheid because it blocked the employment of coloured and black nurses in white wards, although things were slowly changing. When, in 1981, a student burned a South African flag – or bunting as the students preferred to call it – on campus in protest at 20th anniversary Republican celebrations, Barnard, a Senate member, leapt to his defence. The student, Nazeem Mahatey, was fined R75 by the university. Barnard told other members of the Senate they had overreacted. Bob Molloy recalls, 'I remember him saying about Mahatey: "That boy showed bloody good taste. I never did like that damn flag." His view of the Senate was that they were "just a bunch of old farts". He said they "grow old but they never grow up".' Mahatey, now a speech writer for President Thabo Mbeki, says, 'I know Chris Barnard spoke up for me. He was aghast that I should be punished.'

Barnard's stance on patriotism in general had been laid out in provocative style several years earlier, again in a *Cape Times* column: 'Patriotism for me, for this country at this time, isn't narrow sectarianism, it isn't some kind of totem pole to which I bow before I start thinking. And it certainly isn't a set of rigid tribal rules. I am an Afrikaner. My forefathers have been in this land for more than three centuries. My blood, like the rest of my tribe, is a mixture of Dutch, German, French, British and a medically proven percentage of Black, Coloured and Malay race groups, according to research by an Afrikaner who also happens to be one of South Africa's leading haematologists. It is said that blood dictates patriotism. If that is so then it dictates my wish to preserve a country we have fertilised with our dead, made wealthy by our living and, if called on, will maintain by our dying. It also dictates that I try to make that country liveable for my children and that means ultimately for the children of all who live here. And that is why my patriotism might blow cold on flag and anthem when these are but preludes to sabre-rattling, and blow hot on the throwing down of totem poles that delay real progress.'

Against the backdrop of rising violence around the country – this was the decade that would see apartheid finally being broken down – he rarely missed an opportunity to cause a political stir. He took on the Roman Catholic Church in South Africa over its call, in a Sunday school circular handed to Frederick and Christiaan, to boycott Republic Festival activities. He accused the church of encouraging violent demonstrations. 'I'll celebrate our Republic's 20th birthday in the hope that it stays stable long enough to grow up to allow a vote for everyone,' he said in a widely reported speech to a construction industry gathering.

His profile abroad as an apparent defender of the apartheid regime also remained a sensitive issue. In 1982 an invitation to receive an honorary doctorate from the University of Eastern Michigan, and to make a speech there, had to be withdrawn after black students threatened violent protest. Barnard fired off a furious letter which he asked to be read out at the ceremony in his absence, denying any support for apartheid: 'My published writings clearly oppose such policies and call for selection of public representatives on the grounds of competency only. The South African dilemma is being exploited by the mass media, by politicians, by certain groups and certain national interests for reasons unconnected with real concern for the sufferings of the oppressed people of my country. I leave it to you to decide whether your action to exclude me from your presence today may eventually prove to be a stumbling block or a stepping stone.'

Announcing Barnard's retirement the following year, the man in charge of hospital services for the Cape provincial administration, Piet Loubser, described him curiously as 'one of the most important export products of our country', adding, '... his name will be inscribed indelibly in the annals of our history'.

Typically Barnard used his official retirement speech at Groote Schuur to complain of the 'lack of support' from the hospital authorities for organ transplant work. He told 300 guests that the hospital was sliding towards Third World standards. Sixteen years earlier he had put Groote Schuur on the world map. Now he was leaving it with a bitter taste in his mouth. He was given the title Professor Emeritus, and with the aid of a R20 000 grant from the Chris Barnard Research Fund, UCT planned to set up the first Chris Barnard Chair of Cardiothoracic Surgery.

Barnard later confessed he was rather irked that his retirement gift was not a Rolex watch, but a hospital tie. Scornful of bureaucracy, he had neglected his responsibilities as head of cardiac surgery for too long. 'He left the department in a mess,' says Joe de Nobrega. Hannah-Reeve Sanders, then medical superintendent, says, 'He believed we had rejected him, but I believe he rejected us.' His official resignation letter to Sanders has two notes scrawled underneath in different hands. 'I thought he had already left,' said one, and the other: 'No, he was on the QE2.'

A second retirement function followed at the Red Cross Children's Hospital where André now worked as a paediatrician. A third was held at La Vita in Newlands. Barnard persuaded a pharmaceutical company to sponsor the party for 150 guests, so his restaurant made money. Karin, Deirdre and her husband Kobus were there, as were André and Gail. Some of Barnard's greatest successes also made it – Edith Black, who had received a new kidney in 1967; Leonard Goss, the second 'piggy-back' transplant patient; and Dirk van Zyl, who had been given a new heart in 1971 and would survive another ten years. (Dorothy Fisher had died in 1981, nearly 13 years after her heart transplant.) Barnard was presented with a bronzed pair of his surgical boots.

Shortly before his retirement another significant event had taken place in Barnard's life – the opening of the Chris Barnard Exhibition in the Beaufort West Museum. He had donated hundreds of medals and awards handed to him since the first heart transplant. Many represented the highest civilian award a country could give, although it would not be until 1992 that South Africa would honour one of its most famous sons by bestowing upon him the Order of the Southern Cross – Gold, for 'achievements in the interests of South Africa'. The original heart-lung machine he had brought back from Minneapolis in 1958 was placed in a corner of the exhibition. The old rectory that had been his family home had been restored, and its rooms recreated as closely as possible to how they had been when he was a boy. He gave to the house the only thing he said he had inherited from his parents: a stinkwood chair that today stands in the corner of the dining room. His father's mission church was also restored and, with the rectory, declared a national monument. In 1979 Barnard had been made a Freeman of Beaufort West.

This embracing of the family by a town that had, to their minds, shunned what their father stood for again divided the brothers. Initially Marius seemed enthusiastic, even helping to find some of the original furniture for the rectory and church. He also attended the official opening of the exhibition on 3 December 1983 by Lapa

Munnik, who was then minister of posts and telecommunications. But later Marius said he had not forgiven the white people of Beaufort West for the way they had ostracised his family. He would eventually go so far as to insist that all references to him in the rectory be removed.

*

The years following Barnard's retirement were to be as hectic as anything that went before, and no less controversial. He moved into an office given to him by Gloria Craig, and she found herself acting as his secretary despite having to run a busy fashion business. But almost before he had got started on his new life, Barnard was to be struck by a tragedy no-one could have foreseen. He was in Singapore relaxing after another QE2 cruise when he took a call from Fritz Brink. Karin had just left for the airport to return to South Africa, and Barnard was planning to go on to London. 'Chris, André committed suicide last night,' said Brink.

Barnard made what he later described as 'the saddest journey of my life': back to Cape Town via London, the quickest route. He arrived to find himself at the centre of another world story, only this was the most personal and painful of them all. He had known of André's problems for many months. For some years he had been trying to move on in his career and had recently been studying hard for examinations. Friends believed he had always felt 'in the shadow' of his illustrious father. 'Chris wanted André to be the best like him but the truth was he couldn't be,' says one friend. Others blamed Barnard's lifelong neglect of his son in favour of Deirdre. André's descent into drug addiction and depression seems to have begun after he was knocked down by a car outside Groote Schuur in January 1981. Father Tom Nicholson remembers him as a dedicated young man who loved his wife and two small children. 'André was a lovely man. He always sought the approval of his father and he never got it. He always felt he had to prove himself.'

On 29 February 1984 André's wife Gail had left him in charge of their two children to do a night shift at the Red Cross Children's Hospital. During the evening he had phoned Deirdre, telling her he was in the bath. When Gail returned home early next morning she could not get into the ground-floor bathroom, and went outside to walk round to the window. She saw André slumped in the water. A syringe lay on the floor close by. He had injected himself with a large dose of a painkilling drug which he had grown dependent on since his accident.

Colleagues at Groote Schuur had long warned Barnard that André was stealing prescription drugs from the hospital pharmacy. When he had emerged from the hospital after treatment following the accident he found a wound in one leg refused to heal properly and he became depressed by the pain. He was later admitted to the hospital's psychiatric wing where staff imposed a rigid regime of non-contact with family for some weeks. When this rule was relaxed Barnard visited his son, but seemed incapable of understanding the sensitivities of his illness. 'He would go there and chat up the nurses, which was hardly what André needed,' says Gail.

Barnard was convinced André had committed suicide: 'As a proponent of euthanasia and suicide ... I found great comfort in the thought that he'd gone to a far better place than that from which he'd come,' he later wrote. 'The quality of his life had deteriorated to the extent where there was no joy in living.' He pointed out to friends that André, being a doctor, had made sure he would die by sitting upright in a full bath of water before injecting himself. He knew when he became unconscious he would fall forward and drown. But Gail and other members of the family insist to this day that it was an accident, and that was supported by the verdict of the coroner, 'accidental death by drowning'. Gail says André was simply too devoted a father to have killed himself deliberately knowing that Adam, five, and Ashlea, three, would be left alone in the house all night. She believes he took the drug because he intended to do some studying that night and wanted to feel better. He had left Groote Schuur psychiatric unit only five months earlier and was tense about the forthcoming exams. 'He was scared of failing,' said Gail.

Louwtjie took herself off to a mountain to berate God. 'I really used abusive language. It was the worst thing to have happened to me,' she says. 'André's death destroyed everything.'

Media coverage inevitably focused on Barnard's relationship with his son. One newspaper published a critical letter André had written to his father 15 years earlier at the time of the divorce from

Louwtjie. One long-standing friend of the family believes Barnard repeated his mistake with André with the children from his later marriages to Barbara and Karin. 'We saw him favouring one over another in just the same way he had done with Deirdre and André,' she says. 'There was always one who could do no wrong.'

André's attitude towards his father had mellowed over the years. At the time of his qualification as a doctor at UCT in 1975 (he achieved higher grades than his father) he had chosen to miss the graduation ceremony rather than have his divorced parents attend together. He took off on a trip to South America. But whatever pressure he may have felt to emulate him, he was proud of his father's achievements. At his black tie graduation dinner he had invited Barnard as his guest, believing South Africa's most famous doctor would be asked to make a speech. When he wasn't, André was devastated.

At André's funeral, held at the Maitland Crematorium in Cape Town, Barnard openly sobbed. All the family members were there. So too was Barbara. Karin stayed away. At the inquest into his death later that year evidence was given that André had suffered 'an acute reaction' to the painkilling drug Wellconal, rendering him unconscious, rather than an overdose. He had died from drowning as he slumped forwards in the bath. André had put crushed Wellconal tablets, mixed with saline, into a syringe. A needle was found hanging from his arm. The pathologist had found 'a number of old and recent puncture marks' on his body. The head of the Groote Schuur psychiatric unit, Eleanor Nash, told the inquest that André had been treated for 'drug dependency, depression and significant personality problems'.

When André had asked his father for a loan to help him buy a small house in 1979 Barnard, who had never bought a house himself, told him: 'It will just be a noose around your neck,' and said no. André got the money from his mother. Now that his son was dead, Barnard seemed to want to make up for the past. At Deirdre's suggestion he took Gail to dinner and told her not to worry about money. He would pay her R500 a month to enable her to give up night work so that she could look after Adam and Ashlea. He also promised to pay for the children's education. In fact he paid for Adam's prep school but Gail received nothing for Ashlea. When she remarried in 1988 she got a letter from Barnard's attorney saying the children were no longer his responsibility. 'He could have called me up to tell me himself but I think he was too embarrassed,' says Gail.

André's childhood was a happy one, according to Gail. But as an adult he could never meet his own expectations. 'He never felt he was good enough, especially after the breakdown. He lost a lot of confidence and he couldn't cope with the pressure of work and studying for his final exams in paediatrics. It was stress. He was taking things to pep him up and things to slow him down. It was a roller coaster. I had Louwtjie telling me it was my fault because he wasn't like that when he left her. The intensive therapy he received opened a can of worms. His true feelings came out, about the divorce, how his mother treated him and how his father treated him. He'd been bottling it up until then. Louwtjie blamed Chris, and Chris said André hadn't lived, that he should have had loads of girlfriends, and that he was too much under the influence of his mother and the DRC. André had had one or two girlfriends but I was his first serious one. We were very happy, but he had this fight within himself all the time.'

To this day Gail remains angry with Barnard for insisting André committed suicide. 'Saying his son killed himself allowed Chris to do the "Oh, woe is me" bit. He said André had a death wish because he was injecting himself and he should have snapped out of it. He said André had no backbone. But André didn't have a death wish. He was very sensitive. He was a thinker.' André loathed his father's pursuit of young women. 'Why should I eat biltong when I can have fillet steak?' was Barnard's stock, and rather shallow, refrain. He threw a big party at La Vita in Newlands to celebrate Karin's 21st birthday – at which he proudly displayed a blown-up version of the picture of Karin on his knee when she was six – and André and Gail reluctantly went. 'He hated every minute of it. He felt deeply embarrassed. It hurt him too much to think of his father with this reputation. He had been indoctrinated by Louwtjie that his father was a dirty old man who just wanted to sleep with young girls. But André would never have stood up to Chris over that. He wanted approval from him.' Years later Barnard would tell André's children, tearfully: 'I wasn't there for your dad. I could have done a lot more for him.'

In *The Second Life* Barnard did at least acknowledge Gail's view that André died accidentally, but adds: 'I didn't dwell on it too much. All I knew was that my son was dead ... I should have given him the love and affection he needed when he was a little boy. It was my fault.' Strangely, whenever Barnard was asked about the worst moment of his life, he never mentioned André's death. It was always his divorce from Barbara, or, much later, his divorce from Karin.

André's death focused attention again on Barnard's relationship with Deirdre. They had always been extremely close. In 1987 Barnard admitted in an interview how close: 'I must be honest. I think Deirdre is very jealous. She got really fed up with me about a year ago when I told her, "Deirdre, you can't be my daughter and my girlfriend, it's not possible." She really doesn't like me being with other girls. I think it must be very difficult and upsetting for her to see pictures of me with beautiful women all the time. I think she really wants to be the only girl in my life.' He would not like Karin and Deirdre to live across the street from one another. 'That would cause trouble, because not only is Deirdre jealous of Karin, but Karin is jealous of Deirdre – it works both ways.' In the same article Deirdre confirmed she was 'sometimes a bit jealous' of her father's girlfriends. She had even had a relationship with a man who was a reflection of her father 'and he broke my heart in two'. She had married a man who was completely the opposite. Barnard, she revealed, still gave her 'a pretty generous allowance'.

*

Barnard's association with Armin Mattli would earn him a huge amount of money and an even greater amount of ridicule. The two men would become close friends for some years but fall out suddenly and permanently in bizarre circumstances. Mattli ran a centre near Basle, Switzerland, called Clinique La Prairie, where rich people had themselves injected with the cells of aborted lamb foetuses. It was supposed to rejuvenate a person's own cells, curing disease and reversing the ageing process. Barnard, a man of science whose own views on ageing were well known and whose lifestyle seemed to be dedicated to staving off the inevitable – he had long dyed his hair and despite his denials was widely believed to have had face-lifts – was a perfect front for such a product. Years earlier he had gone to the clinic twice at Mattli's invitation to see if the injections of lamb foetal cells could cure his arthritis. (According to Fritz Brink, who said he had had to put up new shelves at his home to accommodate Barnard's arthritis pills, he showed a 'remarkable improvement' after these injections.) Now Barnard agreed to get involved in the 'cellular therapy' research. Even when pathologists at Groote Schuur, including Ernette du Toit, carried out some laboratory tests for him and told him the idea was 'rubbish', he went ahead and signed a three-year contract to head a team of 12 researchers.

Mattli, who still runs the clinic, says he offered Barnard a role exploring possible treatment for cancer cells, a spin-off from the rejuvenation research. 'We had many professors there of international reputation from many countries. Such research naturally had to be conducted in absolute secrecy until a patent was presented. But Barnard began talking about it and the team got upset, so he had to quit.' He had been paid Sfr 250 000 (around £70 000), and had enthusiastically endorsed the rejuvenation treatment by telling newspaper and television interviewers that he had had several courses. Mattli was now developing an anti-ageing cream, Glycel, based on the research at Clinique La Prairie, and he offered Barnard a lucrative deal to help market the product internationally. Barnard, conscious of his reputation, insisted his name should be strictly linked to the research rather than the product; but he would be mentioned on the label and to most people that was a clear endorsement. The two men travelled throughout America, Latin America and Asia. Despite having Karin, Barnard behaved wildly on these trips. 'I found him a very difficult man,' says Mattli. 'One day he was full of sunshine, the next day he was in a very bad mood. He always seemed to have to be the big conqueror of women. He would brag about all the famous women he had slept with. I had to present him with girls all the time, and I paid for them.'

Barnard's book career had taken a problematic turn. *The Faith* had at last been published in London but had not sold particularly well, although one reviewer in South Africa praised it generously as 'a thriller with depth' and urged anyone who agreed with the *Immorality Act* to read it because its portrayal of a white doctor's love for a coloured nurse exposed the inhumanity of such a law.

Barnard also published a second collection of his *Cape Times* columns with Bob Molloy, *The Best of Barnard* (the columns ended the following year after Molloy emigrated to New Zealand). In the same year, 1984, Barnard published *The Arthritis Handbook*, compiled with a BBC journalist, Peter Evans. On the face of it, it should have been a straightforward book giving millions of arthritis sufferers worldwide some useful tips on how to cope with their condition. It turned out to be a legal disaster, thanks to Barnard's highly personal account of how his arthritis had been to blame for his divorce from Barbara.

In a chapter headed *The Personal Dimension* Barnard wrote of how his arthritis had virtually disappeared after he married Barbara because he was 'emotionally settled' and 'physically very active'. It would flare up at times of stress, though, and in later years he often had to rest at weekends rather than play with the children. 'Then came the bombshell. Barbara came to me one day saying she wanted a divorce. She had met a younger man, a fine active guy who, she said, could give her the sort of life I could not.' He had stated earlier in the chapter that his marriage to Louwtjie had ended after he had first fallen in love with Barbara, suggesting their affair was the reason for the divorce. He went on to claim that the stress of the break-up from Barbara had caused a flare-up in his arthritis which prevented him from winning her back. 'I honestly believe I might have won Barbara back if it was not for my condition.' It was a grossly distorted picture of events, and Barbara was infuriated, threatening legal action. Eventually her lawyers and Barnard's lawyers agreed that an apology and statement should be pasted into all the unsold copies of the book. It said Barnard had met Barbara only after his marriage to Louwtjie had got into 'serious difficulties', and that Barbara had not told him she wanted a divorce to marry a younger man.

The publicity surrounding Barnard in the mid-1980s seemed to go from bad to worse.

A hunting trip to Botswana with George van Wyk and a documentary crew went wrong when the party came across two lionesses with their cubs. One lioness was run over by a truck, and the other was shot and wounded but not killed. As the animals staggered around in agony some of the hunting party hurled tin cans at them in front of the camera. The trip had been infiltrated by a wildlife campaigner, Carol Hancock, who was the cameraman's girlfriend. A few weeks later an article appeared in a magazine, *Scope*, under the heading *Bloodbath in Botswana.* It said as well as the cruel killing of the lionesses the hunters had slaughtered five buffalo, six zebra and a protected brown hyena. They had hunted at night and shot animals from moving vehicles, both offences. Barnard, who was supposed to be providing celebrity appeal for the pro-hunting film, was described in the article as a 'horrified observer'. But in the court case that followed, Hancock said it was Barnard who had finally killed the two lionesses with shots from inside his vehicle (he said he did this as an 'act of mercy'). When he realised things had turned sour Barnard left the party and flew back to Cape Town. He escaped prosecution – only three men from Botswana who had been part of the twelve-strong group were charged. Botswana's assistant attorney general called the hunting trip 'criminal and savage'.

Barnard's involvement first with the cell therapy and then with Glycel spawned vast numbers of features in newspapers and magazines. Then it ran into problems with the Federal Trade Commission, which monitors the claims made for products, and the Food and Drug Administration. Barnard was called to give evidence by the FTC. Both bodies felt Barnard's association suggested Glycel was more than a cosmetic and should perhaps be registered as a drug, with the properly approved tests. At around $200 Glycel was not cheap. It was, though, very successful – Harrods in London and Bloomingdales in New York sold it in record quantities. But it gave cynical interviewers all the scope they needed to poke fun at Barnard, a Lothario well into his sixties who was still running after young girls, and his 'magic potions'. Privately, Barnard often admitted the claims made for Glycel were 'nonsense'. Yet he carried on taking the money, increasing doubts about his ethics.

In 1986 his embarrassment in the eyes of his medical peers was complete when the American College of Surgeons, which had made him a Fellow in 1963, summoned him to a disciplinary hearing for 'unprofessional behaviour' over his links to Glycel. Barnard insisted he did not endorse the cream but he had allowed his name to be used on the jar labels describing his research work – the co-development of the key ingredient, glycosphingolipids (GSL), which he said protected cells from damage from ultraviolet light. Rather than suffer the indignity of the hearing he resigned from the organisation in a huff.

By now Barnard had also accepted a post as 'scientist in residence' at the Baptist Medical Center in Oklahoma, where an old friend from Minneapolis, Nazih Zuhdi, was setting up a heart transplant unit. He would be paid $200 000 a year for two years. He did not have to operate – he was not licensed to practise in the US – but merely act as a consultant.

They provided him and Karin with top-class accommodation and a car. Barnard couldn't cope with driving on the right-hand side of the road so Karin did most of the driving, and generally acted as his personal assistant. She remembers Barnard's arthritis being so painful at this time that she had to dress him in the morning. Mattli had sold the patent and distribution rights for Glycel to an American, Irwin Alfin. Karin began working for Alfin and would travel extensively around America, training staff in shops that sold Glycel. (After the investigation by the FDA, leading stores in America and Britain would withdraw Glycel from sale.)

Barnard was earning serious money. His boyhood dream of becoming wealthy had been realised. It was ironic that he had achieved riches at the temporary expense of his professional reputation – until he publicly admitted his involvement in Glycel was a mistake for a man of serious scientific standing, his ethics were seen to be questionable. Yet the money was too good to turn down. Mattli says he paid him a total of around Sfr 1 million (around £300 000). Irwin Alfin paid him $220 000. Mattli and Barnard became such good friends that when, in 1989, Karin gave birth to their first child, they named him Armin, and Mattli was his godfather.

But Barnard's business relationships usually collapsed in rows and recriminations at some point, and this one was perhaps the most bitter fallout of all. In 1992 Mattli was seriously injured in Switzerland by a gang wielding wooden bats. He was left for dead in the street. For 75 days he was hooked up to a life-support machine at Zurich's University Hospital. 'That is when Barnard visited me,' he says. 'He stayed at the Eden Au Lac in Zurich. The bill for his expenses he sent to my office for payment. He told the team of professors who took care of me it was a waste of money – they should stop the life-support machine, it was useless. Two days later he went with an American man to Clinique La Prairie and told him this clinic will soon be up for sale and we could make a very good business together. But I came round eventually. All this came to my ears and naturally our friendship was over.'

Mattli gave the South African franchise for marketing Glycel to Karin, rather than Barnard, giving her the 5% commission on sales. Barnard later launched a court action in Switzerland, claiming he was owed royalties by Mattli. It failed. 'He said I was misusing his name, that he had never received a penny from me and he asked the court to close down my factory. I presented to the court all of my signed contracts with Barnard, together with all the receipts which showed a total of about Sfr 1 000 000. The judge could hardly believe his eyes.' The two men never spoke again. Friends of Barnard say he wanted to change Armin's name, but Karin refused. At the end of his life, when he grew fond of talking sentimentally about his regrets, he would say his involvement with Glycel had been his biggest mistake. Nonetheless, it had helped him build up a small fortune.

*

Confirming Barnard's perennial belief that he was appreciated more abroad than at home, the 20th anniversary of the Washkansky heart transplant in 1987 was barely marked in South Africa, although the *South African Medical Journal* published a special article by Barnard. But in Oklahoma they were not going to let such a milestone pass without a fuss. Heart transplants had become acceptable again thanks to cyclosporin and other improvements that guaranteed a better success rate. There was a jubilant atmosphere at the swish black tie gala dinner, $18,50 a head, held in Barnard's honour at the Oklahoma City Golf and Country Club on 4 December 1987. Walt Lillehei and Denton Cooley, two of the very greatest names in heart surgery, were there to pay warm, personal tributes, proof that not all Americans saw Barnard as the upstart who stole their glory. Cooley told the guests that the first heart transplant had been 'like the assassination of John F Kennedy or the bombing of Pearl Harbour. You never forget where you were and what you were doing when you heard of it.' Lillehei, a man with a wry sense of humour, said: 'Chris generously admits that I taught him everything he knows about cardiac surgery. I have to remind him periodically that I haven't taught him everything I know.' The joke didn't please Barnard – he barely spoke to Lillehei for the rest of the evening.

Barnard often gave more candid interviews when abroad: in Italy in 1974 he had told a magazine he wanted to set up a cardiac clinic there because there was more poverty in Europe than in South Africa, a statement he would surely not have dared make at home. In the run-up to the 20th anniversary celebrations he told the local Oklahoma newspaper that he did not miss surgery at all. He went further: 'I have never been very keen on the operating room side. I only enjoyed it when it was something new I was trying. When it came to routine, I didn't enjoy it any more.' What he did miss was operating on children. 'I always said that if people ask me what I want to be remembered for, it's not the transplant. I'd like to be remembered for the surgery I did on children born with abnormal hearts. The results are really very gratifying because you can change a child who has never enjoyed normality to a child who has a normal life expectancy and normal activity.'

At 65 he appeared to be in reflective mood during this interview, admitting that he had 'made mistakes' and would do things differently if given the chance. For one thing, he would not have accepted all the invitations he received after the first heart transplant. 'If I did it over, I would be much more selective.' He had never sought publicity, he said, yet he believed 80 per cent of doctors hated him for it. 'The unpopularity I have hurts me especially because of the fact that I have really contributed very little towards it.' He even confessed to becoming increasingly nervous about giving lectures as he got older because of the pressure on him to perform well.

While Barnard spent most of the year in America, South Africa was going through ever more tumultuous times. PW Botha's Rubicon speech in 1985, in which he rejected the concept of one man, one vote and said he would not lead South Africa down the road to 'suicide', had led to a tightening of international sanctions and a further mass withdrawal of foreign companies and investment. Oliver Tambo and the ANC in exile in Lusaka had called for the country to be made ungovernable, and the youths in the townships were obliging. It was known by very few people that informal contacts were being forged between Nelson Mandela and the government.

Barnard had long urged the release of Mandela – now in Pollsmoor prison – but on the grounds that the apartheid regime had turned him into a hero by keeping him in jail. He had no doubt that Mandela was a communist terrorist who deserved his punishment, as he wrote in a letter to the *Washington Post* in June 1987: 'From television and newspaper reports I gather that the experts on South Africa on Capitol Hill, supported by your newspaper, are again devising ways and means of saving my Fatherland. One of their demands was and still is the release of Mr Nelson Mandela and the political prisoners from our jails … I am also in favour of releasing Mr Mandela and the political prisoners, but for different reasons. While they remain in jail they are considered martyrs and folk heroes. Once outside the protection of the prison walls they become ordinary men who have to face the realities of the day. They will have an opportunity to justify the esteem in which you hold them, and demonstrate their democratic orientation like Fidel Castro and the Ayatollahs, your previous champions of Freedom.' Elsewhere he said he wanted apartheid scrapped but argued fiercely against sanctions, claiming it would place 15 million children under threat of famine.

Despite the turmoil, Karin was keen to return to South Africa. Barnard had shed all but two of his restaurants – he would keep his connection with La Vita in Newlands until 1998 – but he had bought a large farm in the Karoo near Richmond, about a hundred kilometres from Beaufort West, where he planned to raise sheep. He had been reluctant to commit himself to a third marriage. But Karin was growing restless. She told him she wanted a baby.

13

Marriage and Divorce (Again!)

Barnard's engagement to Karin had been an emotional one. When she landed in New York after a flight from South Africa she discovered some of her luggage had gone missing. In tears she phoned Barnard, who reminded her of a saying he claimed Sophia Loren had once told him: 'Never cry over something that can't cry over you.' When she got to Oklahoma he presented her with a solitaire engagement ring. The spectacularly large diamond turned out to be flawed, but later he bought her a ring with a properly certified diamond. Karin wanted marriage and dismissed Barnard's fears for the health of any child they might have – he still held a superstitious belief that the baby of an elderly father ran a greater risk of being born with defects. 'I desperately wanted a child,' says Karin.

They had found a three-bedroom townhouse in Welgemoed, close to Karin's parents. It was the first family home Barnard had bought himself outright. (In 1986 he had bought a house at an auction belonging to George van Wyk in Plettenberg Bay, complete with furniture, and would, many years later, sell it at a huge profit without compensating Van Wyk for the furniture, another bone of contention between the two men, according to Van Wyk.) In January 1988, nearly four months after their engagement, Barnard and Karin were married in Cape Town, in a civil ceremony before a magistrate. The following evening Father Tom Nicholson – who had undergone heart bypass surgery in 1981 under Barnard – conducted another, symbolic marriage ceremony, more of a blessing, during a 'champagne-and-lobster' party for 140 people at La Vita in Newlands. Deirdre, by now long resigned to her father's taste in ever-younger women, attended, as did Frederick and Christiaan, now teenagers.

Exclusive rights to cover the La Vita event were sold to *Rapport*, the Afrikaans Sunday newspaper. But the paper's rivals, the Johannesburg *Sunday Times*, caused an uproar by digging up a copy of the picture of Karin sitting on Barnard's knee when she was six, and plastering it across the front page. (It led to a court case in which Karin's mother, who had taken the picture, was compensated by the newspaper.) With a select few friends the newlyweds honeymooned on the Blue Train, which stopped in Beaufort West where many of the town's coloured community turned out to cheer them; and then at Mala Mala game reserve, their stay a wedding gift from the owner, Mike Rattray.

Before the wedding, an antenuptial agreement was drawn up – as it had been before his marriage to Barbara – by Noel Tunbridge. This time it was Barnard who had most to protect. In the event of a divorce Karin would not be automatically entitled to half of Barnard's estate, or to half his post-marriage business profits (or losses). They would be married out of community of property.

After the wedding it was just a few months before Karin fell pregnant, despite Barnard's increasing worries about his virility. At one point he consulted a geneticist to allay his fears that his age might be the cause of defects in the child. Armin was born, perfectly healthy, in February 1989 by Caesarian section. Barnard was against the idea of Karin enduring a natural birth. 'He was not in favour of natural birth because he felt medicine had moved on,' she says. 'I was happy to go along with it and so was my doctor because I have a slightly small pelvis.' For the first time Barnard was present at the birth. 'It was such an emotional experience for him that he was almost blown off his feet,' says Karin.

Barnard hit upon a novel idea for the baptism: it would take place in his father's old mission church in Beaufort West. Armin Mattli was to be godfather. Again, an exclusive deal would be done with a magazine. 'I decided the media had made enough money out of me and it was time I made some,' said Barnard. The town's coloured community once more turned out to cheer and applaud the returning Barnard boy.

Wealthier than he had ever been, Barnard was active in the property market. He bought a house in Bloubergstrand which he would later convert to three apartments and sell. He also bought some land at Pringle Bay where he built a holiday cottage that has remained in the family. La Vita in Newlands was still doing well, but he parted company with Chris Lesley after a fire destroyed the Welgemoed restaurant. Again, a business partnership ended in acrimony.

At the end of the 1980s the momentum of violent protest, coupled with the crushing pressure of international sanctions, was pushing the country towards an historic breakthrough: the unbanning, in February 1990, of the ANC and PAC and, a few days later, the release of Nelson Mandela after 27 years in jail. For some time secret negotiations had been going on between the ANC and Pretoria, with several other leading figures including Walter Sisulu having been freed from jail shortly before Mandela. Yet, to the delight of those Afrikaners who equated black rule with Armageddon, a bloody conflict between the Inkatha Freedom Party of the Zulus and the ANC-supporting United Democratic Front was escalating.

Perhaps encouraged by the fact that PW Botha had now gone and the more reasonable FW de Klerk was NP leader and state president, Barnard decided to throw his hat into the political ring again. In late 1989 he campaigned for the newly formed Democratic Party, which had grown out of the PFP, speaking at election rallies and sounding off wherever possible in interviews about the state of the country. (Marius, who had been a PFP MP and party health spokesman, had decided against becoming a member of the DP and did not stand in the 1989 election.) In one day Barnard spoke at no fewer than four rallies. Explaining why he had given up hoping that the NP would reform the country, and why others should do the same, he said: 'If a patient goes to a doctor for 40 years and finds he has still not been cured of his illness, then it is surely time to go to another doctor who can do the job.' His efforts were not in vain. The DP won 33 seats, behind the Conservative Party's 39 and the NP's 94. More importantly, the DP had taken 12 seats from the NP. 'We got excellent exposure in the press for a couple of days after Chris Barnard announced his support,' says Colin Eglin. 'He certainly helped to move the tide along. That election was very good for us.'

But the freeing of Mandela did not, as hoped, stem the mounting and terrifying blood-letting between Inkatha and ANC supporters. Nightly the world's television screens were filled with scenes of carnage, the conflict portrayed as a black power struggle over who should control a post-apartheid South Africa. Another faction entered the fray: right-wing extremist Afrikaners, led by Eugene Terre'Blanche, were embarking on a campaign of violence designed to wreck what hopes remained of a peaceful transition to black majority rule. It looked every day as though the country must be engulfed in an internecine civil war. Barnard announced he wanted to quit and live in Switzerland with his young family. Such was the concern over the negative impact his stance might have that FW de Klerk asked to see him in Pretoria.

'The violence in the black townships is unbelievable,' Barnard told Fred Bridgland in April 1991, just ahead of his meeting with De Klerk. 'I'm witnessing the worst atrocities I've seen in my life, with people being hacked and burned to death every day. I don't want my two-year-old son to grow up in such an atmosphere. I don't want him to face the possibility of being necklaced.' Barnard talked to Bridgland on his farm near Richmond, Ratelfontein. In the four years he had owned the farm he had stocked it carefully with the aim of creating a nature reserve – zebra, springbok, caracal, kudu and ostrich roamed freely. A year earlier he had spent £20 000 on bringing in wild animals. Eventually these would include rhino – not very successfully – and the goal would alter: he hoped to set up a game reserve for hunting as well as conservation, but would die before he could see the dream fully realised.

In the same Bridgland interview Barnard gloomily predicted that tribal warfare would reduce South Africa to 'the condition of an Angola, Mozambique or Zambia'. He again condemned sanctions, blaming them for creating the poverty that he saw as being at the heart of the violence and crime wave sweeping the country: 'The promise of one man, one vote is no magic wand. What comfort is a vote if you lack the very means of survival, if you're dying from starvation, as so many of our black people are? People in the townships get violent because there's nothing there to live for. We have to give them a physical and financial stake in our country. Alongside the slogan of One Man, One Vote, we also need the slogan One Man, One Job, One Child.' Coming from a man who had married three times and fathered five children, the last remark, suggesting population control of blacks, provoked a flood of indignant letters. He had also suggested elsewhere that if each man was entitled to a vote, highly educated people like himself should get ten votes. But overall his views touched nerves and were given widespread foreign coverage. With hindsight, they were typical of the doom-mongers of the day.

Characteristically, Barnard had publicly announced his intentions of emigrating without consulting the one person whose approval he needed – Karin. It was not long before she was making plain her utter refusal to live abroad again. 'Nobody asked me what I wanted to do, and my views happen to differ from some of my husband's,' she said. 'We are not leaving the country. We are not even planning on leaving. We are merely looking at the possibility of dual citizenship. I still love South Africa. We have a good quality of life here and I don't think we would be able to find that kind of life anywhere else.' She admits now they fought over his bleak assessment of the country's future: 'We argued a lot about how depressed he was. He told me I buried my head in the sand like an ostrich.'

Barnard's meeting with De Klerk, and his award the following year of the Order of the Southern Cross – Gold, for his outstanding contribution to South Africa, seemed to go some way to allaying his worst fears. But with a large farm and a new young family to support, he was desperately in need of money. In the 1990s he appeared in various television and newspaper advertisements, selling products from engine oil to breakfast cereals. But ever since the success of *One Life* Barnard had been considering writing a sequel that would tell the story of his life after the first heart transplants. *One Life* had been a huge success but he had, of course, donated all his royalties from that book to the Chris Barnard Fund for research. Under the terms of the original contract for *One Life* he was entitled to keep any money paid for film rights. Now and again a Hollywood film company had come along and paid him a tidy sum, perhaps $20 000, for an option on the film rights. But no film was ever made. *One Life* had portrayed him as a driven but altruistic, morally upright man battling a crippling disease, who prayed before operations. This time he intended to cash in on his reputation as a playboy and produce what he believed would turn the book into a bestseller – racy tales of his sexual exploits. This would be priapic Barnard.

He needed a writer and first he approached his old collaborator, Bob Molloy, still living in New Zealand where he ran a newspaper business. When Molloy turned him down – a decision he later admitted he regretted – he linked up with Chris Brewer, a journalist and public relations consultant. They were paid an advance of R100 000, believed to be the biggest advance ever paid then in South Africa, and a further R100 000 in advances from foreign publishers.

The Second Life turned out to be a commercial flop. It was published in South Africa by Vlaeberg, and in France, Germany, Greece and Australia but not in Britain or America. Brewer believes it was not properly marketed, although it did get plenty of press coverage. Barnard's tales of his fling with Gina Lollobrigida and how she had driven him back to his hotel dressed in nothing but a mink coat inevitably made headlines. So too did his admission that he had once smoked marijuana with Peter Sellers and, on another occasion, tried cocaine. DRC ministers called for the book to be banned, and one psychologist said it suggested Barnard had gone senile. In general these memoirs were condemned for being too sleazy, and Barnard was branded a 'kiss-and-tell-merchant'. Louwtjie called it 'an ugly book'. 'Within half an hour of the book coming out I got calls from Louwtjie, Barbara and Karin,' says Father Tom Nicholson. 'Actually I don't believe most of those things happened, the sex I mean. Chris knew sex sells and he wanted the book to sell.'

Barnard blamed Brewer for the backlash over *The Second Life.* Once again a partnership dissolved in bitterness and anger. 'He exploded one day and told me I'd written a crap book,' says Brewer. The two men did not speak for several years.

Barnard was not put off writing books, though. He had an idea for another novel, about a dynamic heart transplant surgeon who gets involved in shady goings-on at a big hospital, named Groote Schuur: he and a crazed research scientist with a Nazi past set up a ward of potential donors who are kept 'alive' so that their organs can be used at any time for transplant. The surgeon, Rodney Barnes, is horrified when his lover falls from a horse and, after being declared brain-dead, becomes the first inhabitant of the ward. In an effort to stave off her use as a donor, he instigates various unethical experiments on the bodies in the ward. After a promising start the novel descends into farcical scenes involving a dominatrix, a cross-bred baboon-child and the artificial insemination of Barnes's clinically dead lover. The novel would be called *The Donor*.

The kernel of this idea seems to stem from an outline sent to Barnard by Siegfried Stander back in the 1970s. Barnard appears to have suggested what Stander calls a 'sub-plot' about a scientist falling in love with a corpse. But the main theme was Stander's. Stander headed his note to Barnard: *Thoughts on the 'Body-Snatchers' book.* He wrote that a young scientist at a military research centre 'discovers there is a security area in the lab to which only senior researchers are allowed access. There's a hint that it conceals military secrets ... Then he discovers the truth: that they are keeping a number of dead people "alive". This is where we can use the sub-plot you suggested i.e. a scientist falling in love with one of the corpses.'

Barnard makes no acknowledgement in *The Donor* to any debt he may have owed Stander for the central theme of the story, but that may well be for the best as far as Stander's reputation is concerned. He did, however, thank a number of colleagues, including Eugene Dowdle and, especially, Bob Molloy; also Hamilton Naki, one of the key black research workers who had developed remarkable surgical skills in the Groote Schuur animal laboratory. Fittingly for a novel published in the era of the new South Africa, Barnard devoted much space to describing how a black man called Samuel Mbeki, nicknamed 'Boots' as one of his real-life laboratory staff had been (Frederick Snyders), had hauled himself up from being a gardener to learn how to carry out heart transplants on animals. (In 2003 Naki, who had started as a gardener, was awarded an honorary Master of Science degree in Medicine from UCT in recognition of his research work, which included transplanting the liver of a pig.)

There is no evidence that Barnard himself had ever dabbled in the kind of genetic engineering and tasteless experiments featured in *The Donor* (barring his two-headed dog) but the book does contain another macabre concept that he certainly had seriously considered once: using the hearts of hanged men. It was a throwback to the early anatomists who advanced their science using the corpses of executed criminals. They had worked mostly at night and in secret, and the hearts they examined were dead. Barnard thought about keeping these condemned men's hearts alive in the bodies of other people, a grotesque image. He was against capital punishment, but, faced with a dire shortage of donors after the early transplants, he had raised the idea with Wally Beck. 'We decided it would cause too much of an outcry,' says Beck.

For all its absurdities, on one level *The Donor* contains a serious warning: Barnard was fascinated by genetics and research on the boundaries of human knowledge, yet here he shows that 'playing God' can lead to disastrous consequences. Even the 'good' Rodney Barnes joins the evil Nazi scientist in stepping over the borders of ethical and medical decency – one man driven by a twisted love, the other by a consuming hatred of his fellow man, especially those not of his 'pure' race. Sadly, the novel's lack of quality blunts the impact of any message it might convey.

For Molloy, *The Donor* was a major mistake: 'I keep a copy to remind me that we all screw up sometimes but now and then we screw up spectacularly.' He wrote the first draft from 'a basic plot' supplied by Barnard. He knew nothing of Stander's involvement. Molloy wanted to take out the research scientist's Nazi past, which he felt was 'dated'. Barnard insisted it stayed in. When the publishers wanted punchier sex scenes and an almost human personality for the crossbred baboon-child, Molloy pulled out. 'I felt this wasn't my forte and said so. Chris got quite humpy about it and fired off the second draft to someone else.' Molloy did not see the novel again until it was published. 'My input had been progressively mangled from about midway until eventually the plot took off into the weirder realms of gee-whizzery, unexplored even by the most classic Hammer film. Mary Shelley must have been turning in her grave. I wouldn't have cared a damn as I had disliked the whole project from the beginning, but to my embarrassment my name appeared in the credits. It was originally intended as an exploration of the emotional stresses engendered in those involved in transplant medicine; donor families, recipients, medical staff et al. It ended up in the lower reaches of airport junk reading.'

The book, labelled a 'medical thriller', was published by Michael Joseph in London in 1996. It may not have been literature but it did stir plenty of media interest in Barnard, and he approached Steven Spielberg in the hope of a film being made. Spielberg passed. The book's launch in London saw Barnard as much in demand for interviews as ever. One particularly forthright piece, which appeared in the *Daily Mail* in August 1996, caused Karin huge embarrassment. Headlined, *I love young women.*

They don't need brains, just glorious bodies, it was Barnard at his most egotistical, patronising, insensitive and, at times, openly dishonest. He told Angela Levin: 'It was the circumstances of my life that led to the problems. After the (first) heart transplant I had to travel a lot. As a result of my travelling I was exposed to women and parties ... Even then, I was faithful to my first wife and most of my affairs during my second marriage occurred after we had stopped living together as man and wife.'

Levin comments, 'Barnard is now 73, although still going on 21, shamelessly ageist, still happy to boast about his sexual prowess, and overflowing with ego. At times he sounded so outrageous I asked him why he didn't try to modify his words.' Barnard's reply: 'I'm a very honest person. The trouble is most people don't want to see a doctor as a human being. I've always had a big ego. It's driven me all my life. I have to feed it all the time.' He sounds off about age: 'Age is abnormal. A disease. I hate ageing because it causes a tremendous deterioration in the quality of my life.' His arthritis was now crippling: 'Sometimes I cannot open a bottle or turn on a tap. My feet are so bad I cannot walk properly. I can no longer run. My reflexes are slow.' Then it's back to sex, with a wide smile: 'That's why I stick to things that I can do in bed which don't use my joints. Arthritis is the cause of my hypersexual activities. I am fortunate I am still very active. My wife is only 33 and if I don't have sex with her someone else will. Of course, I could never have sex with a woman my own age ... But I don't force my wife to have sex with me. She wants to. I prefer younger women because they are more naive and easier to mould. Although I do like to talk to them, they don't need a lot of brains, just beautiful bodies.'

He ends with a few emotional words about Armin: 'I have never loved anything in my life like that little boy. As I am at home so much more, I see him grow up. I couldn't possibly divorce Karin and hurt him. He's the best thing that has ever happened to me.'

When Barnard returned to Cape Town he walked into a row with Karin. South African newspapers had carried details of the *Daily Mail* interview, homing in on the remark that if Barnard did not have sex with Karin, 'someone else will'. It had made her sound as if she had a line of men waiting to step in the moment Barnard failed in the bedroom. 'I asked him why he made that awful remark about someone else having sex with me and he denied he'd said it,' says Karin. 'But I knew it was the kind of thing he would say. He would always put his foot in it. He would also make remarks about the children without thinking how they would be affected. He'd say he loved Armin more than anything without stopping to consider how that must make Frederick, Christiaan and Deirdre feel. But then, when his children were very small he showed an almost abnormal interest in them. When they grew older he would lose that interest, just when they needed him most.'

In early 1995 they had moved into a new house – a large, elegant mansion in Rondebosch with a swimming pool and driveway, and a distant view of Groote Schuur and UCT against the backdrop of Table Mountain's rear slopes. It was put in Karin's name. Even at his advanced age Barnard still bounded with mental energy, sometimes waking in the night with ideas that he would have to write down immediately.

But the marriage was going through a difficult period. Karin wanted to build a steady family life, but Barnard seemed unhappy when he was at home for more than a few days. Without the adrenalin rush of travel and the boost to his ego brought by the attention he got abroad he easily became depressed. He was disappointed, too, that Karin seemed less than enthusiastic about staying on his farm in the Karoo. He had had ambitions for her to learn to fly to make the travelling between Cape Town and Richmond easier, but they came to nothing. (When he went to the farm he often took Armin, who soon grew to love the place and would later become a confident huntsman.)

To make his restlessness worse, the new South African government seemed to be uninterested in him. He complained he had not been invited to the inauguration of Nelson Mandela as president, although rather than vote in the country's first free elections he had decided to travel with Karin and Armin to collect an honorary doctorate from the University of Ulster. 'He thought it best to be out of the country because there was so much talk of possible violence,' says Karin. Now he moaned to friends that, just as under the old apartheid regime, he was never invited to official government functions. Gloria Craig, well known in Cape Town for her charity work, spoke to a contact at Mandela's office on his behalf. 'I was told someone, somewhere was blocking it,' she says.

'It was embarrassing for Chris when he went abroad and people would ask if he had met Mandela and he had to say no.' Eventually, he did get his invitation to meet Mandela and the photograph duly appeared in the newspapers.

Barnard had lost none of his taste for controversy. When Karin was beaten into second place at a contest to find South Africa's Best Dressed Woman, Barnard stormed up to the judges' table at the gala dinner and publicly accused them of rigging the outcome. More importantly, when in 1995 a French heart surgeon, Christian Cabrol, who had also been in Minneapolis in the 1950s, was reported to have called him 'a fake hero' for claiming the glory for the first heart transplant without crediting Norman Shumway, a deeply hurt Barnard fired off a lengthy letter to the *South African Medical Journal* and South African newspapers that had run the story, setting the record straight. He sued too, winning an out-of-court settlement from one newspaper of R75 000.

His deteriorating health was another strain on the marriage. Arrogantly he had always insisted he knew best when it came to treating his arthritis. He had rarely consulted rheumatologists. Over the years he had experimented with a vast range of remedies, both conventional and alternative. Many of the letters that had poured in to him at Groote Schuur were from well-meaning people suggesting herbal cures, and even magnetic rings or heated pads for his hands. He had tried taking capsules of powdered gold, which seemed to help for a while. But mostly he used methotrexate, an anti-rejection drug commonly given to transplant patients in the late 1960s and 1970s, before the arrival of cyclosporin. (Rheumatoid arthritis is an auto-immune disease where the body attacks, or rejects, some of its own tissue – hence the idea of using immuno-suppressive drugs to fight it.) The problem was that, being Barnard, he did not follow the rules. Methotrexate counteracts folic acid in the body, a vitamin essential for the production of red blood cells. Patients given methotrexate are also given folic acid to balance this. Barnard didn't believe in taking medication which in his opinion would counter the effects of methotrexate. He suffered regular gastro-intestinal problems as a result.

It was not until around 1996 that he approached Johan Brink, Professor of Cardiothoracic Surgery at UCT and head of the heart transplant programme at Groote Schuur, to provide him with cyclosporin. Brink, concerned by his condition, persuaded him to see a rheumatologist again. Six months of cyclosporin boosted his health but what really made the difference was that the rheumatologist eventually convinced him of the need to take folic acid with methotrexate. 'His problem was that he treated himself, something doctors are not supposed to do,' says Brink. 'He thought the rheumatologists knew nothing. He'd treated himself all those years with his own medication – he would read things in medical journals, and try it. When he came to me for cyclosporin I had to say it was a highly toxic drug if not monitored diligently – the deal we eventually made was that he would see a rheumatologist and come to me regularly for blood cyclosporin level and general health monitoring. He became a patient in our heart transplant clinic for six months until his folic acid supplementation allowed him to tolerate methotrexate again and he came off cyclosporin.' Barnard, like all retired staff then, qualified for free medical treatment at Groote Schuur.

He made no mention of it to Brink, but another serious health problem had started to afflict him several years earlier. Had he been aware Brink would have persuaded him to get urgent treatment. In 1993 a small patch had appeared on the right side of his nose which was diagnosed as skin cancer. He had a skin graft done using skin from behind an ear which, according to Karin, was 'very successful'. But later it flared up again, and instead of having it dealt with surgically he decided to apply various creams to control and disguise it. He also went to a dermatologist to burn the area with dry ice. The delay in treating the cancer would, of course, prove disastrous and lead to far more severe facial surgery later. 'He knew he had to do something about it but he always postponed the idea of further surgery,' says Karin.

Later there would be ominous signs of asthma, too. Again, out of vanity, he did his best to hide it, but fits of laughing would sometimes trigger the problem and he would vanish to another room to use his inhaler or use it discreetly under his hand.

Despite the trauma of his divorce from Barbara, and the details of his infidelities that partially emerged afterwards, Barnard had managed to resurrect his close relationship with her parents. Fred Zoellner had long retired. He and Ulli had moved to the tax haven of Zug in Switzerland. Through contacts Zoellner had helped Frederick get a job at the Union Bank of Switzerland after graduating from the University of the Witwatersrand. Barnard often visited the Zoellners with their grandsons.

Ulli was struck down by breast cancer in 1995. As she lay dying in hospital, Zoellner sent for Barnard. He also sent for Father Tom Nicholson to minister the last rites. When Barnard walked into the hospital room he was appalled by the lengths to which the doctors were going to keep Ulli alive, and told them to stop. Quality of life, not quantity, was the goal of medicine, he reminded them. He could have no idea, but within three years he would be witnessing Barbara's harrowing death from the same disease. A few months before his own death, Barnard was interviewed by a British magazine on the subject *It's Your Funeral.* 'I have recently been involved in the care of terminally ill people who were very dear to me, and persuaded their doctors to give them double doses of morphine,' he said, without naming who. 'There was no fuss about it or special arrangements. I just told their doctors that I thought that was the right thing to do. I would very much like someone to do that for me in the same situation.' He wanted to die from something sudden like a heart attack or, bizarrely, 'I could be killed when a bomb explodes in a plane I'm travelling in, something quick and fierce and clean, leaving no messy remains.' No concern was expressed for the other passengers.

Barnard and Barbara flew back to Cape Town together. He told friends that Barbara had said she still loved him and would like them to be together again. It was an absurd notion, according to Tony Ingala. 'By then Barbara had lost her feelings for Chris. She was happily married to Joe.' But Barnard did persuade Zoellner to establish a legacy in the name of his wife. He donated £1,5 million to Cambridge University to set up the Ursula Zoellner Professorship in Cancer Research. Other than the fact that Zoellner had spent a year at Gonville and Caius more than sixty years earlier, no-one at Cambridge seemed to know much about their generous benefactor. By the time the first appointment had been made to the chair in 1998, Barbara was also battling cancer.

The mania surrounding Princess Diana was at its height when Barnard met her for the first time. In October 1996 he was invited to attend a dinner in Rimini, Italy, by the Pio Manzu Centre. Diana, increasingly being recognised for her charity work, was to be given an award for her humanitarian efforts, just as Barnard had been honoured once by the organisation for his medical achievements. They sat together at the top table – 'The King and Queen of Hearts' as one newspaper headlined it – with Barnard's charm and charisma in full flow. He made a typically emotional speech in which he retold one of his favourite stories, about a black boy he had operated on unsuccessfully whose dying wish had been for a simple piece of bread, something he had been denied too often in life. 'He got it, but for him that piece of bread came too late.' Diana, clearly moved, leaned over to him and said: 'That was a wonderful story.' They met for lunch the next day, and Diana offered some advice on a handbag Barnard wanted to buy for Karin, who was at home. She also suggested he should set up a foundation to help children in the Third World get proper medical treatment, an idea he would later pursue.

Despite their widely differing backgrounds and ages, they had plenty in common – Barnard was perhaps one of the few people Diana had met whose exposure to sudden, overwhelming fame had matched her own. Both professed a horror of media pressure, yet both were seen as skilful operators of the publicity machine. Part of Barnard's appeal to younger women was his almost hypnotic ability to make them feel secure and relaxed: they felt they could confide in him. 'Diana opened up to Chris quite a lot about how she was being treated by the royal family,' says Karin. 'They found they shared the feeling that as a public figure people felt they owned you.' It was not long before Diana was writing to Barnard in the hope that he could help her solve a highly personal dilemma – she had fallen in love with a heart surgeon, Hasnat Khan, and wanted to marry him. She even told Barnard she wanted to have two daughters to balance the two sons from her marriage to Prince Charles. Khan had made it clear he could not cope with the kind of media attention they would have to endure in Britain, and Diana wanted to move abroad. Her first choice was Cape Town, where her brother, Earl Spencer, already lived. Could Barnard secure a job for Khan, she wondered?

Barnard, genuinely keen to help, and his ego nourished by the personal calls, letters, faxes and cards that flowed from Kensington Palace, did his best. He went to see people at Groote Schuur and elsewhere but found hospitals were cutting back, not hiring. Later, in London, he met Khan and discussed the situation. Khan confessed he could not cope with the publicity surrounding Diana. 'In all our conversations it was clear to me that she was deeply in love with Khan,' said Barnard, after Diana's death in a car crash in Paris in 1997. 'In the meeting I had with Khan I could not work out whether he loved her in the same way, but he clearly knew she loved him very much. I thought he was a remarkable man because here was one of the world's most sought-after women madly in love with him, but he was cool about it. He just told me he couldn't handle the publicity.' Barnard also went to dinner at Kensington Palace where Diana gave him a blue silk tie. He wore it to public engagements as often as he could, never forgetting to point out who gave it to him.

When Diana visited Cape Town briefly in March 1997, she called Barnard – who was on his farm at Richmond – from her brother's home. She told him she wanted to return the following year with her 'two boys' and stay at Ratelfontein. He invited her to open the Transplant Museum at Groote Schuur on 3 December that year, marking the 30th anniversary of the first heart transplant. Controversially to some, Louis Washkansky's original, oversized heart was to be put on display alongside the much smaller heart he had been given, Denise Darvall's, in which Barnard's silk sutures were still visible. The rooms used during the historic operation, including A and B Theatres, were to house the museum. Mannequins dressed in gowns and clutching instruments would be used to recreate the scene in the room where Washkansky received Darvall's heart. An inquiry was made to Madame Tussaud's in London to ask if the waxwork of Barnard that had been on display there for years was available, but it had been melted down. Two mannequins would portray Washkansky, one on the operating table in A Theatre and one in a bed in the recovery room. But plans to use a female mannequin to represent Denise Darvall on the operating table in B Theatre were deemed to be in bad taste. The Darvall brothers were said to be unhappy with the decision to display their sister's heart in a museum, but they were powerless to stop it. (The museum today is highly popular with tourists and school groups.)

Diana later told Barnard by letter that she could not make the museum opening because of another engagement. In the event she died three months before the opening.

Barnard said at the time that he kept a 'pile of Diana's correspondence which I shall always treasure'. But in truth Barnard treasured very little. He hadn't the patience for it. He later told friends he had felt 'used' by Diana. 'She just wanted me to get a job for her boyfriend,' he said. Karin says, 'He had thrown some of her letters out already when I stopped him one day and told him he must keep them. He had no appreciation of their sentimental value at all.'

There was a highly controversial codicil to the friendship between Barnard and Diana. In May 2001, some six months before he would die himself, Barnard published a book called *50 Ways to a Healthy Heart,* a populist manual that seemed to condone moderate hedonism as the surest way to ensure cardiac fitness. The book was gratuitously packed with the names of famous people Barnard had met and become 'friends' with over the years. In a strange chapter about how sunlight is good for people suffering bereavement, he writes interestingly, but very briefly, about how some of his patients who had needed resuscitation had had 'near-death' experiences, seeing bright lights at the end of a long, dark tunnel, before coming round. He then introduces, completely irrelevantly, his theory that Princess Diana could have been saved if French doctors had acted more quickly to get her to hospital after the car crash. 'Her death stunned me all the more as I was able to get a look at the particulars of the autopsy findings very soon after her death … I think she could have been saved, because according to the report which I have seen, she died of internal bleeding. The injury which caused the bleeding was to a vein which doesn't bleed particularly quickly, in fact it bleeds rather slowly. What I want to say here is that – if Princess Diana had been brought to hospital within ten minutes of the accident – something which should have been easily possible – and, once there, cared for properly, she could have survived.' He went further in interviews: 'I could have opened her chest myself in five minutes and stemmed the haemorrhage.'

It was a shameless piece of grandstanding, condemned in France and elsewhere. Doctors had spent 30 minutes trying to stabilise Diana at the scene of the crash, and it had then taken an hour to get her to hospital. She had suffered two heart attacks, and one of her pulmonary veins, vital for sending oxygenated blood back to the heart for pumping round the body, was ruptured. 'The severity of the Princess's chest injuries, which included heavy blood loss, broken ribs and multiple lacerations, made her chances of survival remote. It was hopeless,' insisted the French doctors who had treated Diana. The Princess's mother, Frances Shand Kydd, also weighed in with criticism of Barnard: 'If he was a friend of Diana's he should say nothing and leave the family in peace.' But the publicity caught the eye of Mohammed Al Fayed, the Harrods owner and father of Dodi Al Fayed, Diana's boyfriend at the time who also died in the crash. Al Fayed was keen to see if Barnard could be of use in his campaign to prove that the crash had been set up by British intelligence because the royal family was unhappy with Diana's association with his son. 'Al Fayed and my father met in London,' says Barnard's daughter Deirdre. 'They had a very friendly conversation but Al Fayed decided my father could not help him, and gave him a Harrods tie.'

Barnard became a father again, for the sixth time, in June 1997 at the age of 74. Again he was present, and again it was a Caesarian. Lara was named after *Lara's Theme,* the signature tune of the *Dr Zhivago* film that was one of Barnard's favourites. (It was also, of course, the melody Denise Darvall and her brother Keith had been singing in the car on that fateful day 30 years earlier.) Another well-publicised baptism in Adam Barnard's mission church followed. Gloria Arendz, who with her fashion designer brother Errol had been close friends with Barbara and now Karin, was Lara's godmother. 'I convinced Karin to have another baby,' she says. 'I told her Chris loves youth, he loves to have children around. Give him that pleasure. She thought it would bring back that whole family energy into their lives again.' But however much Barnard revelled in the company of his children, he was never satisfied when at home. 'It was the choice between fame and adulation and travelling, and the "boredom" of being at home,' says Gloria. 'He would rather travel. He had an insecurity about himself, and the one thing that made him feel secure was his fame.'

Errol had once had first-hand experience of the Barnard ego when travelling. 'We were sitting together on a flight to Johannesburg, in first class. When a flight attendant came over to us, Chris pointed at me and asked him, "Do you know who this is?" The attendant said, "Yes, I know who he is, but who the hell are you?" and walked off. Chris had wanted *me* to be embarrassed. He was horrified. He said, "He's insulted me!" A little later some German passengers came up to him and asked for his autograph. He stood up absolutely beaming, and called the flight attendant over. "See!" he told him. "You might not know who I am, but these people do!" The attendant just looked at him and said, "Professor Chris Barnard, please calm down. I was cracking a joke." That was a measure of how terribly insecure he was.'

Errol, openly gay, was often questioned by Barnard about his sexuality. 'He was fascinated by genes – he wanted to know what that one gene was that made one person artistic, another person gay, and so on.' His interest in genes had a rather more serious purpose: like many he believed the future of heart transplantation, which depended on a ready supply of donor organs, lay in the development of cloned animals, such as pigs, which could be genetically modified to produce organs that would not be rejected by humans. (When the world's first cloned piglets were born in Virginia, USA, in March 2000, one was named Christa after Barnard, and two were named Alexis and Carrel after the French transplant pioneer of the early 20th century. It was the first step in the production, two years later, of cloned piglets with a particular tissue rejection gene 'knocked out' so that theoretically their organs could be transplanted into humans without provoking rejection.)

In the immediate aftermath of the first heart transplant Barnard had seemed keen to acknowledge the help of the team involved, including Rod Hewitson, Terry O'Donovan, and his brother Marius. Yet he told Chris Brewer that it had been 'virtually a one-man show', a remark that understandably failed to make the pages of *The Second Life.* Publicly, at least, he remained grateful: in 1997 a party was held at La Vita to mark the 30th anniversary of the Washkansky operation, and he presented to all the members of the team who were there a plaque bearing the words, 'To be first'. Underneath ran the words: 'In recognition of the fact that it could never have been done without you. Thank you for being part of the team that made history.' It was his last party at La Vita – the following year he sold his interest in the restaurant.

The birth of Lara, sadly, did not cement the family. In fact, according to one very close friend of the couple, Karin soon moved out of the marital bedroom on the pretext of wanting to be close to her baby at night. By now, in any case, Barnard was travelling again as much as ever. He had joined forces with an agent in Vienna, Walter Lutschinger, who had big plans for him. 'Walter reinvented Chris,' says Karin. When most septuagenarians would be content to stay at home and relax, Barnard found himself commuting between Cape Town and Vienna. He set up the Christiaan Barnard Foundation with Lutschinger, partly with the aim of arranging vital surgery in Cape Town for children from poorer countries under Susan Vosloo at the private City Park Hospital (after his death, in what the Groote Schuur authorities saw as a 'piece of marketing opportunism', it would be renamed the Christiaan Barnard Memorial Hospital). There was a new 'heart nutrient' called Terrasyn Formula 50 to promote in Austria, a book to prepare, and he would soon meet another much younger woman, Gudrun Heidler.

But between Lara's birth and his successful 'reinvention' with the publication of *50 Ways to a Healthy Heart* came a series of emotional and physical hammer blows. Barely two years after her mother's death, Barbara, living in Cape Town with her husband Joe and daughter Bianca, was diagnosed with breast cancer. It progressed rapidly, and Barnard took to spending as much time as possible at her bedside. Before she became bedridden he would ferry her to and from hospital for regular treatment. 'He did everything he could think of to find new ways of treating her,' says Gloria Craig. 'He flew around the world speaking to people.' But the cancer spread to Barbara's brain, and in December 1998 she died aged 48. Only the day before, her father Fred Zoellner, broken by the prospect of losing his daughter, had died of a heart attack at his home in Switzerland at the age of 86. His enormous fortune would pass in the main to Barbara's children.

Karin had shown a mature understanding of her husband's devotion to Barbara during the course of her illness. But at the funeral, which she attended, she was embarrassed by his overtly distraught behaviour. 'Chris was sobbing aloud and practically threw himself over the coffin. He had to be pulled away,' says a close friend. 'He was telling people, "She was the one. She really loved me." Karin was absolutely furious.'

In the aftermath of Barbara's death Barnard's marriage to Karin deteriorated further. They decided to try marriage guidance counselling. 'Chris was enthusiastic until the counsellor suggested he should do this or that and he disagreed,' says Karin. Close friends say Barnard's frequent absences gave Karin the chance to mix with people of her own age. She was still young, attractive and lively, and she enjoyed the company of similar types. The 41-year age gap in the marriage was bound to tell in the end. For his part, Barnard could be vicious: he often taunted Karin by comparing her sexual performance unfavourably with Barbara's. It was as if he was hell-bent on destroying the marriage, yet somehow he never believed it would end. He expected Karin to stay with him until he died, no matter what.

He was wrong. In July 1999 Karin decided she wanted a divorce on the grounds of an irretrievable breakdown of the marriage. 'We had gradually drifted apart,' she says. Barnard, faced with spending his last years alone, insisted the marriage was salvageable. So Karin left no room for doubt: she said she had found the male sex stimulant Viagra and a condom in her husband's wash bag at a time when they were no longer sleeping together; he had regularly flirted with other women in her presence, and threatened to seek sex outside the marriage; he had denigrated her as a wife and lover and made unflattering and insulting comparisons between her and Barbara; he had constantly threatened to divorce her and leave her with nothing; he had had one affair (believed to be with a make-up artist he met while filming an edition of the BBC's religious programme *Songs of Praise)*; and he was believed to be having another affair with a younger woman.

Barnard was livid when details from the divorce papers emerged in South African newspapers, and then around the world. He said he did not want a divorce, 'but there is bugger-all I can do about it'. Reluctantly he agreed to leave the house in Rondebosch. 'He pleaded with Karin to be allowed to stay in a room in the house so that he could be close to the children,' says Maureen Brink. 'But she wouldn't let him. He was devastated. He had always believed Karin would stay with him until the end.' The collapse of the marriage plunged Barnard into a maelstrom of loneliness and despair. He may have spent most of his time travelling, but he doted on his two small children. Loneliness, to him, was as terrifying a state as old age. Now he was faced with both. 'I begged Karin not to divorce him,' says Brink. 'I said to her, why can't you hang on, he hasn't got long to live. She would have had everything then, but she couldn't do it.'

Karin tried to have the antenuptial agreement she had signed overturned so that her settlement would reflect Barnard's vastly increased wealth. She had claimed that she had contributed to his earnings – he had 'substantial assets' abroad, she told the court – by travelling with him, helping him and enhancing his image. She also claimed she had been too young and naive to fully understand what she had signed. She had been no match, she said, for the worldly and sophisticated Barnard. The court rejected her application.

Once again Maureen Brink (Fritz had died in 1999) watched Barnard dissolve helplessly. 'It was worse than the divorce from Barbara. He sobbed and sobbed,' she says. But worse fortune was to come. Barnard had always been a vain man, and his finely chiselled nose was, he believed, one of his best features. By the end of the year he could put off the inevitable no longer. The cancer in his nose had flared up again and needed urgent treatment. A plastic surgeon, Hilma Luckhoff, based at the Panorama Medi-Clinic near Cape Town, inserted a balloon to stretch the skin on Barnard's forehead. Later, once the cancerous cells had been cut out, a flap of skin was taken from the forehead and used to cover the hole. More skin was taken from beneath the right eye to build up this area. Radiation treatment was also used to kill any remaining cancer. The result was that Barnard's nose was grotesquely swollen for months, and he took to wearing large clear-glass spectacles to soften the impact.

Even friends, while feeling sorry for him, could not help but see an irony: they made cruel comparisons behind his back with Dorian Gray, the sinister Oscar Wilde character who enjoys eternal youth while living a life of depravity, as a hidden portrait of him physically ages and bears all the scars of his corrupted soul. When Gray finally decides to destroy the painting he in fact kills himself: the portrait immediately resumes its original youthfulness while Gray instantly becomes old and wrinkled, as if his sins have caught up with him. By this reckoning, presumably, Barnard's dramatic loss of his boyish good looks was the price he was paying for his pursuit of eternal youth and the company of beautiful young women. It was payback time, said those clearly jealous of his success and fame.

But, courageously, he did not hide away. He tried to live a normal life, and even went on television to talk about his treatment. He still attended functions, although Lutschinger, who had secured fees as high as $7 000 for after-dinner speeches for Barnard, put things on hold in Vienna while he recuperated in Cape Town.

Barnard's traumatic split from Karin had one positive side effect: it drew him closer again to Deirdre, and even to Louwtjie. He bought an apartment in Higgovale, around the corner from Deirdre's home, and spent increasing amounts of time with her. Louwtjie also lived close by, and despite the long years of estrangement they occasionally had dinner together at Deirdre's house. Louwtjie gracefully agreed to alter his trousers and shirts again, and cooked tripe for him, one of his favourite Karoo dishes. (Despite the decades of world travel Barnard's tastes remained distinctly simple and South African – his favourite car was the 'bakkie' he drove to Ratelfontein and his favourite writer was Bosman, whose classic stories capture the humour and pathos of life in the platteland.) 'It was as if we, the original family, had come over him again like a protective umbrella,' says Deirdre. 'It was wonderful to see my mother and father sitting at the dinner table talking again.' Karin and Deirdre had generally got on well, but now the relationship changed. 'She always said to me she didn't know how I could live with her father. Then when I decided I couldn't any longer she changed towards me,' says Karin.

Deirdre's close friend Dene Friedmann says, 'Deirdre never got over the loss of her father when she was a young girl. She always wanted that attention back. When he and Karin broke up Deirdre was the one who looked after him. She went to him every day to have tea so he wasn't alone. He would have been completely lost without her.'

Deirdre had her father back at long last.

14

Homecoming

During these years Barnard often sought refuge in the beauty and tranquillity of his 32 000-acre Karoo farm. He converted what had been a basic farmhouse into a luxurious game lodge with a view to attracting foreign hunters. He had also set up a small biltong factory there, and even helped make it himself. (Woolworths was so impressed by the quality of the biltong that they offered him a lucrative contract to supply its shops, but he knew he couldn't meet the demand and turned it down.) He would also spend weeks at a time with George van Wyk at his Loxton farm. There he particularly liked the remote hunting lodge that overlooks a large, still lake. 'There are no phones there,' says Van Wyk. 'That's what he said he loved most.' They often discussed payment for the sheep Van Wyk had given him to breed from when he first bought Ratelfontein. 'He told me I'd be looked after in his will,' says Van Wyk.

Whenever possible, Barnard would take Armin to stay with him at Ratelfontein. They were close. Barnard had made a point of preparing his son for the inescapable reality: he did not expect to see him mature to a young man. But he knew Armin loved Ratelfontein and he promised him repeatedly that one day, when he was gone, it would be his. Piet van der Merwe, the manager at Ratelfontein, says, 'Chris and Armin hunted a lot together, mainly springbok. Many times he told Armin he would inherit the farm.'

Through long evenings at Ratelfontein Barnard often spoke to Van der Merwe about his career as a heart surgeon: 'He said he always remembered in particular the children he had operated on, especially the ones where it had gone wrong. He could tell you exactly which child it was and when, what kind of operation, even their names sometimes. They had all stayed in his mind. He said he always remembered how it felt when he had to go to a mother and tell her he couldn't fix her child's problem. He told me it was one of the things you never forgot. It was obvious he was very sad about it.'

Gudrun Heidler was a 28-year-old medical student in Vienna when she was introduced to Barnard by Lutschinger. 'It had been my dream to meet him and it came at the right time for me,' she says. 'I was struggling to complete my final exams and he gave me the encouragement I needed. He was desperately lonely in Vienna. He missed his children and he wanted Karin back. He talked every day about her. He was terribly depressed.' Gudi, as she was known, accompanied Barnard to functions and on trips abroad. She was not paid but her expenses were covered by the Christiaan Barnard Foundation. It was the image of Barnard everyone expected to see, no matter how old he was: arriving with a blonde, blue-eyed, beautiful young girl on his arm. 'He opened up a world of glamour I was not used to,' she says. 'I saw him with Muhammad Ali and Mikhail Gorbachev, and he loved every minute of it. On the first day we met we sat together in a pizza restaurant and he held my hand and said to me, "Can I die in your arms?" Nearly every week he would tell me he was not long for this planet. He often thought he was ill. Once he was convinced he had prostate cancer.' Barnard had let it be known in South Africa that he was quitting the country to move to Vienna, this time blaming criticism in the press – one magazine article in particular, he felt, had ridiculed him – and pointing out that '99 per cent of my interests are overseas'. But, says Gudi, 'he never really intended to do that. He didn't seriously look for a place to buy.'

Lutschinger originally put him up in an elegant city-centre hotel. But the mainly grey-haired clientele made Barnard feel what he dreaded feeling most – old. Instead he moved into the Sports Hotel, a former sports centre in a colourless, industrial part of the city. Here the staff and guests were young. He and Gudi spent many hours sipping drinks in the bar. 'We often talked about marriage and sex. I told him he should try to see a woman who was more his age but he said he wasn't interested. He said he preferred innocence and youth in a woman. I would never say yes, I'd marry him, or no, I wouldn't. But I did tell him that I would want a husband who would still be alive when my child was 20. If he'd asked me seriously I think I would have said no. At the end of the evening I would give him a kiss and go home. It was hard for me because I knew he wanted more. He didn't want to accept that there was a 50-year age gap between us so it couldn't happen. He would joke about wanting me to have his baby. It didn't stop our relationship. We would hold hands and cuddle. All his life he had been with women, he couldn't help it. I often asked him why he had to be with much younger women and he said it was because they had such lovely skin. Everything for him was about looks. He seemed to need the company of young women all the time. We celebrated his 78th birthday in the hotel and all the young girls who worked there made a big fuss of him, which he loved.'

Barnard got to know Gudi's parents well, sometimes going over to their home to cook springbok which he had brought from his farm. Her father, who was 20 years younger than Barnard, says of his daughter's relationship with him: 'It was a love story.' Gudi visited him in Cape Town several times, staying at his home. After his nose operation she flew to South Africa to look after him. Close friends of Barnard who saw them together were convinced that Gudi was keen to marry him. Gudi denies this, but she does admit that during trips they sometimes shared a bed. She insists they did not have sex, however. 'It was out of the question for me,' she says. 'We might share a bed in a hotel if we had to be up very early to catch a flight.' Despite his many years of world travel Barnard was notoriously nervous about missing flights. Always punctual, he often arrived at airports hours earlier than necessary. But it is not an excuse commonly used to share a young woman's bed.

Just before Christmas 2000 Barnard damaged his left hip in a fall at the hotel in Vienna. Doctors there inserted a pin but he was unhappy with the results and decided to return to Cape Town, where he had the hip replaced. It was another reminder that even he could not defeat age.

The publication of *50 Ways to a Healthy Heart* in Britain and South Africa, with the surrounding controversy sparked by his comments on Princess Diana's death, catapulted Barnard back into the limelight he had always craved. 'Any man who says he doesn't like applause and recognition is either a fool or a liar,' he had said once.

In the book's introduction he took the opportunity to rewrite some of his personal history. Where before he had always been frank about wanting to be a doctor to earn good money and help his father (ironically he never succeeded in making money directly from surgery until his retirement because he stayed in a state hospital), now he was 'never in it for the money'. He had even turned down the chance, soon after the first heart transplant, to be represented by a leading international agent who would have made him a fortune. 'I always wanted to be a doctor,' he adds, contradicting what he had said all his life. In his account of his childhood there is, oddly, no mention of Abraham, the little brother who had died from a heart defect before Barnard was born. 'Today I survive on a £400 a month pension,' he writes. In reality Barnard was by now an immensely wealthy man. Apart from his properties, close friends said he had told them of having R14 million in a Swiss bank account.

As usual with a Barnard book there was plenty of the confessional, laced with hindsight. 'I am of the opinion that the first heart transplant was not a great medical breakthrough and certainly not a major scientific discovery of our century,' he says. 'It was something we had practised many times, nothing really magic.' He thought the same at the time, he claims, once more pointing to the fact that there was no photographer on hand to record that historic operation. In fact, it's just as reasonable to believe that there was no photographer because Barnard was understandably concerned about having a failure on his hands and he did not want photographs getting out. Since that transplant he had frequently complained privately that he had not been given the Nobel Prize for Medicine, although he had always accepted that the first heart transplant was essentially based on the research work of others. He simply believed if he had been American or a black South African he would have won the Nobel Prize.

There is more rewriting of his life as the book goes on. Singing the praises of sex as a good way to stay healthy, he says, 'I have had a lot of sex in my life, and the older I got the more important it became for me. However, I believe that sex should always be in the context of a love affair – however short-lived or minor. This may sound a bit strange coming from a man who has always been described by the media as a kind of 'womaniser'. But I ask you to believe me when I say that a married man should try to be faithful. That is my firm conviction. I realise today that my marriages never ended because of unfaithfulness but only because I neglected my partner at the time.' It is hard to make sense of this in relation to the failure of his three marriages and his self-confessed serial infidelity.

For good measure, he adds, bizarrely: 'I have also developed a few additional principles … Never have sex outside the bedroom; never have sex in strange beds; never pay for sex.' More seriously, he answered one of the allegations made against him by Karin. In a chapter about impotence, he says the Viagra found in his wash bag was 'not for me but for a woman friend'. He insists he has never taken Viagra. 'I don't know why my wife made such a big deal about it. We had separated some time previously.' Elsewhere in the book Barnard recommends listening to classical music, especially Brahms, as an antidote to modern stress, and, less predictably, recommends a belief in God. 'I have a firm belief in God and I used to say a prayer before every operation.'

Father Tom Nicholson recalls how Barnard's views on God and the afterlife 'changed regularly'. Others say he believed in God but not, paradoxically, in an afterlife. Just four months before he died, he said in an interview: 'Everyone, especially as they get older, thinks about death – I think about it constantly. The biggest problem with death is the uncertainty of the afterlife. I often claim that if we could be rid of that, there would be no need for organised religion, which exploits our fear of the unknown. The afterlife is something I believe in, but with a hint of scepticism. I have no proof of it … Both my parents believed implicitly in God and the devil and in heaven and hell, so I was exposed to that a lot but, as one gets older, one tries to find a more rational explanation for events. I often asked my father why people suffered and he had a very simple explanation. He said: "It's God's will." As a scientist and doctor concerned with alleviating human suffering that's not good enough for me.'

The divorce had come through with Karin getting, among other things, a R700 000 settlement and the house in Rondebosch. Barnard had also altered his will by now to reflect his bitterness towards Karin and his renewed closeness to other members of the family. Sadly, despite the promises, there would be no farm for Armin – it would be sold after Barnard's death and the money added to the estate. ('It broke Armin's heart when he discovered the farm was being sold after his father died,' says a close friend. 'He spent a few days there with the new owners and Piet van der Merwe and brought back everything he could.') Nor would anything be left to others, such as George van Wyk, who had been led to expect something.

Barnard, whose facial features had begun to settle again after his cancer treatment, was back on the publicity bandwagon and in good form. In what would be his last interview – it was published after his death – he spoke reflectively, almost wistfully, to Peter Hawthorne for *Time* magazine. He talked of his plans to write a book that would show people how they were being 'bluffed' by their doctors into having injections, drugs and even surgery. 'The treatment of people today is dishonest,' he said. Of the operation that made him famous, and the way he took to being a celebrity, he said: 'The heart transplant wasn't such a big thing surgically. The technique was a basic one. The point is I was prepared to take the risk. My philosophy is that the biggest risk in life is not to take a risk. But the operation, and its significance as the first of its kind, took me into another world. Not just professionally but personally and socially. I loved it. I'm a guy who loves people, I love the female sex and I like to enjoy life. You think I was under stress meeting Gina Lollobrigida? Not on your life. I'm easy to get on with, to party with. The professors in Europe, they couldn't understand me. I wasn't fat and bald and didn't wear glasses. I was a pretty good-looking guy and I could put a lot of entertainment and emotion into my lectures. A journalist in Germany once told me I'd never be recognised as a professor in his country because I wasn't serious enough.' His revived friendship with Louwtjie prompted this scathing review of his wives: 'I've been married three times and all the credit must go to Louwtjie, my first wife, who took the strain and stood by me when we were young ... Louwtjie married me for love, my second wife married me for my fame, and my third because of my fame and money.' It was not original – Louwtjie had recently been telling him the same thing.

At a packed gathering of the *Cape Times* Breakfast Club even the old chauffeur story went down well. As usual he had made little written preparation for the speech, preferring to assess the audience first and speak 'off the cuff'. In August 2001 Barnard addressed a meeting of the Organ Donor Foundation in Cape

Town. To his dismay, Karin attended with the new man in her life, Saul Berman, who had been a friend of the family for several years. (They later married.) Yet Barnard gave a vintage performance, by all accounts.

The next morning he had to catch an early flight and Deirdre drove him to the airport. He was on his way to Israel where he was to meet doctors involved in stem cell research – a key subject for him because it held such promise for heart surgery – and appear on a television show. It was the last time Deirdre saw him alive. After Israel, Barnard was due to fly to Germany, where he hoped to sign a contract to supply springbok meat from his farm, and to America, to publicise his new book; but he also had to go to Cyprus to negotiate a deal to market olive oil. First he flew to Vienna where he asked Gudi to go with him to Cyprus. She told him she couldn't because she had to work. She had now qualified – Barnard had attended her graduation – and she was working in a laboratory. 'About a month before he had spoken to me about his funeral and said he wanted me to be there. He told me he had arranged with Walter for money to be set aside to pay for my air fare to Cape Town. He kept saying "tomorrow" would be his last day. When we spoke in Vienna before he flew to Cyprus he did not say, as he usually did, that he would be back soon. He bought a one-way ticket because he intended to go on to another country.'

Barnard called Gudi from Cyprus in a particularly depressed state. He told her that he had been given honorary Austrian citizenship, but even this did not buoy his spirits. 'He also told me again he would die the next day and would be coming back "in a different way". He said he had had enough, but you never knew when he was telling the truth because he lied a lot. He called them "white lies" and I forgave him because he was old.'

On Saturday 1 September Barnard called home to speak to Armin and Lara, but found an answering machine and left a message. That evening he had a severe attack of asthma while at dinner in his hotel in Paphos. He always carried a pump, and he recovered quickly. But the next day was swelteringly hot and humid, conditions known to aggravate asthma. He went to the gym, then for a swim, and after getting out of the pool collapsed with another asthma attack. Witnesses said they saw him grappling with his inhaler before he lost consciousness and died.

Others claimed he had left the inhaler in his room, which was unlikely. Some suggested mischievously that he had been reading one of his own books when he collapsed.

The suddenness of his death prompted immediate speculation that he had died of a heart attack, common after a serious asthmatic seizure. That was the story that initially went round the world in the few hours after his death, and it naturally appealed: Barnard the 'King of Hearts' dies from heart attack. But the post-mortem carried out in Cyprus confirmed that he had died from bronchial blockage brought on by an asthma attack. The pathologist, Eleni Antoniou, said his heart had been 'in excellent condition'. Lutschinger said: 'It was always his biggest fear that he would die like that.' Despite his asthma, arthritis and skin cancer he had remained lean and fit for a man of his age: 'He ate fresh fruit, salad and fish and had meat only once a week. He worked out in the gym every day. He was in great physical shape.'

Back in Cape Town, amid the family grief and shock, preparations were made to fly Barnard's body back to South Africa. Deirdre began making plans for a burial, but says she learned from a television interview aired on the night of his death that he wanted to be cremated, and his ashes buried in the rose garden of the family home in Beaufort West.

On the day of his death, at least, there was no desire to criticise. Sincere tributes were paid. Nelson Mandela described him as 'one of our main achievers' who had 'also done very well in expressing his opinion on apartheid'. President Thabo Mbeki was rather more forthright, praising his 'scientific excellence and humanism' and adding: 'I think he really ought to serve as an inspiration to our people, to the youth generally, to strive for that discovery, that excellence.' Susan Vosloo, the first female heart surgeon in Africa and a close friend of Barnard, said: 'We have lost someone who made the greatest contribution to medical history. He had a brilliant and innovative mind.' At Groote Schuur – where in recent years the high cost of a single heart transplant to save one person has been weighed unfavourably by its state paymasters against the need to fund widespread vaccinations and the fight against AIDS – Johan Brink said Barnard had 'done more for medicine in South Africa than any other person ... He put us on the world map.'

Perhaps the most surprisingly laudatory comment, in view of the reticence he had always shown towards Barnard, came from Norman Shumway. The rivalry between the two had been built up to legendary status. Shumway was said to have avoided attending any medical congress where Barnard was to appear. He declined to be interviewed for this biography. In the official account of the Washkansky transplant in the *South African Medical Journal* of 30 December 1967 Barnard's debt to Shumway had been made plain: 'The recent history of transplantation of the heart began with the experiments of Carrel and (Charles) Guthrie in the early years of this century. Gradually our knowledge increased and progress towards this goal continued through the years with the work of many other brilliant men and, in particular, through the invaluable contributions of Shumway and his associates.'

But in later years Barnard, tired of the repeated claim that he had triumphed on the back of Shumway's work, insisted the technique he used in 1967 had been based on Cass and Brock's paper, published a year before Shumway and Lower's, although the Stanford pair had performed their first successful dog heart transplant earlier, in 1958. Shumway, however, who rarely gave interviews, now applauded Barnard's use of a brain-dead accident victim as his first heart donor. It had 'made the use of brain-dead victims acceptable for organ transplantation ... at a time when there was a terrible furore about the brain-death issue in the United States'. Without Barnard's bold step transplants would not have become 'standard therapy' at that time. 'It was a monumental advance, more societal perhaps than medical, because it applied to all organ transplants.'

Barnard had also done more than anyone else to popularise medicine. As the journalists who arrived in Cape Town to cover the Washkansky story discovered, here was a surgeon who loved to communicate. Until then the medical fraternity had hidden behind a veil of secrecy and scientific jargon. Barnard blew it all away, and from then on doctors began to realise they had an obligation to explain. Barnard would later take his appetite for performing to dubious lengths – bullfighting in Madrid, crooning on stage on the QE2, playing his ukulele in charity television shows – but it was more than opportunistic showmanship. It was a zest for living. The goal of medicine was to improve the quality of life, he always said, and no-one enjoyed life more than Barnard.

His mentor Walt Lillehei, perhaps the most respected figure in cardiac surgery, pointed out that even before the first heart transplant his achievements were remarkable: 'I would say he accomplished a great deal in enhancing the technical and innovative aspects of surgery up until the transplant, and maybe for a year or two after ... During the period before the first few heart transplants he did more than most surgeons ever accomplish in a lifetime.' There was high praise in these words, but also a hint of condemnation for years wasted. 'Walt felt Chris had destroyed his medical personality with his behaviour after those early transplants,' says Lillehei's widow, Kaye.

Deirdre made no secret of the fact that she believed her father had died 'of a broken heart', whatever the findings of the pathologists. She says she does not blame Karin, but she feels that her father found himself alone at the most vulnerable stage of his life and never recovered. It took a day or so after his death before Karin felt up to talking about him. He had remained in many ways 'a child', she says. Yet she had learned a lot 'from his tremendous insight into life'. 'I will remember him as a unique individual, someone who always challenged everything – he tried to make the impossible possible.'

Several of those interviewed for this book used the word 'amoral' when describing him, and it was only a matter of days after his death before opinion turned sour, indeed vicious, with the familiar accusations: egotism, opportunism, racism (his 'ambassadorial' role in the 1970s), and emotional cruelty towards his wives and family. He had said, 'The heart is just a pump,' and many believed Barnard's own heart was nothing more than that. He was 'a smooth phoney ... a professional charlatan', according to one British critic who remembered arguing with him on television over ways to fight apartheid. 'He was extraordinarily narcissistic,' says Frances Ames. 'He wasn't a reflective person and he brushed aside concerns over immuno-suppression in his rush to do the first heart transplant. Freud said men wanted fame, fortune and beautiful women, and Chris Barnard achieved all three. They were his priorities.'

Indeed, he chased girls young enough to be his granddaughters.

Was it an obsession with youth, a refusal to grow old or simply, as many suspected, the compulsive, undignified lust of an ageing man who used his charm and charisma to target the young and vulnerable? 'Chris never had a normal youth and that's why he pursued it in others,' is Father Tom Nicholson's explanation. But perhaps Barnard was simply afraid of the challenge women of his own age presented. He had grown up under a strong, overbearing mother who suffocated his instincts. His marriage to Louwtjie, a woman of independent mind and tough character, foundered when she stood between him and his freedom. He went for the 19-year-old Barbara, but the marriage collapsed as she matured and learned to stand on her own feet. The 'glowing youth' that had attracted him had gone and with it the naivety that allowed him to control her. He pursued another 19-year-old but his marriage to Karin failed as she reached her early thirties and was no longer prepared to accept the lifestyle her husband, 41 years older, preferred.

Did Barnard's self-confessed need to feed the ego that drove him override all else? From Washkansky onwards, his ego certainly seemed to many to be out of control. Asked if he'd like his picture taken with Frank Sinatra, he replied, seriously: 'Or would Frank Sinatra like to have his picture taken with me?' Invited by one of the world's leading chefs to visit his restaurant in France for a sumptuous meal on the house, he responded: 'He wants a picture of me enjoying his food in his restaurant to put up on his wall. The price is too high.'

Had he been less self-serving, could he have used his status to make more of an impact on the fight against the racial oppression that dominated his country in his lifetime? In his final years Barnard often said he 'could have done more' to protest against apartheid. He admitted: 'I spoke out against it when I could, but I didn't stick my neck out.' But nor did he seem anxious to help those who did what they could to alleviate suffering among the victims of apartheid. Those in SHAWCO, the UCT students' organisation that works to improve health care among the poor black and coloured communities, were often dismayed by his lack of support. It had been founded in 1943 when Barnard was a medical student but, despite his background, he resisted the efforts of others to involve him. In later years, while many doctors offered their services free to the cause, Barnard would not even dip his hand in his pocket. Pleas for small donations were met with standard refusal letters from Barnard's secretaries stating that 'Professor Barnard is only a salaried man'. Yet he enjoyed the life of a celebrity and was married for much of this time to an heiress who wanted for nothing. He could not afford to make donations to SHAWCO, but he made sure his annual subscriptions to the Cape Town Press Club were kept up to date.

Medically, could he have dedicated his immense talents to the establishment of a lasting legacy in his name, such as a specialist heart centre, which would have kept Cape Town in the forefront of cardiac research? A new Christiaan Barnard Institute of Cardiovascular Medicine is being set up at UCT. The university has also renamed the research centre built from the R1 million donation from the Chamber of Mines in 1968 after Barnard. But many of his former colleagues say he could have done more during his life to create a permanent medical legacy. They felt then and feel now that it was an opportunity tragically missed in the vortex of glamour, fame and global travel that swallowed Barnard after the first heart transplant.

Johan Brink, who has performed nearly 200 heart transplants at Groote Schuur, says, 'He could have done a tremendous amount more to build our Department up to being a great cardiac centre – firstly while still in our Department, and particularly over the almost twenty years after he retired. There was no support, not only financially but more importantly politically or influentially for our Department after he retired – he literally turned his back on us. However I do believe that his name can and should be used to help academic medicine – cardiovascular medicine in particular – in our university and hospital, which are going through terrible times during the restructuring of our country in the post-apartheid era. Governmental support for high-cost medicine such as cardiology and cardiac surgery has plummeted, and we are really struggling to maintain the highest standards because of this. During Barnard's time he had a very good infrastructure by international standards, and a high level of competence and support in all fields of medicine at GSH and UCT on which he could build his career successes. Hopefully his name will be able to "pay back" some of this success to cardiovascular medicine at GSH and UCT.'

Barnard's dramatic breakthrough in 1967 – and it was a drama like no other – inspired a generation of youngsters to become doctors. In 2003 *Time* magazine polled its readers to name *80 Days That Changed the World.* Two South African events made the list: the first heart transplant and the release of Nelson Mandela. Bill Frist, an American heart surgeon and politician, wrote in *Time*: 'I was 15 years old when Christiaan Barnard performed the first heart transplant. I still have the *Life* magazine cover. My dad was a cardiologist, so the drama carried out in the public's imagination was reinforced by my respect for the practice of medicine and discovery. My ultimate choice of going into surgery and then into heart surgery and then heart transplantation I trace back to that single operation.'

Barnard was a serious medical pioneer, but also a showman and a playboy. He was the 'film star surgeon' and the 'surgeon who dared'. To Siegfried Stander he was an adventurer. To the three wives who loved him and the women he seduced he could be, above all, a misty romantic, the spirit of Louis Armstrong's *Give Me a Kiss to Build a Dream On*, one of his favourite singers and songs. He was all these things, at different times. He was easily moved to tears, like his father; his life rose and fell in waves of emotional highs and lows. Three marriages ended in failure, yet each contained something remarkable and durable: 'I make beautiful babies,' he liked to say well into his seventies. Those drawn by his charm, a mischievous sense of humour and a glittering and incisive intellect tended to forgive him his worst faults. Those whose lives he saved, especially the ones who became friends, worshipped him. His enemies point to his ego, his ruthless ambition and his vanity, his searing rudeness and his failings, rather than strengths, as a surgeon. He was, he said himself, 'a very ordinary surgeon', although he had 'worked hard at it'; he even admitted that, for a surgeon, he was 'too emotional'.

But, at least before fame took hold and his ego soared, he was never less than committed. He once said that when he was young, and faced with equipment shortages at Groote Schuur, if given the choice between a woman and a new pair of surgical gloves, he would have chosen the gloves. His obsessive attention to his patients' post-operative welfare helped establish intensive care in South Africa. Many colleagues who disliked him admired his ability to improvise, a rare trait in a surgeon, and his perfectionism: they admit now that had they or their families needed heart surgery years ago they would have wanted Barnard to do the operation.

The first human heart transplant was not, as Barnard liked to see it at the time (though he denied it afterwards, warding off accusations of opportunism) the finishing line of a race, the breasting of the tape. It was the starting shot. More than 40 000 have been carried out worldwide since, and today someone given a new heart has a 60 per cent chance of surviving more than ten years. But progress has not been smooth everywhere, and controversy over brain-death is still potent for some. Japan's second heart transplant did not take place until 1999, some thirty years after the first when the surgeon found himself charged with murder for removing the donor's heart. He was later acquitted, but Japanese heart surgeons dared not risk another transplant until the concept of brain-death was legally accepted there in 1997. With increasingly effective anti-rejection drugs, some transplant patients today are given more than one new organ during the same operation: heart and lungs, heart and kidney, liver and heart. Critics, especially in South Africa and other countries where poverty is rife, point to the high cost of a heart transplant to save one life and the fact that patients spend the rest of their lives on expensive drugs. Figures for heart bypasses dwarf those for transplants, but a transplant is still the best hope for those brought to the very brink of death by terminal heart failure. It remains a modern-day, everyday miracle.

*

When Barnard's body was back on South African soil his family arranged for a second post-mortem to be carried out at Groote Schuur. There were nagging doubts about whether he could have died in the way he was reported to have died. He had always been meticulous about having his inhaler to hand. Lutschinger, for one, was said to have been suspicious. After all, Barnard had been in a highly emotional and depressed state of mind in Cyprus, as both Gudi and Deirdre, who also spoke to him shortly before he died, recalled. He was desperately missing Armin and Lara – the only personal effects police found in his hotel room were their photographs. He was a self-professed advocate of suicide and euthanasia. As a doctor he also had the knowledge and could acquire the means to kill himself – for example, with an injection of potassium, known as 'the perfect killer' because it strikes instantly by paralysing the heart and is undetectable, being lost through urine before any post-mortem is performed. But there was no evidence of suicide at the scene, and the second post-mortem merely confirmed the results of the first. Barnard had died of an asthma attack, the way he had long feared he would.

Gudi contacted Lutschinger to discuss flying to Cape Town with him for the funeral. 'He told me there were lots of women who had called him, all with the same story,' she says. 'I was heartbroken. This man had changed my life. But I simply couldn't afford to pay for my air fare to South Africa.' Lutschinger said: 'There were various women in different countries. They would call him when he was there. There was no-one special.'

Three memorial services were held: at Groote Schuur, at Cape Town city hall and in his father's old mission church. The funeral service also took place in his father's church, although Barnard had said he did not want a church service because he had spent so much time in churches as a boy. His death brought his three families together. His oldest child, Deirdre, was 51; his youngest, Lara, was four. There were four grandchildren. Frederick and Christiaan spoke at the memorial services. Frederick, choking with tears, recited *A Bag of Tools* at one, and spoke of his father's love for South Africa. Marius, Barnard's only surviving brother, had often described him to friends as 'the Chris I have to bear'. Now he was reported to have said he would not attend the funeral in his home town. Karin accused him of being jealous of his brother's success. Marius says now, 'I can't win. If I say good things about Chris I'm bragging. If I say bad things, I'm jealous.' In fact he did attend the funeral. On 14 September, Barnard's ashes were buried in the rose garden in Beaufort West. As he had wished, the inscription on the simple stone which marks the spot, in English and Afrikaans, reads: 'I came back home.'

He might fittingly have added the words of a note he had sent some months earlier to Susan Vosloo while recovering from his broken hip. Unable to attend a meeting of the Organ Donor Foundation she was chairing, Barnard asked her to tell the audience: 'You only have one life. Make sure to make the best of it. From someone who lived a life worth living.'

Bibliography

Books by Christiaan Barnard referred to in this biography (publication details are those of editions I have used):

One Life, with Curtis Bill Pepper (Harrap, London, 1970)
The Second Life, edited by Chris Brewer (Vlaeberg, 1993)
Heart Attack – All You Have to Know About It (published outside SA as *Heart Attack – You Don't Have to Die*) (Hugh Keartland, 1971)
South Africa: Sharp Dissection (Tafelberg, 1977)
The Best Medicine – a collection of his *Cape Times* and *Rand Daily Mail* columns, edited by Bob Molloy (Tafelberg, 1979)
Good Life, Good Death – A Doctor's Case for Euthanasia and Suicide (Howard Timmins, 1980)
The Body Machine, with John Illman (Multimedia Publications, 1981)
The Arthritis Handbook, with Peter Evans (Multimedia Publications, 1984)
The Best of Barnard – columns from the *Rand Daily Mail* and *Cape Times*, edited by Bob Molloy (Molloy Publishers, 1984)
50 Ways to a Healthy Heart (Thorsons, London, 2001)

NOVELS:
The Unwanted, with Siegfried Stander (Tafelberg, 1974)
In the Night Season, with Siegfried Stander (Prentice-Hall, USA, 1979)
The Faith, with Siegfried Stander (Hutchinson, London, 1984)
The Donor (Michael Joseph, London, 1996)

OTHER BOOKS BY BARNARD:
Surgery of the Common Congenital Cardiac Malformations, by CN Barnard and V Schrire (Staples Press, London; Hoeber Medical Division, Harper and Row, New York, 1968)

The Junior Body Machine, with Christopher Fagg (Kestrel, London; Crown, New York, 1983)
The Living Body, with Karl Sabbagh (Macdonald, London; Plaza and Janes, Barcelona, 1984)
Your Healthy Heart, with Peter Evans (Macdonald, London, 1985)
Barnard also published or co-published nearly 200 papers in medical journals during his career.

BOOKS BY OTHER AUTHORS USED AS SOURCES FOR THIS BIOGRAPHY:
Barnard, Louwtjie *Heartbreak* (Howard Timmins, 1971)
Blaiberg, Philip *Looking at my Heart* (Heinemann, London, 1969)
Brotz, Howard *The Politics of South Africa* (Oxford University Press, 1977)
Bunker, John P *The Anesthesiologist and the Surgeon* (Little, Brown, 1972)
Cooper, David (compiler and editor) *Chris Barnard – By Those Who Know Him* (Vlaeberg, 1992)
D'Oliveira, John *Vorster – The Man* (Ernest Stanton, 1977)
Duin, Nancy and Sutcliffe, Jenny *A History of Medicine* (Simon and Schuster, London, 1992)
Hawthorne, Peter *The Transplanted Heart* (Hugh Keartland, 1968)
Johnson, RW *How Long Will South Africa Survive?* (Macmillan, London, 1977)
Jones, JDF *Storyteller: The Many Lives of Laurens van der Post* (John Murray, London, 2001)
Kirsch, Ralph (ed) *The Forman Years* (Department of Medicine, UCT, 1984)
Liebenberg, BJ and Spies, SB (eds) *South Africa in the 20th Century* (JL van Schaik Academic, 1993)
Lock, Margaret *Twice Dead: Organ Transplants and the Reinvention of Death* (University of California Press, 2002)
Louw, Jan H *In the Shadow of Table Mountain: A History of the University of Cape Town Medical School* (Struik, 1969)
Miller, G Wayne *King of Hearts: the True Story of the Maverick Who Pioneered Open Heart Surgery* (Times Books, New York, 2000)
Paton, Alan *Hope for South Africa* (Pall Mall Press, London, 1958)
Piller, Laurence William *The Cardiac Clinic: Groote Schuur Hospital 1951-1972, The Schrire Years* (comPress, 2000)

Rees, Mervyn and Day, Chris *Muldergate* (Macmillan South Africa, 1980)
Rhoodie, Eschel *PW Botha – The Last Betrayal* (SA Politics, 1989)
Rhoodie, Eschel *The Real Information Scandal* (Orbis SA, 1983)
Richardson, Robert G *The Surgeon's Heart – A History of Cardiac Surgery* (William Heinemann Medical Books, London, 1969)
Saunders, Stuart *Vice-Chancellor on a Tightrope – A Personal Account of Climactic Years in South Africa* (David Philip, 2000)
Schreiner, Olive *Thoughts on South Africa* (AD Donker, 1992, first published 1923)
Shaw, Gerald *The Cape Times – An Informal History* (David Philip, 1999)
Sparks, Allister *The Mind of South Africa* (Mandarin, 1991)
Stark, Tony *Knife to the Heart: The Story of Transplant Surgery* (Macmillan, London, 1996)
Starzl, Thomas E *The Puzzle People: Memoirs of a Transplant Surgeon* (University of Pittsburgh Press, 1992)
Tapson, Winifred *Timber and Tides: The Story of Knysna and Plettenberg Bay* (Juta & Company, 1961)
Welsh, Frank *A History of South Africa* (HarperCollins, 2000)
Young, Louisa *The Book of the Heart* (Flamingo, London, 2002)
Various *They Shaped Our Century – The Most Influential South Africans of the Twentieth Century* (Human & Rousseau, 1999)

As well as the above books, I used as written sources various medical publications, in particular the *South African Medical Journal* and the *British Medical Journal;* and a vast range of newspapers and magazines in South Africa, Britain, America and Italy. Other public sources included the archives of the BBC and the SABC. I found the website *pubmed.com* an invaluable lead to relevant articles published in medical journals throughout the world.

Index

A Bag of Tools 183, 326
Abrahams, Chief Rabbi Israel 162
African National Congress (ANC) 111, 251, 288, 292
Afrikaanse Sakekamer 194
AIDS 133, 319
Al Fayed, Dodi 306
Al Fayed, Mohammed 306
Albert Einstein College of Medicine 111-113, 115, 118
Alfin, Irwin 286
Ali, Muhammad 313
American College of Surgeons 285
Ames, Frances 181, 254, 269, 321
Amin, Idi 244
Amnesty International 259
ANC *see* African National Congress
Anglo American 171
Anti-apartheid movement 149, 186, 207
Antoniou, Eleni 319
Appies, Tom 27
Aragon, Bill 197
Arendz, Errol 306, 307
Arendz, Gloria 306
Argyriou, Aris 263
Armstrong, Louis 324
Aufrichtig, Harry *see* Webber, Harry

Baptist Medical Center 286
Barlow, Neville 9, 10
Barnard Faces His Critics 173
Barnard, Abraham (Chris's brother) 9, 17-21, 36, 58, 69, 315
Barnard, Adam (Chris's grandson – André and Gail's son) 269, 279, 280
Barnard, Adam (married 1734 – an ancestor of Chris) 22
Barnard, Adam Hendrik (Chris's father) 16-24, 26-28, 34-39, 41, 45, 48, 53, 58, 60, 103, 104, 126, 306
Barnard, André (Chris and Louwtjie's son) 28, 74, 75, 78, 89-91, 93, 99, 102, 116, 120, 125, 126, 135, 180, 188, 190, 197, 198, 201, 203, 213, 222, 227, 228, 269, 277-282
Barnard, Armin (Chris and Karin's son) 291, 298, 299, 312, 316, 318, 325
Barnard, Ashlea (Chris's granddaughter – André and Gail's daughter) 279, 280
Barnard, Barbara (Barbara Zoellner – Chris's second wife) 188, 190-192, 196, 197, 202-205, 209, 210, 213, 214, 216, 220-224, 227-229, 239, 241, 244, 263, 265-271, 280, 282, 284, 291, 295, 301, 302, 308-310, 322
Barnard, Chris (the writer) 215
Barnard, Christiaan Alexander (Chris and Barbara's son) 221, 223, 228, 275, 290, 299, 326
Barnard, Deirdre Jeanne (Chris and Louwtjie's daughter; *see also* Visser, Kobus and Visser, Karen) 71, 72, 75, 89-91, 93, 95, 99, 102, 114-116, 120, 125, 126, 135, 177, 180, 184, 188, 190, 197, 198, 203, 269, 277, 278, 280, 282, 290, 299, 306, 311, 318, 319, 321, 325, 326

Barnard, Dodsley (Chris's brother) 19, 20, 29, 30, 33, 35-39, 44, 53, 104, 228
Barnard, Elizabeth (Chris's grandmother) 22
Barnard, Frederick Christiaan Zoellner (Chris and Barbara's son) 184, 209, 222, 228, 230, 275, 290, 299, 302, 326
Barnard, Gail (André's wife) 227, 228, 269, 277-281
Barnard, Hendrik (son of Adam Barnard and Lea le Roux) 22
Barnard, Jan (Chris's grandfather) 22
Barnard, Johannes ('Boetie'; 'Barney' – Chris's brother) 17-20, 23, 25, 27, 32, 33, 35-37, 42-49, 52-54, 57, 58, 109
Barnard, Johannes (arrived in South Africa 1708 – an ancestor of Chris) 22
Barnard, Joyce (Johannes's wife) 44, 47, 48, 51, 54, 57, 58
Barnard, Karin (Karin Setzkorn – Chris's third wife) 270, 271, 274, 277, 278, 280-283, 286, 287, 289-291, 294, 295, 297-301, 303, 305, 306, 308-311, 313, 316, 318, 321, 322, 326
Barnard, Kay (Kay Veldman – Dodsley's wife) 36, 104, 228
Barnard, Lara (Chris and Karin's daughter) 306, 308, 318, 325, 326
Barnard, Louwtjie (Aletta Louw – Chris's first wife) 13, 26, 28, 58-60, 63, 65, 69-77, 80, 83, 84, 86, 88-95, 98, 99, 101, 102, 104, 106, 109, 116, 120, 121, 126, 128, 129, 135, 147, 155, 162-164, 171, 174-180, 183, 184, 187-190, 192, 197-205, 212, 228, 267, 279, 281, 284, 295, 311, 317, 322
Barnard, Maria (Chris's mother) 9, 16-24, 26, 28, 33-35, 37-39, 41, 45, 53, 58, 60, 103, 104, 126, 127, 228
Barnard, Marius (Chris's brother) 26, 27, 33, 45, 69, 104, 121, 122, 124, 126, 139-143, 146, 148, 149, 152-154, 160, 162, 167, 200, 211, 214, 228, 241, 253, 259, 260, 264, 265, 272, 277, 278, 292, 307, 326
Barnes, John 143
Barnes, Rodney 295, 297
Baron, Sydney 253
Barreiros, Eduardo 180, 183, 184
Baskin, Mickey 48
Beaufort West 15, 16, 18, 20, 23, 25-28, 30-32, 36, 51, 55, 58, 60, 64, 74, 103, 171, 194, 200, 214, 217, 222, 230, 260, 278, 291, 319, 326
Beaufort West Courier 37
Beaufort West Museum 277
Beaufort, Duke of 15
Beck, Walter 'Wally' 205, 213, 222, 223,
Bekker, Fanie 69, 200
Belfond, Pierre 220, 227, 248, 250
Bennett, Benjamin 170
Berman, Saul 318
Biko, Steve 246, 254, 255
Bini, Alfredo 174
Black, Edith 126, 127, 132, 277
Blaiberg, Eileen 167, 179, 182
Blaiberg, Jill 167
Blaiberg, Philip 151, 161, 162, 165-170, 176, 179, 182, 184, 186, 190, 193, 194, 208
Boerekerk 16, 26, 27
Bolus scholarship 46
Boots *see* Snyders, Frederick
Bosman, Annette 149, 182, 229
Bosman, Bertie 136-138, 146, 149, 153, 154, 172, 182, 229
Botha, Louis 17
Botha, Martinus 'MC' 126, 129, 131, 137, 138, 146, 162, 167, 172, 173
Botha, PW 232, 261, 288, 292
Botha, RF ('Pik') 165, 194, 242, 244
Brassil, Aileen 188
Brewer, Chris 295, 307
Breytenbach, Breyten 169, 236, 250, 251
Bridgland, Fred 293
Brink, Fritz 13, 121, 133, 147, 263, 265, 267, 268, 270, 278, 283, 310
Brink, Johan 300, 301, 319, 323

Brink, Maureen 133, 265, 267, 268, 270, 309, 310
British Medical Journal 173
Brock, John 56, 84
Brock, Russell 108, 173, 320
Bulawayo 23
Burger, JG 12, 146, 147
Burger, Willie 29, 30
Burton, Richard 171, 269

Cabrol, Christian 97, 300
Calne, Roy 114
Calvinism 26, 59, 74, 84, 171
Cambridge University 191, 302
Campbell, Gil 92, 122
Cantini, Gianfranco 174, 200
Cape Argus 215
Cape Times 105, 128, 147, 148, 160, 179, 189, 211, 224, 238, 260, 264, 274, 275, 283, 317
Cape Town Press Club 323
Carnegie Corporation 115
Carrel, Alexis 80, 320
Carter, Jimmy 249
Castro, Fidel 289
Cavvadas, Cathy 78
Central High School 29-31, 36
Ceres 65-67, 69-74, 76, 85, 104, 121
Chamberlain, Richard 151
Charles Adams Memorial Scholarship 84, 89
Charles, Prince 244, 303
Chris Barnard Chair of Cardiothoracic Surgery (UCT) 276
Chris Barnard Exhibition 277
Chris Barnard Research Fund 156, 158, 159, 174, 199, 212, 276, 294
Christiaan Barnard Foundation 308, 313
Christiaan Barnard Institute of Cardiovascular Medicine (UCT) 323
Christiaan Barnard Memorial Hospital 308
Cillie, Piet 193
City Hospital for Infectious Diseases 73, 74, 76-78
City Park Hospital *see* Christiaan Barnard Memorial Hospital
Clinique La Prairie 282, 283, 287
CN Barnard Investments 263
CN Barnard Properties 263
Communism 51, 199
Communist Party 44
Conservative Party 292
Cooley, Denton 99, 122, 124, 140, 149, 164, 184, 287
Cooper, David 107, 127, 141
Craig, Gloria 263, 267, 268, 278, 299, 308
Crichton, Cuthbert 57, 60, 61, 69, 71
Cywes, Marlene 121
Cywes, Syd 84, 121

D'Oliveira, Basil 186
Daily Dispatch 212
Daily Mail 160, 168, 212, 297, 298
Daily Mirror 160, 182
Daily Sketch 150
Darvall, Denise 11, 134-145, 155, 157, 200, 304, 306
Darvall, Edward 134, 136, 137, 147, 149, 152, 156, 157, 160, 229
Darvall, Keith 134, 136, 157, 306
Darvall, Myrtle 134, 135, 157
Darvall, Stephen 134, 136, 157
Darwin, Charles 51, 139
Day, Leontine 90, 91, 93, 98
Dazian Foundation Bursary 84
De Beers 171
De Klerk FW 292-294
De la Porte 221
De Nobrega, Joe 109, 110, 133, 241, 251, 252, 254, 276
De Villaverde, Marques 180
De Villiers, Kay 181, 182
DeBakey, Michael 99, 124, 149, 163, 164, 226
Demikhov, Vladimir 108
Democratic Party (DP) 292

DeWall-Lillehei bubble oxygenator 85, 98, 104
Diana, Princess 302-306, 314
Die Beeld 195
Die Burger 193
Diederichs, Nico 195, 203, 243, 259, 260
Dodsley-Flamstead, Miss 19, 24, 53
Dowdle, Eugene 77, 210, 296
DP *see* Democratic Party
Dr Kildare 151
Drennan, Maxie 49, 50
Du Toit, Ernette 106, 120, 182, 283
Dutch East India Company 22
Dutch Reformed Church 15, 16, 23, 26, 106, 167, 222, 281, 295

Eglin, Colin 255, 292
Elgin 69
Elseviers 240
Erasmus Commission 236
Erikson, Dolores 87
Etoe, Sheila 270
Evans, Peter 284

Face the Nation 162-164
Fair Lady (magazine) 224, 266
Fehrson, Doctor 20, 73
(Fifty) 50 Ways to a Healthy Heart 305, 308, 314
Fischer, Bram 251
Fisher, Dorothy 190, 194, 205, 277
Foreign Affairs Association 240
Forman, Frank 56, 57
Fortuin, Barbara 75, 76, 78
Fourie, Pieta 32, 34
Franzot, Martin 126, 135, 212, 213, 222
Frater, Bob 116-119
Freud, Sigmund 321
Friedmann, Dene 120, 216, 222, 311
Frist, Bill 324
Frost, David 258, 259
Fry, Richenda 62

Gandhi, Indira 246, 247
Gelb, Sandy 271
Getty, Paul 201
Gettysburg Address 93
Gibbon, John 81
Gillespie, Gene 76
Glycel 283, 285-287
Gone with the Wind 71
Gonville and Caius, (Cambridge College) 191, 302
Good Life, Good Death 264
Goosen, Carl 104, 109
Gorbachev, Mikhail 313
Goss, Leonard 222, 223, 277
Gott, Vincent 88
Graaff-Reinet 23
Grace, Princess of Monaco (Grace Kelly) 184
Gray, Dorian 310
Great Fire of Knysna 22
Groote Schuur Hospital (GSH) 45, 49, 56, 61, 63, 71, 74, 76, 79-81, 83, 84, 94, 101, 102, 104, 105, 107, 109, 113, 116, 120-122, 128, 130, 133, 135, 136, 138, 140, 144, 146, 147, 149, 152, 156, 158, 160-162, 166-169, 171, 175, 179-182, 184, 186, 188, 192, 194, 196, 205, 206, 211-215, 224-226, 229, 240, 241, 251, 252, 254, 256, 259, 264, 265, 271-274, 276, 278-280, 283, 295, 299-301, 303, 304, 308, 319, 323-326
Guthrie, Charles 320

Hain, Peter 207
Hall, Georgie 158
Hancock, Carol 284, 285
Hans, Leontine *see* Day, Leontine
Hardy, Francoise 179, 187
Hardy, James 119, 155
Harper's Bazaar 204
Harvey, William 191
Haupt, Clive 165-169
Hawthorne, Peter 153, 317
Heard, Tony 260

Heart Attack – All You Have To Know About It 210
Heart Attack – You Don't Have to Die see *Heart Attack – All You Have To Know About It*
Heartbreak 59, 70, 84, 177, 198, 200
Heidler, Gudrun (Gudi) 308, 313, 314, 318, 325, 326
Helpmekaar Fund 38, 45, 46
Hendrik Verwoerd Award 180
Herbert, Adrian 209
Hersman, Gordon 226, 227
Hertzog, General Barry 36, 44
Hewitson, John 212, 273
Hewitson, Rodney 12, 45, 53, 105, 110, 139, 145, 146, 180, 212, 273, 307
Heydenreich, Jo *see* Stander, Jo
Hippocrates 80
Hitchcock, Francois 126, 128, 129, 144, 146, 180
Hoffenberg, Bill 166, 167
Hope, Alastair 138
Horwitz, Mark 77, 221
Horwood, Owen 234
Hume, David 112-114, 122, 123
Hunter, John 97

Illman, John 264
Immorality Act 218, 267, 283
In the Night Season 217, 218, 221, 264
In the Shadow of Table Mountain 43
Ingala, Tony 227, 228, 263-266, 270, 302
Inkatha Freedom Party 292
Institute for the Study of Plural Societies 240
It's All in the State of the Mind 225

Jackie (*see also* Stevens, Katharine) 41
Jacobs, Evelyn 184, 185, 258
Jaffe, Basil 44, 48, 53
Johnson, Lyndon B 164
Jones, JDF 208
Jordaan, Peggy 138, 144
Jordan, Norma 267
Jorgensen, Herga 94
Jorgensen, Sharon 94, 95, 98, 100, 101, 108, 109
Joubert, 'Pikkie' 44, 62, 65-72
Joubert, Truida 66-68, 70, 76
Joubertina 23

Kahn, Harry 199
Kantrowitz, Adrian 149, 161, 163, 165, 169, 179
Kaplan, Barry 131
Karoo 15, 34, 39, 46, 49, 215, 217, 239, 261, 289, 299, 311, 312
Kelly, Grace *see* Grace, Princess of Monaco
Kelly, Rowena 54
Kennedy, Jacqueline 202
Kennedy, John F 151
Kennelly, Brian 206
Kerkbode 167
Khan, Hasnat 303, 304
Killops, William 190, 194
Kirklin, John 98
Kissinger, Henry 248, 249
Kronkite, Walter 164
Kruger, Jimmy 236, 252, 254, 255
Krynauw, Frank 30, 34, 35, 37
Krynauw, Willem 30

La Corniche Estates 263
La Perla (*see also* La Vita) 264
La Vita 264-266, 269, 271, 273, 277, 281, 289-291, 307
La Vita Grill 265
Lambrechts, Tollie 138
Lande, Marilyn 88, 91, 93, 94, 96
Lara's Theme 134, 306
Laughton, Charles 59
Lawler, Richard 155
Le Roux, Eileen 270
Le Roux, Lea 22
Lesley, Chris 265, 292
Levin, Angela 298

Lichfield, Patrick 224
Life 324
Lillehei, Kaye 86, 321
Lillehei, Walt 81, 85-88, 95-97, 99, 110, 111, 114, 163, 165, 231, 287, 288, 321
Lindbergh, Charles 193
Litrico, Angelo 171, 187, 188, 201, 204, 267
Litrico, Franco 267
Lollobrigida, Gina 171, 172, 174, 177, 187, 200, 201, 295, 317
Longmore, Donald 129
Lord, Graham 220
Loren, Sophia 171, 174, 187, 204, 290
Losman, Jacques 223
Loubser, Piet 276
Louw, Aletta *see* Barnard, Louwtjie
Louw, Eric 60, 212
Louw, James 71
Louw, Jannie 43, 49, 63, 71, 80-83, 101, 102, 105, 107, 113, 166, 180, 229
Louwrens, Jan 28, 29
Lower, Richard 108, 122, 123, 128, 135, 173, 194, 231, 320
Luckhoff, Hilma 310
Ludolphi, Bertha 227, 265-267
Lutschinger, Walter 308, 311, 313, 318, 319, 325, 326

Mackenzie, Don 173, 176, 183, 200
Macmillan, Harold 111
Mahatey, Nazeem 275
Mail on Sunday 273
Malan, Nico 12, 146, 176, 183, 195, 204
Mandela, Nelson 103, 111, 113, 124, 196, 289, 292, 299, 300, 319, 324
Marcos, Imelda 240, 244
Marcos, President Ferdinand 240, 244
Marks, Solly 191, 202, 204
Marx, Karl 51
Mattli, Armin 274, 282, 283, 286, 287, 291
Mayo Clinic (Rochester) 98, 117
Mbeki, Samuel 296
Mbeki, Thabo 275, 319
Mbengo, Mountain 254
Meany, George 253
Men Never Die (*The Unwanted*) 220
Metrowich, Redvers ('Red') 249, 250
Middleton, Paul 264
Miller, G Wayne 86, 96
Mississippi Medical Center 119
MK *see* uMkhonto weSizwe
Mohammed Al Fayed *see* Al Fayed, Mohammed
Molloy, Bob 189, 238, 239, 261, 275, 284, 294, 296, 297
Mondadori, Giorgio 171, 174, 177
Mondadori, Paolo 174
Mondale, Walter 178
Moodley, Strini 259
Morgan Grampian 233
Morkel family 16
Morkel, Hercules 25, 27
Mostert, Justice Anton 232, 236
Mowbray Maternity Hospital 209
Muggeridge, Malcolm 173, 199, 207
Muizenberg cemetery 9
Mulder, Connie 208, 232-234, 241-243, 246, 249, 252, 256, 261
Multimedia 264, 270
Munnik, Lapa 12, 146, 176, 277
Murray, Andrew 23
Murray, Lionel 212
Myers, 'Bullet' 272
Myers, Martin 272

Naki, Hamilton 151, 296
NASA 192
Nash, Eleanor 280
National Heart Hospital 121, 149, 150, 208
National Institutes of Health 97
National(ist) Party 16, 36, 37, 51, 64, 101, 186, 191, 195, 196, 208, 212, 213, 250, 255, 256, 292
Neethling, Midwife 73
Nellen, Maurice 81, 82
New Scientist 173
New York Times 164

Newman, Paul 174
Newsweek 143, 154, 177
Nicholson, Father Tom 222, 278, 290, 295, 302, 316, 322
Ningi *see* Stevens, Katharine
Ninky *see* Stevens, Katharine
Njonjo, Charles 257
Nordstrom, Trudy 87, 88
Novati, Aldo 264
Novitsky, Dimitri 272
NP *see* National Party
Nuffield Scholarship 84

O'Donovan, Jenny 140, 141
O'Donovan, Terry 140-143, 181, 212, 307
O'Molony, Tim 65-68, 70-72
Observer 199
Onassis, Aristotle 202
One Life 40, 43, 49, 56, 59, 60, 65, 69, 73, 76, 82, 86, 89, 93, 95, 103, 122, 125, 128, 131, 136, 139, 141, 142, 198, 199-201, 210, 241, 245, 271, 294
Oosthuizen, Stella 31, 32, 41
Oppenheimer, Harry 194, 241
Order of the Southern Cross 277, 294
Organ Donor Foundation 317, 326
Ozinsky, Joe 138, 141, 142, 208

PAC *see* Pan-Africanist Congress
Pacemaker (*boat*) 115
Pacemaker, device 99, 132
Pan-Africanist Congress (PAC) 111, 124, 251, 253, 292
Panorama Medi-Clinic 310
Pappas, George 123
Paul VI, Pope 171, 172
Peck, Gregory 174
Peninsula Maternity Home 57, 64
Pepper, Beverly 192
Pepper, Curtis Bill 136, 139, 177, 182, 192, 198, 204
Perry, Genevieve 92, 93
Perry, John 92, 97
PFP *see* Progressive Federal Party
Phillips, Walter 105, 109
Pick, Joan 9, 104, 105
Pick, Victor 151
'Piggy-back' heart transplants 223, 265, 273, 277
Piller, Bill 107, 121, 206
Pio Manzu Centre 302
Pitanguy, Ivo 229, 230
Player, Gary 261
Pogrund, Benjamin 152, 204, 253, 254
Ponti, Carlo 172, 204
Pravda 150
Pretoria News 220
Prins, Friedrich 134, 156, 157
Progressive Federal Party (PFP) 255, 259, 292

QE2 270, 271, 277, 278, 320

Rabie, Daantjie 29, 86, 135
Rabie, Dominee 20, 24, 27
Rabkin, Rachel 78
Rainier, Prince of Monaco 184
Ralph, Johnny 70
Rand Daily Mail 204, 237, 238
Raphaely, Jane 224
Rapport 290
Rattray, Mike 271, 291
Rautenbach, Amelia 138, 145
Red Cross War Memorial Children's Hospital 84, 107, 109, 110, 187, 206, 212, 227, 277, 278
Rhoodie, Denys 242, 243, 261
Rhoodie, Eschel 232-250, 252, 253, 257-259, 261, 262
Rhoodie, Katy 242, 262
Rhoodie, Nic 240, 261
Rivonia Trial 113
Roman Catholicism 27, 61, 104, 171, 203, 222, 275
Ross, Donald 44, 53, 61, 121, 149
Rossouw, Michel 45, 58, 210
Rossouw, Sannie 138

Royal College of Surgeons 72, 173
RSA Sport 256, 257
SACS *see* South African College School
Salvation Army 23
Sanders, Hannah-Reeve 76, 276
Sandri, Emiliano 183, 264
SAP *see* South African Party
Saunders, Stuart 102, 119, 196, 206, 214
Schlebusch, Alwyn 241
Schrire, Robert 261
Schrire, Velva (Val) 12, 81, 82, 105, 107, 110, 113, 117, 127, 128, 131, 132, 136, 137, 148, 151, 161, 165, 180, 205, 206, 222, 261
Schweitzer, Albert 192
Scope 285
Scott, John 147, 153
Sellers, Peter 259, 295
Setzkorn, Karin *see* Barnard, Karin
Shah of Iran 180
Shand Kydd, Frances 306
Shapiro, Bennie 121, 144, 206
Sharp Dissection see *South Africa: Sharp Dissection*
Sharpe, RL 183
Sharpeville 111, 211, 246, 251
Shaw, Gerald 211
SHAWCO 322, 323
Shean, Terry 189
Shearer, Henrietta 94
Shelley, Mary 297
Sheppard, David 207
Shumway, Norman 97, 108, 122, 128, 129, 135, 149, 155, 163, 164, 169, 170, 173, 178, 179, 182, 194, 222, 231, 300, 320
Silva, Bianca 308
Silva, Joe 268-270, 302, 308
Sinatra, Frank 322
Sisulu, Walter 292
Sklar, Solly 129
Smith, Pieter 184-186, 190, 194, 205, 258
Smuts, Jan 16, 36, 37, 43, 44
Snyders, Frederick ('Boots') 115, 296
Sobukwe, Robert 124, 251-254
Somerset, Lord Charles 15
Sonnenberg, John 76-78
South Africa Foundation 194
South Africa: Sharp Dissection 245-248, 250, 259, 264
South African Broadcasting Corporation 154
South African College School (SACS) 120
South African Medical and Dental Council 60, 151, 254, 274
South African Medical Association 180, 255
South African Medical Journal 73, 142, 143, 170, 287, 300, 320
South African Party (SAP) 16-18, 36
South West African People's Organisation 258
Southern African Freedom Foundation 249
Sparks, Allister 238
Spencer, Earl 303
Spielberg, Steven 297
SSP *see* Students' Socialist Party
St George's Cathedral 211
Stander, Jo 215, 216, 220, 221
Stander, Siegfried 63, 215-222, 258, 264, 296, 297
Starzl, Thomas 114, 115, 122, 123
State, David 115
Stern 159, 185, 201
Stevens, Katharine 39-43, 217
Stevenson, John 150
Steyn, Joan 120
Stoffberg, Desmond 128, 176, 180, 183, 187, 189, 201
Storay-Dowdle, Karen 270, 271
Story, Jim 87, 88
Storyteller 208
Strand, Sara Pieterz 22
Strijdom, Prime Minister JG 101
Students' Socialist Party (SSP) 44, 51
Sunday Express 221
Sunday Times (Johannesburg) 186, 291

Sunday Times (London) 125, 152
Suppression of Communism Act 199
Suzman, Helen 236, 255
Swanepoel, André 105
SWAPO *see* South West African People's Organisation

Tambo, Oliver 288
Taylor, Elizabeth 269
Taylor, Ivan 223
Terblanche, John 118
Terre'Blanche, Eugene 293
Thal, Alan 84, 85
The Arthritis Handbook 284
The Beat of My Heart 32, 33, 36, 127, 139
The Best of Barnard 284
The Body Machine 264
The Cardiac Clinic – The Schrire Years 206
The Citizen 232
The Donor 295-297
The Faith 218, 258, 264, 283
The Open Heart of South Africa 235
The Paper Curtain 245
The Private Life of Henry VIII 59
The Puzzle People 122
The Question Why 207
The Real Information Scandal 241, 253
The Second Life 164, 167, 172, 177, 185, 187, 192, 195, 196, 207, 222, 233, 255, 258, 281, 295, 307
The Standard 257
The Transplanted Heart 153
The Unwanted 54, 63, 209, 214, 217-221, 244, 245, 248, 264
Time 114, 153, 154, 317, 324
Times 150
To the Point 242
Tobruk 37, 53
Treason Trial 103
Tunbridge, Noel 218, 291

uMkhonto weSizwe (MK) 111, 207
United Democratic Front 292
United Party (UP) 36, 196, 208, 212, 214
University of Minnesota Hospital 85, 94, 179
UP *see* United Party
Usakos 60, 61

Van den Berg, WM 185
Van den Bergh, Hendrik 233
Van der Merwe, Jacobus 54
Van der Merwe, Piet 312, 317
Van der Post, Laurens 208
Van der Riet, Dion 217, 221
Van der Walt, HN 234, 235
Van Rensburg, Andries 66
Van Rensburg, Marie 65, 66
Van Wyk, George 230, 284, 290, 312, 317
Van Zyl, Dirk 208, 277
Varco, Richard 85, 95, 111, 112, 163
Veldman, Kay *see* Barnard, Kay
Venter, Coert 136
Verwoerd, Prime Minister Hendrik 101, 111, 124, 191
Visser, Karen (Chris's granddaughter) 269
Visser, Kobus 269, 277
Vivier, WGH 28
Vogue 204
Vorster, Prime Minister JB 12, 14, 124, 146, 162, 170, 180, 186, 196, 199, 211, 232-234, 241, 242, 246, 249, 251, 255, 257, 261, 262
Vosloo, Susan 308, 319, 326

Wall Street Journal 161
Wangensteen, Owen Harding 84-99, 101, 163, 179
Washington Post 289
Washington Star 233
Washkansky, Ann 12, 129-133, 135, 137, 148, 152, 154, 156, 160, 162
Washkansky, Louis 11, 12, 97, 126, 127, 129-133, 135-138, 140, 143-145, 148-156, 158-162, 165-168, 170, 179, 182, 185, 187, 200, 287, 304, 307, 320, 322

Washkansky, Michael 132, 137, 156
Webber, Charlotte 47, 48, 60
Webber, Harry 44, 50-54, 56, 57, 59, 60, 199
West, Frederick 173
Wicomb, Winston 273
Wilderness 34, 35, 39, 46, 48, 49, 69, 70
Willers, Piet 44, 49, 53, 57, 210
Williams, Roger 211, 224, 225
Wintle, Walter D 226
Woods, Donald 212, 243, 252, 253
Young, Andrew 249, 253
Younghusband, Peter 168, 212

Zoellner, Barbara *see* Barnard, Barbara
Zoellner, Fred (Friedrich) 190-192, 196, 201, 202, 204, 208, 210, 249, 265, 269, 301, 302, 308
Zoellner, Ulli (Ursula) 190-192, 202, 249, 265, 269, 301, 302
Zuhdi, Nazih 286